NATIONAL UNIVERSITY
LIBRARY

D0370957

THESE
YET TO BE UNITED
STATES

NATIONAL UNIVERSITY
LIBRARY   SAN DIEGO

THESE
YET TO BE UNITED
STATES

Civil Rights and Civil Liberties in America since 1945

Jeanne Theoharis
BROOKLYN COLLEGE

Athan Theoharis
MARQUETTE UNIVERSITY

WADSWORTH

THOMSON LEARNING

Australia • Canada • Mexico • Singapore • Spain
United Kingdom • United States

WADSWORTH

THOMSON LEARNING

Editor: Clark Baxter
Developmental Editor: Sue Gleason
Assistant Editors: Julie Iannacchino, Kasia Zagorski
Editorial Assistant: Jonathan Katz
Marketing Manager: Caroline Croley
Marketing Assistant: Mary Ho
Project Manager, Editorial Production: Elaine Hellmund
Print/Media Buyer: Rebecca Cross
Permissions Editor: Bob Kauser
Production Service: Impressions Book and Journal Services, Inc.
Photo Researcher: Sue Howard
Copy Editor: Susan Ryan
Cover Designer: Elizabeth Ragsdale
Cover Image: © Corbis
Cover Printer: Transcontinental Printing
Compositor: Impressions Book and Journal Services, Inc.
Printer: Transcontinental Printing

COPYRIGHT © 2003 Wadsworth, a division of Thomson Learning, Inc. Thomson Learning™ is a trademark used herein under license.

ALL RIGHTS RESERVED. No part of this work covered by the copyright hereon may be reproduced or used in any form or by any means—graphic, electronic, or mechanical, including but not limited to photocopying, recording, taping, Web distribution, information networks, or information storage and retrieval systems—without the written permission of the publisher.

Printed in Canada
1 2 3 4 5 6 7 06 05 04 03 02

For more information about our products, contact us at:
Thomson Learning Academic Resource Center
1-800-423-0563
For permission to use material from this text, contact us by:
Phone: 1-800-730-2214
Fax: 1-800-730-2215
Web: http://www.thomsonrights.com

Asia
Thomson Learning
5 Shenton Way #01-01
UIC Building
Singapore 068808

Australia
Nelson Thomson Learning
102 Dodds Street
South Melbourne, Victoria 3205
Australia

Canada
Nelson Thomson Learning
1120 Birchmount Road
Toronto, Ontario M1K 5G4
Canada

Europe/Middle East/Africa
Thomson Learning
High Holborn House
50/51 Bedford Row
London WC1R 4LR
United Kingdom

Library of Congress Control Number: 2002102241

ISBN: 0-155-06989-6

Contents

PREFACE

This is a new story of America—of the ways ordinary citizens pressed the nation to live up to its professed ideals of liberty, justice, and equality for all regardless of race, gender, and sexual orientation. It is simultaneously a story of the ways those movements were thwarted and contained by other Americans, both ordinary and powerful. Looking at civil rights and civil liberties over the past fifty years reveals the character of the United States following World War II. The country had fought and won a war to defend democracy and self-determination abroad yet would be challenged to make real these principles at home. The war effort had encompassed men and women of all races. Yet within the United States, access to jobs, public spaces, housing, schools, unions, and political power was allocated and determined by race and gender.

This book differs from others on postwar America because it looks at civil rights and civil liberties in tandem and does so over the past fifty years. It merges two historical approaches—of looking at America from the view of those in the highest seats of power and from the perspectives of those too often denied political and economic access. It shows that the civil rights movement was not just a southern movement but spanned the nation; not just a movement for African Americans but waged by other people of color, including Latinos and Native Americans as well as women of all races; and not just a struggle that began in the mid-1950s and ended in the mid-1960s. It was more varied (from voting rights to garbage pickup to bilingual education, from the right to form unions to the right to live in any neighborhood to access to a diverse and challenging curriculum), more grassroots, and more broad than many other studies of the postwar period have shown. And the resistance that civil rights workers faced from their neighbors as well as local, state, and federal officials was more multifaceted and long-lasting than has previously been revealed. While the history of civil rights is often told as a story of leaders—Martin Luther King Jr., Malcolm X., César Chávez, Betty Friedan—these movements were led and organized by local people across the country. Many of their stories appear here, threading the struggle for justice from Cambridge, Maryland, to Mayersville, Mississippi, to East Lost Angeles, to Wounded Knee. Some of these individuals are familiar like Rosa Parks, but their experiences are not so widely known. Parks, for instance, had been politically active for decades, including being secretary of the Montgomery NAACP. Some, like Johnnie Tillmon, who helped organize the National Welfare Rights Organization; Harry Moore, who fought to enfranchise black voters in Florida; or Dolores Huerta, who was key to the founding and organizing of the United Farm Workers, have not been so widely included in the history books.

Despite popular memorializations that celebrate the civil rights movement (particularly around Martin Luther King Day), Americans who fought for civil rights stood in the minority of their communities and were the target of community ostracism, economic pressure, and physical violence. Only over time and great effort were the issues these movements fought for recognized as matters that should be addressed by the nation. The challenge to racial segregation and racial discrimination gave rise to movements such as the Young Lords, the United Farm Workers, the American Indian Movement, the National Organization for Women, and the Gay Liberation Front, which served to change the role of other ethnic groups, women, and gays and lesbians in post-1945 America.

Civil rights struggles did not end in the 1970s. In Part 3, we look at the enduring nature of racial and gender discrimination (in school segregation, the exploding prison industrial complex, the widening gap between rich and poor, and the persistence of racial and gender stereotypes to drive public policy) and how these movements have been transformed over the past 25 years. Civil rights and civil liberties—and the forces and assumptions that worked to limit them—took new, and sometimes more covert, forms in the post-1973 period. The backlash against civil rights, for instance, was often premised on the assumption that racism was over. The protection of civil liberties in this period, particularly the notion that individual rights were harmed by group protection, was used to erode the civil rights gains of previous decades. Thus, opponents of civil rights have been consistent in protecting educational, economic, and political privilege and yet differed in ideology and tactic over the past fifty years.

At the same time, civil liberties issues—free speech and fair trial, the right to dissent, and protection from political repression—have too often been treated in passing in studies of the postwar period and then with a focus almost exclusively on the phenomenon of McCarthyism. We highlight that the threats to civil liberties were far broader than the tactics and charges of Senator Joseph McCarthy and the House Committee on

Un-American Activities (HUAC). Indeed, the ways Joseph McCarthy has come to personify anti-Communism diverts attention from the ways that the American public and a broad range of institutions bought into the idea that the nation would be safe from Communism only through limiting civil liberties.

Civil liberties were endangered less by prosecution than by the covert monitoring, harassment, and disruption of groups and activists critical of U.S. policy. Recently released records confirm the central role of the Federal Bureau of Investigation (FBI), and how secrecy and surveillance policies affected the right to privacy, to advocate for one's rights, and to dissent free of political persecution. The FBI used extralegal means to monitor individuals as varied as suspected Communists, civil rights activists, and gay federal employees, disseminated information to discredit them and their movements, and devised methods to shield their antidemocratic tactics from public scrutiny. FBI surveillance did not end in the early 1970s; the need to compromise civil liberties in the fight against communism was picked up in post–Cold War America in the fight against terrorism.

Looking at civil rights and civil liberties at the end of the millennium reveals an America still short of its celebrated ideals but also shows the lengths to which many Americans continue to go to make those principles reality.

We would like to thank Dick Etulain and the late Gary Nash for their interest in publishing a comparative, critical history of civil rights and civil liberties. Dick Etulain read this manuscript extremely carefully and provided numerous useful ideas for revision and steady encouragement to facilitate getting this work out.

We would also like to thank and dedicate this book to our family: Nancy Theoharis, Scott Dexter, George Theoharis, Elizabeth Theoharis, Julie Causton-Theoharis, and Chris Caruso. While others have argued that writing a book as a father-daughter team is a sign of good character, they knew better but encouraged our work all the same.

Jeanne Theoharis
Athan Theoharis

I would like to thank my students at Brooklyn College of the City University of New York and at the University of Michigan, who learned much of the details of this history as I did. By their thoughtful questions, persistent interest, and frequent suggestions, they continually showed me the value of the word in changing the society we live in. I have been lucky to have a wealth of friends and academic mentors who have provided me a rich foundation upon which to work and grow: Moustafa Bayoumi,

Jennifer Bernstein, Sean Buffington, Brenda Cardenas, Julie Cooper, Tamara Duckworth, Jason Elias, Michael Elsila, Lauren Fox, Arnold Franklin, Roderick Harrison, Amy Schmidt Jones, Robin Kelley, Barbara Krauthamer, Peter Laipson, Earl Lewis, Stephanie Melnick Goldstein, Karen Miller, Nancy Romer, Kelly Stupple, Alexis Stokes, Katherine Tate, and Mark Ungar.

Matthew Countryman provided rich commentary on parts of this manuscript and generously endured innumerable conversations about civil rights in post-1945 America. This book grew profoundly through Alejandra Marchevsky's critical insights, unqualified enthusiasm, and abiding friendship. Paisley Currah's companionship—intellectual and emotional—sustained and nourished me in finishing this book. I am greatly indebted to Scott Dexter, who has leavened this project's many stages and my life with love, wit, and intellectual grace. This is an undeniably richer and clearer book for his careful eye, steady patience, and keen criticisms. I can only hope that this work does justice to such support.

Jeanne Theoharis

INTRODUCTION

The history of civil rights and civil liberties in post-1945 America is a history of movements that challenged Americans to bring the practices of their society into conformity with the nation's stated ideals of "liberty and justice for all." It is, as well, a history of movements that evolved along parallel *and* divergent paths. Both movements shared a common goal to advance individual rights. They differed in their methods, with civil rights advocates endorsing government action to remove barriers to equality and civil liberties advocates seeking to preclude government restrictions on dissent. Changes in national politics and values, precipitated by crises at home and abroad, also disparately influenced the ability of these movements to achieve their objectives.

The goals of civil rights activists varied over time as did their purposes. They consistently demanded legal equality and the full opening of economic and educational opportunities to all Americans. Their initial objective was to rescind state laws denying blacks equal access to education, voting, housing, and public services and to end segregation in the federal bureaucracy and the military services.

Despite the abolition of slavery with the end of the Civil War, the majority of African Americans lived in the South and were employed primarily as tenant farmers, sharecroppers, and domestic workers. In response to the impact of the boll weevil, the mechanization of southern agriculture, the upsurge of lynchings, and the lure of employment opportunities in northern industries, many African Americans migrated from the rural South to the urban North dating from the 1910s but this migration accelerated in the 1940s. There, rather than the promise of equality, blacks encountered a different form of segregation than in the South. They lived in racial ghettoes, were denied corporate or skilled jobs, and attended predominantly black, underfunded schools. But they could vote and command support for the goal of a racially free and just society. In the aftermath of the Great Depression and the Roosevelt New Deal, they became an important constituency of the revived, and more liberal, Democratic party.

The predominant objective of civil rights activists, moreover, changed during the 1960s in two fundamental ways. They no longer sought only to end racial discrimination but to ban as well sexual (both gender and orientation) and ethnic discrimination. This goal was to be achieved by rescinding discriminatory state laws and also by enacting federal laws or executive orders guaranteeing equality. Affirmative action programs symbolized this new approach—federally imposed initiatives to ensure that women and minorities were awarded government contracts, assured of participation in intercollegiate sports, informed of job and educational opportunities, and admitted to undergraduate and professional schools.

An important catalyst to this changed objective was the twin emergence of more militant black, women, ethnic, and gay and lesbian movements and new national priorities ushered in first by the New Deal and then by World War II and the Cold War. Social equality soon became a key part of the nation's reform agenda and international image. A new liberalism had emerged from the New Deal's assault on limited government and states rights. In their responses to the socioeconomic crisis of the Great Depression, New Deal liberals endorsed the principle of federal responsibility to promote economic recovery and relief (incorporated in legislation establishing the Agricultural Adjustment Administration, Social Security, and the National Labor Relations Board). The federal government's role, they had come to believe, should no longer be confined to promoting economic growth through tariffs and land grants or to acting as an impartial mediator to curb monopolies and abusive corporate practices. Federal responsibility should also include programs alleviating social and economic injustice, protecting workers' rights, and providing a safety net for Americans hit by hard times. Specific New Deal programs of the 1930s might not have directly challenged, and in some cases exacerbated, an existing system of racial segregation in the areas of agricultural relief, public housing, and public works. Still, these programs changed people's relationship to the federal government. In the process, New Deal liberals rejected an earlier Progressive era liberalism that had sanctioned the institution of Jim Crow laws (by southern legislators) and a racially segregated federal bureaucracy and military, based on the premise of the inherent inferiority of blacks.

This departure in New Deal politics was limited, reflected in liberal members of Congress's demands (notably, New York Senator Robert Wagner) for federal antilynching legislation. Then, with the onset of World War II, President Franklin Roosevelt, on June 25, 1941, by Executive Order 8802 prohibited racial discrimination in hiring by government agencies, in federally funded job training programs, and in those industries receiving federal defense contracts. The combination of Roosevelt's limited antidiscrimination order, the increase in defense production during World War II, and the declining availability of white male workers (triggered by the conscription of men in a still-segregated army) opened new economic opportunities for blacks and women.

In 1940, only 240 of the 100,000 aircraft workers were blacks, and then mainly janitors. Blacks comprised less than 1 percent of the workforce in the electrical machinery industry and less than 3 percent in the rubber industry. Black employment in federal agencies increased sharply owing to a wartime shortage of workers (from 60,000 to 200,000). For the first time since the federal bureaucracy was officially segregated in 1913, black women were hired as clerical workers (although they were assigned to segregated offices and promoted six times less than whites). Black employment in war industries also increased sharply (from 3 percent of all war workers in 1942 to 8 percent in 1945), while the number of black skilled workers doubled. One million black Americans, two-thirds women, obtained jobs during the war years. Yet despite these increased job opportunities, blacks continued to encounter occupational discrimination, as most white-collar and managerial positions were reserved for whites.

More strikingly, between 1940 and 1945, over 6 million women entered the workforce, increasing the number of employed women from 12 to 18 million. Between 1940 and 1945, the net gain for working women almost equaled that of the previous forty years. By 1945, women constituted 38 percent of all federal employees, more than double that of 1941. Women's employment gains were greatest in defense work, their employment increasing 460 percent. Concurrently, women's median wages (adjusted for inflation) increased by 38 percent, with married women receiving 72 percent of this increase. Nonetheless, most newly employed women were assigned jobs based on the conviction that they could not perform so-called man's work. A 1943 Detroit survey confirmed that more than one-half of employed women were employed in 5 of 72 job classifications, whereas only 11 percent of men were employed in these five categories.

These slight changes were also triggered by government pressure on employers to abandon prejudices that women were unable to perform many jobs. The trade journal *Automotive War Production* in 1943 articulated this prejudice: "woman power differs from manpower as oil fuel differs from coal" and recognition of this difference was necessary "for obtaining best results." Federal officials instead argued that the wartime employment crisis could only be resolved by employing women "on a scale heretofore unknown." By April 1942, government-supported vocational training of women increased from 1 percent to 13 percent, while the number of job categories for which employers were willing to consider women applicants increased from 29 percent to 55 percent. As strikingly, the army broke with tradition and in 1942 enlisted women in the Women's Army Corps (followed by the creation of women's units in the navy and the coast guard). Harvard Medical School first admitted women in 1944, and many hospitals accepted women interns for the first time.

A DIFFERENT POLITICS OF CIVIL LIBERTIES

Civil liberties advocates endorsed a contrasting conception of individual rights. Their principal objective, incorporated in the First Amendment's ban, was that "Congress shall make no law . . . abridging the freedom of speech, or of the press; or the right of the people peaceably to assemble and to petition the Government for a redress of grievances." The First Amendment did not guarantee unfettered speech and personal privacy but limited federal authority over speech and association. Thus, civil liberties advocates demanded limits to governmental action.

This conception of a negative guarantee had first been tested in World War I. When enacting the Espionage Act of 1917, Congress had specifically prohibited any spoken or written statements that "willfully" or "falsely" interfered "with the operation or success of the military or naval forces of the United States," promoted "the success of its enemies," caused "insubordination, disloyalty, mutiny, or refusal of duty" within the military services, or "willfully obstruct[ed]" military recruitment.

Free speech was not an absolute right, the Supreme Court ruled in 1919 in *Schenck v. U.S.* when upholding the constitutionality of the Espionage Act. "When a nation is at war," the Court affirmed, "many things that might be said in time of peace are such a hindrance to its efforts that their utterance will not be endured as long as men fight." The Court imposed a high standard for such restrictions: such speech must pose "a clear and present danger." That is, speech could be barred if the immediate result was harmful to legitimate security interests of the state.

This narrow exception was soon qualified further, in response to domestic and international developments triggered by the new internal security concerns of the New Deal and World War II eras. The socioeconomic crisis of the Great Depression led many Americans (though a numerical minority) to join fascist and communist movements. The ideological alignment of these movements with Nazi Germany and the Soviet Union acquired a more sinister significance with the outbreak of World War II in 1939. Concerned about the loyalty of American fascists and communists, Congress and the Roosevelt administration purposefully limited the ability of these potentially "subversive" movements to influence governmental policy.

This containment objective, however, was not to be advanced solely through legislative restrictions and criminal prosecution. Congress did curb suspected foreign-directed subversion under the Foreign Agents Registration Act of 1939, requiring any individual who "within the United States acts at the order, request, or under the direction of a foreign principal" to register with the Justice Department as a foreign agent. Congress also passed the Hatch Act to bar from federal employment any individual who was a member of "any political party or organization which advocated" the violent overthrow of government. The Alien Registration (or Smith) Act of 1940 extended these restrictions on radical activities by making it a crime to conspire to "knowingly or willfully advocate, abet, advise, or teach the duty, necessity, desirability, or propriety of overthrowing or destroying" the government "by force or violence." The act also criminalized membership in an organization, and publication and distribution of literature, that advocated the violent overthrow of government.

In contrast to World War I, government restrictions on civil liberties after 1936 also arose from secret executive directives. These directives expanded federal surveillance of radical activists for the purpose of anticipating and thereby containing possible subversion.

In August 1936, President Roosevelt secretly authorized FBI investigations of the suspected links between American fascist and communist movements and Nazi Germany and the Soviet Union. Interpreting Roosevelt's directive broadly, FBI officials launched a massive investigation of left-wing and right-wing activities—focusing primarily on left-wing trade union and political organizations (the U.S. Communist party, the International Longshoremen's Union, United Mine Workers, the Newspaper Guild) and secondarily on profascist organizations (the German-American Bund). Then, with the onset of World War II in Europe in September 1939, President Roosevelt sanctioned FBI surveillance of anti-interventionist organizations and pressured the FBI to monitor the "subversive" press (including profascist periodicals and mainstream isolationist newspapers the *Chicago Tribune* and *New York Daily News*).

President Roosevelt also sought to anticipate any espionage threat. In May 1940 he authorized FBI wiretapping during "national defense" investigations. To limit the risk that this secret wiretapping order could be discovered, Attorney General Robert Jackson purposely decided not to maintain the records of approved wiretaps. Jackson's decision undercut his own and his successors' abilities to monitor FBI wiretapping and emboldened FBI Director J. Edgar Hoover to devise special records procedures to preclude discovery of the FBI's more intrusive investigative techniques. In 1942, for example, Hoover instituted a Do Not File authorization procedure for the conduct of "clearly illegal" break-ins (employed to photograph sensitive records or install microphones targeting radical activists and organizations).

These illegal investigative techniques (wiretaps violated the 1934 Communication's ban and the Fourth Amendment which prohibited unreasonable searches and seizures) and the FBI's massive monitoring of subversive activities were not intended to prosecute individuals for violating national security laws. In contrast to World War I espionage cases, the scope of such surveillance remained unknown to the public. Premised on the need to acquire advance intelligence about the tactics and plans of dissident activists, FBI investigations enhanced the ability of executive branch officials to contain dissent. Two examples highlight how this secrecy undermined accountable government, and even presidential oversight.

In 1942, FBI agents broke into the New York headquarters of the American Youth Congress (AYC, a radical student organization) and in the process photocopied First Lady Eleanor Roosevelt's correspondence with AYC officials. FBI Director Hoover demanded that FBI officials review and prepare a report on Mrs. Roosevelt's correspondence, but President Roosevelt was not informed about this surveillance and analysis.

Again in 1942, FBI officials launched a massive investigation, which continued until 1956, to ascertain communist influence in the motion picture industry. This inquiry was triggered by FBI officials' concerns over the content of wartime films. Ironically, given U.S. alignment with the Soviet Union against fascist Germany, the suspect films were pro-Soviet—*Mission to Moscow*—or antifascist—*Hangmen Also Die*. FBI agents attempted to identify those producers, directors, actors, and stagehands who were members of the Communist party or Communist front organizations. This investigation promoted no legitimate national security objective, as the suspected actors and writers were neither engaged in nor had any opportunity to engage in espionage.

The AYC and Hollywood investigations highlight two potentially troublesome developments. First, seemingly legitimate national security concerns could result in investigations of political and personal activities. Second, FBI bureaucrats could use the acquired information not to prosecute but to stigmatize radical ideas and associations as inherently dangerous.

THE LEGACIES OF THE NEW DEAL AND WORLD WAR II

The New Deal and World War II bequeathed differing legacies for the post-1945 civil rights and civil liberties movements: sanctioning, on the one hand, the principle of federal responsibility to promote social and economic reform and, on the other, the legitimacy of security measures to ensure that subversives could not undermine governmental policy.

Internal security priorities posed new challenges for the post-1945 civil rights and civil liberties movements. Militant activists who demanded expanded government power to ensure racial equality were in effect challenging the interests of the nation's political and business leadership because such changes would entail restrictions on personal and property rights. These essentially radical demands rendered civil rights activists vulnerable to the charge of "subversion." To achieve their goal of fundamental social change, militant civil rights activists were dependent on a politics more tolerant of unpopular dissent.

Advocates of gay and lesbian rights were even more dependent on tolerance for civil liberties. Dating from 1937, FBI agents had begun collecting information about homosexuals (then termed "sex deviates") on the premise that homosexual federal employees could be blackmailed to betray the nation's secrets or to subvert government policy. Furthermore, every state had criminalized homosexual activities, and local police vice squads monitored places frequented by homosexuals.

A new politics of civil rights catalyzed by the antifascist tenets of World War II offset these restrictions. The democratic antiracialist rhetoric of the wartime antifascist alliance against Nazi Germany's Aryan white supremacist theories lent legitimacy to antisegregation demands. Threatening to organize a March on Washington in 1941, A. Philip Randolph and other civil rights advocates demanded that the federal government end racial discrimination in the armed services and in the hiring practices of defense contractors. In response, FBI agents intensively monitored the March on Washington movement and wiretapped its leadership.

Prominent black sociologists W. E. B. Du Bois and E. Franklin Frazier, the NAACP, and a catch-all category—"Negro Organizations"—were investigated owing to their "subversive tendencies." FBI officials were particularly interested in efforts "for the purpose of teaching negroes how to become qualified voters." A nationwide code-named RACON program instituted in June 1942 to survey the "extent of agitation among Negroes which may be the outgrowth of any effort on the part of the Axis powers or the Communist Party" uncovered no instance of espionage or sabotage but did obtain intelligence about the political strategies and tactics of black activists. As a byproduct of this survey to uncover "foreign inspired agitation among the Negroes in the country," FBI officials learned of rumors "concerning the formation of Eleanor or Eleanor Roosevelt Clubs among Negroes." The first lady's public support of racial justice led many conservative southerners to fear that white activists planned to travel to the South to recruit black domestics to join

Eleanor Clubs around the slogan "A White Woman in the Kitchen by Christmas." While a figment of southern segregationists' antipathy toward Mrs. Roosevelt, this rumored recruitment effort nonetheless triggered an intensive FBI investigation to ascertain whether Eleanor Clubs were being organized and black domestics "demanding their own terms for working."

With one glaring exception, the political activities of the targeted activists and organizations were not directly affected by such wartime surveillance. The sole exception involved ethnics suspected of disloyalty. On September 2, 1939 (the day after the German invasion of Poland and the start of World War II in Europe), FBI Director Hoover ordered FBI officials to identify all "persons of German, Italian, and Communist sympathies" and other persons "whose interest may be directed primarily to the interest of some nation other than the United States." All such "dangerous" or "potential dangerous" individuals, both alien residents and citizens, were to be listed in a Custodial Detention index and "watched carefully." This program acquired a different purpose in 1940 when Hoover obtained Attorney General Robert Jackson's approval of a plan to "arrest" these listed individuals " in the event the United States becomes involved in war." Intended to anticipate possible espionage and sabotage, FBI investigations focused on ethnic and radical activities and associations. Agents identified possible detainees by reviewing subscription lists of German, Italian, and communist newspapers; membership records and reports of informers who had infiltrated fascist and communist organizations; and the letterhead stationery of suspected profascist and procommunist groups.

The FBI's Custodial Detention program did not become fully operational in December 1941 following the Japanese attack on Pearl Harbor and the German declaration of war on the United States. Relying on the alien detention provisions of the 1798 Alien and Sedition Acts, President Roosevelt on December 8, 1941, authorized the detention of those German, Italian, and Japanese alien residents "deemed dangerous to the public peace and safety of the United States."

Federal officials, however, instituted another internment program in February 1942, restricted to all Japanese West Coast residents, three-quarters of whom were Japanese-American citizens. This internment program had been triggered by demands of military officials and West Coast political leaders based on racialist assumptions. As General John DeWitt argued, "The continued presence of a large, unassimilated, tightly knit racial group, bound to an enemy by strong ties of race, culture, custom and religion along a frontier [the Pacific Ocean] vulnerable to attack constituted a menace which had to be dealt with." California Attorney General Earl Warren similarly demanded the mass evacuation of all Japanese Americans, warning that "every alien Japanese should be considered in

Japanese Americans being relocated to internment camps.

the light of a potential" saboteur and that the absence of sabotage to date constituted proof of future sabotage planning.

On February 19, 1942, President Roosevelt issued Executive Order 9066 authorizing the secretary of war to designate war zones "from which any or all persons may be excluded." Military officials ordered the evacuation of 120,000 Japanese alien residents and Japanese-American citizens from California, Oregon, and Washington to be relocated in what were essentially concentration camps. In rulings of 1943 *(Hirabayashi v. U.S.)* and 1944 *(Korematsu v. U.S.)*, the Supreme Court upheld the constitutionality of the president's evacuation and detention order. Japanese-American citizens had not been discriminated against, the Court reasoned, adding that "residents having ethnic affiliations with an invading enemy may be a greater source of danger than those of different ancestry." National security considerations were given greater weight than individual rights. Government officials were not required to prove that all Japanese Americans posed such a danger (they could not) or that there were no other alternatives than treating all Japanese Americans as a class.

The German and Italian alien and the Japanese internment programs directly affected civil liberties. The FBI's intensive monitoring of radical dissent, homosexuality, civil rights, and labor activism during the New Deal and World War II eras might not have uncovered evidence that these activists (whether profascist or procommunist) were involved in espionage or sabotage. But they had collected massive amounts of derogatory information (some unsubstantiated hearsay) on the personal and political activities of suspected subversives. These surveillance records were retained. Supplemented by investigations that continued after 1945 to create massive files recording subversive beliefs and associations, these files acquired a different significance in the more alarmist security climate of the Cold War era. Increasingly after 1945, FBI officials secretly disseminated this information to conservatives in Congress (Senators Joseph McCarthy and Patrick McCarran, Congressmen Richard Nixon and J. Parnell Thomas, the House Committee on Un-American Activities and the Senate Internal Security Subcommittee) and in the media (the Hearst newspapers, *Chicago Tribune* Washington bureau chief Walter Trohan, and *New York Herald Tribune* Washington bureau chief Don Whitehead).

Two examples highlight the legacy of the FBI's wartime surveillance activities. In 1942, FBI officials launched an investigation of Washington *Times-Herald* gossip columnist Inga Arvad, in response to uncorroborated allegations that she might be a German spy. Despite closely monitoring her writings and various associations (including wiretapping her phone, reviewing her published column, and breaking into her apartment to photocopy her papers), FBI agents uncovered no evidence of espionage but did discover that Arvad was having a sexual affair with then–naval ensign John F. Kennedy. Through a bug installed in her hotel room (during two weekend visits with Kennedy in Charleston, South Carolina), FBI agents learned that Kennedy and Arvad engaged in "sexual intercourse on numerous occasions" and that Arvad had attempted to pressure Kennedy to marry her by implying that she might have become "pregnant as a result."

FBI officials recognized the political sensitivity of investigating a columnist employed by the isolationist, anti–New Deal *Washington Times-Herald*. This file on Arvad had to be safeguarded because the newspaper's editors would "be quick to expose" the FBI investigation. Maintained separate from the FBI's central records system, the file was transferred to FBI Director Hoover's office on July 14, 1960, the day Kennedy won the Democratic presidential nomination. It is unclear how FBI officials used this information during Kennedy's presidency. FBI officials did at minimum brief Nixon White House aide Charles Colson in 1971 about the Kennedy-Arvad affair. At the time, the Nixon White House had begun collecting derogatory information about the Kennedys, fearing that the former president's brother, Senator Edward Kennedy, might emerge as the Democratic presidential nominee in 1972.

The second incident involved Pulitzer Prize-winning *New York Times* reporter Harrison Salisbury. Based on the uncorroborated allegations of a suspicious neighbor, FBI officials listed Salisbury in 1941 in the Custodial Detention index. In 1942, Salisbury's UPI (United Press International) employer decided to assign their valued reporter to cover the war in Europe—requiring accreditation from the War Department. Before granting clearance, military officials checked with the FBI, and learned of his inclusion in the FBI's Custodial Detention index, deemed a "code expert" and "in the employ of the German government." Based on this misinformation, the War Department rejected UPI's request. Unwilling to lose Salisbury's services, UPI officials pressed the matter. Conducting their own investigation, War Department officials discovered that the FBI's sole source, Salisbury's neighbor, was "unreliable" and came from a family "known to be nefarious prevaricators."

The Arvad-Kennedy and Salisbury incidents underscore the long-term threat to civil liberties posed by the scope, purpose, and secrecy of FBI investigations. Both were mainstream reporters, and yet never knew about (and could not refute) the secret collection of misinformation and derogatory personal information. Retention of such accumulated information offered new opportunities during the vastly different national security politics of the Cold War era.

Part One

1945–60

World War II profoundly influenced civil rights and civil liberties at home. As a world leader of a democratic crusade against fascist racism and imperialism, the United States had helped ensure an Allied (U.S., British, and Soviet) victory over the Axis powers (Germany, Japan, and Italy). Military victory and the creation of the United Nations offered the promise of an enduring peace and the expansion of democratic principles. When trying leaders of Nazi Germany and Japan for war crimes, Allied leaders legitimated the punishment of perpetrators of racist oppression.

The promise of continued postwar cooperation was not to be realized. Both nations soon became enmeshed in diplomatic conflict over the shape of the postwar world. With German and Japanese military withdrawal from occupied territory in Eastern Europe, China, and Southeast Asia, Soviet troops moved into Eastern Europe and part of prewar China and Japan. In addition, the social and economic costs of the war and the brutality of German and Japanese occupation unleashed democratic, anticolonial movements in the Balkans, the Middle East, Asia, and Africa that challenged the restoration of European colonialism. The United States and the Soviet Union emerged from the war as international rivals, abandoning cooperation for a politics of confrontation. This conflict differed from earlier political–military rivalries between nation-states. Competing ideologies (a conflict between capitalist democracy based on free trade and individual rights, and communist centralism based on state trading systems and the primacy of the Communist party and the state) underpinned this bipolar world conflict. Increasingly after

1947, U.S. officials represented the Soviet Union not simply as a militarily powerful adversary but as a subversive clique bent on world domination.

This conception of the Soviet threat was incorporated in what became the blueprint of U.S. policy during the Cold War era, National Security Council directive 68 (NSC 68). The "integrity and vitality of our system is in greater jeopardy than ever before in our history," the framers of this directive posited, threatened by the "Kremlin design . . . which would destroy our free and democratic system." To stem this threat would require a substantial increase in defense spending to address the conventional military threat posed by a heavily armed Soviet Union and to counter the unprecedented threat posed by revolutionary movements. Soviet agents, moreover, would attempt to recruit sympathetic individuals to commit espionage or influence U.S. policy. This fear of Soviet subversion legitimated efforts to monitor movements and activists advocating radical economic and political change. One by-product was the meteoric rise of the nation's most prominent anti-Communist, Senator Joseph McCarthy.

The framing of the Cold War as an ideological conflict between individual liberties and freedom and totalitarian repression, however, also legitimated efforts to ensure political equality and racial justice. U.S. professions of freedom and democracy were contradicted by the reality of racism infecting the nation's schools, housing patterns, the right to vote, blood supplies, and distribution of services. An amicus brief challenging racial segregation filed in the 1954 *Brown v. Board of Education of Topeka* case highlights this interconnection: "It is in the context of the present world struggle between freedom and tyranny that the problem of racial discrimination must be viewed. . . . Racial discrimination furnishes grist for the Communist propaganda mills, and it raises doubts even among friendly nations as to the intensity of our devotion to the democratic faith." The *New York Times* similarly editorialized, "When some hostile propagandist rises in Moscow or Peking to accuse us of having a class society we can if we wish recite the courageous words of yesterday's opinion. The highest court in the land, . . . has reaffirmed its faith—the undying American faith—in the equality of all men and children before the law."

Chapter 1

THE EMERGENCE OF A NEW CIVIL RIGHTS MOVEMENT

American participation in World War II rested on a contradiction. This was a "good war," fought against the imperialism and racism of Germany, Italy, and Japan. Yet, the ideals of self-determination, liberty, and democracy that U.S. officials claimed distinguished the Allied cause from that of the Axis seemed little more than slogans when viewed through the unjust treatment of people of color in the United States. As First Lady Eleanor Roosevelt explained, "The nation cannot expect colored people to feel that the United States is worth defending if the Negro continues to be treated as he is now." The split between these wartime ideals and the practice of democracy within the United States became the ground from which postwar freedom struggles grew. The economic and social changes produced by the war, the experiences of people who served in the war, and the changing consciousness that resulted in the aftermath of the war formed a critical springboard for the postwar civil rights movement.

Called to serve their country on the battlefield, blacks were treated as second-class citizens at home and largely excluded from the growing defense industry and government jobs. Many black leaders sought to use this moment of expanding economic opportunity to change the status of African Americans. For example, the socialist labor activist A. Philip Randolph threatened in 1941 to mobilize blacks to march en masse on Washington to protest discriminatory labor conditions. Randolph had earlier founded the black radical newspaper the *Messenger* and had helped organize a union for black railroad porters, the Brotherhood of Sleeping Car

Porters. As the nation entered World War II, Randolph again saw the United States calling on the loyalty and service of African Americans to risk their lives abroad without treating them as equal citizens at home. He explained, "One thing is certain and that is that if Negroes are going to get anything out of this National Defense, we must fight for it and fight with the gloves off."

Fearful of the negative international publicity of a mass march of blacks on Washington, President Roosevelt met with Randolph. Roosevelt agreed to prohibit discrimination in war industries and government positions in exchange for Randolph calling off the march. To do this, Roosevelt issued Executive Order 8802 establishing the Fair Employment Practices Commission (FEPC) and prohibiting discrimination in defense industries and in the government. The symbolic importance of the president acceding to the demands of a mass movement and affirming the principle of antidiscrimination policy within the executive branch was significant. The effect of Roosevelt's action, however, was limited. The FEPC was given no teeth to enforce these antidiscrimination provisions. In addition, of the nearly two million blacks employed in the munitions industries, most were confined to the lower-paying, menial jobs. Some black women for the first time did find industrial jobs, but most continued working as domestic labor. The armed forces were not desegregated, much to the consternation of most blacks.

WARTIME MIGRATION AND URBANIZATION

The opening of economic opportunities in the North combined with the dire situation blacks faced in the South led to a second great migration of blacks to the North. The mechanical picker, along with the effects of the Great Depression, had wreaked havoc on the livelihoods of sharecroppers and small tenant farmers in the South. Across the region, the price of cotton plummeted from $.35 per pound in 1919 to $.06 in 1931. Increased mechanization reduced the need for workers. By the 1960s, modernized plantations needed one-fifth of their workforce. Since Reconstruction the economic, political, and physical intimidation of black people had been the law and custom of the land. As a result, more than one million blacks migrated to the North in the 1940s, and another 1.5 million did so in the 1950s. Most blacks continued to live in the South—with many migrating from the rural to the urban South. Between 1940 and 1960, Birmingham's black population increased 84 percent, Montgomery's 40 percent, and Baton Rouge's a tremendous 453 percent. Thus, by 1950, the majority of blacks lived in cities in the North and in the South.

African Americans were not the only ones migrating because of the war. During the Great Depression, many Mexicans had been forcibly deported from the United States, viewed as a threat to "American" jobs. The war brought a new policy, the bracero program. Mexican workers were recruited to the United States. Congress appropriated $100 million for this wartime labor recruitment program and 250,000 workers migrated to the United States. Bracero workers helped grow and harvest sugar beets, tomatoes, peaches, plums, and cotton in 21 states and worked on the railroad. In 1944 alone, they harvested crops worth $432 million.

Found to be extremely profitable to the growing U.S. agribusiness, these bracero labor programs continued through the 1950s and 1960s. More than 4.5 million Mexicans migrated to the United States between 1948 and 1964 to do farm work, making up 25 percent of all farm workers in the United States. Alongside this recruitment program, from 1954 through 1958, the Immigration and Naturalization Service (INS) began a program called Operation Wetback, which deported nearly two million persons of Mexican descent from the United States to Mexico, responding to inflammatory press coverage of alien workers constituting a foreign menace to the nation's moral fabric. These nativist sentiments, fueled by the anti-Communist politics of the period, conflicted with corporate desire for cheap, vulnerable labor, as southwestern agribusiness relied on the economic advantages of immigrant labor. Owners paid bracero workers pittance wages and also used them to prevent unionization among farmworkers, playing immigrant and native-born workers against each other. Even when the bracero program officially ended in 1964, braceros continued to be recruited to do farm work.

People of color began to crack another barrier to employment during the war years—unions. As some unions began to open their ranks in large scale to black workers, particularly within the Congress of Industrial Organizations (CIO), blacks joined in high numbers. Black union membership increased from two hundred thousand in 1940 to 1.25 million in 1945. Many white workers reacted with violence to protest having to work and live alongside blacks. Hate strikes—where whites would walk off the job to protest the hiring of any black workers—shut down factories in Detroit, Chicago, Baltimore, and Philadelphia. Many unions, particularly in the skilled trades, remained entirely closed to blacks.

Racial tension simmered in cities like Detroit, as increasing numbers of blacks migrated to the city to work in the war industries and were often harassed verbally and physically at schools, in city parks, on the street, and in factories. Violence erupted in January 1942, when the first black families moved into the Sojourner Truth housing projects. Between 1941 and 1944, white factory workers held dozens of wildcat strikes to protest the hiring or upgrading of black workers. In June of 1943, the worst riot of the war years occurred when black and white teenagers clashed on Belle Isle (a local park and picnic spot for black and white Detroiters). Looting and rampaging erupted across the city, while the police killed 17 blacks but no whites. In the end, 25 African Americans and 9 whites were killed and hundreds of thousands of dollars of property destroyed.

THE CONTRADICTIONS OF MILITARY SERVICE

During the 1930s, many blacks had sharply criticized rising fascism in Europe and rallied behind the cause of antifascism, particularly Italy's military aggression against Ethiopia. One of only two nations to escape European colonialism, Ethiopia was seen by many black Americans as the heart of Black Africa. When Italy invaded Ethiopia in 1935 and forced Emperor Haile Selassie into exile, blacks across the United States raised money, formed committees in New York City, Chicago, and Los Angeles, and agitated the League of Nations to intervene against Italy on behalf of Ethiopia's sovereign status.

Five hundred thousand blacks served overseas during World War II. More than three million black men registered for the war, and about one million black men and women served in the armed services (roughly equal to the black percentage in population). However, blacks served in separate units, and black troops were often assigned menial work in the armed forces. Racial tensions at army bases in the United States and among the troops stationed overseas was high. Similar discriminatory treatment affected the Latino, Native-American, and Japanese-American communities. A half a million Chicanos served in segregated units in World War II, as did 100,000 Puerto Ricans and 44,500 Native Americans. Many Japanese enlisted, often joining the army straight from the internment camps where they were being held.

Even enlisting was often segregated. A black high school teacher in Charlotte, for example, was beaten severely for taking four of his students to the "whites only" army enlistment station. One great irony in the fight against Hitler's Nazi Germany (and its policy of biological determinism) was that the American blood supply during the war was separated by race—all the more ironic because the research of a black doctor, Charles Drew, had made blood banks possible in the first place. Drew ultimately ended up resigning from the Red Cross over their policy.

Another irony of the war involved the use of Navajo code talkers to communicate military secrets during the war—many of whom had attended government boarding schools where speaking in Navajo was forbidden. Because of the complexity of the Navajo language (referred to by the U.S. military as "the unbreakable code"), 420 Navajo code talkers proved indispensable to the U.S. war in the Pacific. Yet on numerous occasions, their fellow soldiers captured or attacked them, thinking they did not "look American."

Many people of color refused to accept this discriminatory treatment. By late 1943, blacks comprised 35 percent of the nation's delinquent registrants, and between 1941 and 1946, over two thousand black men were imprisoned for not complying with the Selective Service Act. Some blacks, like the young Malcolm X, purposefully acted crazy at their induction hearings to get classified psychologically unfit for war. Many Japanese Americans held in internment camps also chose to resist the draft and face jail sentences (and often ostracism within the Japanese-American community) to protest being interned without cause. Twenty-two percent of draft-age Japanese-American males answered "no," qualified their answer, or refused to answer questions regarding their willingness to serve in the U.S. army and swear unqualified allegiance to the United States. They felt that other Americans were not required to fill out such a form so neither should they. As Frank Emi, a young father interned at Heart Mountain camp, explained, "The more I looked at it the more disgusted I became. We were treated more like enemy aliens than American citizens."

At home, black leaders continued to agitate over unequal treatment in the armed forces and in society at large. Black writer George Schuyler explained, "Our war is not to defend democracy, but to get a democracy we have never had." In 1942, the black newspaper the *Pittsburgh Courier* called for a "Double V Campaign"—Victory at Home, Victory Abroad. Joining with blacks across the country, the *Courier* demanded that the struggle for equality for African Americans continue, even amidst the war. Strident in criticizing discrimination, many black newspapers were threatened with censorship and loss of access to rationed newsprint.

One particular manifestation of this tension came to a head around clothing in Los Angeles in June of 1943. U.S. servicemen rioted by stripping young black and Latino men of their zoot suits and beating people of Latino descent regardless of what they were wearing. Baggy suits tapered at the ankle with a hat to match, zoot suits were popular with young blacks and Latinos. The suits took on a subversive meaning, emphasizing a bold new identity for young African Americans and Chicanos. In contrast to the white custom of calling black men "boy," zoot suiters called each other "man," talked fast, and refused to be subservient to authority. This proud posture—and fabric rationing regulations that outlawed these baggy suits—made wearing a zoot suit an anti-American gesture.

At the end of the war in 1945, white and nonwhite GIs returned to the United States to dramatically different receptions. Whites came home to a jubilant United States that honored their service and provided education, health, and pension benefits to mark their dedication. Black and Latino soldiers returned to an America unwilling to acknowledge fully the bravery of their service or treat them as first-class citizens. Their benefits were administered in segregated fashion and sometimes in ways that made them nearly impossible to obtain and use. This double standard was strikingly evident in Salina, Kansas, where German prisoners of war were served at a lunch counter while black soldiers who accompanied them were refused service; in Alabama, where a black army nurse boarded the bus before the white passengers and was beaten and then jailed for her presumption; and in Three Rivers, Texas, where a funeral home refused to bury a Chicano soldier killed in the Pacific during the war. In some places, from Liberty, Mississippi, to Columbia, Tennessee, whites rioted and lynched black servicemen—attempting to extinguish black aspirations that might have grown during the war. But the war had changed these men and women. Many like Mississippian Medgar Evers, North Carolinian Robert Williams, Georgian Jackie Robinson, Kansan Oliver Brown, and Californian César Chávez soon took the struggle for equal rights to new, more militant places. They came back from the war unwilling to tolerate second-class status at home and committed to working to eliminate it.

The nation itself faced new international realities. The contradictions between the United States' international posture and domestic practice became clearer in the postwar period. In prosecuting Nazi leaders for war crimes in the Nuremberg trials, the nation's leaders helped make racial persecution an international issue. Nazi predilection for eugenics made theories of biological racism increasingly suspect in the United States. The United States also emerged from World War II in a mounting Cold War with the Soviet Union. Hoping to win the hearts and minds of the world towards capitalist democracy, U.S. officials became more conscious of how civil rights protests highlighting the lack of democracy within the United States impacted the nation's global image.

The struggle for civil rights in the United States also became embedded in a larger struggle of people of color abroad. With the convening of the Fifth Pan-African Congress in Manchester, England, in October 1945, Africans, African Americans, and Afro-Caribbeans met to forge an international alliance to promote independence for African nations and justice in the United States. U.S. scholar and writer W. E. B. Du Bois joined African independence leaders such as Jomo Kenyatta and Kwame Nkrumah to "make the world listen to the facts of our condition. We will fight in every way we can for freedom, democracy, and social betterment."

Challenges to U.S. colonialism in Puerto Rico had also been brewing for decades. Bought by the United States from Spain in 1898, the island gained U.S. citizenship in 1917; Puerto Ricans could migrate to the United States without a visa but were subject to being drafted. With the 1950 Puerto Rican Federal Relations Act, the island gained the right to draft its own constitution as long as it followed the limitations placed on a U.S. territory. This did not give Puerto Ricans any representation in Washington, D.C. In 1952, a majority of Puerto Ricans voted to become a commonwealth, having been denied the option to vote for statehood. Some Puerto Ricans opposed commonwealth status and the role President Truman had played in insuring it, seeing it as continued Puerto Rican subservience to the U.S. political economy. Angered at Truman's support of U.S. military and economic control of Puerto Rico, on November 1, 1950, Puerto Rican nationalists unsuccessfully tried to assassinate the president. Over three years later, on March 1, 1954, four Puerto Rican nationalists, members of the Independence movement, attacked the United States Congress, wounding five congressmen.

THE SEGREGATED UNITED STATES AND THE LEGAL FIGHT TO CHANGE IT

Segregation had long been a method of protecting white economic and social privilege and maintaining black second-class status. Southern segregation—often called "Jim Crow," after a popular minstrel dance of the 1800s—was assured through separate drinking fountains, bathrooms, trains, schools, public spaces, blood supplies, lunch counters, movies, and churches. Racial codes constrained social interaction. Blacks were addressed only by their first names and stepped aside on the sidewalk so that whites could walk freely by. In places throughout the South, whites were sworn in at court using one Bible and blacks another (and blacks were forced to hold the Bible themselves so the court officer did not have to touch it). At a South Carolina cotton mill, blacks and whites were even forbidden to look out the same window. With the tacit and often explicit aid of the courts and police, groups of whites meted out their own justice against blacks through public hangings, burnings, or torture. An upsurge in antiblack violence in 1945 and 1946 was another sign that many whites were willing to resort to violence to keep blacks as second-class citizens.

School segregation was the centerpiece of this system of unequal rights. Across the country, white schools had better facilities with newer books and more resources. Per-pupil spending across the country depended primarily on the race of the pupil. In many schools across the South, white students attended school two months longer than black students. In Mississippi in 1950, for example, the state spent $122.93 per pupil on whites versus $32.55 for blacks; white teachers made $1,861 a year, black teachers averaged $711. Whites had free transportation where blacks had to pay. Only 7 percent of black students finished high school in Mississippi—one-sixth the number of whites.

The South was not the only segregated region in the United States. Northern segregation operated slightly differently but ensured white privilege just the same. Public spaces—bathrooms, trains, movie theaters, and lunch counters—were not legally separated for blacks and whites. But schools, housing, and jobs operated on a strict racial hierarchy with whites at the top. And many public spaces, although not explicitly marked "for whites only," were effectively restricted to whites. Housing was one of the most blatant areas of discrimination—carried out through the collusion of the federal government, local banks, real estate agents, private citizens, and homeowner associations. Blacks who dared move into white neighborhoods were met with violence. In Chicago, between 1945 and 1946, whites attacked 46 black homes, and, in the next three years, four riots erupted as blacks attempted to move into all-white areas.

The Federal Housing Authority (FHA), established during the New Deal to facilitate home ownership for working Americans, helped enable segregation. The process of standardization that the FHA introduced included a system of rating neighborhoods from A through D. The neighborhoods that received A ratings were invariably all white, with no blacks, Chicanos, or Jews, and deemed most favorable for loans. The neighborhoods receiving D ratings were neighborhoods where people of color lived and considered very high risk for loans (or red-lined). These ratings often were not based on the quality of housing or buildings in the neighborhoods but on prevalent societal ideas about the people who inhabited them. Predictive rather that descriptive, these ratings did not just reveal segregation—they caused it. Blacks often could not get bank loans—and when granted loans, they were restricted to certain parts of the city. Favoring new construction over rehabilitation, new suburban homes over old city ones, FHA standards also set in motion a process of urban decay.

THE NAACP'S CAMPAIGN AGAINST SEGREGATION

Opposition to racial inequality and segregation did not surface only after 1945. Founded in 1909 after a brutal lynching in Springfield, Illinois, the interracial National Association for the Advancement of Colored People (NAACP) had protested racial injustice since its inception. The NAACP was not started as a mass-based organization but focused on winning legislative and judicial action and using its public voice to secure change by working within the law. Under the leadership of Walter White, the NAACP in the 1930s through the 1950s waged a national legal campaign to dismantle segregation while, for the first time, simultaneously beginning to build a local base.

The organization's leaders saw that it needed to build its local presence to grow and also to counter grassroots organizing by radical organizations such as the Communist Party. Between 1931 and 1954, the NAACP's membership increased dramatically from 70,000 to 400,000. By cultivating an indigenous leadership and a grassroots presence, local branches provided a foundation for the movement to grow in the 1950s and 1960s. The organizing strategies and political vision of these local leaders often exceeded the national office's ideas about appropriate action or politically effective strategy, and the national office often tried to rein in the work of its local leaders.

At the same time, through a series of court cases aimed first at graduate and professional schools, the NAACP chipped away at the legal basis of educational segregation and the Supreme Court's 1896 decision in *Plessy v. Ferguson*, which had legalized "separate but equal" facilities. These cases demanded the persistence of the plaintiffs and the NAACP to follow them for years through the courts and laid the groundwork for the landmark Supreme Court decision of *Brown v. Board of Education of Topeka* in 1954, which outlawed segregation once and for all.

For instance, in Maryland, where there was no separate law school for blacks, the Maryland Supreme Court ruled that the University of Maryland must let Donald Murray into the law school immediately in 1935. In 1938, in *Gaines v. Missouri*, the U.S. Supreme Court struck down the state's provisions to send black defendant Lloyd Gaines to another state for law school since a separate black law school did not exist in Missouri. These two decisions opened formerly all-white institutions to black defendants but retained the separate-but-equal logic of *Plessy v. Ferguson*.

The NAACP, through a team of lawyers headed first by Charles Hamilton Houston and then by Thurgood Marshall, chiseled away at the laws and policies that allowed for racial discrimination. Under Oklahoma law, school officials could not admit so-called colored students to white schools or teach classes of mixed races. In 1946, Ada Sipuel applied to University of Oklahoma Law School, the only law school in the state. Ordered by the Supreme Court in 1948 to provide facilities for her, the university established separate ones. She declined to attend and, with the help of the NAACP, sued again. In 1949, the Supreme Court ruled that she must be admitted to the regular university.

In 1950, the University of Oklahoma graduate school admitted G. W. McLaurin but segregated him in the classroom and placed a curtain in front of his library carrel. McLaurin sued, and on June 5, 1950, the

Supreme Court found these practices unconstitutional. In 1950, the Court also ordered the University of Texas law school to admit the black defendant Herman Sweatt even though separate black facilities existed, ruling that the provisions between the white and black schools were not equal. In two unanimous decisions, the Court, though not overturning the logic of *Plessy,* had begun to take seriously the *equal* in "separate but equal."

The NAACP also challenged discrimination in public transportation and housing. NAACP attorneys also succeeded when the Court ruled against segregated interstate travel in 1946 and Jim Crow dining cars in 1950. In response, in 1947, the Congress of Racial Equality (CORE) organized a Journey of Reconciliation through the upper South to test the Supreme Court ruling desegregating interstate buses. Founded in 1942 by James Farmer, CORE was inspired by Mahatma Gandhi's civil disobedience in India and A. Philip Randolph's March on Washington movement. Gandhi had led thousands of East Indians to disobey the laws that propped up Britain's colonial rule in India, and these militant nonviolent actions succeeded in winning India's independence. Farmer believed that such protest tactics could be used in challenging racial inequity in the United States. The riders, a mixed group of blacks and whites, were harassed and then arrested in North Carolina for violating the state's segregation laws, despite the Supreme Court's having ruled that interstate buses must be desegregated. Although illegally cut short, this ride served as a precursor for the Freedom Rides that CORE sponsored in 1961.

NAACP attorneys also attacked housing segregation. Segregation was enforced in part through restrictive covenants, provisions written into housing contracts and neighborhood association bylaws whereby the new buyer promised not to sell the house to blacks. In 1945, the McGhees, an upwardly mobile black family in Detroit, bought a house in a white neighborhood. The neighbors strenuously objected, citing a restrictive covenant that made it illegal for any black family to move into the neighborhood. With the help of the NAACP, the McGhees challenged this in court. In 1948, the Supreme Court decided unanimously in *Shelley v. Kraemer* that restrictive covenants could not be enforced by the state. This ruling helped enable an open housing movement, but housing discrimination did not end. As late as 1968, the FHA regularly approved housing covenants that denied blacks the right to rent or buy a home. This open housing movement, moreover, revealed class tensions already present within the black community, as some middle-class blacks sought to distance themselves and their character from poorer blacks.

As middle-class blacks began to test their new mobility, white homeowner associations and civic groups lashed back. Whites drew imaginary boundaries around their neighborhoods and used rocks and pickets, taunts and arson to harass those blacks who dared cross the invisible line. In an unanticipated way, the Eisenhower administration helped some whites flee racial integration through the Federal Highway Act of 1956. Combined with earlier mortgage assistance to middle-class Americans, federal funding of highway construction contributed to the migration of white professionals and skilled workers from the nation's cities to outlying suburbs. The racial and economic resegregation of the nation's cities had long-term consequences for race relations in the subsequent decades.

During the 1940s and 1950s, moreover, a number of Chicano organizations, including the American GI Forum and the League of United Latin American Citizens (LULAC), also pursued cases that laid a precedent for overturning segregation. Middle-class Mexican Americans formed LULAC in a 1929 fight for expanded opportunities. Then, after the Three Rivers funeral home refused to bury Félix Longoria, a soldier who had died in the Pacific, Mexican-American veterans founded the GI Forum to press for equal treatment. In *Westminster v. Méndez* (1946), lawyers challenged the segregation of Mexican children under the Fourteenth Amendment and won their most important legal victory when a U.S. district court ordered the desegregation of a number of Southern California schools. The Court of Appeals for the Ninth Circuit affirmed the verdict, stating that neither race nor language could be used to segregate children.

Challenges to segregation extended to sports. Black baseball players worked only in the Negro Leagues, not on any major or minor league teams. Since the 1930s, blacks had demanded the integration of organized baseball, and World War II intensified these demands. As one black newspaper mocked, "Let's have the Negro have his name on the casualty lists of Pearl Harbor or Batan or Midway. But, for heavensakes, let's keep his name out of the boxscores." Prodded by New York's mayor Fiorello La Guardia, Branch Rickey, the president and general manager of the Brooklyn Dodgers, decided to sign a black player, Jackie Robinson, as part of a plan to bring young players to the Dodgers. He picked Robinson, one of a number of extremely talented ballplayers, because his army background, college education, race pride, and willingness not to retaliate when taunted made him the kind of respectable choice that Rickey was seeking. Assigned to the Dodgers' farm team, the Montreal Royals, in 1946, Robinson was called up for spring training with the Dodgers on April 10, 1947. The black press was jubilant, having promoted the strengths of Negro League players for years. The Dodgers trained in Cuba that year to make Robinson's training easier. In spring training, about a half dozen players threatened to mutiny if Robinson played. Rickey threatened their jobs, and they backed down.

On opening day against the Boston Braves, Jackie Robinson played first base and changed America's national pastime. To do this, Robinson endured public abuse from fans, opposing teammates, and even members of his own team. Other teams called him "snowflake" and shouted, "Hey, nigger, why don't you go back to the cottonfields where you belong?" Robinson received hate mail at home, and the Philadelphia Phillies and St. Louis Cardinals threatened to refuse to take the field if Robinson played. But slowly he won over his Dodger teammates and fans across the nation. At the end of the year, having led the Dodgers with 29 stolen bases, 125 in-run scores, and a batting average of .297, Robinson was named National League Rookie of the Year by the magazine *Sporting News*. The editors wrote, "That Jackie Roosevelt Robinson might have had more obstacles than his first year competitors, and . . . a harder fight to gain even major league recognition, was no concern of this publication. . . . He was rated . . . on the basis of his hitting, his running, his defensive play, his team value." By the end 1947, 15 other blacks were playing in organized baseball, about half in the Dodgers' minor league clubs. Two years later, in 1949, Robinson was chosen Most Valuable Player. The integration of the major leagues spelled the end of the Negro Leagues, one of the largest black-owned and operated businesses at the time.

The foundations of racism were slowly beginning to crack. In 1946, President Truman appointed a Committee on Civil Rights to prevent discrimination and investigate civil rights. In 1947, the NAACP petitioned the newly formed United Nations to demand that the United States protect black rights and black lives at home. Playing to the emerging global politics of the Cold War, the NAACP argued, "It is not Russia that threatens the United States so much as Mississippi." That same month, the president's Civil Rights Committee issued its report entitled *To Secure These Rights*. After detailing incidents of lynchings and police brutality and the refusal of state and local governments to protect basic human rights, the committee recommended a series of modest changes in federal public policy: expanding the Justice Department's civil rights section to a division; enacting legislation banning lynchings and the poll tax; making the FEPC permanent and creating a joint congressional civil rights committee; and ending racial discrimination in federal employment and the military services. The committee emphasized that the nation could no longer ignore the "growing international implications of civil rights violations." Over one million copies of the report were sold and distributed over the next year. However, the powerful block of Southern Democrats (who held leadership positions on key congressional committees) filibustered to preclude immediate legislative action on the committee's recommendations.

Then, in 1948, under pressure from Randolph, who again threatened massive civil disobedience, Truman issued an order to desegregate the military. Like Roosevelt, Truman feared international attention to America's race problem, particularly as the Cold War heated up. Running for reelection in 1948, Truman used this desegregation order to shore up black support and to undercut the challenge of Henry Wallace, who was running as a candidate of the left-wing, antisegregationist Progressive Citizens of America party with support from W. E. B. Du Bois, actor Paul Robeson, and many southern black activists. By integrating the armed forces and red-baiting Wallace for his bold political stands, Truman bolstered his own popularity with blacks and New Deal liberals. He was reelected in 1948, with black votes making the crucial difference in Ohio, Illinois, and California.

By 1950, NAACP lawyers decided to confront school segregation head-on. They brought suit in five cases challenging primary school segregation, arguing that black children were denied the quality of education available to white children in Clarendon County, South Carolina; the District of Columbia; Topeka, Kansas; Prince Edward County, Virginia; and Wilmington, Delaware. These cases were ultimately consolidated under *Brown v. Board of Education* (the name of the Topeka case) to emphasize the national character of school segregation. In Topeka, Rev. Oliver Brown's seven-year-old daughter had to cross the railroad tracks and wait for a worn-down bus to drive her to the black school across town when a white school was much closer to their house. In Clarendon County, the county spent $179 per capita on white students but only $43 on black students. When the community asked for a bus for black children in 1947 and the superintendent refused, the community decided to fight for full equalization of schools. All of the people connected to the NAACP's petition in Clarendon County were fired. The leader of the struggle, J. A. Delaine, lost his job, as did his wife, two sisters, and niece. Whites burned his house, stoned his church, and fired shots at him in the dark. In Prince Edward County, the black Moton High School held twice as many students as it was designed for and had no cafeteria or gym. When the school system dragged its feet on improving the school, sixteen-year-old Barbara Johns organized her classmates to strike to demand a better school. The NAACP originally hesitated to support the strike, believing it was too risky given how few moderate whites lived in the county. NAACP lawyer Spotswood Robinson met with the students on the third day of the strike. Impressed by Johns and the striking students, he agreed to take the case as long as the parents agreed to a direct attack on segregation.

NAACP lawyers challenged the constitutionality of segregation on two fronts. They argued that segregation itself was damaging and violated the Fourteenth Amendment's guarantee of equal protection. They also argued that the only way to make schools and school resources truly equal was to integrate them. Thurgood Marshall and the other NAACP lawyers called this double attack the "bow with two strings." Key to the first approach was the research of black psychologist Kenneth Clark, who showed the psychological damage of segregation on black children using experiments with black and white dolls. Most of the black children questioned during the experiment called white dolls "nice," while describing the black dolls as "bad." Clark concluded, "These children saw themselves as inferior, and they accepted the inferiority as part of reality." The Department of Justice joined the NAACP's efforts by filing an amicus brief that asserted that school desegregation was critical to the United States' international position.

Chief Justice Earl Warren played a pivotal role in making *Brown v. Board* one of the landmark cases of the twentieth century. New to the Supreme Court, Warren recognized the historical importance of the *Brown* case and the opportunity to overturn decisively the *Plessy* decision. Aware of the controversy it would spark, he labored to ensure a unanimous decision, believing that unanimity would make it more difficult to undermine. On May 17, 1954, the Supreme Court ruled unanimously in *Brown v. Board of Education* that "separate educational facilities are inherently unequal," overturning the legal basis of school segregation. The Court also cited the need to protect the international reputation of the United States as part of its reason to put an end to school segregation. Monroe, North Carolina's NAACP president, Robert Williams, eloquently articulated the meaning of the decision for many black Americans. "On this momentous night of May 17, 1954, I felt that at last the government was willing to assert itself on behalf of first-class citizenship, even for Negroes."

To accomplish this unanimity, however, Warren agreed to delay the implementation of the decision for another year. After hearing more testimony over the next year, in *Brown II* (1955), the Court called for desegregation to happen "with all deliberate speed." Asking for "a prompt and reasonable start towards full compliance," the Court returned the cases to the states for implementation, setting no definite timeline for desegregation and, instead, putting the burden back on civil rights activists to press for compliance. The elation of the previous year gave way to discouragement; the vagueness of the wording invited delay and outright rebellion on the part of segregationists. As Charles Houston pointed out years earlier, "Nobody needs to explain to a Negro the difference between the law in books and the law in action."

THE AFTERMATH OF *BROWN*

The *Brown* decision asserted black citizenship—that blacks were entitled to the same quality of education in the same school as whites—and became another weapon in the arsenal of civil rights workers. But it provided no real protections for that citizenship in a society where many were willing to fight to deny blacks equal rights. Indeed, some white southerners came to refer to the day the *Brown* ruling was handed down as "Black Monday." As Mississippi Senator James Eastland explained, "On May 17, 1954, the Constitution of the United States was destroyed because of the Supreme Court's decision. You are not obliged to obey the decisions of any court which are plainly fraudulent." President Eisenhower made no effort to stem this resistance to the decision of the highest court in the nation. He tried to stay out of matters relating to desegregation, remarking, "I don't believe you can change the hearts of men with laws or decision," while characterizing people who worked for compliance with the Court's *Brown* decision as "extremists." Eisenhower even called his decision to appoint Earl Warren to the Supreme Court "the biggest damn-fool mistake I ever made."

Southern governors and legislators endorsed a strategy of massive resistance to interpose state power to prevent school integration. In March of 1956, 101 of the 128 southern congressmen signed the Southern Manifesto, vowing to resist school desegregation by all available legal methods. White southern citizens, seeing themselves as a society under siege, also mobilized to prevent integration. White Citizens Councils sprang up in nearly every southern city, formed primarily of middle-class whites who sought to protect their racial interests through allegedly respectable means. Over a quarter of a million whites eventually joined these councils. Often with funding from the state, the councils operated initially through economic intimidation, although later many turned to violence. As one council member put it, their role was "to make it difficult, if not impossible for any Negro who advocates desegregation to find and hold a job, get credit, or renew a mortgage." Membership in and activities of the Ku Klux Klan (KKK) surged as many saw violent intimidation as the best way to maintain the racial caste system in the South. Conservatives nationwide supported this antidesegregation stance. The *National Review,* founded in 1955 by Yale graduate William Buckley, staunchly opposed integration. In 1957, the editors wrote that white southerners were justified in resisting civil rights: "the white community is so entitled, because, for the time being, it is the advanced race."

A third group of whites made the enforcement of *Brown* nearly impossible. They did not join the Klan or work with the Citizens Councils. But they did not speak out to support civil rights or even to condemn the bitter, at times violent resistance of their neighbors. As Alabama federal judge Frank Johnson explained, "The biggest problem was white folks' not doing anything. . . . The large majority of white people were not active in opposing the rights of blacks. Their inactivity allowed those that were willing to be active in opposing to be more effective."

In retaliation for the *Brown* decision, from 1956 through 1959, southern state governments also focused on destroying local NAACP chapters. They banned the organization as subversive and demanded its membership lists. The NAACP refused to hand over lists. Disclosing their membership meant turning over black names to whites who would make trouble for them. The South Carolina legislature passed a law prohibiting any city or state employee from belonging to the NAACP; in Louisiana, Alabama, and Texas, injunctions brought the state branches to a halt by tying them up in litigation. Some, like the Alabama branch, shut down completely. The NAACP's legalistic strategy meant that the organization focused its efforts fighting in court rather than organizing their constituents to resist on the ground. This left local blacks even more vulnerable to retribution and red-baiting.

RED-BAITING AND THE CIVIL RIGHTS MOVEMENT

Civil rights activism was often equated with Communism during the Cold War era. The logic was circular: Communism threatened American democracy by its very antidemocratic nature, so those who questioned American democracy were Communists trying to destroy America. Radical organizations that had been crucial to grassroots organizing in the South in the 1930s and 1940s, such as the International Labor Defense and the Southern Conference for Human Welfare, found their membership and support decimated by this anti-Communist fervor. Red-baiting also crippled the more moderate NAACP, which had publicly shunned any sort of radical allegiances but still lost 246 branches and nearly fifty thousand members in the South in the 1950s. Many Latino activists faced similar charges of Communism. Community activist César Chávez explained, "If you talked about civil rights, you were a Communist, no doubt. Organizing, you were a Communist. Police brutality, you were a Communist. It was just fantastic."

One target of such vigorous attack was Paul Robeson. Master singer, actor, lawyer, and All-American athlete, Robeson had navigated the tricky waters of racial representation for decades. From *Emperor Jones* to *Black Boy*, Robeson's acting roles were confined to the prevailing, demeaning ideas of blacks at the time. Robeson longed to play uplifting black characters that would ring true to black people yet was constantly thwarted in his efforts to do so. His experiences politicized him tremendously. "The artist must take sides," Robeson declared. As one of the most well-known and popular entertainers in the world, Robeson became a spokesman for the United States during World War II. After the war, however, Robeson spoke out more and more forcefully against the racial caste system in the United States, called for friendship with the Soviet Union, and attacked American capitalism. For his criticisms, Robeson became the subject of intensified Federal Bureau of Investigation (FBI) surveillance, while 85 of his U.S. concerts were canceled. Even black leaders and organizations like the NAACP lined up against him. Jackie Robinson, in a move he later regretted, testified against Robeson at the House Un-American Activities Committee hearing.

Robeson remained steadfast in his criticism and his devotion to U.S. ideals. "I defy any part of an insolent, dominating America, however powerful. I defy any errand boys, Uncle Toms of the Negro people, to challenge my Americanism because by word and deed I challenge this vicious system to the death. I'm looking for freedom, full freedom, not an inferior brand." He criticized U.S. involvement in the Korean War and told blacks "that the place for the Negro people to fight for their freedom is here at home." For this and his association with many African independence leaders, the State Department revoked his passport in 1950. When Robeson was asked at a HUAC hearing why he did not just move to Russia, he replied, "Because my father was a slave, and my people died to build this country, and I am going to stay here and have part of it just like you."

Robeson was not the only civil rights activist branded a subversive for criticizing the economic and racial structures of the United States. Highlander Folk School was another prominent target. Founded in 1932 by a white man, Myles Horton, in Monteagle, Tennessee, the integrated Highlander Folk School sought to train poor rural whites and blacks to become their own leaders to solve their own problems. The school encouraged its participants, most of whom were whites from rural Appalachia, to return to their communities and work for social change. But by the late 1940s and 1950s, many blacks also attended Highlander workshops, including Septima Clark, Esau Jenkins, Rosa Parks, and Nashville students such as Marion Barry, Diane Nash, and John Lewis. For many of the participants, this was their first opportunity to share ideas and to eat alongside people of another race. Highlander's work—its philosophy of participatory democracy and commitment to integration—subjected the school to continued calls of communism and a police raid in 1959.

One victim of this raid and the red-baiting of the era was Septima Clark. Born May 3, 1898, in Charlestown, South Carolina, Clark completed 12th grade at Avery Institute, which enabled her to teach in rural areas. (Blacks were not allowed to teach in the public schools in Charlestown.) In 1956, she lost her teaching job of 40 years and her pension because she refused to stop her activities with the NAACP—South Carolina had required all state employees to give up their membership in the organization or lose their jobs. "[A]nyone who was against segregation was considered a Communist," she remarked. "White southerners couldn't believe that a southerner could have the idea of racial equality; they thought it had to come from somewhere else." Her family was unsupportive of her work with the NAACP. "They didn't feel as if they could fight for freedom or for justice."

At this point, Myles Horton asked Clark to become Highlander's director of workshops. She and Esau Jenkins, a black farmer, bus driver, and longtime activist on Johns Island, realized the need for a program to teach adults how to read as the first step in getting them to register to vote and participate in the political process. "[W]hen we looked through these election laws, we knew what we had to do with those people. We had to get them trained to read those laws and answer those questions." They set the school up behind a grocery store so that local whites would not know what they were doing and hired Bernice Robinson, a black hairdresser who was not a trained teacher but "knew how to listen," to teach at the first night school for adults. Between 1956 and 1961, Clark traveled throughout the south setting up these schools and recruiting over seven hundred teachers to run them. These became known as the citizenship schools and, through them, thousands of people were registered to vote.

Since the 1930s, Highlander had faced charges of Communism, but these heated up when Martin Luther King Jr. spoke at the 25th anniversary of the school in 1957. A picture of King sitting in the midst of an integrated audience near a writer from the *Daily Worker* (a Communist paper) was circulated through the South as so-called proof that King had attended a Communist training center. In 1959 Tennessee police raided Highlander. Septima Clark was leading a workshop when 18 officers burst in, arresting her and tearing through the school looking for evidence to shut it down. But Clark and Horton fought back, refusing to be intimidated.

One of the ironies of the Cold War was that while activists were silenced at home, the United States was trumpeting its commitment to democracy abroad. Red-baiting did not destroy southern grassroots activism, however. When long-established civil rights organizations were weakened by intense anticommunism, new organizations and voices emerged to forge a mass movement for civil rights in the 1950s and 1960s. The changing consciousness and urbanization that resulted from World War II and court victories like *Brown* provided the soil for this mass movement to grow. The seeds that many at Highlander, the NAACP, the radical labor movement, and local black churches and organizations had sown during the 1930s and 1940s began in the 1950s and 1960s to bear fruit.

These postwar movements faced similar violence, economic pressure, and government surveillance. But more and more people willingly risked such reprisals, and by the 1950s and 1960s, the courts were more receptive to ruling in favor of black rights. Such rulings, while not guaranteeing rights, gave blacks and committed whites new tools in the fight for racial justice. Television and newspaper coverage, in addition, brought national attention on racist incidents, systematic repression, and civil rights strategies that had occurred for decades outside the protection of such scrutiny. By the mid-1950s, 66 percent of the nation's homes had a television, and by 1960, 80 percent of rural homes had a television set. Television coverage drew Americans from disparate backgrounds into stories of the courageous acts, fierce determination, and brutal repression of civil rights workers.

This growing awakening should not obscure how few people participated in the civil rights movement. Most middle-class whites and many middle-class blacks—journalists, ministers, teachers—accommodated racial injustice and many benefited, at least economically, from that accommodation. Many poor and working-class whites took solace in their own racial privilege, despite economic circumstances that could have allied them with their nonwhite brothers and sisters. And many poor and working-class people of color were unwilling to risk their livelihoods and lives by speaking out—many believing that respectable behavior, not confrontational protest, was the way to defeat racism. Thus, many blacks who joined the movement, like Septima Clark, faced deep criticism and sometimes ostracism from their families as well as from the larger black and white communities for their civil rights work. Yet their determination to prod the nation to live up to its ideals soon sparked a mass movement that changed the nation.

EARLY SEEDS: EMMETT TILL, THE MONTGOMERY BUS BOYCOTT, AND THE DESEGREGATION OF CENTRAL HIGH SCHOOL IN LITTLE ROCK

Three events of the 1950s planted the seeds of change that inspired far greater numbers to become active in the 1960s: the lynching of Emmett Till, the Montgomery bus boycott, and the desegregation of Central High School in Little Rock, Arkansas. In August 1955, 14-year-old Chicago-native Emmett Till was on vacation in Mississippi visiting his uncle. Joking with his friends and cousin, he committed the unpardonable offense of saying, "Bye, baby," to the white woman working at a local store. Three nights later, the storekeeper's husband, Roy Bryant, and J. W. Milam seized Till from his uncle's house and brought him down to the Tallatchie River where they beat him, shot him, tied his body to a cotton gin, and threw it in the water. Already that year a number of blacks had been killed by whites in Mississippi; for example, Rev. George Lee was lynched in Belzoni, Mississippi, after attempting to register to vote.

Till's mother, Mamie Bradley, and his uncle, Mose Wright, made this case something different. A Chicago schoolteacher, Mamie Bradley insisted on bringing her son's body back to Chicago and having an open-casket funeral. "I wanted the whole world to see what they had done to my boy." Emmett Till had a bullet in his skull, a crushed forehead, and one eye gouged out. *Jet* magazine published a picture of his mutilated corpse that reverberated through black America.

Bryant and Milam were indicted and charged with kidnapping and murdering Till. As national attention to the case grew, white Mississippi rallied around the two white men. Their attorneys argued that the body was not identifiable as Till's and appealed to the all-white jury's racial pride: "I'm sure that every last Anglo-Saxon one of you has the courage to free these men in the face of that [outside] pressure." Till's uncle, Mose Wright, chose to testify at the trial. Asked to identify the men who had come to his house and taken Till, Wright identified Bryant and Milam (an extremely dangerous and rare act for a black man in a southern court). The NAACP moved all of the black witnesses out of state to ensure their safety; after he testified, Mose Wright never returned to Mississippi. The all-white jury deliberated for an hour and then acquitted the two men. Two months later, for a payment of $4,000, Bryant and Milam admitted to a white journalist, William Bradford Huie, to having killed Till. Despite the verdict, Mamie Bradley and Mose Wright became powerful symbols of black resistance and public courage.

The racial situation in Mississippi was not unique. Mississippi was among the poorest and harbored some of the most entrenched racism of any state in the union. Nonetheless, in New York, blacks in the 1940s could not find a single place outside of Harlem to eat, and in 1943, police shot black army private Robert Bandy for stepping to the defense of a black woman. In Florida, NAACP leader Harry Moore and his wife, Harriette, were killed by a bomb that exploded beneath their house on Christmas Day, 1951. Fired from his job as a schoolteacher after 20 years for his civil rights work, Harry Moore had agitated against lynchings, fought for equalizing teacher's salaries, and cultivated NAACP chapters in small towns and cities across Florida. As a cofounder of the Progressive Voter's League, he also helped launch a campaign to register one hundred thousand blacks, then cultivated them into a political force in local elections. His unflagging activism made him a much-hated man in white Florida circles and had even distanced him from the national NAACP, which began to regard him as too much of a troublemaker.

In Montgomery, Alabama, blacks were the majority of bus riders but could be asked to move at any time if there were not enough seats for white passengers. Since whites sat from the front and blacks from the back, blacks had to pay in the front and then go around to the back door to board. Many drivers pulled away while blacks were reboarding, called black passengers names like "cows" and "niggers," and were authorized to carry guns and nightsticks, at times threatening black riders. Thus, experiences on the bus had become a source of anger and frustration in Montgomery's black community—and many were determined to change it.

The Montgomery bus boycott of 1955 was not the first bus boycott. In 1953, in Baton Rouge, Louisiana, under the leadership of Rev. T. J. Jemison, blacks boycotted city buses for a week. They demanded and won a first-come, first-serve policy—blacks would sit from the back and whites from the front, but if a black person was seated, he or she would not be asked to move.

The boycott in Montgomery, furthermore, was the product of deep-seated frustrations and years of groundwork, particularly by E. D. Nixon and Jo Ann Robinson. Born in 1899 and only able to attend school through the third grade, E. D. Nixon became a lifelong organizer. The longtime president of the local Brotherhood of Sleeping Car Porters, an organizer of the Montgomery's Voter's League, president of Montgomery's NAACP from 1939 to 1951, and the head of the state conference from 1951 to 1953, by 1955, Nixon was looking for a test case to attack bus segregation head-on. Jo Ann Robinson was an English professor at Alabama State College. In 1949, she had been thrown off the bus and physically threatened in the process. She vowed that the Women's Political Counsel (WPC), an organization of middle-class black women in which she was active, would change bus policy. Becoming president of the WPC in 1950, Robinson began to formulate ways to protest bus segregation, including making plans for a boycott. In May of 1954, Robinson wrote the bus company a letter on behalf of the WPC stating that if things did not change, blacks would boycott the buses.

Rosa Parks, the woman who sparked the movement, also had a history as an activist. In 1943 and 1944, Rosa Parks tried to register to vote and finally succeeded in 1945. She then had to pay a poll tax of $16.50—$1.50 for each of the 11 years when she had not been registered but had been over the age of 21. Becoming a member of the local NAACP in the 1940s, she was elected secretary in 1943 and worked with the NAACP's Youth Council. In the summer of 1955, Rosa Parks attended Highlander Folk School. "[I]t was one of the few times in my life up to that point when I did not feel any hostility from white people. . . . I felt that I could express myself honestly without any repercussions or antagonistic attitudes from other people."

Rosa Parks was not the first black Montgomerian that year to refuse to give up her seat on the bus. In early 1955, Claudette Colvin was arrested in Montgomery for the same act. At first, the NAACP wanted Colvin to be the test case but dropped her when they found out that she was pregnant and unmarried. Another young woman, Mary Smith, had also been arrested for demanding to keep her seat on the bus. But her family was poor, and there were rumors that her father had a drinking problem. So she, too, was rejected as a test case for the NAACP to stand behind.

Then, on Thursday, December 1, 1955, bus driver James Blake asked four black people to move when one white passenger boarded the bus. Three did, but Rosa Parks remained seated. Parks had previous trouble with this bus driver and decided that she was not going to move this time. "People always say that I didn't give up my seat because I was tired but that isn't true. I was not tired physically, or no more tired than I usually was at the end of a working day. I was not old, although some people have an image of me as being old then. I was forty-two. No, the only tired I was, was tired of giving in." She was arrested and taken to jail.

The word spread. Virginia and Clifford Durr, a liberal white couple who had long been active in civil rights, and E. D. Nixon bailed Parks out. Nixon was thrilled, believing Parks to be the kind of person the NAACP could rally around. Parks agreed to be the test case and was defended by Fred Gray, a black lawyer. Advised of Parks' arrest, Robinson decided the WPC would call for a one-day boycott on Monday, the day that Parks would be arraigned in court, and told Nixon of her plans. She and two students sneaked into the college late that night and duplicated and distributed over fifty thousand copies of a leaflet announcing the boycott.

Meanwhile, very early Friday morning, Nixon called Rev. Ralph Abernathy, with whom he had worked in the NAACP, and a new minister in town, Rev. Martin Luther King Jr., to mobilize a meeting that day of Montgomery's black clergy to support the one-day boycott. Nixon wanted King's help and the use of King's church for the clergy's meeting. King and his family had recently moved to Montgomery so he could take on his first congregation at Dexter Avenue Baptist Church. The church's previous minister, Rev. Vernon Johns (the uncle of Virginia high school activist Barbara Johns), had been a bit too radical for the congregation when he pushed every church member to register to vote. To the congregation, King, at first, seemed like a welcome change.

Born on January 15, 1929, to a prominent Baptist minister's family in Atlanta, Martin Luther King Jr. attended Morehouse College in Atlanta at the age of 15 by passing a special exam. Filled with spiritual doubt as a teenager, King thought the black church overly emotional. At Morehouse, he began to realize the intellectual and protest underpinnings of black religion. He remained critical of those who "reduc[ed] worship to entertainment" and preachers who "confuse[d] spirituality with muscularity." Yet, seeing the possibility of a more active Christianity, he decided

Carpools helped sustain the 13-month boycott in Montgomery.

to pursue religious training at Crozer Theological Seminary in Boston and received his doctorate at Boston University's School of Theology. In Boston, he met and eventually married Coretta Scott, who was studying vocal music at Boston's New England Conservatory of Music.

When Nixon asked King's help that December morning, King hesitated, requesting time to think about it. Nixon refused, telling King that he had already invited the other ministers to a meeting to be held at King's church. King then agreed. At first, the clergy were timid about getting involved with the one-day boycott. The community was going forward with this boycott, the impatient Nixon argued, and they had better go forward with them. Seeing Nixon's point, many pastors preached about the boycott on Sunday. Nixon also took a leaflet to reporter Joe Azbell of the *Montgomery Advertiser,* who printed it on the cover of Sunday's newspaper.

At first, the WPC had called for only a one-day boycott. On Monday, the community stood together, and the buses were nearly empty of black riders. That night, fifteen thousand people attended a huge mass meeting. King spoke, "And we are not wrong. . . . If we are wrong, the Constitution of the United States is wrong. . . . And we are determined here in Montgomery to work and fight until justice runs down like water and righteousness like a mighty stream." Excited and uplifted by the day's success and the unity the community had achieved, the people decided to continue the boycott and formed an organization called the Montgomery Improvement Association (MIA). The leadership of this organization was dominated by the clergy, despite the role many women of the

WPC played in organizing the boycott. The MIA began with three demands: courteous treatment towards black riders; a first-come, first-serve policy where whites would sit from the front, blacks from the back, and no one would be asked to give up their seat; and the hiring of black drivers. As the ongoing boycott radicalized the community, the MIA came to demand full integration of the bus.

The boycott was sustained through the determination of working-class people, mostly women, who walked miles to work. King captured this sense of purpose, "[W]hen the history books are written in future generations, the historians will have to pause and say, 'There lived a great people—a black people—who injected new meaning and dignity into the veins of civilization.'" Black taxis made regularly scheduled stops and charged black riders bus fare in order to get them to work. Many blacks (and some whites) who had cars volunteered to drive people to and from work. Trying to break the boycott, the city outlawed the carpools and ruled that taxis could not charge cheap fares. Ninety African Americans were arrested for their roles in the carpools. Both King's and E. D. Nixon's houses were bombed.

The boycott captured national television and newspaper attention. Month after month, the country watched black Montgomery refuse to ride segregated buses. Blacks and whites across the nation saw a united black community unwilling to tolerate second-class treatment and willing to sacrifice to attain their rights. On February 1, 1956, the MIA took the fight to a second front, filing suit in federal court to challenge the constitutionality of bus segregation. Finally, on November 13, 1956, the Supreme Court ruled in favor of Montgomery's blacks. Three hundred eighty-two days after the boycott began, on December 20, 1956, the boycott ended as Montgomery's black community took their seats in the front of the bus.

The Montgomery bus boycott provides a preview of the mass movements of the 1960s. It was neither a spontaneous uprising nor the product of one charismatic leader and one "tired, old woman." Well-planned and organized, the boycott succeeded because of the efforts of many people who laid the groundwork for years. The movement created Martin Luther King, not vice versa. The struggle was not just male-led (although male leadership was often more visible) nor was it a middle-class fight. Working-class people were the bus riders, had the most to gain by equitable treatment, and, for over a year, put their commitment into daily practice by walking miles to work. Rosa Parks lost her job at Montgomery Fair, and her husband resigned from his when his white boss forbid discussion of the bus protest or Rosa Parks. Jo Ann Robinson ended up resigning from her job at Alabama State in 1960 because of the school's objections to faculty involvement in civil rights. Before the movement began, few were convinced that the community could stay unified and withstand the economic and violent backlash to maintain such a lengthy fight against unequal public transportation. The boycott instead proved the power of people to change things—that the community could be organized and stay mobilized around a common cause. As participants became radicalized, their aims grew to demand complete integration, and they were willing to adopt new strategies and risk continued retaliation.

On January 10 and 11, 1957, nearly a month after Montgomery's buses had been desegregated, King, Ralph Abernathy, Rev. T. J. Jemison of Baton Rouge, Rev. Fred Shuttlesworth of Birmingham, and several other black activist ministers from around the South met at Ebenezer Baptist Church in Atlanta to take the work begun in Montgomery to a national level. They formed a permanent Christian organization, the Southern Christian Leadership Conference (SCLC), elected Martin Luther King as its president, and established its purpose "to redeem the soul of the nation." Explicit in the SCLC's mission was that the United States had compromised its ideals through its treatment of African Americans, and the SCLC would save the nation through this movement for social change.

Despite their strong commitment to social justice, these ministers had little experience as community organizers. They recruited a non-clergy woman—Ella Baker—to set up the organization and be its first executive director. Born in Norfolk Virginia, Baker had attended Shaw University and then moved north, drawn to the allure of Harlem's black community. She worked for the NAACP in the 1940s, becoming the southern field secretary and then secretary of branches. Traveling throughout the South to work with local branches, she expanded the reach of the NAACP in the South and brought the concerns of the membership to the national office. Her efforts helped expand the NAACP's membership in the 1940s, which brought "a new surge of identity" within the black community. But Baker became frustrated with the hierarchy of the NAACP and its lack of commitment to local organizing and resigned. She believed that local people had both the power and the need to make their own decisions, but the national office, set on pursuing its own agenda, rejected this model of grassroots leadership. She joined Bayard Rustin and Stanley Levison to start the northern group In Friendship to raise money for southern civil rights activities. Her work there led to the request for her to direct the SCLC and launch the fledgling group's Crusade for Citizenship. In 1961, Baker left the SCLC over conflicts about leadership and organizing, finding the SCLC too elitist and male-dominated. "The basic attitude of men, and especially ministers, as to . . . the role of women in their church setups is that of taking orders not providing leadership." Baker criticized the SCLC for relying too heavily on charismatic leadership.

SCLC's role in the struggle for civil rights did not reflect that of the black church as a whole. Many black churches opposed the movement, fearing trouble with the local white power structure. As Mississippi activist Fannie Lou Hamer explained, "Most black preachers had to be dragged kicking and screaming into supporting the movement." Nonetheless, many leaders came out of the church, and black Christian views undergirded many people's decision to join the struggle. From Montgomery to Little Rock to Mississippi, the foot soldiers of the civil rights movement often relied on their religious faith to bolster and sustain their struggle against racism. God was on the side of the oppressed, they believed, and justice would be served in this world, not only in the next.

School segregation remained a central issue to blacks across the country. Despite the landmark *Brown* decision, few schools were actually integrated. For example, when Autherine Lucy enrolled at the University of Alabama in 1956, white students and local citizens rioted. Through the efforts of the NAACP, she succeeded in getting reinstated; however, her criticisms of the university for conspiring with the mob led the school to expel her. President Eisenhower refused to intercede.

Eisenhower's lack of leadership soon exacerbated a national crisis over school desegregation. In Little Rock, Arkansas, the school board had been the first to announce its willingness to comply with the *Brown* decision. Set to begin a very limited desegregation of one high school, Central High School, in 1957, the board chose nine black students, six girls and three boys, based on their good grades, their willingness to be a part of the case, and their acceptability (originally, 75 had signed up). According to Melba Pattillo Beals, "I wanted to go to Central High School because they had more privileges." Daisy Bates, president of the Arkansas NAACP, coordinated the struggle on behalf of the black students and their families. She and her husband had a long history of community involvement, having started the *Arkansas State Press* in the early 1940s to provide fair coverage of issues concerning blacks.

Arkansas Governor Orval Faubus, however, decided to take a hard-line stand against this limited integration. Running for reelection, Faubus saw opposition to desegregation as a way to boost his popularity across the state. As whites from around the state mobilized to protest desegregation, Faubus called out the National Guard to prevent the nine students from entering the school on September 4. Eight of the nine met at Daisy Bates's house. But Elizabeth Eckford, who had not received the message, went to school alone and was turned away by the National Guard surrounding the school. This left her at the mercy of a jeering mob. Ernest Green, another of the nine students, explained, "It had to be the most frightening thing, because she had a crowd of a hundred, two hundred, white people threatening to kill her. She had nobody. . . . Nobody that she could turn to as a friend except this white woman, Grace Lorch, came out of a crowd and guided her through the mob and onto the bus and got her home safely." The other eight were also refused admittance when they sought to enter the school. Daisy Bates and the NAACP went back to court to get the young people safely into school. Hoping to avoid confrontation, President Eisenhower tried to reason with Governor Faubus. To meet the letter but not the spirit of the law, Faubus removed the National Guard, leaving only the local police to protect the students. On September 23, the Little Rock Nine went into school for the first time, only to be trapped inside a few hours later by the growing mob. The police were not able or willing to disperse the angry crowd. Melba Patillo Beals recalled the "stark terror" she felt. "Someone made the suggestion that if they allowed the mob to hang one kid, they could then get the rest out. And a gentleman, who I believed to be the police chief, said 'unh-uh, how are you going to choose? . . . I'll get them out.'"

Faubus's defiance of the federal court's order transformed the issue into a challenge of federal authority and forced Eisenhower to act. The president declared in a nationally televised address that "mob rule cannot be allowed to override the decisions of our courts." Eisenhower called in the 101st Airborne to escort the students into and throughout school. Ernest Green described that first day, "Walking up the step that day was probably one of the biggest feelings I've ever had. I figured I had finally cracked it." Melba Patillo Beals agreed, "There was a feeling of pride and hope that yes, this is the United States; yes there is a reason I salute the flag." Even with the protection of 101st Airborne, the Little Rock Nine faced verbal and physical harassment, tripping, name-calling, shoving, and kicking over the course of the school year. Frustrated with months of constant harassment, in December, Minniejean Brown dumped a bowl of chili on a taunting classmate's head. For this action, she was thrown out of school. White students began passing around cards. "One down, eight to go." Still, the other eight endured. On May 29, 1958, Ernest Green became the first black student to graduate from Central High.

The next year, emboldened by continuing white protest, Faubus closed all the Little Rock public schools to avoid continuing with desegregation. Most black children went without school, as did many white children whose parents could not afford to send them out of the city or to private school. The Supreme Court ruled this action unconstitutional, an "evasive scheme" to get around desegregation. The following year the schools were reopened.

Faubus was reelected governor in July 1958 with an unprecedented 69 percent of the vote, and one Gallup Poll of 1958 found Americans picking him as one of their 10 most admired men. In contrast, the Bateses' commitment to desegregation placed them in physical and economic danger. A cross was burned on their roof and a rock thrown through their window bore the message, "Stone This Time. Dynamite Next." Support for the *Arkansas State Press* waned during desegregation, and the Bateses finally had no choice but to file for bankruptcy.

These events—the lynching of Emmett Till, the Montgomery bus boycott, and the desegregation of Central High—laid the groundwork for the mass movement soon to come. As Cleveland Sellers, who became a full-time activist in the 1960s, recalled, "I watched television news reports of the school integration crisis in Little Rock, Arkansas, and the heroic Montgomery bus boycott. . . . I was extremely proud of them. They were my people. They were standing and fighting a common enemy."

Chapter 2

THE COLD WAR AND THE DECLINE OF DISSENT

WOMEN AND THE PARADOXES OF THE COLD WAR

World War II had eroded some of the barriers to equal rights for women, opening employment opportunities in what had been exclusively male jobs. Between 1940 and 1943, 4.4 million women became salaried workers, 3 million more than under normal peacetime conditions. These employment gains, however, occurred in those geographic areas having the highest concentration of defense industries. In Detroit, for example, the female workforce increased from 182,000 to 387,000. By 1944, more women were employed in factories than had been in the entire workforce of 1940.

The end of the war in 1945, however, did not usher in a return to the prewar employment situation. Women comprised 60 percent of all workers whose jobs were terminated in the early weeks after the end of World War II. This downturn was quickly reversed, as almost two-thirds of employed women remained in the workforce but often in clerical rather than manufacturing jobs. By the early 1950s, the number of gainfully employed women exceeded that of the highest wartime level in 1944, and by 1960, women comprised 33 percent of the nation's workforce. Of employed women, moreover, 54 percent were married and 33 percent were mothers; 30 percent of all married women and 39 percent of mothers having children of school age were employed.

Women's wartime advances did not automatically lead to support for sexual equality. Whereas 80 percent of the respondents to a 1938 poll opposed married women working, by 1943 over 60 percent approved such employment. This shift conformed with the increase in the proportion of married women who were employed, from 15 percent in 1940 to 24 percent in 1945, and with the economic needs of many families for the wife to work while the husband used his GI benefits to attend college. Wartime gains in employment and in admission to new job classifications, moreover, had not resulted in equal pay; in 1945, as in 1940, women employed in manufacturing earned only 65 percent of what men did. Women were principally employed in sex-segregated and sex-typed occupations (clerical, sales, and service positions). Black women, who encountered both racial and sexual discrimination, were employed primarily in service and domestic work. The limited wartime gains women had made in more highly paid, skilled jobs were reversed, with women's employment in the automobile industry declining from 25 percent of all auto workers in 1944 to 7.5 percent in April 1946. By the 1960s, women constituted only 3 percent of the nation's lawyers; only 186 of the 2,708 lawyers employed in the nation's top 40 law firms were women. Not until 1951 did Harvard Law School admit its first woman student. Medical schools continued to impose a 5 percent quota on female admissions, with 70 percent of all hospitals refusing to accept women interns. Moreover, although 25 percent of all federal employees were women, only 3 percent held high-level positions. During the 1950s, women's educational parity with men actually fell. Proposals to provide federal funding for child care and job training, to ensure equal pay, or to enact an Equal Rights Amendment to the Constitution commanded little support. Few women considered themselves feminists. The National Woman's Party, for example, formed in the 1920s to lobby for enactment of the Equal Rights Amendment, had only 4,000 dues-paying members in 1945 (from 60,000 in the 1920s), declining to 627 active members in 1947 and to 200 in 1952.

Federal policies like the GI Bill, home loans, and federally funded highway construction enhanced postwar employment and housing opportunities for male workers while strengthening a patriarchal family system. Thus, the celebrated 1950s family was not so much traditional as new. War veterans (98 percent of whom were male) were eligible for grants under the Servicemen's Readjustment Act of 1944 (the so-called GI Bill) to attend college while the newly established Veterans Administration offered mortgages at low interest rates. In addition, the wartime Selective Service Act gave job preference to returning war veterans. If these federally funded programs contributed to increased postwar affluence and new social and economic opportunities, the resultant cult of domesticity and consumerism led to an increase in early marriages and birth rates. The median age of marriage, which had remained constant at 22 from 1890 to 1945, declined to 20.1 by 1956 at the same time that fertility rates increased from 2.3 in 1937 to a peak of 3.7 in 1957.

Belying the image of family prosperity, a full 25 percent of Americans were poor, with one-third of America's children living below the poverty line. For black families, childhood poverty rose to 50 percent. Teenage pregnancy, moreover, soared during the 1950s—in 1957, for example, 97 out of every 1,000 American girls aged 15 through 19 gave birth (compared to 52 out of 1,000 in 1983). Finding traditional home life stultifying, many women turned to tranquilizers in the 1950s. Virtually nonexistent in 1955, 1.15 million pounds were consumed by 1959. American popular culture, in contrast, simplistically conveyed a sense of women's dependency and roles as housewife and mother, captured in popular television shows such as *Father Knows Best* and *Ozzie and Harriet*. In December 1953, a new magazine, *Playboy*, appeared, graphically portraying women as sex objects and popularizing a hedonistic sexuality.

Cold War security concerns, in addition, deterred women from seeking occupational and economic independence. Women's magazines, like *McCall's* and *Ladies' Home Journal*, celebrated women's role as mother and housewife and the nuclear family as a secure haven in an ever-dangerous world. Writing in the *Atlantic*, Agnes Meyer identified women as "the cement of society" and urged women to recapture "the wisdom that just being a woman is her central task and her greatest honor . . . no job is more exacting, more necessary, and more rewarding than that of housewife and mother."

The Soviet Union's launching of Sputnik in 1957 indirectly opened educational opportunities for women. Concerned that the United States was falling behind in the areas of science and technology, Congress enacted the National Defense Education Act in 1958, providing loans and grants to college and graduate students majoring in science and foreign languages. In contrast to the GI Bill, this act benefited both male and female students. By expanding graduate school enrollments, federal assistance enabled more women to earn Ph.D.s. The Women's Armed Services Integration Act, enacted in 1948, also gave women permanent status in the military services—although women were banned from combat and were not promoted to command male troops.

McCARTHYISM AND HOMOSEXUAL RIGHTS

Although women made slight gains, the post-1945 period ushered in the dark ages for gays and lesbians. Service in the military during World War II broke down the isolation of rural males while physical separation from women and the close bonding of armed combat increased gay experiences. As many men quietly acknowledged a homosexual identity, a gay and lesbian subculture emerged. A small minority formed the Mattachine Society in 1951 in Los Angeles, and lesbians in San Francisco formed the Daughters of Bilitis in 1955. These organizations, however, did not seek to mobilize gays and lesbians to demand equal rights but to promote greater self-esteem among and tolerance toward gays and lesbians. In contrast to racial and gender discrimination (and the attendant belief in the inferiority of blacks and women), homosexuals bore a different burden; their conduct was seen to be both immoral and abnormal (the latter view sanctioned by the medical community).

These fears were heightened in the security-driven atmosphere of the 1950s catalyzed by Senator Joseph McCarthy. When a Washington, D.C., vice squad detective testified that as a "quick guess" 3,500 "sex perverts" were employed in the federal bureaucracy (300 to 400 as State Department employees), Assistant Secretary of State John Peurifoy responded that the State Department had fired 91 "sex perverts" since 1947. Prominent Republicans jumped on this admission, accusing the Truman administration of tolerating homosexuals in government. In April 1950, for example, Republican National Committee Chair Guy Gabrielson contended that the "sexual perverts who have infiltrated our government in recent years" posed "perhaps" as dangerous an internal security threat as "the actual communists" in the State Department cited recently by Senator McCarthy. Echoing this view, Republican Senator Kenneth Wherry repeated this warning when denying that homosexuals could be separated from subversives. "I don't say every subversive is a homosexual. But a man of low morality is a menace to government whatever he is, and they are tied up together."

In June 1950, a special Senate inquiry was launched to investigate this homosexual crisis. Because of privacy concerns, the so-called Hoey Committee (named after its chair, North Carolina Senator Clyde Hoey) conducted its investigation in secret. In December 1950 the committee concluded that employment of "sex perverts" constituted a dangerous security problem, owing to homosexuals' lack of "emotional stability" and the "weakness of their moral fiber." Strict screening procedures were required, as the nation's security was threatened by "even one" homosexual employee: their influence could entice "moral individuals to engage in perverted practices" and their fear of exposure could render them vulnerable to being blackmailed into betraying national secrets or adversely influencing public policy.

The Hoey Committee's demand for more effective screening procedures was quickly implemented. Testifying before a House appropriations subcommittee in April 1951, FBI Director J. Edgar Hoover claimed that

FBI investigations had uncovered "derogatory information" on 14,484 of the 3,225,000 incumbent and applicant employees, of whom 406 were "sex deviates." Then, on June 20, 1951, Hoover authorized a code-named Sex Deviates program to ensure "a uniform policy for furnishing information concerning allegations [of homosexuality] concerning present and past employees" of the executive, legislative, and judicial branches. Great care was taken to identify suspected homosexuals. FBI agents monitored gay bars, other places patronized by gays, and gay publications and developed liaison relations with local police vice squads. Such information was then disseminated to officials responsible for purging suspected employees.

The FBI's initiative commanded the full support of the Eisenhower White House. Having won election by pledging to institute more effective internal security procedures, President Dwight D. Eisenhower in April 1953 by executive order explicitly barred the employment of any homosexual in the federal bureaucracy. The number of employees discharged because of suspected homosexuality doubled during the 1950s (particularly in military service), increasing another 50 percent in the early 1960s. Such purges were not confined to federal employees. FBI officials soon expanded the Sex Deviates program to include dissemination to "institutions of higher learning or law enforcement agencies" in "appropriate instances where the best interest of the Bureau is served."

Even before issuing his executive order, President-elect Eisenhower encountered a particularly delicate personnel problem. In December 1952, he appointed Arthur Vandenberg Jr. (the son of a prominent Republican senator) White House Secretary. Having campaigned on the need for tighter federal security procedures, the president-elect required security clearance investigations for all White House appointees. In the course of their investigation of Vandenberg, FBI agents discovered that he was gay. Briefed on this matter, Eisenhower agreed to an arrangement whereby no FBI report would be filed (or Vandenberg's homosexuality disclosed) in return for Vandenberg withdrawing his name for appointment for health reasons.

Syndicated columnist Joseph Alsop's experience highlights how political considerations affected privacy rights. While in Moscow to interview Soviet Premier Nikita Khruschev in February 1957, Alsop was entrapped by Soviet security officials in a homosexual affair. These officials unsuccessfully attempted to blackmail the columnist to assist "the cause." Alsop was able to flee Moscow in return for providing the Central Intelligence Agency (CIA) a detailed, confidential report on this matter and his own sex life. This information was shared with FBI officials who had already compiled reports on Alsop's alleged homosexuality. FBI Director Hoover briefed Attorney General Herbert Brownell and Deputy

Attorney General William Rogers and then Assistant to the President Sherman Adams, with CIA director Allen Dulles concurrently briefing Secretary of State John Foster Dulles and Under Secretary of State Christian Herter. Hoover's rationale for briefing these men was "in view of the implications" of discovery—namely, Alsop's prominence and an unsubstantiated rumor that British Prime Minister Anthony Eden was "in the same category." Alsop's acquaintance with Eden, "though there was no indication of impropriety," and the possibility that Alsop might in the future contact the White House, the FBI director concluded, required that the president be "informed of this recent information."

This discovery soon acquired a different value. An ardent anti-Communist, the syndicated columnist had consistently advocated a more militant anti-Communism. Indeed, after 1957, Alsop criticized the Eisenhower administration's fiscal conservatism as having caused a "missile gap" between the United States and the Soviet Union. Infuriated by Alsop's commentary, Rogers (now attorney general) demanded an FBI report summarizing whatever information the FBI had on Alsop. He intended to brief senior administration officials (including Secretary of Defense Neil McElroy, Air Force General Nathan Twining, and President Eisenhower) "concerning the incident in Moscow" and "Alsop's propensities." Rogers, however, "would not take responsibility for such information going any further."

THE INSTITUTIONALIZATION OF SECURITY

The handling of the Alsop and Vandenberg cases, the Hoey Committee report, and the FBI's initiation of a Sex Deviates program highlight how Cold War security and homophobic concerns created a climate hostile to civil liberties and privacy rights. Security considerations led to a breach in the zone of privacy that previously precluded intrusive investigations into an individual's sex life. Such intrusive investigations were institutionalized by an employee loyalty program.

The federal employee loyalty program was created in response to three events: the June 1945 arrest of six individuals (three editors and writers associated with the radical journal of Far Eastern affairs *Amerasia,* and three federal employees suspected of having leaked classified documents to these editors); the November 1945 defection of Elizabeth Bentley, a courier for a wartime Soviet spy ring that had obtained classified information from Communist sympathizers employed in various federal agencies; and a June 1946 report of a Canadian commission on a wartime Soviet espionage operation in Canada that had relied on information provided by Igor Gouzenko, a Soviet consular official who defected in 1945.

Responding to the *Amerasia* case developments, a House committee in July 1946 examined current federal security procedures. The committee demanded changes to ensure "a complete and unified program that will give adequate protection to our Government" against disloyal individuals. To co-opt congressional action, on November 25, 1946, President Truman appointed a Temporary Commission on Employee Loyalty to study current security procedures and recommend any needed changes.

The commission concluded that the "employment of subversive persons presented more than a speculative threat" and urged the establishment of a permanent federal loyalty program. By executive order on March 22, 1947, Truman instituted a Federal Employee Loyalty Program, requiring agency and department heads to ensure the loyalty of all incumbent and applicant employees. Individuals about whom "reasonable grounds exist for the belief that the person is disloyal to the Government of the United States" were to be dismissed; accused employees could appeal adverse rulings to specially established review boards.

Denials of clearance, however, were not based solely on conduct but membership or association with individuals who were members of organizations that the attorney general deemed subversive. During appeal hearings, the accused individual could not directly challenge the sources of reports that led to a denial of clearance because FBI officials had insisted on confidentiality for their sources, and thereby effectively denied accused employees the opportunity to challenge the veracity of FBI-reported information. Confidentiality also enabled FBI officials to launder information that could not have been presented during court proceedings (because obtained illegally through a wiretap, break-in, or mail intercept).

McCarthyism and a Politics of Anti-Communism

The creation of the Federal Employee Loyalty program did not silence the president's critics. Dating from 1948, conservatives in Congress criticized the president's loyalty program as inadequate (citing cases where individuals had received a loyalty clearance despite FBI reports questioning their loyalty). In addition, they portrayed the president's refusal to grant Congress access to FBI reports on specific federal employees as an attempted cover-up of his administration's indifference to the Communist threat. Indeed, in February 1950, Senator Joseph McCarthy catapulted to national prominence by claiming to have uncovered 205 "known Communists in the State Department."

The timing of McCarthy's charges proved crucial, leveled in the heightened security atmosphere following the arrests of suspected Communist spies (most notably, Alger Hiss, Judith Coplon, and Ethel and Julius Rosenberg). These cases seemed to confirm the existence of a serious Soviet espionage threat to which the administration was indifferent. They also led many to equate membership in subversive organizations or association with subversives with actual espionage. Forced on the defensive, President Truman, in April 1951, revised the loyalty program from basing dismissal "on all evidence, reasonable grounds exist for the belief that the person involved is disloyal" to whenever "there is a reasonable doubt as to their loyalty to the Government of the United States." Truman's revised order precipitated a re-review of those loyalty cases where an accused employee had been cleared on appeal. This action raised further questions about the effectiveness of the president's original program and whether Truman administration officials tolerated communistic activities.

From 1950 through 1952, Republicans in Congress and Republican presidential candidate Dwight Eisenhower condemned Truman's loyalty procedures as inadequate and dangerous. Their "softness toward Communism" charge struck a responsive chord, as Republican candidates won sweeping victories in the 1952 presidential and congressional elections. Having pledged more effective internal security, the newly elected president instituted strict security procedures on April 27, 1953. Agency and department heads were directed to dismiss summarily any unfit or unsuitable employee; an individual's employment had to be certified as "clearly consistent with the interests of national security"; and all employees had to be "reliable, trustworthy, of good conduct and character, and of complete and unswerving loyalty to the United States."

The Supreme Court and the Loyalty Dilemma

The Truman (loyalty) and Eisenhower (security) programs in effect equated disloyalty with adherence to allegedly subversive ideas or associations. Considerations of fairness and due process were no longer elemental rights but matters to be weighed in the light of more important security needs. These procedures—and specifically the denial of clearance based on membership in organizations proscribed subversive by the attorney general—precipitated a series of court cases. The Supreme Court's rulings in *Bailey v. Richardson* (1951), *Cole v. Young* (1956), and *Greene v. McElroy* (1959) had far-reaching importance for civil liberties and further underscored the limits of the role of the federal judiciary in protecting civil liberties.

The *Bailey* case posed the first challenge to the constitutionality of President Truman's loyalty program. Bailey had been denied a loyalty clearance based on allegations of an anonymous source whom the FBI certified was reliable. Bailey's attorneys argued that their client had been denied the right to challenge the veracity of this source during appeal hearings. In addition, owing to the vagueness of the program's dismissal standards and "the sole and unfettered discretion of [hearing] board members," Bailey was punished by the loss of livelihood and respect.

Bailey lost her case at the federal district court level and on appeal to the circuit court. The procedures of the loyalty program, the courts conceded, were "contrary to every known precept of fairness to the private individual." Nonetheless, the serious internal security crisis confronting the nation justified giving greater weight to secrecy than fairness. The justices further ruled that hearings procedures, while not complying with the standards of evidence of a normal court trial, were permitted under Truman's executive order. Bailey's First Amendment rights had not been violated because she had simply been denied employment, not labeled disloyal. The Supreme Court's 4–4 split vote on her appeal in effect sustained the ruling of the lower federal courts.

The Supreme Court in 1956 revisited the issue of the government's absolute discretion to dismiss an employee without providing that person an opportunity to challenge the claimed evidence. President Eisenhower based this claimed power on Public Law 733. Enacted in August 1950, this law authorized summary dismissal for national security appointments (Defense or State Department). Ruling narrowly in *Cole v. Young*, involving the dismissal of an employee of the Department of Health, Education, and Welfare, the Court held that defendant Cole's dismissal lacked legal authority given his nonsensitive appointment in the Department of Health, Education, and Welfare. The Court again avoided the larger question of whether federal loyalty programs must adhere to the same standards as court proceedings.

The issue of the fairness of dismissal proceedings surfaced again in 1959 in *Greene v. McElroy*. This case raised a broader constitutional issue because the dismissed individual was not employed by a federal agency but by a firm holding a defense contract. The Court once again issued a narrow ruling: President Eisenhower had not specifically authorized nonconfrontation of witnesses during defense contracting programs and thus the secretary of defense (McElroy) lacked authority to prohibit confrontation. These narrow rulings (in these and other cases involving federal loyalty programs) reflected the federal judiciary's deference to security considerations and unwillingness to protect individual rights from government surveillance. This unwillingness underpinned the Court's rulings in the so-called Smith cases.

On June 28, 1948, a federal grand jury indicted the 12 top leaders of the U.S. Communist Party for having violated the Smith Act's prohibition against organizing to violently overthrow the government. Following a lengthy, contentious trial, a federal jury convicted 11 of the Communist leaders (the case of the 12th having been severed for health reasons). The principal evidence offered by government attorneys to sustain conviction involved Communist party publications (including Marxist-Leninist classics such as Lenin's 1917 tract *State and Revolution*) and the testimony of FBI informers that the Communist leaders adhered to and established schools to teach Marxist-Leninist doctrines of revolutionary change.

In June 1951, in *Dennis v. U.S.*, the Supreme Court upheld the conviction of the Communist Party leaders and the constitutionality of the Smith Act. The Court held that the government need not await the planning of a revolutionary act but could take anticipatory action based on a standard of "appreciable probability." Communist Party leaders were rightfully convicted, Chief Justice Fred Vinson ruled, having formed a "highly organized conspiracy, with rigidly disciplined members" and in light of "the inflammable nature of world conditions, similar uprisings in other countries, and the touch-and-go nature" of U.S. relations with the Soviet Union, "with whom petitioners were in the very least ideologically attuned." In a powerful dissent, Justice Hugo Black challenged the Court's majority for restricting the First Amendment's protections to "'safe' or orthodox views." Black expressed the hope that "in calmer times when present passions and fears subside, this or some later Court will restore the First Amendment liberties to the high preferred place where they belong in a free society."

In 1957, the Supreme Court in effect rescinded the effect of the *Dennis* ruling. By then, the Cold War had waned in intensity, and new justices (notably Earl Warren's replacement of Fred Vinson as chief justice) made the Court more sensitive to First Amendment and privacy rights. In *Yates v. U.S.* (an appeal of the conviction of second-level Communist Party officials under the Smith Act), the Court held that conviction under the Smith Act required evidence not simply of advocacy of revolutionary change but "advocacy of action, not ideas . . . that those to whom the advocacy is addressed must be urged to *do* something, now or in the future, rather than merely to *believe* in something." By this ruling, the Court reverted to the *Schenck* case standard of weighing equally security and civil liberties considerations.

The *Yates* ruling dovetailed with similar Court rulings of 1955, 1956, and 1957 that challenged the premise that individual liberties had to be sacrificed to preserve national security. In *Quinn v. U.S.* (1955), the Supreme Court overturned the contempt of Congress conviction of radical labor leader Thomas Quinn, observing that the "power to investigate, broad as it may be, is also subject to recognized limitations" incorporated in the Fifth Amendment. In *Jencks v. U.S.* (1957), the Court ruled that defense attorneys had a limited right of access to FBI files to challenge the veracity of FBI informers' court testimony and then, in *Pennsylvania v. Nelson* (1956), struck down state loyalty statutes as intruding on exclusive federal authority in internal security matters. In a 1965 case, *Albertson v. Subversive Activities Control Board,* the Court held that Communist Party officials could not be compelled to identify their officers, members, and publications because this would violate the Fifth Amendment.

Reacting bitterly to the Court's narrowly crafted rulings, congressional conservatives introduced a spate of bills to curb the Court's authority to assess the constitutionality of national security policy. This attack on the Court was rebuffed. The only measure enacted into law, in August 1957, narrowed the scope of defense attorneys access to FBI files, confining it to direct testimony of government informers during security trials.

THE THREAT TO CIVIL LIBERTIES: SURVEILLANCE, NOT PROSECUTION

Because the Court limited its oversight to "cases and controversies," far more serious civil liberties issues were never addressed—particularly the unique character of federal surveillance activities during the Cold War era. Federal surveillance was not confined to prosecuting individuals and organizations suspected of violating federal laws but focused on obtaining advance intelligence about the activities and objectives of targeted individuals and organizations. In effect, this nonprosecutive purpose immunized such secret activities from court review. The policy and uses of federal wiretapping and bugging highlight how secrecy adversely affected civil liberties.

Despite Supreme Court rulings of 1937 and 1939 that required the dismissal of any indictment based on evidence obtained by federal agents through an illegal wiretap, President Roosevelt secretly authorized FBI wiretapping during "national defense" investigations in May 1940. President Truman expanded national defense wiretaps in 1946 to "subversive activities" investigations and "cases vitally affecting the domestic security, or when human life is in jeopardy [e.g., kidnapping]."

These directives could not legalize wiretapping. Such "intelligence" wiretaps posed serious constitutional problems insofar as their subjects were never only foreign agents but included radical activists, labor unions, and civil rights groups. The embarrassing exposure of FBI wiretapping practices during a 1949 espionage case, moreover, had the ironic consequence of ensuring further secrecy.

In March 1949, FBI agents arrested Judith Coplon, a low-level Justice Department employee, as she was about to deliver 28 FBI reports to Valentin Gubitchev, a Soviet agent employed on the United Nations staff. Coplon was convicted on charges of unauthorized possession of classified documents and intending to deliver them to an agent of a foreign power. Her conviction, however, was reversed on appeal and her case remanded for retrial.

The *Coplon* case threatened to expose the scope and political purposes of FBI investigations, their wiretapping activities, and their attempts to mislead government attorneys and the courts. For one thing, Coplon's attorney succeeded in having the 28 FBI reports submitted as evidence. Their release confirmed that FBI investigations focused on political activities and that information in 15 of the 28 reports had been obtained through wiretaps. Coplon's attorney thereupon petitioned the court for a pretrial hearing to ascertain whether her phone had been tapped. These hearings disclosed that the FBI had in fact tapped Coplon before and after her arrest (raising the additional question of whether Coplon's privileged conversations with her attorneys had been shared with prosecutors). In addition, the FBI agent who originally denied any knowledge of Coplon's being tapped had reviewed the Coplon wiretap logs (which were destroyed in view of "the imminence of her trial").

The court's rulings granting defense attorneys the right to review the 28 FBI reports and then exposing the FBI's illegal methods seemingly highlight the civil liberties safeguards of the American judicial system. Nonetheless, the consequences of the *Coplon* case were that the FBI took steps to prevent further scrutiny. In December 1949, FBI Director Hoover barred any FBI agent or supervisor who might in the future be assigned to a particular case from engaging in searches or other intrusive investigations. Any agent who might subsequently be called as "a competent witness" in a case should "have no testifiable knowledge of the existence of a technical surveillance [wiretap] in that particular case." (Wiretaps and break-ins were to be conducted by agents who would not appear as witnesses.)

Hoover, in addition, authorized a special June Mail records procedure. FBI agents were to caption "June" all reports derived either from "highly confidential sources" (i.e., sources illegal in nature such as wiretaps, break-ins, bugs, or mail intercepts) or from "most secretive sources, such as Governors, secretaries to high officials who may be discussing such officials and their attitude." June-captioned reports would not be filed in the FBI's central records system but would be routed to a Special File Room where they would be maintained "under lock and key." The next month, Hoover authorized a second records submission procedure under which FBI agents were to report on a separate, detachable "administrative page," and not in the text of their official reports, "facts and information which are considered of a nature not expedient to disseminate, or which would cause embarrassment to the Bureau, if distributed."

The court's review of suspected FBI wiretapping during the *Coplon* trial also precipitated an internal Justice Department–FBI review in October 1951 of FBI wiretapping (and bugging) practices and procedures. FBI wiretapping was "essential for national security," Hoover emphasized, but should the courts honor defense attorneys' petitions for similar discovery, "cases of vital importance to the protection of the United States" would be compromised. Hoover then briefed Attorney General J. Howard McGrath directly about another possible problem involving FBI microphone (bugging) practices, installation of which in most cases required trespass (in violation of the Fourth Amendment). Microphones, the FBI director emphasized, were used only for intelligence purposes and were "highly pertinent to the defense and welfare of the nation."

Attorney General McGrath, on February 26, 1952, reaffirmed existing wiretapping policy (prior review and approval in each case by the attorney general) but stated that "I cannot authorize the installation of a microphone *involving a trespass* under existing law." McGrath did not prohibit the continued uses of such illegal techniques but simply required that FBI officials "advise" the Justice Department. Thus notified, Justice Department officials could forego prosecution rather than risk exposing FBI illegal practices.

FBI agents continued to install bugs through trespass after February 1952. Eisenhower's election led to a more permissive bugging policy. In 1954, FBI Director Hoover convinced Attorney General Herbert Brownell to authorize "unrestricted" bugging "when the intelligence to be gained was a necessary adjunct to security matters and important investigations in instances where prosecution is not contemplated."

A NEW POLITICS OF EXPOSURE

Unwilling to ensure that FBI practices were lawful, Attorneys General McGrath and Brownell invited extensive use of these wiretaps and bugs. The richness of the intercepted information motivated FBI officials to seek alternative (nonprosecutive and extralegal) uses of oftentimes politically invaluable intelligence.

Stymied by recent Supreme Court rulings in Smith and McCarran Act cases, FBI Director Hoover in 1956 authorized a code-named COINTELPRO–Communist Party. Hoover's purpose was to contain the Communist party's "influence over the masses, ability to create controversy leading to confusion and disunity, penetration of specific channels in American life where public opinion is molded, and espionage and sabotage potential." The approved tactics included preparing and mailing anonymous letters to Communist activists to promote factionalism and leaking derogatory personal information about prominent Communists to reliable reporters and columnists. The inception of this program had broad civil liberties consequences. It marked the FBI's formal abandonment of a law enforcement mission for a course of political containment. FBI officials concurrently instituted safeguards to ensure that their disruptive actions could not become known, successfully precluding judicial, congressional, or even presidential oversight.

The COINTELPRO–Communist Party formalized practices instituted on a more limited and secretive basis eight years earlier. The purpose then was the same: to contain radical activists without risking disclosure of FBI officials' violations of the law. Fearful in the early Cold War years that Communist influence in the labor union and civil rights movements and in the popular culture would threaten the nation's security in the event of a future national emergency or war with the Soviet Union, FBI Director Hoover sought Attorney General Tom Clark's approval for a program to identify "all members of the Communist Party or any others who would be dangerous" for possible detention. Since prospective detainees should include "Communist sympathizers," Clark urged Hoover to launch an "educational campaign" to alert the public to the seriousness of the Communist threat. Then, after further deliberation, on August 3, 1948, the attorney general secretly authorized the FBI to prepare a list of dangerous individuals for possible detention.

Quite independently and unaware of this secret ongoing program, in September 1950, Congress enacted the Subversive Activities Control (McCarran) Act. Communist and Communist-infiltrated organizations were required to register with a newly established Subversive Activities Control Board, and Communists were prohibited from employment in defense industries, holding office in labor unions, and obtaining passports for foreign travel. The act also authorized the preventive detention of dangerous citizens. Its standards for apprehending and detaining such dangerous citizens, however, were more cognizant of civil liberties than those of the Justice Department's secret 1948 program. Unwilling to comply with the McCarran Act's standards, FBI and Justice Department officials secretly decided to continue listing suspect individuals under the 1948 guidelines. This preventive detention program was never implemented during either the Korean or Vietnam wars, so the question of the Justice Department's authority to ignore congressionally mandated standards was never tested. Nonetheless, the privacy and civic rights of those listed on the FBI's Security Index were compromised.

In February 1951, FBI Director Hoover secretly authorized a code-named Responsibilities Program to disseminate secret information concerning individuals on the Security Index to state governors and other reliable public personalities and organizations. Hoover claimed an obligation to protect public facilities "serving large portions of the people" and thus responsibility to alert public and private officials if any individual listed in the FBI's Security Index was employed in a public utility or in a public or semipublic organization (e.g., elementary and high schools, state colleges, the Red Cross, police departments). More than eight hundred state and local employees (over half of whom were public school and college teachers) were identified and then fired during the four-year operation of this program.

Skeptical reporters and union officials, however, demanded to know why these individuals were dismissed. Some governors then admitted having obtained the unverified information from the FBI, violating the explicit condition governing the Responsibilities Program—that they not disclose the FBI's assistance. To preclude further questioning of the FBI's role, Attorney General Brownell and FBI Director Hoover terminated the Responsibilities Program in March 1955.

The FBI's COINTELPRO and Responsibilities Program were not unique. Based on the proposition that communism is dangerous and convinced of the public's indifference to this threat, in February 1946, FBI Director Hoover launched an educational campaign to ensure "an informed public opinion" about the "basically Russian nature of the Communist Party in this country." Hoover explicitly intended to undermine Communist support among labor unions, "persons prominent in religious circles," and "the Liberal elements." "Educational material" was released through "available channels" (certifiably reliable reporters and members of Congress). In 1956, Hoover expanded this educational campaign to carefully selected reporters and columnists to ensure the continuous dissemination of derogatory political and personal information— again on the condition that the FBI's assistance was not to be disclosed.

Favored reporters willingly participated in this educational campaign, some for the scoops and others for ideological reasons. One example of this mutually beneficial relationship involved *New York Herald-Tribune* Washington bureau chief Don Whitehead. In 1955, Whitehead contacted the FBI's media liaison for assistance on a proposed article on "the fight against Communism and what the Communists are doing." Whitehead was instead offered privileged, if controlled, access to FBI files to write a history of the FBI. Provided an office at FBI headquarters, Whitehead was spoon-fed selected FBI documents, and his manuscript was reviewed— and specific changes were recommended— by FBI officials. Whitehead's history (which became a best-seller, *The FBI Story,* and a popular movie the next year) extolled and promoted the Bureau's role in combating the Communist menace.

THE HIDDEN HISTORY OF MCCARTHYISM

FBI dissemination programs were intended to influence public opinion and to redefine what constituted disloyalty. Such covert dissemination efforts included assisting the highly publicized campaigns of the House Committee on Un-American Activities, the Senate Internal Security Subcommittee, and Senator Joseph McCarthy.

Created as a special committee in 1938 (and becoming a standing committee in 1945), HUAC had consistently sought to expose the threat of "un-American" ideas and associations. Focusing at first on the alleged influence of Communists in shaping New Deal reform programs, the onset of the Cold War created a more receptive political climate for investigations into un-American activities. Indeed, the committee first achieved nationwide prominence in 1947 when launching an investigation into Communist influence in Hollywood (the center of the nation's film industry). As the targeted individuals were employed in the private sector and had no opportunity to engage in espionage, HUAC's proposed inquiry provoked controversy at first. Could Congress demand that subpoenaed witnesses respond to questions about their political associations and beliefs? Would the employment of Communists as producers, directors, writers, or actors threaten the nation's security because of their potential to influence the popular culture?

These hearings and the House of Representatives' decision to cite 10 recalcitrant witnesses for contempt of Congress (for refusing on First Amendment grounds to answer the committee's questions about their relationship to the Communist party) highlighted the priority of security considerations during the early Cold War years. As one by-product of the hearings film executives instituted an informal blacklist. Within days of the House vote of November 1947 to cite the 10 Hollywood directors, writers, and producers for contempt of Congress, film studio executives announced their intention not to rehire the so-called Hollywood Ten until each "had purged himself of contempt or been acquitted or declared under oath that he was not a Communist." Studio executives further affirmed their future intent not to employ Communists knowingly.

Unknown at the time, HUAC's congressional inquiry of October 1947 had depended on the covert assistance of FBI officials. In May 1947, HUAC Chair J. Parnell Thomas and HUAC Counsel Robert Stripling traveled to Hollywood to initiate a preliminary inquiry to ascertain whether the committee could successfully launch a full-scale, public hearing into Communist influence in the film industry. Thomas and Stripling immediately solicited FBI assistance. A leery FBI director at first demurred, fearing that the FBI's image would be tarnished by being directly linked to the controversial committee. Assured that the committee would not insist on direct FBI participation, and that "under no circumstance will the FBI source of this information be disclosed," FBI Director Hoover agreed to assist them "in order that they might better put the spotlight of public opinion on the Communist movement." This assistance included providing summary memoranda on 9 individuals whom Thomas and Stripling identified as being of particular interest, identifying another 9 "cooperative and friendly witnesses" (including Ronald Reagan and Robert Montgomery) and 24 "hostile witnesses" who were "identified with the communist movement."

The FBI's limited assistance to Thomas and Stripling in May convinced the full committee to authorize a full investigation, culminating in the October 1947 public hearings. Following this committee decision, Thomas personally solicited Hoover's assistance "for leads and information of value." Assured that this assistance would never become known, Hoover agreed to help. "It is long overdue for the Communist infiltration in Hollywood to be exposed," Hoover reasoned, "and as there is no medium at the present time through which this Bureau can bring that about on its own motion I think it is entirely proper and desirable that we assist the Committee in Congress that is intent upon bringing to light the true facts in the situation."

Since 1942, the FBI had intensively investigated Communist influence in Hollywood. Through its paid and volunteered informers and break-ins to photocopy Communist membership lists, FBI agents had successfully identified those individuals employed in the film industry (whether as producers, directors, screen writers, actors, or stagehands) who had joined the Communist party and various Popular Front or pro-Soviet groups during the 1930s and 1940s.

This information was secretly provided to HUAC. During the hearings, immediately after each of the 10 subpoenaed witnesses refused to answer the committee's questions, Committee counsel introduced into the record a list of the Popular Front and pro-Soviet organizations to which they had belonged and a photostatic copy of their Communist party membership (having obtained this information from the FBI). These disclosures changed the dynamics of the proceedings from the principled First Amendment stance of the 10 witnesses and their supporters to the question of whether their refusal to answer was intended to preclude discovery of the extent and purposes of Communist influence in Hollywood.

The FBI's quiet role did not cease with the termination of the October hearings. In the ensuing months and until the conclusion of the contempt trials, FBI agents continued to monitor the activities of the Hollywood Ten and their attorneys to rally public support for their stand. This intrusive surveillance included wiretapping two of the Ten's attorneys (Bartley Crum and Martin Popper), in the process acquiring invaluable advance intelligence about the defense's public relations and trial strategies. FBI Director Hoover immediately shared this privileged information with Attorney General Tom Clark and Assistant Attorney General T. Vincent Quinn (who supervised the prosecution of the Ten on contempt charges).

FBI officials continued after 1947 to promote HUAC's exposure efforts although the extent of their assistance varied owing to the penchant of committee members and staff to seek publicity (at times publicly compromising the FBI's covert role). In 1951, the committee revisited the issue of Communist influence in Hollywood. By then fully aware of the names of former Communists, the committee insisted that subpoenaed witnesses admit to their past membership and publicly identify any associate who had also been members. A willingness to inform became a condition for clearance and continued employment. Ironically, if the purpose was to preclude Communist influence over the content of films, the operation of the blacklist primarily penalized actors and directors—blacklisted screen writers were able (though at less pay) to submit commissioned scripts under pseudonyms. Indeed, one of the Hollywood Ten, Dalton Trumbo, won an Academy Award in 1956 for best screenplay, "The Brave One," which he wrote under the pseudonym Robert Rich.

This politics of tainting radical ideas and associations as inherently subversive influenced the content of films. During the early Cold War era, studio executives studiously avoided controversial themes. When the blacklisted producers, writers, and directors, moreover, pooled their talents and resources to produce a left-oriented film about a strike by Mexican-American miners, *Salt of the Earth,* their efforts encountered concerted opposition from HUAC, radio commentators, and conservative activists. Film laboratories and sound studios were pressured not to process the film, commercial theaters not to book the film, and newspaper and radio stations not to accept advertisements for the film's showings. These efforts ensured the film's commercial failure and served as a powerful deterrent to the production of future films offering a radical message on labor, civil rights, and controversial political issues.

FBI officials similarly assisted the Senate Internal Security Subcommittee. Created in November 1950 to oversee implementation of the recently enacted Subversive Activities Control Act, the Senate Internal Security Subcommittee almost immediately established a covert liaison relationship with the FBI. In contrast to HUAC, however, this liaison relationship was sanctioned by Attorney General J. Howard McGrath. FBI officials processed the subcommittee's name-check requests and provided "appropriate leads and suggested clues" for the subcommittee's "confidential use and guidance." This assistance was predicated on the understanding that the subcommittee would "strengthen internal security for the good of the United States but to help the Bureau in every possible manner." Like the Responsibilities Program, this covert liaison relationship was terminated in 1954 owing to the recklessness of its then-chair William Jenner and high-level staff aides.

FBI officials developed a similar covert liaison relationship with Senator Joseph McCarthy. First elected to the Senate in 1946, McCarthy languished in obscurity until February 1950 when he catapulted to national prominence, claiming to have documentary evidence that the State Department knowingly employed Communists and, further, that the Truman administration tolerated Communist influence on the nation's foreign policy. Coming shortly after the recent perjury conviction of Alger Hiss (a former State Department official who denied having given State Department documents to a Communist agent), McCarthy's dramatic charges tapped into a widespread public belief that existing security procedures were inadequate and that the Truman administration was unwilling to institute needed changes. He popularized the notion that Communists (and Communist sympathizers), by infiltrating sensitive State Department positions, were able to influence government policy, thereby posing a more serious threat than espionage.

McCarthy's growing national reputation was the unintended by-product of a strategic political decision of the Senate Democratic leadership. Doubting that McCarthy could substantiate his charges—in a February 20 Senate speech the senator had scaled the number of known Communist State Department employees down to 81 from the 205 he had cited in a February 9 speech in Wheeling, West Virginia—Senate Democrats on February 22 introduced a resolution to create a special committee to investigate these 81 cases. Their purpose was to discredit McCarthy and, in the process, nip in the bud an emerging Republican strategy, dating from 1949, of tarring the Truman administration's foreign policy as "soft on Communism."

With limited expertise in the areas of foreign policy and internal security, McCarthy had not played a prominent role in the Senate before February 1950. The decision of Senate Democrats to make McCarthy's 81 cases the central issue caused conservative reporters and members in Congress to rally behind the senator. Indeed, Republican Senate minority leader, Robert Taft, urged McCarthy to "keep talking and if one case doesn't work out, proceed with another one." The special committee failed to discredit McCarthy. The committee divided along partisan lines, and its highly publicized hearings precipitated a rancorous debate over Communist influence in the federal bureaucracy. In effect, the committee's hearings and reports sustained a new definition of espionage, equating membership in suspect organizations and holding dangerous ideas with a proclivity to promote Soviet objectives.

From 1950 through July of 1953, conservative reporters (some who joined McCarthy's staff and others in a private capacity) wrote the senator's speeches and, through their own research (and privileged access to the FBI), sought to document his accusations. Their evidence did not include a single new example of espionage but only the accused individual's membership or association with organizations deemed subversive. They focused on the Truman administration's alleged indifference to the Communist threat, confirmed by the president's refusal to fire individuals who sympathized with Communism or the Soviet Union.

Despite the partisan dimensions of McCarthy's attacks on the Democratic Truman administration, FBI officials did not remain above the fray. Committed to a more militant anti-Communist politics than the Truman administration, FBI officials willingly acted to sustain McCarthy's charges but took special care to preclude discovery of their covert assistance. McCarthy was not given FBI files or reports but information conveyed in blind memorandum form (i.e., on plain, nonletterhead stationery). Information was at times summarized to make it appear that the senator had "secured a CSC [Civil Service Commission] file rather than a Bureau file," while at other times FBI-supplied "information would be completely paraphrased making it impossible for any observer to determine that the information was actually taken from a Bureau report." McCarthy also relied on FBI officials for advice on strategy and to identify skilled investigators.

From 1950 through 1952, McCarthy's impact derived from press reporting of his speeches in the Senate or in public forums. After Republicans won the White House and majorities in the House and Senate in 1952, McCarthy's political fortunes changed. He became chairman of the Senate Committee on Government Operations and its Permanent Investigations Subcommittee. As chairman, he had both a more powerful forum and staff resources to sustain an anti-Communist crusade. The ambitious senator nonetheless recognized the need for expanded FBI assistance. Accordingly, on November 28, 1952, he proposed "closer cooperation with and extended use of the FBI" with the beginning of the new session of Congress in 1953 and solicited Hoover's recommendations on committee staff appointments. The FBI director willingly responded, ordering FBI officials to give this request prompt attention. Then, at a January 12, 1953, personal meeting with Hoover, McCarthy outlined his and the committee's plans and intention "from time to time" to seek Hoover's counsel.

FBI assistance to McCarthy ranged from advice about staffing, administration, and planned strategy to information from FBI files. This mutually cooperative arrangement continued until July 1953, in response to the senator's appointment of a current FBI agent, Francis Carr, as his committee's chief of staff. Having learned of Hoover's reservations about this proposed appointment, McCarthy directed two of his aides—Jean Kerr and Roy Cohn—to discuss this matter personally with the FBI director (preferring this arrangement because it allowed him to deny having cleared the matter with Hoover). At this meeting, Hoover refused to concur in or veto any McCarthy staff appointment, but then spelled out the reason for his reservation: "the appointment of an Agent now in the [FBI's] service and engaged upon work dealing with subversive activities would, no doubt, be seized upon by critics of the Senator and of the FBI as a deliberate effort to effect a direct 'pipe line' into the FBI and that would make it necessary for the Bureau to be far more circumspect in all of its dealings with the McCarthy Committee should Mr. Carr be appointed." When McCarthy nonetheless appointed Carr, all future FBI assistance to McCarthy was terminated.

McCarthy's recklessness ultimately led the Senate to vote in December 1954 to condemn him for "conduct unbecoming a member of the U.S. Senate." It would be mistaken, however, to conclude that the Senate's condemnation meant the end of *McCarthyism* (the term coined to describe the senator's role in promulgating a virulent anticommunism). Even during the height of his influence, McCarthy was never a lonely operator. Nor was he alone in capitalizing on a politics that equated radical political associations and the questioning of Cold War internal security and foreign policies with disloyalty. McCarthy commanded the support of a broad network of politicians, reporters, bureaucrats, and self-proclaimed patriotic citizens and organizations until 1954. This network, and the companion set of beliefs about the unquestioned primacy of security considerations, did not dissolve in December 1954. A far less personalist McCarthyism continued to shape American politics until the early 1970s.

During the height of the Cold War, few radicals were prosecuted for speech or associations that did not meet the test laid down in the Supreme Court's ruling in the *Schenck* case of posing a "clear and present danger" to the state. The exception was the conviction of the top leadership of the Communist party in the *Dennis* case. Security concerns, however, resulted in other (primarily covert) attempts to contain those individuals who either advocated dangerous ideas or alleged subversives who could influence public opinion in ways that challenged Cold War priorities: advocating cooperation with the Soviet Union, opposing loyalty oaths, criticizing the FBI, or defending the rights of Communists to free speech.

This obsession over security risks was not confined to employees in sensitive federal agencies (the State and Defense Departments, the FBI, and the CIA). Loyalty oaths were also required of state employees (particularly those employed in higher education), of individuals seeking a license to wrestle in Indiana, and of those seeking a permit to fish in New York City's reservoirs. Under Pennsylvania's Pechan Act of 1951, any public official could investigate whether a teacher or other public school employee is "a subversive person," and "any state-aided institution of learning not part of the public school system" would have to file a report describing its procedures against employing subversive persons. Private corporations (CBS, for example) emulated the Federal Employee Loyalty Program, while the American Medical Association, the American Bar Association, and the National Education Association required loyalty tests for membership. Furthermore, in 1950, the American Bar Association's House of Delegates required all attorneys to file affidavits that they were not Communist Party members and urged state regulatory bodies to expel any Communist or advocate of Marxism-Leninism from practicing law. Attorney General J. Howard McGrath articulated this sense of an omnipresent security threat: "There are today many Communists in America. They are everywhere—in factories, offices, butcher shops, on street corners, in private businesses. And each carries in himself the germs of death for society."

In this climate, citizens had to be careful about their associations and publicly-expressed convictions. Even Supreme Court Justice Hugo Black found it expedient to avoid controversial social relationships. Sensitive to southern criticisms of the Court's ruling in *Brown v. Topeka,* Black forbade his daughter Josephine from attending her cousin's wedding in Montgomery, Alabama, fearing the possible "unpleasant" result should it become known that she attended a reception at which alleged Communists would be present.

Who might be tainted became an open-ended question. Indeed, the FBI investigated civil rights leader Martin Luther King Jr. and the Southern Christian Leadership Conference; staff members and leaders of the American Civil Liberties Union and the radical National Emergency Civil Liberties Committee; and the recently formed gay and lesbian organizations the Mattachine Society and the Daughters of Bilitis. Left-liberal periodicals the *Nation* and *New Republic* were monitored, as were Democratic presidential candidate Adlai Stevenson Jr., famed architect Frank Lloyd Wright, and prominent writers (Ernest Hemingway, Nelson Algren, Dashiell Hammett).

In 1960, FBI officials created a special Reserve Index of those individuals who posed a "potential threat in time of [national] emergency." Those listed included Martin Luther King Jr., Norman Mailer, and a college professor who had spoken sympathetically about the Soviet Union in one of his classes. Special attention was to be given to "writers, newsmen, entertainers, and others in the mass media field." FBI Director Hoover cited the need to list those who were "in a position to influence others against the national interest or are likely to furnish material financial aid to subversive elements due to their subversive associations and ideology."

Part Two

1960–73

The 1960s and early 1970s were marked by significant advances in the rights of people of color and women and by increased sensitivity toward the right to dissent and privacy rights. National security justifications no longer commanded the unquestioned support as they had during the late 1940s and 1950s, triggered by the relaxation of U.S.-Soviet tensions, an increasingly controversial Vietnam War, and revelations of FBI and White House abuses of power. Through sustained protest and dramatic sacrifice, African Americans and women helped shape a new national consensus endorsing equality of opportunity. At the same time, the civil rights and women's rights movements were riven by internal conflicts— between those willing to work from within the system to reform the nation's laws and those demanding radical systemic changes through more militant tactics and separatist strategies.

The civil rights movement shaped national politics during the 1960s. Civil rights activists adopted tactics of mass mobilization and civil disobedience to highlight injustice and appeal to the nation's moral conscience and constitutional ideals. In the process, they challenged Cold War priorities, demanding that the nation focus on ensuring freedom and democracy *within* the United States. Civil rights activists invigorated American democracy by championing the right to petition the government for the redress of grievances (the underlying rationale for the First Amendment), heightening public awareness of the value of dissent, and exposing the limits of those rights as activists were repeatedly denied free speech, fair trial, and equal protection under the law.

As civil rights, women, and student activists moved from reform to radical politics, their militancy provoked a sharp increase in federal surveillance. FBI containment tactics succeeded in promoting factionalism within these movements. FBI and White House officials once again publicly characterized militant activism as subversive and anarchic, increasing public fear of these movements. The unanticipated exposure of these surveillance practices during the mid-1970s ironically promoted a new political culture that valued privacy rights and that questioned claims of national security.

The growth and tactics of militant groups, race riots in northern cities, and often-violent student-led protests against the Vietnam War precipitated an immediate backlash. A new conservatism erupted, symbolized by the 1968 presidential campaigns of George Wallace (the nominee of the American Independence Party) and Richard Nixon (the Republican nominee). Wallace appealed to southerners opposed to racial integration, to many northern white and blue-collar workers and white ethnics who thought that civil rights reforms had gone too far and impinged on their own economic and social rights, and to many Americans disenchanted with the elitist thrust of liberal reformers (whom Wallace contemptuously derided as "overeducated, ivory-tower folks with pointy heads"). Nixon's appeal was broader, aimed at the "forgotten Americans . . . who do not break the law, who pay their taxes and go to work . . . who love their country . . . [and] cry out . . . that is enough, let's get some new leadership."

At their core, Wallace and Nixon capitalized on the distinctive law-and-order concerns of the late 1960s. American conservatives repeated the anti-Communist themes of the McCarthy era that foreign-directed subversives threatened to the nation's internal security. Conservatives more pointedly questioned the costs of liberal domestic programs and elite politics and whether the federal government should address economic and social injustice. Resenting many of the changes of the 1960s, they claimed that liberal programs had created a climate that undermined respect for law and had given women and blacks special rights and unfair advantages over hard-working Americans. Their protests' moral basis underpinned a powerful cultural conservatism. By the end of the 1960s, a new moral concern had emerged: that liberal programs to promote equality undermined respect for "traditional values," contributed to the breakdown of the family, and encouraged an unbridled hedonism.

This emerging anti-civil rights and anti-civil liberties politics, however, was almost immediately counterbalanced by revelations of FBI and White House abuses of power during highly publicized Senate hearings of 1973 into the Watergate Affair. The twin developments that year of the Supreme Court's controversial ruling in *Roe v. Wade* and the Senate's investigation of the Watergate break-in and cover-up made 1973 a watershed year. The Court's landmark *Roe* decision affirming women's right to privacy (and prohibiting the state from infringing on women's control of their bodies) invigorated an emerging cultural conservatism to arrest and reverse those policies ensuring greater equality for women and blacks. Conversely, the Watergate revelations precipitated a reassessment of the major institutional and value changes of the Cold War era—and specifically whether government secrecy and unchecked surveillance ensured abuses of power and unwarranted violations of privacy rights.

The impact of *Roe v. Wade* and Watergate contributed to a new antigovernment politics. Many Americans questioned whether the government should ensure racial or sexual equality and should infringe on privacy rights. A post–civil rights politics emerged, defining reform as rewarding individual merit, affirming personal responsibility, and curbing government regulatory power.

Chapter 3

A MASS MOVEMENT
FOR CIVIL RIGHTS

STUDENTS TAKE THE LEAD

On February 1, 1960, four freshman at North Carolina A&T—Franklin McCain, Ezell Blair, David Richmond, and Joseph McNeil—defied local law and custom, sat down at Woolworth's lunch counter in Greensboro, and asked to be served. Frustrated with people talking about change but not acting on it, the four friends had decided the night before to take action. Having no idea what would happen, they pledged to continue their stand until they were served. The next day, they all purchased school supplies to emphasize Woolworth's willingness to take their business but not serve them equally, and then they requested service at the lunch counter. Visibly flustered, the waitress called in the manager. He told them to go home, insisting untruthfully that the policy was set at corporate headquarters, and closed the lunch counter. McCain described his feelings that first day, "If it's possible to know what it means to have your soul cleansed—I felt pretty clean at that time."

Word about their action spread across campus. The next day, the four young men were joined by twenty-three men and four women from a neighboring women's college. By the third day, the protesters occupied 63 of the 65 seats. By the fourth day, three white women joined the sit-ins, and the protests had overflowed Woolworth's and moved on to Kress, another downtown department store. A protest that had begun with four people was now a movement. Although Woolworth's first tactic was to ignore the young people, hoping they would go away; as the sit-ins continued, whites began to harass and attack the protesters, and the store began arresting the protesters.

News of the Greensboro sit-ins spread throughout the South. Young people inspired by the Greensboro sit-ins saw a blueprint for their own actions. As one student explained, "It's like waiting for a bus, man. You know where you're going all the time but you can't get there 'til the right vehicle comes along." One week later, on February 8, Winston Salem and Durham/Duke also had sit-ins. By February 9, the sit-ins spread to Charlotte; by the 10th, to Raleigh; and by the 11th, to Hampton, Virginia.

On February 13, 76 people were arrested in Nashville. Students in Nashville had been studying, planning, and training in nonviolence for months. They had conducted a trial sit-in in the fall of 1959, had been refused service, and then left. One of the leading students there, Diane Nash, came from Chicago and confronted the rigidity of southern segregation. "I didn't agree with the premise that I was inferior, and I had a difficult time complying with it. Also, I felt stifled and boxed in since so many areas of living were restricted." Nash's frustration led her to seek out Rev. James Lawson's workshops on nonviolence. Lawson had come to Nashville as the Fellowship of Reconciliation's first southern field secretary and had enrolled in Vanderbilt's School of Divinity. Imprisoned as a conscientious objector during the Korean War, Lawson was committed to the moral and practical value of nonviolent civil disobedience and had traveled to India to study Gandhi's nonviolent methods. His workshops brought this training in the theory and practice of nonviolence to Nashville students. Lawson was later expelled from Vanderbilt University's Divinity School for his role in the sit-ins.

Out of these workshops, Diane Nash, John Lewis, and other students started the Nashville Student Movement. Refusing to obey unjust laws and at the same time not responding with hate or violence, they believed, was the only way to undermine the foundations of racism and build the "beloved community." Diane Nash explained the power of this movement, "The movement had a way of reaching inside you and bringing out things that even you didn't know were there. Such as courage."

The movement spread beyond Greensboro, beyond Nashville, to Chattanooga and Houston and Atlanta. A few days after the Greensboro sit-ins began, Morehouse University's star football player Lonnie King confronted Julian Bond, a budding literary talent, to "make it happen" in Atlanta. The two were an unlikely match—King had grown up poor, his mom was a maid, and he had joined the navy to escape the South. Bond had grown up in a prominent black family in Atlanta, his dad was the dean of Atlanta University, and he had gone to private school in Pennsylvania before attending Morehouse. The two canvased the coffeehouse to announce a noon meeting to discuss a possible sit-in. That day's small gathering became a larger meeting the next. The students wanted to act immediately. The president of Atlanta University urged caution instead, and he provided funds for a full-page ad in Atlanta's newspapers listing their grievances and the steps to be taken to remedy them. When this produced no change, two hundred students converged on 10 eating places on March 15. Students also called on the community to stop shopping at Rich's, the leading department store for most blacks in Atlanta. "Close out your charge account with segregation, open up your account with freedom," demanded their campaign.

That summer the Atlanta sit-in movement targeted businesses that discriminated against blacks, and it catapulted another student, Ruby Doris Smith, into leadership. Raised in a middle-class black family in Atlanta, Smith was attending Spelman College when the Greensboro sit-ins began. "I began to think right away about it happening in Atlanta . . . when two hundred students were selected for the first demonstration, I was among them." Assigned to the A&P grocery store, she often marched alone in her daily pickets in front of the A&P. Smith explained, "We do not intend to sell our dignity for a few dollars."

By the end of 1960, nearly seventy thousand people had sat-in in 150 cities. Three thousand six hundred people had been arrested. At least 50

Students did homework while sitting-in to demand equal service.

percent of those who participated were women. Having started with four students, the sit-ins had become a mass movement, drawing in young people across the South. There had been sit-ins in the 1950s, but none caught fire with the public or the media these had. The new sit-inners had come of age during *Brown,* the Till lynching, the Montgomery bus boycott, and the desegregation of Little Rock. As Joseph McNeil, one of the initial Greensboro sit-inners, explained, "I was particularly inspired by the people in Little Rock. . . . We knew what they were going through was not easy, but somehow many of us wanted to . . . be a part of something like that." These events convinced them of the need and, more importantly, of the possibility for change.

Part of what gave the sit-ins momentum was that blacks throughout the South had long suffered the indignities of downtown segregation. They could identify with the anger of those in Greensboro or in Nashville and use those actions as a model for their own. It was not that the risks diminished as the sit-ins went on. If anything, the violence and arrests increased. Many protesters also faced anger and ostracism from their families and disciplinary action from their schools. Yet the numbers continued to swell. As one student put it, "I myself desegregated a lunch counter, not somebody else, not some big man, some powerful man, but little me. I walked the picket line and I sat in and the walls of segregation topple. Now all people can eat there."

Identifying with Martin Luther King, Jr., black students modeled their actions on Gandhi's tactics of nonviolent civil disobedience. Breaking unjust laws would dramatize the injustice of segregation. Refusing to participate in an unjust system by inserting their bodies and removing their buying power, they attacked the economic roots of segregation by sitting-in and boycotting downtown business. Students joined these protests dressed in their Sunday best and often did homework during quiet moments.

Widespread and sustained, the sit-ins called into question the belief that blacks were satisfied with the status quo and that any protests were orchestrated by outside agitators and communists. Many whites had long chosen to believe that blacks were happy with the system of racial segregation. Whenever protests happened, these whites claimed that the demonstrations were by led by communists or outsiders—that "their blacks" were satisfied. Such beliefs helped discredit those advocating change. But by their numbers and their militancy, the sit-ins of the 1960s unraveled this illusion of contentment. These demonstrations also proved that students could organize orderly, well-executed actions outside of the realm of the NAACP, upsetting the NAACP's position as the dominant civil rights group and their focus on legalistic tactics as opposed to mass mobilization.

With young people taking the lead in the struggle for equal rights and willingly going to jail for their beliefs, the sit-ins revealed a generation gap in the black community. While many older blacks were heartened by the protests, others were scared or put off by the students' militancy. In Atlanta, that rift widened when older community leaders urged students to accept a compromise where they would halt their protests in exchange for the lunch counters being integrated *nine months later.* Lonnie King explained, "The thing was basically a young-versus-old split, and the young folks knew that we had been blackjacked and kind of just bludgeoned in the damn meeting. . . . I had seen people that I had had respect for all my life crumble when faced with an awesome decision." Julian Bond noted how these adults who had urged an end to the protests elbowed the students aside when the lunch counters were finally integrated.

Ella Baker, working as SCLC's executive director at the time and of the older generation, was buoyed by the demonstrations. She realized the "dissatisfaction among the young with the older leadership" and the need for these students to meet and build these downtown protests into a larger movement for social change. To encourage this movement, she called a conference, Sacrifice for Dignity, for April 16–18, 1960, using $800 of the SCLC's money. Between 200 and 300 people attended the meeting at Shaw University, including at least 120 southern black student activists representing 56 colleges, observers from 13 student and social reform organizations, northern black and white students, and 12 southern white students. The vast majority of those attending were black students, although white students were active from the start. Baker helped the students form their own separate organization, the Student Nonviolent Coordinating Committee, or SNCC (pronounced "snick"). The SCLC, the NAACP, and CORE all viewed the students as a potential youth wing of their organizations; Baker, however, urged the young people to go their own way and think more broadly than desegregating lunch counters. Her ideas of democratic leadership and indigenous struggle were to become central to the new organization's emerging agenda and philosophy.

Committed to being an interracial organization, SNCC's original statement of purpose reflected the influence of Lawson and the Nashville group and their commitment to nonviolent direct action as a vehicle for militant social change: "By appealing to the conscience and standing on the moral nature of human existence, nonviolence nurtures the atmosphere in which reconciliation and justice become actual possibilities." Through the sit-ins, these young people had seen through the sit-ins that nonviolent direct action was a weapon of confrontation and a way to achieve substantive social change. SNCC's philosophy rested on the potential of ordinary men and women to create change and focused on grassroots organizing to enable local people to decide where the movement would go. Seeking to encourage as many voices as possible, these young people rejected individual celebrity and organizational hierarchy. As Ella Baker explained, "Strong people don't need strong leaders. . . . People have to be made to understand that they cannot look for salvation anywhere but to themselves." Disdaining event-based strategies, the student activists favored consensus and group-centered leadership. Drawing young people of many backgrounds as organizers and people of all ages into the struggle, they labored across the South, combining moral righteousness with persistent action. As Julian Bond explained, "We were operating on the theory that here was a problem, you expose it to the world, the world says 'How Horrible' and moves to correct it."

From a staff of 16 people in 1961, SNCC grew to over 150 by early 1964, and by the summer of 1965, over 200 people were full-time staff members, with another 250 people acting as full-time volunteers. Many interrupted their studies to work for SNCC full time. Organizers earned $10 a week. Compared to other civil rights organizations, SNCC had a very small budget. These students often resented how national civil rights organizations raised money for themselves by associating with SNCC's work.

CIVIL RIGHTS AND THE PRESIDENTIAL ELECTION

These students were also able to make their mark on the 1960 presidential contest between John F. Kennedy and Richard Nixon. The Atlanta students had long pressured Dr. King to join their movement. King and his family had moved to Atlanta where he copastored Ebenezer Baptist Church with his father Martin Luther King Sr. and devoted the rest of his time to the SCLC. Returning from the summer break, the Atlanta students decided to delay their next challenge to downtown segregation until October, with the objective of pressuring presidential candidates Kennedy and Nixon to take sides on the sit-ins. They finally convinced King to join them. On October 19, King participated in a restaurant sit-in with Atlanta students, was arrested, and was given an unusually harsh sentence of four months of hard labor. One of John F. Kennedy's advisors convinced him to make a personal call to Coretta Scott King to express his sympathy about King's sentence. Coretta Scott King remembered the call, "Kennedy said, 'I'm thinking about you and your husband and I know this must be a very difficult time for you. If there's anything I can do to help, I want you to please feel free to call.'" Robert Kennedy, John F. Kennedy's brother and campaign manager, worried that the call would cost Kennedy white southern support. Still, that night, Robert Kennedy called the presiding judge, and King was soon released. Richard Nixon, on the other hand, did and said nothing.

Because of those two calls, Martin Luther King Sr., who had previously supported Nixon, pledged "a whole suitcase full of votes that I'm taking up and putting in the lap of John Kennedy." Through King Sr.'s initiative, millions of leaflets were distributed by the Democratic Party through black churches reading, "No Comment Nixon vs. A Candidate with a Heart—Sen. Kennedy: The Case of Martin Luther King, Jr." Chicanos were also organizing to get out the vote, particularly on behalf of local Chicano candidates. Kennedy benefited from this local organizing. Despite the closeness of the election (Kennedy won by less than 1 percent) and the initial coldness of the black community towards his candidacy, over 70 percent of blacks and over 85 percent of Chicanos supported Kennedy. This support proved decisive. Without strong black support, Kennedy would have lost New Jersey, Illinois, Texas, Pennsylvania, Michigan, and South Carolina, totaling 137 electoral votes. A resounding Chicano vote ensured his victory in Texas and New Mexico.

Once elected, Kennedy quickly backpedaled on his commitment to civil rights. In his first years in office, Kennedy introduced no new civil rights legislation and delayed his campaign promise to wipe out housing discrimination in federally funded housing projects with "a stroke of a pen." Kennedy nominated many judges to the bench who proved to be some of the staunchest enemies of racial progress. On the issue of civil rights, Kennedy was a follower not a leader, a politician largely committed to the status quo.

SNCC GOES TO MISSISSIPPI

A cadre of grassroots leaders, such as Bob Moses, helped spearhead a growing movement that in the early 1960s challenged the entrenched system of segregation in Mississippi. Raised in a working-class family in Harlem, Moses attended Hamilton College on scholarship and began his graduate work at Harvard in 1957. When his mother died, he returned to New York City to teach math. The sit-ins drew Moses to the South. "They were kids my age, and I knew this had something to do with my own life. It made me realize that for a long time I had been troubled by the problem of being a Negro and at the same time being an American." Older than most of the students, he gravitated to SNCC and its commitment to organizing and direct action. Ella Baker sent Moses to Mississippi to meet NAACP organizer Amzie Moore. A World War II veteran, a service station–restaurant owner, and a longtime activist, Moore convinced Moses that voter registration was the key to destroying the second-class status of blacks in the South. Moore, along with other older Mississippi NAACP activists like Aaron Henry and Medgar Evers, provided the foundation for SNCC to establish a base in the state.

In 1946, only 5,000 of the more than 350,000 blacks who lived in Mississippi were registered to vote. This increased by the 1950s to nearly 25,000 out of almost 500,000 blacks (or approximately 5 percent of blacks in the state). In some counties, no blacks were registered. Voter applicants had to be of "good moral character" and were subjected to tests of the state constitution. Having the power to decide who passed and who did not, white voter registrars usually failed black applicants. To ensure prospective voters' moral character, their names were published in the newspaper for two weeks. This publicity often brought various forms of harassment and economic intimidation against those blacks who dared to register. Depriving black Mississippians of the right to vote also helped maintain a system of economic disadvantage. Eighty-six percent of all nonwhite families lived below the poverty line in Mississippi. The average annual income of a black family in Mississippi was $606 compared with $2,030 of the average white family. Infant mortality was twice as high for blacks as for whites. Even in 1965, 95 percent of rural blacks in Mississippi had no bathtub, shower, or flush toilet. This political, economic, and social disfranchisement was enabled by violence, enacted by local citizens, protected by the state, and designed to send a powerful message to anyone who got out of line.

For the next four years, SNCC and Moses focused their efforts on voter registration in Mississippi. At first, the SNCC students were suspicious of Moses. According to Julian Bond, "We thought he was a Communist because he was from New York and wore glasses and was smarter than we were." Moses's thoughtfulness and organizing style anchored SNCC's movement in Mississippi. Greenwood native Ida Mae Holland described his style, "At first glance, Moses didn't look like the inspirational leader. . . . Yet as I would soon learn, no packhorse could teach him anything about stamina; no history book patriot or bloodied war hero could show him how to stand firm against his enemies. . . . With quiet, soulful eyes, this math teacher from the Harlem projects shared his creed before each battle: 'Each and every one of us can strike a blow for freedom.' "

SNCC's style of organizing embodied in Moses's belief that everyone can "strike a blow for freedom" differed profoundly from other civil rights organizations. SCLC favored mobilizing the community around a particular campaign to capture national attention. SCLC stayed in communities for shorter periods of time while SNCC remained for the long haul, looking to develop local leadership and address the issues of concern to local people. As Bob Moses wrote from jail in McComb, Mississippi, "This is a tremor in the middle of the iceberg from a stone that the builders rejected." Furthermore, SNCC organizers traveled to communities thought to be too difficult and dangerous to mobilize. Moses continued, "The problem is that you can't be in the position of turning down the tough areas, because the people would simply lose confidence in you." SNCC's commitment led local residents such as Mary Dora Jones, of Marks, Mississippi, to become involved. "They comes in, they mean business. They didn't mind dyin'. . . . I just love that . . . because they was there to help us. And since they was there to help us, I was there to help them."

Mississippi was not SNCC's only battleground. Early discussions of nonviolent strategy led SNCC members to decide not to post bond (which meant serving the full time in jail and putting the burden of the expense on the state). On January 31, 1961, 10 local activists were arrested in Rock Hill, South Carolina, on charges of trespassing for their role in downtown demonstrations. Nine decided not to post bail but to serve their time in jail. They asked for outside help to support their struggle. SNCC responded by sending a delegation of four—Diane Nash, Ruby Doris Smith, Charles Jones, and Charles Sherrod. This jail-in became a broadening experience, providing an opportunity to read, reflect, and sharpen their analysis of the movement and their own sense of purpose.

FREEDOM RIDES THE BUS

A 1960 Supreme Court ruling, *Boynton v. Virginia,* provided the spark for another set of actions—the Freedom Rides. To test this ruling which outlawed segregated interstate bus terminals, CORE, under the leadership of James Farmer, organized the first set of Rides. Only a dramatic confrontation, Farmer believed, would ensure that this ruling was enforced. On May 4, 1961, seven black and six white volunteers, all seasoned activists, left Washington, D.C., for Alabama and then Mississippi. Their goal was to integrate the buses they were riding and each of the terminals where the buses stopped. Prepared for violence, all of the riders had been trained in nonviolence. Some even left letters behind to loved ones in case they were killed.

The buses never made it to Mississippi. The first bus was stopped in Anniston, Alabama, where it was bombed, set on fire, and the riders heavily beaten. The second bus encountered violence in Anniston but managed to continue on to Birmingham where it was met by a mob. Birmingham Police Commissioner Bull Connor gave the crowd and the KKK 15 minutes to attack the riders before sending in the police. Having learned earlier of this arrangement, FBI agents chose to do nothing. James Peck was one of the riders who was brutally attacked. A white pacifist who had served time in prison during World War II as a conscientious objector, Peck described the scene in Birmingham, "The mob seized us and I was unconscious, I'd say within a minute." Peck was refused treatment at the first hospital he was taken to and ultimately required 53 stitches in the head.

The violence in Anniston and Birmingham stopped the buses. However, SNCC activists decided to continue the rides begun by CORE. As Diane Nash explained, "The impression would have been given that whenever a movement starts, all you have to do is attack it with massive violence and the blacks will stop." On May 17, SNCC activists tried to resume the Ride but were trapped in Birmingham, jailed, and then dropped off by Commissioner Connor himself on the Tennessee border. Alone, on foot, and vulnerable to attack if discovered to be Freedom Riders, they sought shelter with a local black family.

SNCC rejected Attorney General Kennedy's call for a cooling-off period. Determined to draw the federal government into protecting them and making good on its own laws, Nash organized this next Ride that began in Birmingham. Despite Alabama Governor Patterson's assurances to the Kennedys that the riders would be protected, the riders encountered violence in Montgomery. John Lewis described the mob. "They carried every makeshift weapon imaginable. Baseball bats, wooden boards, bricks, chains, tire irons, pipes, even garden tools—hoes and rakes. One group had women in front, their faces twisted in anger, screaming, 'Git them niggers. GIT them niggers!'" The crowd of over a thousand people attacked the riders and reporters covering the event; white riders Walter Bergman and Jim Zwerg and black rider William Barbee suffered permanent damage and paralysis from their beatings. Those whites who took part in grassroots direct action for civil rights were often subject to the violence, social and family ostracism, and economic hardships that blacks were. White activists had broken the racial compact, according to many segregationists, and deserved attack for being "race traitors" and "nigger lovers."

Faced with the violence in Montgomery and Governor Patterson's refusal to keep his word, President Kennedy decided to send in 600 federal marshals. The next evening, a large crowd of blacks rallied in support of the Freedom Rides at Ralph Abernathy's church in Montgomery. Dr. King traveled to Montgomery to support the riders and lead the rally. The marshals proved no match for several thousand whites that had gathered outside and trapped the demonstrators inside the church for hours. The incident left all sides angry. Governor Patterson was mad at Kennedy for sending in the marshals, Kennedy was fed up with both the riders and Patterson, and the black community was incensed that the government was not protecting citizens who were exercising their rights under the law. Two days after the church incident, 27 Freedom Riders left

Montgomery for Mississippi. King was not one of them. Still on probation for his part in the Atlanta sit-ins, he refused the student riders' pleas that he join them. "I think I should choose the time and place of my Golgatha."

The ride to Mississippi was a frightening experience; most riders assumed that they would face an even more brutal response than they had in Alabama. Instead, when the riders finally reached Mississippi, they were arrested and sent to Parchman prison. Attorney General Robert Kennedy had secretly reached an agreement with Mississippi Senator Eastland. Trading justice for order to take the movement out of the headlines, the federal government promised not to step in when the state arrested the riders if Eastland promised that there would be no violence. The buses and terminal were legally desegregated, yet Kennedy and Eastland agreed that the riders would be jailed anyway. Fred Leonard, a black freshman at Tennessee State University, described the riders' trial. "[T]he judge turned his back, looked at the wall." Freedom Rides continued over the course of the summer. More than half of the riders were black, more than two-thirds were students, and more than half of the students were women. At least 328 people were arrested. The jail conditions were harsh; the cells were overheated in the summer, dirty, crawling with bugs, and often without mattresses. Still, solidarity and friendship grew in jail despite the conditions. Free-ranging discussions became a form of political education, and singing provided a way to keep their spirits up (and annoy their captors).

A group of middle-class black women in Jackson, under the leadership of Claire Collins Harvey, stepped up to help mitigate these deplorable conditions. Noticing that some of the first Freedom Riders seemed cold, Harvey took extra clothes down to the jail and that Sunday raised money in her church for their needs. These efforts blossomed into a full-fledged organization called Womanpower Unlimited, which established an interracial network that provided food, blankets, clothes, magazines, and books to Freedom Riders in jail as well as information to families of jailed riders. Their efforts were not popular in the black or white communities but underscored the impact of the Freedom Rides on people's consciousness by leading these women to action. The networks that helped shelter civil rights workers became part of the backbone of the struggle throughout the deep South. Moving from supporting to becoming activists themselves, Womanpower Unlimited later became involved in the campaign to register voters and boycott Jackson's white-owned businesses.

The events of 1961 led civil rights workers to be called "freedom riders"—the term connoted deep respect and profound trepidation of their stubbornly fearless stand. The Rides had helped nationalize the movement, increasing donations and the number of volunteers. Like the Montgomery boycott and sit-ins, the Freedom Rides democratized the movement by taking the role of change from the hands of the lawyers into the arms of ordinary people. Young people handled the organization and coordination. As Diane Nash explained, "The media and history seem to record it as Martin Luther King's movement, but young people should realize that it was people just like them, their age, that formulated goals and strategies, and actually developed the movement." The Freedom Rides also changed local policy and federal enforcement by creating the kind of attention that forced the government to uphold the law. The Rides solidified SNCC's policy of not posting bond, as they refused to compromise with a judicial system that jailed them for exercising their legal rights.

After the Rides, a split arose in SNCC between those who favored direct action and those who wanted to focus on voter registration. Voter registration could potentially garner public and federal support, whereas direct action had proven effective in the sit-ins and again in the Freedom Rides. Attorney General Robert Kennedy had promised protection and support if civil rights workers turned their attention to voting rights. Some saw this promise as a tactical advantage that would enable SNCC's work, while others believed that Kennedy was only trying to tone down the movement. Ella Baker proposed a compromise, and two wings were established. SNCC quickly came to realize that voter registration was direct action. Many local whites saw the efforts to register mass numbers of blacks to vote as mass confrontation and responded through bombing churches and houses, attacking or firing civil rights supporters, and arresting activists on false charges. Despite their promises and this violence, federal authorities provided little support.

THE MOVEMENT GROWS IN MISSISSIPPI

In July 1961, Bob Moses returned to Mississippi full time to head SNCC's voter registration project and to challenge the climate of fear that limited activism in the state. One of the first people to join the movement, Herbert Lee, a black dairy farmer and father of nine, was murdered on September 25, 1961. Angered at Lee's civil rights stand, state representative E. H. Hurst, a white childhood friend of Lee's, shot him in broad daylight in front of witnesses. Lee's murder symbolized the resistance SNCC would encounter in its campaign throughout the South—and further the difficulty of convicting a white person for killing a black person in Mississippi. Through the coercion of black witnesses, Hurst was acquitted on the grounds of self-defense. Justice Department officials refused to provide protection for these witnesses who, although willing to testify to what had really happened, feared for their own lives. One of the witnesses, Louis Allen, was murdered in front of his house in January 1964.

SNCC supporters were brutally attacked at a march protesting Lee's murder. White SNCC worker Bob Zellner described the crowd, "I remember the sounds of the black jacks as they hit the heads of Bob Moses and Charles McDew. . . . They had just every kind of weapon you can imagine: baseball bats, pipes, wrenches. . . . [One man] started putting his fingers into my eye sockets and he actually would work my eyeball out of my eye socket and sort of down on my cheekbone." FBI agents stood by taking notes as the SNCC workers were beaten. Even though they were the ones being attacked for peacefully demonstrating, Zellner, Moses, and McDew were each sentenced to four months in jail for their role in organizing the march.

Herbert Lee's murder ushered in a period of soul-searching for SNCC workers in Mississippi. As Chuck McDew put it, "It's okay to put our own lives in jeopardy, but when you can cause somebody else to get killed, then that's a different question. [We] came to the conclusion that nothing would happen in Mississippi, and in the South, unless somebody was willing to die." The Kennedys had promised federal support for voter registration work but SNCC was quickly learning that they were on their own.

Nonetheless, this movement to claim citizenship engendered a profound sense of empowerment for many local black people. As Ida Mae Holland explained, "Being around the SNCC people had turned my narrow space into a country bigger than I'd every imagined." After being raped on her 11th birthday by the white man in whose house she did domestic work, Holland began to rebel openly and turned to prostitution to support her family. Coming into contact with SNCC provided a different outlet for her rebellious energy. Despite her mother's admonitions not to go near any civil rights workers, Holland followed a freedom rider to the SNCC office where they were eager for her help. "I realized I had taken to these newcomers like a duck to water. Being treated with respect was something wholly new for me." Holland began working with the movement in Greenwood and later toured the North for SNCC to raise money and increase publicity for the organization.

SNCC did not have a lot of money, and often organizers had to live in local people's homes. SNCC worker Jean Wheeler Smith described their welcome. "They loved us before they ever saw us. When you showed up, they didn't even ask if you were hungry. . . . They would just do for you like you were their own children." One of the first women to open her home was Mama Dolly Raines, a tiny, 70-year-old sharecropper in Lee County, Georgia. As SNCC's Charles Sherrod observed, "There is always a 'mama.' She is usually a militant woman in the community, outspoken, understanding and willing to catch hell, having already caught her share."

The media, at times, aided the impact of the movement. Such coverage kept some of the violence and other forms of retaliation against civil rights workers in the public eye, broadcast images of determined black people fighting for change in local communities throughout the South, and pulled the nation into local struggles. By making the actions of civil rights activists prominent news, these stories changed the ways blacks had long been publicly portrayed in two significant ways. First, few public images existed of blacks standing up for their rights, even though this had been going on for decades. These new images often provided a catalyst for more demonstrations and further organization. Second, such coverage made violence against blacks important enough to be news, affording a small measure of protection for the dangerous work of civil rights activism. Even though violence against whites had long been and continued to be framed as a matter of national importance, the fact that violence against blacks was covered at all was a change. Not all press coverage enabled civil rights. Much of it, particularly by local newspapers, demonized the movement and stoked the frenzy of local whites. But many people in the movement, like SNCC's Communication Director Julian Bond, understanding the importance of the media to their struggle, worked hard to ensure that their actions would be covered. And some reporters were willing to defy convention to capture the face of racism and the fight against it.

The media played a decisive role in publicizing the desegregation of the University of Mississippi. In January 1961, James Meredith applied for admission to the university and asked the NAACP for assistance. On September 10, 1962, the Supreme Court affirmed Meredith's right to attend the University of Mississippi. Meredith's enrollment at Old Miss touched off a series of riots that revealed the entrenched nature of school segregation. On September 20, 1962, Governor Ross Barnett personally blocked Meredith from entering the university. Determined to hold fast against Meredith's enrollment, Barnett used the full power of the state to resist federal law mandating Meredith's admission, explaining, "We will not drink from the cup of genocide." The governor's defiance of federal law motivated President Kennedy to act. Five hundred federal marshals accompanied Meredith when he attempted to enroll again 10 days later. They proved insufficient for the angry mob that rioted that night and would not disperse even after rounds of tear gas had been fired. At the end of that long night, 2 people were dead, 28 marshals had been shot, and 160 people had been injured. The images of this riot were broadcast through the nation.

FREEDOM NORTH

Even though segregation was seen as a southern issue, black communities throughout the North were also beginning to challenge northern discrimination and segregation. In 1960, a Boston woman named Ruth

Batson called the NAACP after learning that the child of a white friend was taught science in school but Batson's daughter was not. Batson had long been politically active, having been elected Democratic state committeewoman in 1956 and the first woman president of the New England Regional NAACP in May 1958. She persuaded the NAACP to set up a committee where she and a group of parents investigated school segregation and the discrepancies between the city's white and black schools. "When we would go to white schools, we'd see these lovely classrooms, with a small number of children in each class. The teachers were permanent. We'd see wonderful materials. When we'd go to our schools, we would see overcrowded classrooms, children sitting out in the corridors." The group focused on the disparities in resources and the quality of education. "[W]here there were a large number of white students, that's where the care went. That's where the books went. That's where the money went." The city spent 10 percent less on textbooks, 19 percent less on library spending, and 27 percent less on health for black students than for white students. Per-pupil spending averaged $340 for white students but only $240 for blacks. The curriculum at many black schools was out-dated and often blatantly racist, and teachers were less permanent and often less experienced than those assigned to white schools. The district also engaged in differential hiring practices; thus, many schools had no black teachers (blacks made up only .5 percent of the teachers in Boston public schools).

On June 11, 1963, community activists packed the School Committee meeting to present their findings. But the School Committee rejected their report of racial inequity within the system. Batson described the committee's reaction, "We were insulted. We were told our kids were stupid and this was why they didn't learn." Refusing to acknowledge any role in perpetuating unequal schooling in the city, the school committee maintained a racially stratified school system over the next decade. Batson concluded, "[W]e found out that this was an issue that was going to give their political careers stability for a long time to come." The community would have to look for other means to force educational change within the city.

Housing proved another crucial battleground outside the South. In Milwaukee, Father James Groppi, a white priest of a mostly black Catholic parish, helped lead a series of peaceful marches to integrate the city's segregated schools and neighborhoods. Crowds harassed the marchers, yelling epithets, spitting, and at times beating them. But the marchers continued. After 200 consecutive days of marches, Milwaukee aldermen passed an open-housing ordinance. California citizens turned against the passage of open-housing legislation. In November of 1964, California voters overwhelmingly passed Proposition 14, which repealed the state's 1963 law banning racial discrimination in the sale of real estate.

Three of every four white voters supported Proposition 14 to preserve their freedom to discriminate in the sale of their property.

Northern discrimination extended to labor unions. In May 1963, the Philadelphia NAACP launched a construction campaign to protest the exclusion of black workers from construction unions. Not one black skilled craftsperson was employed on any government construction site in Philadelphia in 1963 and only one black electrician was a member in the 7,300-member plumber, electrician, and steamfitter unions. Blacks were overwhelmingly restricted to unskilled jobs—despite their skills— and to membership in the Laborers Local. For three days, growing numbers of picketers tried to prevent workers and materials from entering the construction area. The construction representatives agreed to the NAACP's demands to form a joint NAACP-industry committee and hire five blacks on the spot. But this pressure did not yield long-term change. The next month, the construction representatives broke off talks with the NAACP. In 1966, there were only 50 black union members out of 9,000.

THE MOVEMENT MOVES WEST: THE FIGHT FOR A UNION FOR FARMWORKERS

Chicanos had also long resisted their second-class status. Their efforts to promote change intensified in the period after World War II. One of the central battlegrounds involved the right to join a union, because many farmworkers were Chicanos and Mexicans and farmworkers were not unionized. Migrant workers received substandard wages that could be docked or changed at any moment. They often worked under grueling conditions, not entitled to breaks for water or to go to the bathroom. Many fields did not even have bathroom facilities. Workers who challenged this treatment were quickly fired and sometimes deported. The opportunity to form a union or to earn a minimum wage guaranteed for other workers was not available to farmworkers. The passage of the Wagner Act in 1935 had affirmed the right of Americans to join unions without retribution; this guarantee left out two groups, domestics and farmworkers.

Two organizers—César Chávez and Dolores Huerta—rose to challenge this situation. César Chávez was born in 1927 in Yuma, Arizona, to farmworker parents who often served as community leaders. After losing their farm during the Depression, Chávez's family followed the migrant work to California where he grew up. Chávez was enrolled in 36 schools as his family crisscrossed California harvesting tomatoes, peas, berries, grapes, cotton, sugar beets, and lettuce. Joining the navy at age 17 to serve during World War II, Chávez experienced pervasive discrimination, describing his military service as the two worst years in his life.

After getting out of the military, he married Helen Fabela. Chávez received his initial organizing training in the Community Services Organization (CSO), which combined political advocacy with house-to-house visits to mobilize the community around social action.

Dolores Huerta was born in 1930 in New Mexico. Her mother also instilled in her a sense of justice and self-confidence that sustained her political work and encouraged her to continue her education. Unlike many women of her time, she attended community college and became a teacher. She met Chávez while working for the CSO as a lobbyist. Sharing the dream of building a strong union to address the vulnerable position farmworkers occupied in the labor market, they formed a lifelong organizing team. Yet Huerta has rarely been seen as the co-leader that she was—her important role long obscured by Chávez's public persona. In her decades of political service, she was often criticized for her unfeminine behavior—for her independence, outspokenness, and aggressiveness; for her refusal to stay home to raise her kids; and for her determination to be a full-time organizer.

Despite Chávez and Huerta's enthusiasm for organizing farmworkers, the CSO was reluctant to get involved. According to Chávez, many of the CSO's leaders "lacked the urgency we had to have." Chávez and Huerta decided "to organize the union ourselves." So with a third organizer, Gil Padilla, they left the CSO in 1962 to start the National Farm Workers Association (NFWA). Like Chávez, Padilla came from a farmworker background and had served in World War II.

Traveling the length and breadth of the farmworking communities of California, the three dropped off leaflets and organizing cards for farmworkers, visited homes, and stopped at labor camps along the way. Purposefully avoiding calling themselves a union to avoid harassment, they collected eighty thousand pledge cards, and by 1964, the NFWA had a thousand members. In December of 1964, the association premiered the underground farmworker newspaper *El Malcriado* (meaning "ill-bred" or "children who speak back to their parents"). Published originally in Spanish, the paper was extremely popular with farmworkers and called attention to issues like wages and working conditions. Committed to long-term grassroots organizing to build this movement, the NFWA adapted the tactics of the southern civil rights movement to the farmworkers' struggle.

FROM ALBANY TO BIRMINGHAM: KING AND THE SCLC'S NONVIOLENT WAR

Despite the sit-ins and the Freedom Rides, the *Brown* decision and the Montgomery Boycott, much of the South remained staunchly segregated. Paralleling SNCC's actions, the SCLC under King's leadership launched local campaigns in Albany, Georgia, in 1962 and then in Birmingham, Alabama, in 1963. The active presence of the NAACP, then SNCC, and finally the SCLC in Albany aided a local movement that demanded the right to vote and total desegregation of the city.

While the Birmingham campaign has been memorialized as one of King's most successful, Albany is seen as one of his low points. In large part, the failure in Albany derived from the tactics of the Chief of Police Laurie Pritchett, a calculated segregationist, and the indifference of the federal government and the rest of the nation to the police chief's illegal maneuvers. Pritchett adopted a nonviolent strategy in public in his effort to deny black rights, arresting everyone who protested. He called it "mind over matter. I don't mind and you don't matter." As protests grew in Albany, he filled the jails with demonstrators, contracting out to other local jails for space. As in Mississippi during the Freedom Rides, Pritchett denied protesters their rights to free speech, assembly, and due process, treating them brutally in jail but keeping these actions out of view of the media.

Despite Pritchett's tactics, the number of participants grew, often motivated by their religious faith. According to Bernice Johnson Reagon, a student at Albany State College and the secretary of the local NAACP Youth Council, "In 'We Shall Overcome' there's a verse that says 'God is on our side,' and there was a theological discussion that said maybe we should say, 'We are on God's side.' God was lucky to have us in Albany doing what we were doing." Singing played a crucial role in the mass meetings and in empowering the civil disobedience. "Not only did you call their names and say what you wanted to say, but they could not stop your sound."

To sidetrack the movement, Pritchett was strategic in his campaign of arrests. For instance, after arresting King the first time, city officials moved to avoid publicity and get him out of jail. The city made an oral agreement with the leaders of the Albany movement, promising changes in downtown segregation and the hiring of black workers if they called off the demonstrations. King and the majority of other prisoners accepted release from jail, but city leaders reneged on their promises and consistently refused to negotiate with local blacks in subsequent months. When King was arrested a second time, the police chief personally arranged for the bail money to pay for his release but not for the hundreds of others kept in jail. Pritchett wanted to deny King the publicity of being a martyr in jail. The city also succeeded in getting a federal injunction halting the protests. Even though King and the SCLC had refused to obey unjust state laws, they believed that the federal judiciary was their ally and felt bound to obey the injunction and stop their participation in the protests.

The events in Albany reveal that the American public and the federal government were indifferent to civil rights violations when southern officials did not resort to violence or kept it hidden from view.

Federal officials never intervened against Pritchett's illegal tactics. According to Rev. William Anderson, a local leader who was arrested a number of times (sometimes for walking down the street with a sheet of paper), "To my knowledge, no action was taken relative to the violation of our civil rights." King left Albany discouraged, believing that the federal government had abandoned the movement.

SCLC's short-term direct action approach contrasted sharply with SNCC's organizing work in Albany. SNCC continued their work in the city even after most of the SCLC left. Charles Sherrod explained, "Now I can't help how Dr. King might have felt . . . but as far as we were concerned, things moved on. We didn't skip a beat." Mass meetings in the city continued for 6 years and some of SNCC's organizers remained permanently. They eventually succeeded in desegregating public facilities in Albany, and in 1976, 15 years after he came to organize Albany, SNCC's Charles Sherrod was elected to the city commission.

SCLC's experience in Birmingham was a different story. A founding member of SCLC, Rev. Fred Shuttlesworth had for several years led a movement in Birmingham, the Alabama Christian Movement for Civil Rights (ACMCR). His activism resulted in his home being blown up in 1956; he was chain whipped and his wife stabbed when they went to register their children at the all-white Phillips High School in 1957. Thoroughly segregated, the city was sometimes called "Bombingham," for the number of attacks on churches, synagogues, and local citizens. Many jobs, including the police and fire departments, were not open to blacks. Standing behind Birmingham's social policy, Alabama Governor George Wallace declared in his inauguration speech in 1963, "I draw the line in the dust and toss the gauntlet before the feet of tyranny . . . and I say segregation now . . . segregation tomorrow . . . segregation forever." Indeed, the city had closed its parks and its professional baseball team rather than integrate them.

A feisty organizer, Shuttlesworth invited King and the SCLC to Birmingham to begin a concerted campaign against Birmingham's segregation. Shuttlesworth believed that this would give the ACMCR greater public exposure and ultimately produce a needed victory for the SCLC. Many moderate whites and blacks disagreed with this strategy of direct action. The city had just restructured its government and elected a moderate, Albert Boutwell, as the new mayor. Believing that the city was changing, they counseled patience and criticized the SCLC for leading demonstrations. When demonstrations continued, city officials succeeded in getting a federal injunction forbidding any further protests. Unlike in Albany, however, King and the Birmingham movement decided not to abide by the injunction. On Good Friday, 1963, King and 50 others defied the injunction and were arrested for participating in a demonstration. Placed into solitary confinement, King responded to a letter from white clergy who called the protests "untimely and unwise." On scraps of newspaper and toilet paper, he wrote,

> I have almost reached the regrettable conclusion that the Negroes' great stumbling block in the stride toward freedom is not the White Citizens' "Councilor" or the Ku Klux Klanner but the white moderate who is more devoted to "order" than to justice; who prefers a negative peace which is the absence of tension to a positive peace which is the presence of justice, who constantly says "I agree with you in goal you seek, but I can't agree with your methods of direct action"; who paternalistically feels that he can set the timetable for another man's freedom, who lives by the myth of time and who constantly advises the Negro to wait until a "more convenient season."

King's "Letter from a Birmingham Jail" did not receive much attention in 1963 but over time came to be regarded as one of King's most important writings. Many would see his arrest and the philosophy he laid out in the letter as a turning point in King's leadership. He had decided to break the law and go to jail with no clear path in sight—confident only that the injunction was unjust and the movement needed to go on. King was released eight days later. The protests continued with Police Commissioner Connor and his men arresting all who participated.

The most controversial aspect of SCLC's campaign in Birmingham involved the large-scale participation of elementary and high school students. Eager to march and less economically vulnerable than their parents, hundreds of young people provided the critical numbers in SCLC's spring campaign to fill the jails and bring city officials to the negotiating table. Patricia Harris was one of these children: "I was afraid of getting hurt, but still I was willing to march on to have justice done." When Bull Connor used police dogs and fire hoses to arrest the young people, national television stations broadcast pictures of young black children being bitten by police dogs and lifted off the ground by the power of the fire hoses. Black business leader A. G. Gaston, who had originally opposed the protests, commented in horror, "They've turned the fire hoses on a little black girl. And they're rolling that girl right down the middle of the street."

The sight sickened many in Birmingham and throughout the nation. Bowing to the militancy and the extensive media coverage, downtown merchants finally agreed to desegregate lunch counters and hire black workers in clerical and sales positions. The night after the agreement was publicized, the KKK rallied outside the city, and bombs exploded at the home of Martin Luther King's brother and at the Gaston Motel, where King and much of the SCLC were staying. As crowds of blacks gathered at both places, state troopers attacked black demonstrators with clubs and rifles. Some blacks fought back. Thirty-five blacks and five whites were injured in confrontations that night.

Shortly after the demonstrations in Birmingham brought merchants to an agreement with the movement, President Kennedy proposed a new civil rights bill to Congress. It outlawed segregation in all interstate accommodations, guaranteed equal employment opportunity, allowed the attorney general to file school integration suits, withheld federal money to federal programs that discriminated, and eliminated a voting barrier by certifying that anyone who had a sixth-grade education was literate. The movement in Birmingham had provided the final force for this overdue presidential initiative.

THE COMPLEMENTARY LEGACIES OF MARTIN LUTHER KING JR. AND MALCOLM X

Even though Martin Luther King, Jr. gained national prominence before Birmingham, the movement there and the resulting civil rights bill are among his most celebrated triumphs. Memorialized later as "acceptable" and "passive," King's actions, at the time, were seen as unwise and disruptive. Today, a man who long challenged America to make good on its ideals is, ironically, used as proof of American progress toward equality. Made safe and unthreatening, the man who attacked the unconscionable divide between rich and poor in America, spoke out against the war in Vietnam, and hammered away at the "deep roots of racism" in American society is barely visible in the sea of platitudes that surround his life. King's ability to challenge prevailing wisdom and to change his own thinking made him a great leader. Black activists saw in his courage their own courage; in his vision, their own vision of a better society; and in his actions, their own ability to act. Believing that blacks must sacrifice and go to jail to demand their rights, he himself was jailed at least 15 times. Seeing the transformative power of resisting evil without unleashing evil back, he often criticized white and black moderates for allowing injustice through their inaction. Although King popularized the strategy and theology of nonviolence in the Black South, the movement made King—not King the movement.

King's advocacy of nonviolent direct action is often counterposed to Malcolm X's militancy. This contrast distorts the purposes of both of their struggles—dignity, untrammeled citizenship, real economic opportunity, a breaking of fear, and a powerful sense of black identity. The demands for civil rights and black power grew out of common soil and reflected a shared drive for justice. Stokely Carmichael, a longtime SNCC activist, saw that local blacks often did not distinguish between these men and their adherents, regarding them all as freedom fighters. Armed self-defense and self-reliance had long been part of the southern black landscape; many people saw self-defense and nonviolent direct action as two sides of the same freedom coin. Malcolm X, too, came to criticize these false divisions. "The 22 million Afro-Americans don't seek either separation or integration. They seek recognition and respect as human beings."

Malcolm X was born Malcolm Little in Omaha, Nebraska, in 1925. His father, Rev. Earl Little, was a Baptist preacher, and both of his parents were followers of the black nationalist Marcus Garvey. Facing KKK harassment, the family moved to Lansing, Michigan, where whites attacked and killed Rev. Little. His death was ruled a suicide, and the family was never able to get life insurance, throwing them into financial turmoil and, for a time, onto welfare. Malcolm, nonetheless, excelled in school and hoped to become a lawyer. But his junior high school teacher advised him against it, telling him to be a carpenter instead because "you have to be realistic about being a nigger." After this damning advice, Malcolm drifted out of school and through a number of jobs. Sporting his zoot suit, he lived the fast life: partying, hustling, drinking, drug dealing, and stealing. In February 1946, he was arrested and sentenced to 10 years in prison for theft.

In jail, Malcolm Little got his first exposure to the Nation of Islam, a religious movement founded in Detroit in 1930 by W. D. Fard, who claimed to be the "long-awaited one." The Nation of Islam was at the time led by one of Fard's followers, Elijah Poole (renamed Elijah Muhammad), who was believed to be the messenger sent by Allah to redeem blacks. Combining the basic traditions of Islam with a black nationalism particular to the United States, the Nation of Islam preached that blacks were the original humans, whites the devils, and Islam the black man's religion. The Nation's program of black pride, moral discipline, and economic self-sufficiency drew followers among prisoners, the urban poor, and increasingly from the black middle class. Pointing out the hypocrisies of white America's treatment of blacks, the Nation urged black people to break out of a subservient mentality that had been imposed by whites. The Nation invested in various business, and by 1960, was the largest black-owned business in the United States. Electrified by this message, Malcolm X began regular correspondence with Elijah Muhammad, started a dedicated program of reading, talked to other prisoners about the Nation's teachings, and joined the prison's debating program. "[R]eading had changed forever the course of my life. . . . Some way, I had to start telling the white man about himself to his face."

Malcolm Little emerged from prison a new man in 1952 and changed his name to Malcolm X to rid himself of the last name that was likely the name of the slave master who had owned his family. His full name became El-Hajj Malik El-Shabazz. More a prophet than organizer, Malcolm quickly developed a following. Poet Sonia Sanchez described his charisma, "[H]e drew an audience towards him. Malcolm knew how to curse you out, in a sense, and make you love him at the same time for doing it. He knew how to, in a very real sense, open your eyes as to the kind of oppression that you were experiencing." Even though he urged blacks to defend themselves against violence perpetrated against them, he himself did not engage in acts of violence.

Malcolm's influence in the Nation grew rapidly as he rose from assistant minister of Detroit's Temple Number One to national spokesman for the Nation of Islam. Under his leadership, the organization's membership increased from several hundred to a hundred thousand by the early 1960s, including 40 temples and 30 radio stations throughout the United States. Attacking the ways blacks had been taught to view themselves, Malcolm X worked to get people to celebrate their blackness. "When you teach a man to hate his lips, the lips that God gave him, the shape of his nose that God gave him, the texture of the hair that God gave him, the color of the skin that God gave him, you've committed the worst crime that a race of people can commit. . . . This is how you imprisoned us." One Harlem woman said of Malcolm's importance, "He taught me that I was more than a Little Black Sambo or kinky hair or nigger." A modern nationalist, Malcolm recognized the organizing potential of a newspaper and helped initiate the newspaper *Muhammad Speaks* in 1960 to spread the work of the Nation. Malcolm's role as a media spokesman and in creating *Muhammad Speaks* increased the influence of the organization and inspired political action far beyond his own engagement, but it also caused jealousy from other ministers.

ROBERT WILLIAMS, GLORIA RICHARDSON, AND THE GRASSROOTS OF BLACK POWER

Malcolm X was not the first among his peers to offer a vision of black activism that included self-defense. Another such advocate was NAACP leader Robert Williams. A soldier during World War II, Williams questioned the army's discriminatory treatment of blacks, was discharged, and returned to Monroe, North Carolina, where he had grown up. As the NAACP came under attack following the *Brown* decision, the middle-class leadership of the Monroe chapter flagged and membership fell. Assuming the presidency, Williams revived the chapter by recruiting fellow war veterans and a broad working-class base. The NAACP was reluctant to press on sexual cases, but Williams took on these controversies and, further, worked with the Socialist Worker's Party to bring greater attention to these trials. In his most famous case, the "kissing case," two young black boys, David Simpson, age eight, and James Thompson, age ten, participated in a kissing game with white children. Threatened by a lynch mob because of a kiss, the boys were jailed, supposedly for their protection. Williams responded by seeking national and international publicity, explaining, "If the U.S. government is so concerned about its image abroad, then let it create a society that will stand up under world scrutiny." Three and a half months later, with national and international pressure mounting, North Carolina Governor Luther Hodges conditionally released the two boys. While Williams had built widespread support for the boys' cases, the NAACP disapproved of his alliances with "subversive" groups.

Williams took on other cases but soon became frustrated over the failure of the legal system to protect black lives. He began to call for self-defense against acts of white aggression. "I do not mean that Negroes should go out and attempt to get revenge for mistreatments of injustice but it is clear that there is no Fourteenth or Fifteenth Amendment nor court protection of Negroes' rights here, and Negroes have to defend themselves on the spot when they are attacked by whites." These opinions, his militant tactics, and his political associations led NAACP officials to kick him out of the organization. In response, he started the publication the *Crusader* in 1959 to promote his views, amassing several thousand subscriptions throughout the country. Williams promoted the power of nonviolent direct action but emphasized that many southern racists were immune to the moral politics of nonviolence. "When Hitler's tyranny threatened the world, we did not hear much about how immoral it is to meet violence with violence."

In 1960 Williams was arrested for participating in the student sit-ins in Monroe. Then, in 1961, after two weeks of demonstrations by Freedom Riders, a mob of several thousand whites attacked the demonstrators. Many blacks fought back. In the midst of this violence, Williams gave a white couple who had mistakenly driven into the black section of Monroe safety in his house. For this act of kindness, police accused him of kidnapping the couple. Fearing for their lives, Williams and his family fled to Canada that night and then to Cuba. From Havana, every Friday night, Williams hosted Radio-Free Dixie, a radio show heard from New York to Los Angeles where he played jazz and talked politics. He distributed the *Crusader* from Cuba and wrote *Negroes with Guns,* a book that influenced SNCC members and other radicals like Huey Newton. Williams criticized the divisions between black activists as "too much conflict among our people" and "the new 'militancy' which too often condemns the so-called 'Uncle Tom' without trying to win him over." Williams lamented how America had betrayed its ideals. "I thought [the Constitution] was the greatest document in the world. The problem is [the government and many citizens] didn't respect it." Willing to work with "white people who are willing to give us aid without strings attached," he called on African Americans to "create a black militancy of our own. We must direct our own struggle."

Another black leader, Gloria Richardson of Cambridge, Maryland, also endorsed mixing nonviolent civil disobedience with self-defense. Born in 1922 to a politically active and well-off family, Richardson assumed leadership of the Cambridge Nonviolent Action Committee (CNAC) in 1962, having been impressed by a group of freedom riders from SNCC. "This was the first time I saw a vehicle I could work with. With SNCC, there's not all this red tape—you just get it done." Despite her middle-class background, Richardson identified with Cambridge's working poor black population. "I experienced the same kinds of things that all other Blacks did in Cambridge. My father died because he could not go to the hospital. . . . I was not able to get a job of any kind since I didn't want to teach. I could not go into the restaurants if I wanted to." Cambridge, Maryland, was one-third black; 29 percent of blacks were unemployed and another third underemployed (working less than 30 weeks of the year).

CNAC demanded the elimination of downtown segregation, an end to police brutality, the integration of public housing, jobs for blacks in local industries and stores, and complete integration of schools. Richardson helped organize demonstrations at the movie theater, skating rink, city hall, county courthouse, and jail, which continued for seven weeks in April and May of 1963. In early May, the 80 activists who had been arrested were fined a penny and their sentences suspended; the judge subjected Richardson to a condescending speech about how she had disgraced her family's good name. Following the trial, on May 14, Richardson, her daughter Donna, and her mother Mabel all were arrested in new demonstrations.

Eleven days later, 12 teenagers were arrested for picketing in front of the Board of Education building. Released into the custody of their parents, the 12 were expelled from school. The community was outraged. With tensions mounting, Richardson appealed to Attorney General Robert Kennedy for a federal investigation into civil rights violations in Cambridge. Kennedy ignored her request. Infuriated when two of these students were convicted with indeterminate sentences and fearful of the continuing violence inflicted on black protesters, CNAC activists began carrying guns for protection. In response to the ongoing demonstrations, Maryland Governor Tawes, on June 14, 1963, declared martial law in Cambridge, called in the National Guard, set a 10 P.M. curfew, and prohibited any further demonstrations.

A critical juncture had been reached. As Richardson observed, "The choice that Cambridge and the rest of the nation finally faces is between progress and anarchy, between witnessing change and experiencing destruction. The status quo is now intolerable to the majority of Negroes and may soon be intolerable to the majority of whites. People have called our movement the Negro Revolution. They are right." Finally, on July 22, a meeting between black community leaders, Cambridge city officials, and the federal government was convened in Washington. There they reached an agreement that called for complete and immediate desegregation of schools and hospitals; construction of 200 units of low-rent public housing; employment of a black advocate in the Cambridge office of the Maryland Department of Employment Security and in the post office; and the establishment of a human relations commission. A fifth point, the adoption of a charter amendment desegregating all public accommodations, contained a loophole: if 20 percent of voters petitioned, this charter amendment would have to be put to a referendum. When more than 25 percent of voters did petition, the matter was put to a public referendum. Richardson (and CNAC) then split with the NAACP and other blacks, claiming that "the referendum was unconstitutional, illegal and immoral." Believing that desegregated public facilities were a constitutional right not matters of public opinion, they urged blacks to boycott the polls. Richardson was resoundingly criticized for this decision by many black leaders. The desegregation referendum was defeated.

Many black men and women like Williams and Richardson owned and carried guns before and during the 1960s for self-defense—including Amzie Moore, Medgar Evers, Daisy Bates, and Elizabeth Eckford's mother. In addition, many Mississippians who became active in the movement set up community patrols or took turns staying up through the night to guard their homes. In 1964 blacks in Louisiana formed the Deacons for Defense to provide armed escorts for black activists and protect black neighborhoods from continuing Klan violence. Most SNCC members saw nonviolence as tactically and even philosophically wise; nonetheless, as SNCC's Joyce Ladner pointed out, "All of our parents had guns in the house and they were not only for hunting rabbits and squirrels, but out of self-defense."

WOMEN'S LEADERSHIP, WOMEN'S MARGINALIZATION

Local people, and particularly women, played a crucial role in the growth and impact of the civil rights movement. Gloria Richardson's leadership in Cambridge attests to how militancy and ideological difference crossed gender lines. The prominence of male leaders masked the fact that women led and populated the movement in great numbers. Women's previous activism in the church and participation in community and women's groups facilitated their decision to join the movement. Their religious faith and race consciousness underpinned their desire to secure a different society for their children. As John Lewis explained, "[I]t was these women—wives and mothers in their forties and fifties, hardworking, humorous, no-nonsense, incredibly resilient women who had carried such an unimaginable weight through their own lives and had been through so much unspeakable hell that there was nothing left on this earth for them to be afraid of—who showed us the way to mobilize in the towns and communities where they lived."

Women activists faced no less danger than men. They were jailed alongside men, fired alongside them, and beaten as viciously, even those who were pregnant. Winson Hudson (who along with her sister Dovie became the first black plaintiffs to file a school desegregation suit against the state of Mississippi) remarked, "Our husbands weren't as brave as us." Women had long faced sexual and physical violence in the South despite the more public focus on the violence of lynching, which was aimed at black men.

Nonetheless, although many women played important organizing and leadership roles, the leaders who gained public prominence were largely men. This reflects less their contribution than attitudes within the movement itself and society at large about who should be the leaders. The work of local people was obscured in favor of a set of national leaders, in the process minimizing the hard work and organizing visions that built the civil rights movement. Ella Baker left the SCLC because of these male-centered attitudes. "I had known . . . that there would never be any role for me in a leadership capacity with SCLC. Why? First I'm a woman. . . . The basic attitude of men and especially ministers as to . . . the role of women in their church setups is that of taking orders, not providing leadership." Sexism, ironically, suffused a movement that empowered women. For many women, their participation kindled a new sense of confidence. As Joyce Ladner explained, "But for many of us, I think, SNCC gave us the first structured opportunity to use our skills in an egalitarian way without any kind of subjugation because of our race or our class or our gender."

This false image of a male-led movement was captured in the organization and execution of the 1963 March on Washington. In a day that brought hundreds of thousands of civil rights workers and supporters to the nation's capital, not one woman spoke. The public face presented of the civil rights movement was a male one. The idea for the march came from 73-year-old A. Philip Randolph, who decided in 1962 that it was time to call for another march on Washington. He wanted to commemorate the 100-year anniversary of the Emancipation Proclamation by calling attention to the social and economic inequities that still

wracked the nation. Randolph enlisted Bayard Rustin to help him organize this march for jobs and justice, to call for the passage of the Civil
Rights Act, integration of public schools, a fair employment practices
bill, and job training. Randolph's choice of Rustin as organizer was controversial. A gay socialist and pacifist, Rustin had gone to jail to avoid service in World War II. His personal and political activities brought him
under scrutiny from the FBI and criticism from other civil rights leaders.

To ensure the support of the National Urban League and the NAACP
to join with CORE, SNCC, and SCLC in supporting the march, Randolph
and Rustin abandoned their plans for civil disobedience. President
Kennedy nonetheless feared that the march would be too radical and too
critical of the federal government and would harm the passage of his proposed Civil Rights Bill. He pressured the march's organizers to cancel it.
When they refused, Kennedy lobbied for softening the message and succeeded in changing the march's themes to unity and racial harmony, a
cry to "pass the bill." Many SNCC activists objected. SNCC chairman John
Lewis observed, "What we had hoped would be a protest against government neglect was being turned into a propaganda tool to show the
government as just and supportive." Malcolm X chose not to participate,
referring to it as a "farce on Washington" for the compromises the
march's leadership had made to placate the Kennedys.

The public image of unity masked how women were pushed to the
background of the march. Civil rights activist and Yale divinity student
Pauli Murray protested to Randolph "over the blatant disparity between
the major role which Negro women have played and are playing at the
crucial grass-roots levels of our struggle and the minor role of leadership
they have been assigned in the national policy-making decisions. . . . The
time has come to say to you quite candidly, Mr. Randolph, that 'tokenism'
is as offensive when applied to women as when applied to Negroes." The
only woman on the organizing committee was Anna Arnold Hedgeman,
a longtime colleague of Randolph's and stalwart political activist. Hedgeman later observed that the march demonstrated "that Negro women are
second-class citizens in the same way that white women are in our culture." While women played major roles in fundraising for the march and
in the movement itself, march organizers rejected the idea of letting even
one woman speak, saying that it would cause "serious problems vis-à-vis
other women and women's groups." They preferred that Randolph introduce the accomplishments of some outstanding women—Rosa Parks,
Gloria Richardson, Myrlie Evers, Daisy Bates, and Diane Nash Bevel—in
"A Tribute to Women." These women stood, were applauded, and then
returned to their seats. The wives of the national leaders did not march
with their husbands. Gospel legend Mahalia Jackson and opera singer
Marian Anderson did sing, two of the few women on the dais that day.

The march was dreaded—and feared—by many white Americans. In a premarch poll conducted by the *Wall Street Journal,* two-thirds of Americans denounced the idea. Most newspapers as well as politicians predicted violence and criticized the march as anti-American. According to South Carolina Congressman William Jennings Bryan Dorn, "This attempt to force Congress to bow to demands is a dangerous precedent, and could some day lead to the overthrow of free government and destroy the liberties of our people." NAACP president Roy Wilkins remembered that "the [Kennedy] administration had the army preparing for the march as if it were World War II." Washington "seemed paralyzed with fear of black Americans." Even when the fears of violence proved unfounded, the *Wall Street Journal* remained critical, "This nation is based on representative Government not on Government run by street mobs, disciplined or otherwise."

The march, held on August 28, 1963, was peaceful, with over 250,000 people (some estimated 400,000) traveling to Washington on freedom buses and trains to participate. The first protest activity for many blacks and whites, the march brought together a coalition of religious, civil rights, and labor groups from across the country and broadcast the mass movement to the nation. Television conveyed an image of a unified movement of civil rights activists and supporters demanding that America make good on its ideals. That unity was being tested behind the scenes. SNCC's chairman John Lewis had written a fiery speech denouncing the Civil Rights Act and the federal government as "too little and too late . . . the revolution is at hand and we must free ourselves of the chains of political and economic slavery." Pressured to tone down his speech, Lewis agreed to do so only in deference to Randolph, who had "waited all my life for this opportunity."

Lewis explained, "Cut were the words that criticized the President's bill as being 'too little and too late.' . . . Gone was the question asking, 'which side is the federal government on?' The word 'cheap' was removed to describe some political leaders, though the phrase 'immoral compromises' remained, as did 'political, economic and social exploitation.'" Still, Lewis's speech remained one of the most critical of the day, attacking the false promises of the American democratic system. Lewis was also the only speaker to avoid the word *Negro* and instead to talk of "black people." Citing the violence, harassment, and false incarceration encountered by those seeking to exercise their constitutional rights, Lewis asked, "Where is the political party that will make it unnecessary to have Marches on Washington?"

Martin Luther King delivered the last and most memorable speech of the day. King's speech ended with the now-famous words, "I still have a dream. It is a dream deeply rooted in the American meaning of its creed, 'We hold these truths to be self-evident, that all men are created equal.' I have a dream that one day on the red hills of Georgia, the sons of former slaves and the sons of former slave owners will be able to sit down together at the table of brotherhood . . . ." Not the warm-and-fuzzy version of contemporary memorialization, King's speech demanded that America finally live up to its proclaimed democratic principles. King's vision of an America no longer riven by race emboldened many at the march, putting forth an ideal for a country whose racial caste system had long contradicted its celebrated creeds.

THE BIRMINGHAM CHURCH BOMBING

Eighteen days after the March on Washington, on September 15, 1963, the Sixteenth Street Church in Birmingham, Alabama, was bombed. Four girls—three 14-year-olds and one 11-year-old—were killed, dashing the optimism engendered by the march. On that same day, Birmingham police killed a black youth, and a group of whites killed yet another young black riding his bicycle. This senseless killing of children devastated the civil rights community. According to Coretta Scott King, "We really felt the sense of progress [after the march], that people came together, black and white, even though the South was totally segregated. . . . [A] few weeks later came this bombing in Birmingham, with four innocent little girls. Then you realized how intense the opposition was, and that it would take a lot more than what was being done to change the situation." SNCC activist Anne Moody articulated this disillusionment, "You know something else, God? Nonviolence is out. I have a good idea Martin Luther King is talking to you, too. If he is, tell him that nonviolence has served its purpose. Tell him that for me, God, and for a lot of other Negroes who must be thinking it today."

Bringing the perpetrators to justice in the Birmingham church bombing proved impossible, despite the evidence pointing to Robert Chambliss. According to Assistant Attorney General Burke Marshall, "It certainly turned out in the end that [the FBI] knew who did the bombing. They never gave the Department of Justice a case to prosecute, or identified to the civil rights division the person that did the bombing." Indeed, FBI agents often developed information that could have either prevented further violence against civil rights workers or convicted those engaging in violence against the movement. But senior FBI officials were not committed to preventing violence against civil rights activists, in part convinced that the movement was Communist-influenced. FBI Director

Hoover also demanded that FBI informers must be protected, and he used them to surveil the movement instead. Fifteen years later, on November 18, 1977, Robert Chambliss was convicted of first-degree murder in the bombing of the Sixteenth Street Church. Not until 2000 were two other men, Bobby Frank Cherry and Thomas Blanton Jr., indicted for their roles in the bombing.

Chapter 4

IS THIS AMERICA?:
CIVIL RIGHTS AND THE NATION

President Kennedy failed to ensure passage of a civil rights bill before his assassination on November 22, 1963. When Vice President Lyndon Johnson became president, many black and white civil rights activists feared that the Texan would renege on Kennedy's promises. Johnson, however, recognized the importance of civil rights to his own career. He later confided, "I knew that if I didn't get out in front on this issue, they [the liberals] would get me. They'd throw up my background against me, they'd use it to prove that I was incapable of bringing unity to the land I loved so much. . . . I had to produce a civil rights bill that was even stronger than the one they'd have gotten if Kennedy lived." When some Congressmen sought to weaken the bill's provisions for equal access to public accommodations and equal employment opportunity, Johnson pushed to have the bill passed whole. He rallied an array of groups to defeat a southern-led filibuster in the Senate. Strenuous lobbying from the NAACP, the United Automobile Workers (UAW), and clergy who came from around the country to lobby Congress ensured approval of an intact Civil Rights Act in 1964.

In 1964, the civil rights movement garnered international attention. That December, Martin Luther King Jr. received the Nobel Peace Prize. In his acceptance speech, King characterized the honor as recognition for the movement as a whole. "I accept the Nobel Prize for Peace at a moment when twenty-two million Negroes of the United States of America are engaged in a creative battle to end the long night of racial injustice . . . on behalf of a civil rights movement which is moving with determination and a majestic scorn for risk and danger to establish a reign of freedom and a rule of justice."

FBI officials responded to King's honor by intensifying their harassment, sending a tape recording of King's sexual indiscretions addressed to his wife, Coretta. The accompanying letter urged King to commit suicide: "King, there is only one thing left for you to do. . . . You better take it before your filthy abnormal fraudulent self is bared to the nation." This anonymous letter, written by FBI officials, was typed on plain stationery and postmarked from Florida—to disguise the fact that it was drafted by the FBI. The letter accompanied a tape containing excerpts from King's conversations and sexual activities intercepted by bugs that FBI agents had installed in King's hotel rooms during his trips around the country.

King was aware that the FBI was "out to get me, harass me, break my spirit." Earlier, in 1963, Director Hoover had obtained Attorney General Robert Kennedy's permission to wiretap King's home as well as the SCLC office. Privately referring to King as "the burrhead" and to his speech at the March on Washington as "demagogic," Hoover publicly denounced King as "the most notorious liar in America" and ensured that blacks were not hired as FBI agents through the early 1960s.

MALCOLM X MOVES AWAY FROM THE NATION OF ISLAM

Malcolm X did not join in the international celebration of King's Nobel Prize, explaining, "He got the peace prize, we got the problem." Becoming more political and more powerful, Malcolm sought to turn the Nation of Islam from moral rehabilitation to political action. A riveting public speaker, Malcolm was sharply criticized by other civil rights leaders, including Bayard Rustin and James Farmer, for talking big and doing little. Malcolm was now ready for a new active role. Expressing his reluctant admiration for people like King for taking a stand, he urged the Nation to take part in demonstrations and lay out a plan of action. But Elijah Muhammad, envious of Malcolm's growing public figure and uncommitted to expanding the Nation into political activism, demanded that Malcolm stay away from politics.

The growing division between the two men also widened over Elijah Muhammad's personal life. Muhammad had numerous affairs, having children with a number of his mistresses. For a long time, Malcolm refused to see this side of his Elijah Muhammad, but after talking to a number of the women Muhammad had been involved with, Malcolm's view of his mentor greatly diminished. Putting much weight on living the moral philosophies the Nation espoused, Malcolm X began to see Elijah Muhammad as someone who did not practice what he preached and who punished others for disobeying the moral codes that he himself ignored.

The final straw came at a Black Muslim rally in New York following the assassination of President Kennedy. Malcolm X talked of "reaping what you sow"—the violence the United States had perpetrated, particularly against black citizens, was coming back upon it. Although Elijah Muhammad had explicitly instructed his ministers to say nothing about the assassination, in the question-and-answer session, Malcolm X described the assassination as "the chickens coming home to roost." Extremely angry over this comment, given Kennedy's popularity, Elijah Muhammad publicly silenced Malcolm X for 90 days.

Malcolm penitently accepted this silencing. In March 1964, however, he split from the Nation of Islam, now describing the organization, "Moral reform it had but beyond that it did nothing." At the same time, Malcolm made a pilgrimage to Mecca, required of every Muslim once in his or her lifetime. Malcolm had traveled abroad before, but this trip and worshipping with Muslims of all races began to alter his views about whites. He now spoke publicly that all whites were not the devil—that "the white man is not inherently evil but American's racist society influences him to act evily." His talks with African independence leaders such as Kwame Nkrumah and Gamel Nasser further "awakened me to the dangers of racism" and the value of cooperation among all people of African descent. After his trip to Mecca, he also embraced a more traditional Islam.

In March 1964, Malcolm founded a religious organization called the Muslim Mosque, intended for African Americans seeking to practice Islam outside of the Nation of Islam. Within weeks, the Nation of Islam lost about 20 percent of its members to the Muslim Mosque. Inspired by African independence leaders who had formed the Organization of African Unity, Malcolm then announced the formation of a political group, the Organization for Afro-American Unity. Through these new organizations, Malcolm X began to reach out to other civil rights groups, met with other civil rights leaders, and declared his admiration for the courage and work that SNCC and King were doing in the South. He endorsed community control, independent electoral action, armed self-defense, and cultural efforts to promote a positive black identity. More open to working with whites than he had been previously, he still thought blacks and whites should work separately in their communities. Convinced that Harlem and other predominantly black sections of American cities needed political autonomy, Malcolm emphasized the importance of political power and voter registration in the North as well as the South. He exhorted black people to "wake up, clean up, stand up."

Malcolm X linked the struggles of blacks in America with the independence movements against colonialism in Africa: "[T]he revolt of the American Negro is part of the rebellion against the oppression and colonialism which has characterized this era." Warmly welcomed as he crisscrossed the African continent from Ghana to Egypt to Algeria, Malcolm was convinced that the movement for justice within the U.S. would be strengthened by rebuilding the ties between Africans and African Americans. He urged his supporters "to see beyond the confines of America" and planned to file a petition against the United States with the United Nations documenting how the situation of blacks in America violated the UN's Human Rights Charter. As the Vietnam War escalated, many more white and black Americans came to share Malcolm's vision. Indeed, Malcolm was one of the first American critics of the war, as early as 1963 condemning U.S. support for the corrupt dictatorship in South Vietnam. In January 1965, Malcolm X observed, "[The government] should get down on their hands and knees every morning and thank God that 22 million black people have not become anti-American. You've given us every right to. The whole world would side with us if we became anti-American." These stands were decidedly unpopular with the American public. His break with the Nation, moreover, caused fierce animosity among some of his former followers while some of his supporters outside of the Nation feared that Malcolm was going soft.

Malcolm X would not have time to develop his political ideas into a broad plan of action. His life had been repeatedly threatened as the divisions between Malcolm and the Nation of Islam grew, tensions eagerly promoted by FBI officials. Indeed, the Chicago field office of the FBI bragged about its role in fomenting the deadly conflict. Forced out of his house by the Nation, Malcolm increasingly feared for his own life. On February 19, 1965, Malcolm told photo journalist Gordon Parks, "It's time for martyrs now. And if I am to be one, it will be in the cause of brotherhood. That's the only thing that can save this country." On February 21, less than a year after his break with Muhammad, Malcolm X was shot by three members of the Nation of Islam at the Audobon Ballroom in Harlem while two others distracted the crowd. The next year, three Black Muslims—Norman 3X Butler, Thomas 15X Johnson, and Talmadge X Hayer—were convicted for the murder. Nonetheless, some questioned whether high Nation officials had ordered Malcolm's assassination and whether the New York police and the FBI (both in the crowd the day he was killed) played a role in promoting or protecting the assassins. *The Autobiography of Malcolm X,* told to and written up by Alex Haley, was rushed into print and sold over a quarter of a million copies, increasing Malcolm X's influence tremendously.

MISSISSIPPI BLEEDING: MEDGAR EVERS, FREEDOM SUMMER, AND THE MFDP

Facing persistent violence, the movement in Mississippi was beginning to gather momentum through the work of SNCC and local NAACP organizers, particularly field secretary Medgar Evers. The NAACP's role as a defender of civil rights earned it the bitter hatred of many Mississippi whites. Mississippi Governor Paul Johnson, in a speech in 1964, said the initials of the organization stood for "niggers, apes, alligators, coons, and possums." Evers launched boycotts of the segregated state fair, spoke out against the mayor of Jackson, and instigated sit-ins at the downtown Woolworth's. The NAACP's national office, thinking that this protest strategy was too militant, urged Evers to step back. But he continued, declaring at a rally on June 7, 1963, "It's not enough just to sit here tonight and voice your approval and clap your hands and shed your tears and sing and then go out and do nothing about this struggle. . . . Freedom has never been free." Five days later, on June 12, 1963, Evers was shot in the back in front of his home in Jackson, Mississippi. Despite Evers's prominence and the evidence pointing to Byron de la Beckwith (his fingerprint was found on the gun used, and he had boasted about killing Evers), a jury twice failed to convict him. Myrlie Evers, Medgar's wife, described the special treatment that Beckwith received in jail. "He had a large cell that was open for him to come and go as he wanted. He had television sets, he had typewriters, he had almost all the comforts of home. This man was also accorded a major parade along the route of the highway on his way home . . . The governor, Ross Barnett, actually made a visit to the accused during the first trial." Not until 1993 was Byron de la Beckwith convicted of Evers's murder.

Fannie Lou Hamer, another Mississippian, played a defining role in building the movement. The youngest of 20 children of poor black sharecroppers, Hamer was born on October 6, 1917. Her mother always told her to respect herself—"There's nothin' wrong with you being black, child. God made you black."—and bought her a black doll (the first and only child in Ruleville to have one). At the age of six, Hamer was enticed by the plantation owner to join her family in the cotton fields. He promised the hungry child treats of food in exchange for picking 30 pounds of cotton in a week. This bargain began her daily field labor that continued for the next 40 years. Hamer eventually became the plantation timekeeper—a position that allowed her a measure of control over her livelihood and that of others. Because she was the person who recorded how much each person picked, she surreptitiously brought her own weighted scale to try to compensate for the ways the owner cheated other sharecroppers. Like many African-American women in Mississippi, Hamer was involuntarily sterilized when she went to the hospital to have a small cyst removed from her stomach.

Hamer had yearned for "some way we can change things." After attending her first SNCC meeting in 1962, she decided to try to register to vote. "[I]f I'd had any sense I'd a-been a little scared, but what was the point of being scared? The only thing they could do to me was kill me and it seemed like they'd been trying to do that a little bit at a time ever since I could remember." On her way with others to register, they were all arrested under the charge of the bus being "too yellow." When she returned to the plantation, the owner, Marlow, told her to take her name off the list (even though she had not actually been allowed to register). She refused, telling him, "I didn't register for you. I registered for me." Upon hearing this, he fired her and kicked her off the plantation where she had lived and worked for 18 years. That night she went to stay with a friend, Mary Tucker. The next week, Tucker's house was bombed.

In 1963, Hamer joined the staff of SNCC. Returning from a citizenship school headed by Septima Clark in June 1963, Hamer and four others tried to integrate the bus station restaurant in Winona, Mississippi. Forced to leave by police, they were arrested when one of the women, Annell Ponder, wrote down the license plate number of the police car. All of them were brutally beaten at the jail in Winona. Annell Ponder was hit with "blackjacks, and a belt, fists and open palms. . . . They really wanted to make me say yes, sir . . . and that is the one thing I wouldn't say." Fifteen-year-old June Johnson was beaten so hard she lost consciousness. Calling Hamer "bitch," "fatso," and "whore," the police officers made two black prisoners take turns beating her until they were exhausted while the officers watched. One of the patrolmen pulled her dress up and tried to molest her. When she began screaming in pain, the beating got more brutal. This brutality left Hamer with permanent damage to her kidneys, blind in her left eye, and in pain for years.

For protection, SNCC workers were required to show up or call at predetermined times. If they did not, other staff would begin calling local jails to put the word out about them. In this way, local police and sheriffs would know that they were being watched when they arrested SNCC workers. Thus, when the five activists did not show up in Greenwood as planned, Julian Bond telegraphed the Justice Department and wrote the U.S. Commission on Civil Rights and the Interstate Commerce Commission to demand they investigate. Discovering that the five were jailed in Winona, SNCC sent a delegation headed by Lawrence Guyot to arrange bail. Guyot and the others were arrested—Guyot brutally beaten—and an all-white jury later convicted the entire group of disorderly conduct and resisting arrest. Four days later, they were released on bail. Hamer was taken to the hospital; she would not let her husband or her family see her for a month. The Winona incident, however, was not an aberration. Protected by the courts and promoted by the police, the Ku Klux Klan, and White Citizens Councils, violence against civil rights workers intensified.

Hamer, however, emerged from her prison ordeal resolved to continue in her work. Her faith had lifted her out of the torture and despair she had faced in jail: "It wouldn't solve any problem for me to hate whites just because they hate me. Oh there's so much hate, only God has kept the Negro sane." Hamer's determination brought many into the movement. As fellow activist Annie Devine explained, "Myself with others realized that there is a woman that can do all these things. And when she got herself beat in Winona, there was a greater woman. Why not follow somebody like that? Why not just reach out with one hand and say, just take me along?"

The courage of Hamer and numerous other local blacks proved crucial to SNCC's campaign. One SNCC worker explained, "If I need a couple of bucks or even a ride for a hundred miles or so, there would be people waiting in line. . . . When there's that kind of push behind you, you can keep going." Women, moreover, were core of the Mississippi movement, housing and feeding civil rights workers, trying to register to vote, organizing others to register, and legitimizing SNCC in the eyes of many residents. Nearly all of these women lost their jobs. Many found their houses and churches bombed and were harassed in a variety of other ways. Hamer, for instance, received inflated water and electric bills. One month she received a bill for $9,000, for 6,000 gallons of water the family had supposedly used that month even though their house did not have running water inside.

SNCC's persistence, in turn, provided powerful example for local people. "How they stood," according to Amzie Moore, "how gladly they got in the front of that line, those leaders, and went to jail. It didn't seem to bother 'em. It was an awakening for me." SNCC activists understood that part of their mission was to meet the survival needs of the local people. They distributed food and clothing to people in need while trying to register people to vote. Unita Blackwell, who became one of the leaders of the Mississippi challenge, praised SNCC, who "went where nobody went." "All the educated folk we had known looked at us like we were fools and didn't know nothing and these here talked to us like we was educating them." The daughter of sharecroppers, Blackwell grew up in Sunflower County and was living in Mayersville, Mississippi, in the 1960s when SNCC workers came to her church. "That's the first time in my life that I ever come in contact with anybody that tells me that I had the right to register to vote." A young mother, Blackwell saw that voting could give her family a better life. So angered by the circuit clerk's refusal to register her, Blackwell became a SNCC organizer herself. After that, no one would hire her in the cotton fields, and she was arrested and jailed over 70 times.

Even though more people were joining the movement in Mississippi, SNCC organizers were worried. The economic and physical violence continued unabated. Most people who had tried to register to vote had not succeeded, given the myriad of ways that Mississippi registrars devised to reject their application. Leaders like Bob Moses also feared that the increasing mechanization of southern agriculture made local blacks particularly vulnerable and disposable. Out of this frustration was born the idea of the Mississippi Freedom Democratic Party (MFDP)— Mississippi blacks with SNCC's help would organize their own Democratic party, hold their own elections, and in the process document the discrimination blacks faced in attaining full political participation.

SNCC organizers had concluded that they needed the nation's attention on Mississippi or black Mississippians would continue to be slaughtered. Some SNCC organizers proposed bringing a large contingent of students from across the country to work in Mississippi for the summer. These organizers hoped that these students would bring the attention of the nation and some protection from violence in Mississippi. They believed that the nation would be quicker to respond to violence against outsiders than to the deaths of local Mississippians. The idea sparked debate for months within SNCC. Many worried that these educated (mostly white) volunteers would overwhelm and intimidate the local movement. Some felt that bringing in white volunteers would exacerbate the problem of white life being valued more than black; whites being able to partake in civil rights activity for a short while but then return home, leaving the problems and the people behind. Hollis Watkins worried that while recruiting white students would act as a deterrent to violence, "ultimately it would destroy the grass-roots organizations that we had built and were in the process of building. For the first time we had local people who had begun to take the initiative themselves and do things." Many older local blacks such as Fannie Lou Hamer rebutted, "If we're going to break down this barrier of segregation, we can't segregate ourselves." Moses elaborated, "So it isn't any longer Negro fighting white, it's a question of rational people against irrational people."

In the end, SNCC decided to sponsor Freedom Summer. Over 800 students, three-quarters of them whites from prestigious colleges, traveled south to help organize the Mississippi Freedom Democratic Party and run Freedom Schools. Students were asked if they would "serve under a project director who was black?" and screened for their responses.

The local Mississippi press called the Mississippi Summer Project an "invasion." Some Mississippians, like Klan leader Sam Bowers, saw it as a "nigger-communist invasion," a "crucifixion" of the "innocent people of God" instigated by "the savage blacks and their Communist masters." Mississippi officials responded by expanding the state highway patrol from 275 to 475 and outlawing the picketing of public buildings and the distribution of leaflets about boycotts.

Most local blacks welcomed the volunteers. Unita Blackwell explained, "There was interaction between blacks and whites. . . . I guess they became very real and very human, we each to one another." The Freedom Schools, according to SNCC worker Mendy Samstein, "saw kids getting turned on to reading, to doing math . . . the Freedom Schools changed—started to change because it's a very slow process . . . the children's images of themselves." Freedom Summer, however, exacerbated racial tension in SNCC—provoking debate long after the summer over the racial sensitivity of white volunteers and the issue of interracial sex between local black men and white women volunteers.

While many Freedom Summer volunteers were attending the opening workshops, three civil rights workers—two whites, Andrew Goodman and Michael Schwerner, and one black, James Chaney—disappeared. Coming at the beginning of Freedom Summer, this crisis set the tone for the summer. Schwerner, a native of Brooklyn, New York, and Chaney, a native of Meridian, Mississippi, were already working for CORE in southwest Mississippi, but Goodman was a fresh Freedom Summer volunteer from New York. Schwerner and his wife, Rita, had moved to Meridian in January to direct CORE's Freedom House. By spring, the Klan had come to see the Jewish civil rights worker Schwerner as "a thorn in the flesh of everyone living, especially white people." And plans began to be made to "take care" of him.

The disappearance of the volunteers brought a surge of law enforcement agents to the area to search for the bodies. Rita Schwerner remarked, "It's tragic that white northerners have to be caught up into the machinery of injustice and indifference in the South before the American people register concern." President Johnson sent 400 unarmed sailors to search for the bodies and pressured the FBI to investigate the case. In the process of searching for the three, they found the bodies of other blacks, long missing. Many white Mississippians at first regarded the case as a hoax. Governor Ross Barnett suggested that the three had run off to Cuba. Yet, on August 4, on a tip from an FBI Klan informant, the bodies were discovered buried under a dam on Klansman Olen Burrage's farm.

The disappearance of the three civil rights workers provided the final push for passage of the 1964 Civil Rights Act, signed into law on July 2, 1964, by President Lyndon Johnson. The act created an Equal Employment Opportunity Commission, outlawed discrimination in federally funded programs, and authorized the Justice Department to sue to desegregate public education and other public facilities. It made it easier to remedy discrimination in public accommodations and facilitated the right to vote in national elections. Enactment of this legislation had little immediate impact in Mississippi. By the end of the summer, 68 black churches had been bombed or burned, 35 people had been shot, and hundreds of others beaten and harassed, their houses and stores bombed. And still the vast majority of black Mississippians could not vote.

The goal in creating the MFDP was to dramatize this injustice to the nation. That summer, more than 80,000 blacks registered and voted in separate MFDP elections to select 68 delegates (64 blacks and 4 whites) to represent Mississippi at the national Democratic Convention in Atlantic City. The delegation was optimistic that they would be seated as the rightful delegation from Mississippi if they could capture a national forum. The majority of the delegates were local women—Fannie Lou Hamer, Winson Hudson, Hazel Palmer, Annie Devine, Unita Blackwell, and Victoria Gray. The delegates brought with them notarized depositions from people whose attempts to register were met with violence; photographs of the violence and economic conditions in which Mississippi blacks lived; lists of churches that had been bombed, including the bell from the Mt. Zion Methodist Church; and a burned-out Ford station wagon (like the car Goodman, Shwerner, and Chaney had driven).

Taking their case to the convention's Credentials Committee, the MFDP challenged the seating of the delegates selected by the regular Mississippi party on the grounds that those Democrats did not represent the entire state. Most blacks were not allowed to vote, and the Regulars were not even loyal to the Democratic party. (The Regular party refused to take a loyalty oath to the Democratic party and went on to support Republican Barry Goldwater in the 1964 elections.) If the Freedom Democrats could convince 10 percent of the committee to endorse their challenge, the issue would have to be taken up on the floor of the convention.

President Johnson worked behind the scenes to deny the MFDP this opportunity. Johnson saw this gathering as his convention—the place where he would be chosen as the Democratic presidential nominee. Johnson worried that the growing support for the MFDP's challenge would erode his popularity among white southerners (even though Johnson's support among these whites was already questionable, given his work to pass the Civil Rights bill). When Fannie Lou Hamer's testimony to the Credentials Committee aired on national television, an angry Johnson held his own press conference to take the spotlight off Hamer. Much to the president's chagrin, however, her testimony was rebroadcast in full that night during the nightly news. The country heard Hamer conclude: "All of this on account we want to register, to become first-class citizens, and if the Freedom Democratic Party is not seated, I question America. . . . Is this America, the land of the free and the home of the brave where we have to sleep with our telephones off the hooks because our lives be threatened daily because we want to live as decent human beings in America?"

Fannie Lou Hamer testifying before the Credentials Committee at the Democratic National Convention.

The Johnson White House had also called in the FBI to monitor the convention and the MFDP in particular. With the cooperation of the NBC network, FBI agents posed as reporters to gain off the record information from the delegates. They wiretapped Martin Luther King's hotel room and bugged the storefront SNCC and CORE were using as their headquarters. An informant attended all the MFDP meetings. Through these sources, the White House was kept abreast of all the MFDP's contacts and strategies. Johnson then told Minnesota Senator Hubert Humphrey and Minnesota Governor Walter Mondale that they must convince convention delegates not to support the MFDP in order for Humphrey to be selected as Johnson's running mate. According to SNCC's Courtland Cox, the MFDP was pressured to turn over the list of their supporters on the Credentials Committee. Then, "every person on that list, every member of that credentials committee who was going to vote for the minority, got a call. They said, 'Your husband is up for a judgeship, and if you don't shape up, he won't get it.' 'You're up for a loan. If you don't shape up, you won't get it.'" Influential Democrats also threatened the MFDP directly that if they persisted, the liberal Humphrey would be denied the vice presidential nomination. Hamer responded by asking Humphrey, "Do you mean your position is more important to you than four hundred thousand black people's lives?"

A backroom compromise was worked out and issued as a fait accompli to the MFDP—they would be given two at-large seats designated to white minister Ed King and black NAACP leader Aaron Henry at the convention, with the rest of the delegation "welcomed as honored guests." (President Johnson specifically opposed giving Hamer a seat.) The national party promised to eliminate racial discrimination in all future delegations. Many of the MFDP's allies—Joseph Rauh of the UAW, Bayard Rustin, and even some middle-class MFDP members such as Aaron Henry—supported the compromise as a political victory. King was called in to endorse the compromise but his heart was not in it. At the meeting of the delegates, Gray, Hamer, and Devine called for rejection. "We didn't come all this way for no two seats," said Hamer. She explained, "I don't see how all of these people are stepping on the bandwagon now that didn't come way up there from Mississippi, 69 delegates subject to being killed on our way back, to compromise no more than we'd gotten here." Most of the delegates who were poor and had struggled to get to the convention rejected the compromise. Using the passes given to them by other delegates, they held a sit-in on the convention floor.

The hard work and sacrifice of the MFDP participants had brought the disfranchisement of Mississippi blacks before the nation. But they left with little to show for it. Disillusioned by the outcome, many MFDP activists were convinced they were sold out by the movement's liberal allies. The events in Atlantic City called into question the conviction that revealing injustices and playing by the rules would prompt national action. Many in the movement began a painful reassessment. Hamer explained, "[W]e learned the hard way that even though we had all the law, all the righteousness on our side—that the white man is not going to give up his power to us. We have to build our own power."

Singer Harry Belafonte, a longtime supporter of the movement, understood the level of burnout among SNCC workers. He paid to send 11 SNCC members to Guinea in West Africa in September 1964—an eye-opening trip for the SNCC staff. As SNCC's executive secretary James Forman put it, "We belonged here. . . . My political and historical convictions about the importance of Africa to black people in the United States had become a living experience." Fannie Lou Hamer continued, "I learned that I didn't have anything to be ashamed of from born being black. I saw black people . . . doing everything that I was used to seeing white people do." John Lewis and Donald Harris met up with Malcolm X in Nairobi, Kenya, beginning a relationship that was cut short by Malcolm X's assassination. As John Lewis recalled, "[I]t was clear that Africa was doing for [Malcolm] the same thing it was doing for us—providing a frame of reference that was both broadening and refreshing. . . . This was clearly a man in the process of changing."

After the Africa trip, MFDP attorneys filed notice to contest the seating by the House of five white Mississippi congressmen because blacks had been "systematically and deliberately excluded from the electoral process." They urged instead the seating of Fannie Lou Hamer, Annie Devine, and Victoria Gray, who had been elected in a freedom vote after being denied a place on the official ballot. The House rejected their motion, 225–149, but more than one-third had stood with the MFDP's congressional challenge. The MFDP again challenged the seating of the Regular Democrats at the 1968 National Convention in Chicago. This time, they won; however, their victory was overshadowed by protests over the war in Vietnam that wracked that convention.

Many of the participants in Freedom Summer chose to stay on in the South; others returned to their communities with a changed vision. As Marshall Ganz, a Freedom Summer volunteer who subsequently become an organizer with the National Farm Workers Association, explained, "[W]orking in the civil rights movement gave us what we called 'Mississippi Eyes,' because you'd go back to where you came from and suddenly it would look different. . . . It hadn't changed but you'd changed."

The seeds of mistrust that emerged in Atlantic City drove the movement in many directions in the coming years. In 1964 elections, however, faced with conservative Republican Barry Goldwater, who attacked the welfare state, forced integration, and a foreign policy too soft on Communism, over 95 percent of blacks voted for Johnson. Nonetheless, many civil rights workers (particularly young activists) believed that blacks could not rely on their liberal allies. Johnson won in a landslide, although Goldwater captured the five states of the old Confederacy (Mississippi, Alabama, South Carolina, Georgia, and Louisiana) and helped realign conservative whites to the Republican party. Opposition to civil rights, moreover, was not confined to the South. The ardently segregationist Alabama Governor George Wallace had earlier challenged Lyndon Johnson in the Democratic primaries and drew substantial support outside of the South, polling 34 percent, 30 percent, and 45 percent, respectively, in the Wisconsin, Michigan, and Maryland primaries.

SELMA TO LOWNDES COUNTY: THE FIGHT FOR THE VOTE CONTINUES

Voting rights remained a pivotal problem. Eager to find a place in Alabama to hammer away at the issue, the SCLC chose Selma. The catalyst to this decision was a request for help from Amelia Boynton, Fred Reese, and the Dallas County Voters League. One of the only blacks in Selma who was registered to vote, Boynton and her husband, Sam, had been active since the 1930s to help other blacks register. Fred Reese was a local minister, schoolteacher, and president of the Dallas County Voters League. Together, the two had worked on voting rights for years. Although blacks made up nearly 60 percent of the residents, they were a mere .9 percent of the registered voters. When SNCC began demonstrations in Selma in 1963, Selma Sheriff Jim Clark deputized white men over the age of 21, creating an armed posse at his disposal that did not hesitate to use force. The local courts issued an injunction that made it illegal for more than three black people to walk down the street together or to attend a public meeting without the sheriff's permission.

Responding to Boynton and Reese's invitation, the SCLC began holding mass meetings and then demonstrations in Selma. Sheriff Clark responded by forcibly arresting the protesters. These violent tactics made good copy for newspapers. Over and over, Clark personally—and the police more generally—attacked and jailed protesters. And over and over, particularly as King focused the national spotlight on Selma, national newspapers ran photos of these confrontations.

The movement in Selma was not just a product of the violence they encountered but of ongoing, monotonous action. As John Lewis wrote, "The patience and persistence it took to endure those countless hours of weary boredom in stifling heat or bone-chilling cold, in driving rain and wet, slushy snow, is as admirable as the bravery it took to face the billy clubs of those deputies." This effort received widening support. School teachers and hundreds of school children joined the demonstrations. Because their jobs were controlled by the white school board and because of their influence within the community, the teachers' decision to march proved crucial for the movement. So was the support of Selma's young people. One of the youngest and most stalwart demonstrators was eight-year-old Sheyann Webb. One day on her way to school, she stopped at Brown's Chapel to listen to the adults, including King, plan for the upcoming protests. She kept returning to the church each day, missing school, and soon became a regular participant in the demonstrations.

On February 4, at the invitation of SNCC, Malcolm X joined Rev. Shuttlesworth and Coretta Scott King at a Selma rally. In a press conference, he explained, "I think the people in this part of the world would do well to listen to Dr. Martin Luther King and give him what he's asking for and give it to him fast, before some other factions come along and try to do it another way." In nearby Marion, on February 18, a nighttime demonstration turned violent when police and angry white citizens attacked protesters. While trying to rescue his injured grandfather, 26-year-old Jimmy Lee Jackson was whipped by police and then shot at close range. Jackson died seven days later.

Seeking to turn this tragedy and community outrage into positive action, that Sunday, SCLC organizer and minister James Bevel called for a march from Selma to Montgomery to lay Jackson's coffin at Governor

Wallace's steps. The idea caught fire in the community and with SCLC. SNCC activists, however, feared that the march would put people in unnecessary danger and would do more to publicize the SCLC than help the people in Selma. Some SNCC activists privately referred to King as "de Lawd," critical of King's sense of self importance and his episodic involvement in local struggles. After much debate, SNCC decided not to participate as an organization but some SNCC members, including John Lewis, chose to participate on their own.

Governor Wallace prohibited the march. Nonetheless, on Sunday, March 7, six hundred people set off from Selma to Montgomery. The march was silent, people walking two-by-two, with Hosea Williams of the SCLC and John Lewis at the front. When the marchers reached the Edmund Pettus Bridge on the outskirts of Selma, they were met by a sea of Alabama State troopers, many on horseback. They knelt down to pray. As John Lewis explained, "The troopers came toward us with billy clubs, tear gas, and bullwhips, trampling us with horses. I felt like it was the last demonstration, the last protest on my part." Footage of the violence was broadcast across the country. That night, ABC cut into its show *Judgment at Nuremberg,* a drama about Nazi brutality and the war trials to convict them, to show the Alabama police attacking the marchers on the bridge in Selma. Many viewers took several seconds to realize that the footage being shown was not about the Nazis but of that day's news.

Although he had not participated in the march, King quickly issued a call for people to come to Selma to aid in the demonstrations. And people from across the country, including 450 clergy, began to come. Rev. Reese explained the mood in Selma as initially low. "Then you hear the door of the church opening and there is a group of people, black and white, who came from New Jersey. . . . There was a round of applause in the church and you could feel a change in the atmosphere—a spirit of inspiration, motivation, hope, coming back into the eyes and into the minds of these people." White Unitarian minister James Reeb from Boston was one of those clergy. He was attacked and killed by three white men the night he arrived, and his death made front page news. More people poured into Selma. President Johnson and Vice President Humphrey both called the Reeb family to express their sympathy. The national outrage following Reeb's death contrasted sharply with the silence over Jimmy Lee Jackson's a few weeks earlier, angering many SNCC workers. Four days after Reeb's death, President Johnson introduced the Voting Rights Bill, which prohibited literacy tests and allowed federal registrars to process applications in communities where they had been discrimination. Using the language of the movement, Johnson pledged, "It is not just Negroes but all of us who must over come the crippling legacy of bigotry and injustice. And we shall overcome." Rev. C. T. Vivian explained the significance of the bill. "[M]illions of people in the South would have a chance to be involved in their own destiny."

At the same time, the SCLC had gone to court to obtain a restraining order against the police. Under King's urging, march organizers agreed to wait until Judge Frank Johnson made his ruling. Finally, Johnson issued the restraining order. On March 21, 3,200 marchers left Brown's Chapel for the Pettus Bridge and on to Montgomery. Only 300 marchers were allowed to make the march. They reached Montgomery on March 25, where they were joined by more than 25,000 supporters at a rally at the state capitol. King spoke about the difficult days that lay ahead, even if Congress passed the Voting Rights Act. "We are still in for a season of suffering. . . . However difficult the moment, however frustrating the hour, it will not be long, because truth crushed to the earth will rise again . . . the arc of the moral universe is long, but it bends towards justice." That night white Detroit volunteer Viola Liuzzo was killed by Klan members leaving town. Liuzzo's black teenage passenger Leroy Moton escaped by feigning death.

Stokely Carmichael had joined the Selma-to-Montgomery march. SNCC activists had vowed after Atlantic City to create an independent black political movement outside of the Democratic party and Carmichael used the march to begin organizing in Lowndes County. At the start of 1965, not one black person was registered to vote in the entire county—though blacks comprised the county's majority, twelve thousand out of the fifteen thousand residents. More than half of the black population lived below the poverty line. One hundred and thirty percent of the whites in the county were registered, a sign of the corruption SNCC would encounter.

Alabama law allowed new political parties to form at the county level. Because many Alabamians could not read, each party had to have a symbol to identify it on the ballot. John Hulett, one of the founders of the Lowndes County Freedom Organization (LCFO), explained their choice of the panther, "When we chose that symbol, many of the peoples in our county started saying we were a violent group who is going to start killing white folks. But it wasn't that, it was a political symbol that we was here to stay and we were going to do whatever needed to be done to survive." Organizing the party and the decision to run blacks for seven county offices prompted the retaliation from local whites. Josephine Mayes described the violence, "They would shoot at us and try to scare us, but we wouldn't let them bother us."

LCFO candidates were defeated in November. As SNCC worker Cleveland Sellers explained, the local white leaders "stuffed some ballotboxes; they forced some blacks to use ballots that had already been marked for white candidates; they insisted on helping those blacks who couldn't read; they brought in truckloads of blacks who worked on their farms and told them who to vote for." Still, nine hundred blacks voted for the LCFO, and a new, independent black consciousness had been nurtured in the county. In 1970, John Hulett was elected sheriff of Lowndes County.

The national media first reported on the call to Black Power in Lowndes County, alarmed by Carmichael's declaration, "The only way we gonna stop them white men from whuppin' us is to take over. We been saying freedom for six years—and we ain't got nothin'. What we gonna start saying now is 'Black Power'!" Yet, the idea of Black Power had been part of the movement from the 1941 March on Washington movement to Robert Williams's organization of the Monroe NAACP. At base, Black Power was a critique of American individualism, of the notion of individual rights. Civil rights activists had long argued that rights were denied to blacks as a group and must be won as a group. Carmichael explained, "We are oppressed as a group because we are black, not because we are lazy, not because we are apathetic, not because we're stupid . . . and in order to get out of that oppression, one must feel the group power one has. Not the individual power." The media's knee-jerk criticism of Black Power as fanatical and antiwhite obscured these continuities.

Shortly after SNCC's campaign in Lowndes County, the organization held a controversial and contested election. Stokely Carmichael was elected chairman over the reigning chair John Lewis. Even though SNCC had long advocated organizing local people to secure power for themselves, Carmichael saw his election signaling a new turn for SNCC. "The SNCC people had seen raw terror and they understood properly this raw terror had nothing to do with morality but had to do clearly with power. It was a question of economic power, of the exploitation of our people, and they clearly saw that the route to this liberation came first through political organization of the masses of the people." Since 1964 SNCC members had debated whether more centralized governance was needed and what role whites should play within the organization. The decision to move to a more hierarchical structure and an all-black organization marked a dramatic shift, one that reflected the growing disillusionment of many black SNCC workers with their white liberal allies, the belief that blacks must govern and take care of their own communities, and an increasing emphasis on Third World solidarity. SNCC also began to distance itself from some of its most committed local black activists, such as Fannie Lou Hamer, whose approach some SNCC members dismissed as "no longer relevant" and its longtime white staff members, such as Bob and Dottie Zellner. White SNCC workers were urged to use their talents in organizing white communities. Then, in December 1966, in an extremely divided election, the organization voted to expel whites from SNCC completely.

The changes within SNCC and the organizing in Lowndes County reveal that the mid-1960s were a time of radicalizing consciousness, profound disillusionment, ideological disagreement, and steadfast determination. As had happened in Montgomery, in Mississippi, and in Salinas, as people organized and felt their own power, their demands and sense of what was possible grew. They came face to face with entrenched injustice—and the costs of the struggle for equal rights. Having publicized the profound inequalities of American society, civil rights activists had succeeded in winning only limited change. School desegregation remained largely a court victory, not an American reality.

By 1966, 52 percent of northern whites believed the government was pushing too fast for integration. From 1961 through 1966, physical attacks by whites against activist blacks had increased fivefold, and yet it was nearly impossible for a white person to be convicted for violence against a black person. As Sam Bowers, the Imperial Wizard of the KKK in Mississippi, boasted, "A jury would not dare convict a white man for killing a nigger in Mississippi." The economic gap between whites and nonwhites was worsening. Twenty percent of whites lived below the poverty line compared with 50 percent of blacks. In 1964, infant mortality for blacks was 90 percent higher than whites.

"A JAGGED PLEA": THE URBAN RIOTS OF THE MID-1960s

Persistent social and economic inequality triggered riots in every major American city between 1964 and 1968. These uprisings were often catalyzed by incidents of police brutality. In many black communities, the police (predominantly white) were seen as an occupying force that repeatedly harassed people of color. The Watts section of Los Angeles was 98 percent black, but the officers who policed it were 98 percent white. An extremely poor section of the city, with 34 percent of its male residents unemployed, Watts was four times as crowded as other L.A. neighborhoods, but its poverty was hidden by a maze of freeways that isolated this predominately black section of the city. Watts residents had difficulty even getting the city to pick up their trash. In August of 1965, as President Johnson signed the Voting Rights Bill in to law, blacks in Watts rioted.

The specific event that triggered the Watts riot was a confrontation between a black drunk driver, Marquette Frye, and the police on a stifling hot day in August. As another officer arriving on the scene began hitting the suspect and his family, the crowd that had gathered began throwing stones and bottles. This escalated to looting and burning buildings. Six days later, after 14,000 National Guard members had been called out, 34 people were dead, hundreds were injured, hundreds more were homeless, and 4,000 blacks had been arrested. The damage totaled nearly

$45 million. While the city tried to portray the riot as the actions of "criminal element," most of those arrested had no previous criminal record. One young man explained, "The riots will continue because I, as a Negro, am immediately considered to be a criminal by police." The riot symbolized profound discontent of many within the black community at the ways that affluent America ignored the economic and social conditions facing many Watts residents.

"We won," young people in Watts would tell Martin Luther King, "because we made them pay attention to us." King's visit to Watts convinced him of the need for profound economic change. "I am appalled that some people feel the civil rights struggle is over because we have a 1964 civil rights bill with ten titles and a voting rights bill. Over and over again people ask, What else do you want? . . . Well, let them look around at our big cities." Pointedly questioning the structures of U.S. capitalism, King explained, "[A]n edifice which produces beggars needs restructuring." His concern for economic justice led him in 1967 to begin to organize a Poor People's Campaign; poor people of all races would come to Washington, D.C., and set up an encampment on the Mall, staying until their demands were addressed. Lobbying, civil disobedience, and their physical presence would focus the attention of the federal government on the problems of poverty.

Riots broke out in 150 cities during the summer of 1967. In most of these cities, the demography of the police did not resemble the demography of the community. In Detroit, which was 35 percent black and the site of the worst riot that year, there were only 217 black officers in a force of 4,709. Three of the 220 lieutenants were black, and only one of the 65 inspectors was black. Many blacks saw the police as an arm of state repression, rather than a protective force.

Detroit seemed like it could avoid urban unrest since it was a city with two black congressmen, a strong NAACP, and a prosperous auto industry. Still this did not translate into more power for the blacks as a whole. In Detroit, as in other cities, urban renewal had meant black removal, the disruption of neighborhoods, and increased tensions within the black community. In 1963, the city's plans to tear down ten thousand old structures displaced over 43,000 people, 70 percent of whom were black. Political and class tensions fissured Detroit's black community; some residents benefited from the new political and geographic realities of the city but most did not. The new interstate system sliced through the black community, isolating these neighborhoods from the rest of the city. Black auto workers were restricted to certain jobs and rarely promoted to supervisory positions. In addition, the number of industrial jobs were declining at the very time of significant black migration to the city, falling from 338,000 in 1947 to 153,000 in 1977, while Detroit's black population rose from 300,000 in

1950 to 759,000 by 1980. Detroit's housing was also extremely segregated. Whites reacted violently as blacks moved into some of Detroit's all-white suburbs, like Dearborn or Warren, or white sections of the central city.

At 4 A.M. on July 23, 1967, police raided an illegal after-hours bar. Celebrating the return of two men from Vietnam, more than eighty people were gathered there when police roughly closed it down and arrested all the patrons. The crowd refused to disperse and grew larger and angrier over the next day as the police grew more violent. Newly elected black Congressman John Conyers unsuccessfully tried to disperse the crowd. He described the scene, "People were letting feelings out that had never been let out before, that had been bottled up. It really wasn't that they were that mad about an after-hours place being raided. . . . It was the whole desperate situation of being black in Detroit." At the height of the unrest, the riot encompassed 14 square miles—200 square blocks—of the city.

Governor George Romney asked for federal help, and late on July 24, President Johnson sent in 2,700 army paratroopers. The police continued to respond violently against all blacks, not just rioters. As Congressman Conyers explained, "What really went on was a police riot." In a move that served only to increase the chaos, many officers shot out the streetlights. They raided many apartments where rioters were allegedly hiding, arresting and assaulting many uninvolved Detroiters. On the evening of July 25, three young black men were shot to death at the Algiers Motel by police. While police claimed they died in a gun battle, residents of the motel claimed that the young men were unarmed and shot by police intentionally. At the end of five days, 43 people were dead (30 at the hands of the police) and hundreds were injured, including 85 police officers. Property damage was estimated at $45 million, with 412 buildings completely burned.

The city's leadership along with federal officials downplayed the structural inequalities that fueled these disturbances. Many instead ascribed the riots to the growing danger of Black Power ideology and decried the violence as senseless and self-inflicting. Yet, as Detroit bookstore owner Ed Vaughn explained, "It wasn't Black Power that caused the rebellion, it was the lack of power that caused the rebellions around the country." Roger Wilkins of the U.S. Justice Department who had gone to Detroit, observed, "What I thought I was seeing in these riots was not what J. Edgar Hoover saw, which was a communist plot, but rather hopeful people who believed that the political system would respond to them. And it was kind of a jagged plea to the political system: Pay attention to us, we're left out, we ache."

On July 27, President Johnson convened a commission on civil disorders headed by Illinois Governor Otto Kerner to examine the causes of the riots and to recommend changes to prevent their recurrence. Releasing its findings in February 1968, the Kerner Commission concluded, "our nation is moving toward two societies, one black, one white—separate and unequal." The commission pointedly observed, "What white Americans have never fully understood—but what the Negro can never forget—is that white society is deeply implicated in the ghetto. White institutions created it, white institutions maintain it and white society condones it." With Congress calling for further budget cuts, Johnson ignored the commission's recommendations for federal intervention and increased spending in the areas of jobs and housing. As Roger Wilkins explained, "It was a mandate, had the president chosen to take it. . . . Instead, he refused even to have the commission come over and present it to him."

Johnson's commitment to a War on Poverty had faded when he faced political infighting over the cost of his Great Society initiatives and the inflation resulting from the sharp increase in defense spending for the war in Vietnam. In his inaugural address of 1965, Johnson had employed the phrase *the War on Poverty,* but the idea originated under Kennedy. Johnson asked "for an order of plenty for all of our people." The challenge ahead was "whether we have the wisdom to use that wealth to enrich and elevate our national life, and to advance the quality of our American civilization." The proposed War on Poverty combined new initiatives such as Headstart, Medicare and Medicaid, and Legal Aid, with a significant boost to older programs such as Food Stamps, unemployment insurance, and Aid to Families with Dependent Children (AFDC). An Office of Economic Opportunity was established to fund community initiatives with "maximum feasible participation" of poor people to be hired to formulate and enact solutions for their own communities. This community funding dramatically but briefly changed the American landscape—significantly reducing the proportion of Americans living in poverty from 18 percent in 1960 to 8 percent in 1980, combating hunger in many communities, and for a short time enabling community participation in public policy.

A federal commitment to a War on Poverty was short-lived. Many city mayors did not like the idea of the poor running their own programs and from the outset worked to sabotage the programs. Another limitation in the philosophy fueling the War on Poverty was the conviction that poverty was caused not by a lack of good jobs but rather a lack of skills and cultural deficits among the poor. Redistribution was not the key to the Great Society—tax cuts for corporations and wealthy individuals accompanied the introduction of several Great Society programs. With the Office of Economic Opportunity spending only $70 a year for each poor person, Daniel Patrick Moynihan, assistant secretary of labor in 1964, remarked that the War on Poverty was "oversold and under-financed to the point that its failure was almost a matter of design."

Moynihan himself helped sow the seeds of backlash against the War on Poverty with his publication of *The Negro Family: The Case for National Action*. In it, he wrote of the "tangle of pathology" that affected the urban black family; the "matriarchal" structure of the black family, he argued, was "so out of line with the rest of the American society, [that it] seriously retards the progress of the group as a whole and imposes a crushing burden on the Negro male." Moynihan proposed "a national effort to strengthen the Negro family," in essence to install black men as the head of the household over black women. Despite widespread criticism of his conclusions, Moynihan's report gave a liberal imprimatur to the idea that the black family was pathological and the underlying source of the poverty and alienation facing the black community, not the structures of racism and economic deprivation. These conclusions combined with Johnson's weariness and growing antagonism among many voters towards bold social programs made substantive urban policy initiatives politically unfeasible.

The Detroit riot prompted an upsurge of organizing among many black Detroiters, particularly among black workers. By the late 1960s, a quarter of a million blacks worked in Detroit's factories but few held supervisory or skilled positions. Moreover, the union, the United Auto Workers, had grown so friendly with management that white and black workers had little recourse to address job or promotion grievances and were left behind economically despite the large profits made by the Big Three auto companies. The companies cultivated divisions among diversity of people working in the factories—blacks, Detroit-born whites, Polish Americans, recently migrated Appalachian whites, and Arab immigrants. In the aftermath of the riot, however, workers began to ally in various factories. Understanding the importance of the media and political education, they put out the independent *Inner City Voice* and gained control of the Wayne State University newspaper *South End*.

Formed in May 1968, the Dodge Revolutionary Union Movement (DRUM) launched a wildcat strike at the Dodge main plant over the issue of speed-ups. In 1946, 550,000 autoworkers had produced a little more than 3 million cars; by 1970, 750,000 workers produced a little more than 8 million cars. The company called this automation; black workers called this speed-up "niggermation." Although 4,000 black and white workers participated in this action, shutting down the plant, mostly black workers were disciplined after the strike. One of those fired for his role in the strike was longtime activist General Baker. He wrote an open letter to Chrysler: "[B]y taking the course of disciplining the strikers you have opened that struggle to a new and higher level. . . . You have made the decision to do battle with me and therefore to do battle with the entire black community in this city, this state, this country, and the world." Chrysler's differential treatment drew more black workers into DRUM. Auxiliaries formed at plants throughout the city: ELRUM (at the Eldon Avenue Chrysler plant), FRUM (at Ford), JARUM (at Chrysler's Jefferson Avenue plant), CADRUM (at the Cadillac Fleetwood factory), and DRUM II (at Dodge Truck). In June of 1969, the local RUMs incorporated into a larger coordinated organization, the League of Revolutionary Black Workers.

THE VIETNAM WAR AND THE RESHAPING OF THE FIGHT FOR CIVIL RIGHTS

These smoldering frustrations grew as the country's involvement in the Vietnam War intensified. The war in Vietnam profoundly altered national politics, diverting the country's limited energy and financial resources away from civil rights. The United States sent disproportionate numbers of young people of color across the world to "protect democracy" whose rights to political and social equality were not ensured at home. More people came to see that the quest for justice was an international struggle and that international issues shaped civil rights within the United States.

U.S. involvement in Vietnam predated the 1960s. Opposing the popular independence movement led by Communist Ho Chi Minh, the United States, under both presidents Truman and Eisenhower, helped fund the French in their unsuccessful eight-year war to recolonize Vietnam. Peace talks in 1954 divided Vietnam in half; elections were to be held in 1956 to unify Vietnam and allow the people to choose their leader. The Eisenhower administration blocked these elections as Ho Chi Minh's popularity ensured his election to head a unified Vietnam. Instead, U.S. officials installed a government headed by Ngo Diem in South Vietnam. To counter the NLF's growing base within South Vietnam, President Kennedy decided in 1961 to send in Green Berets and military advisors to train South Vietnamese troops. Under the Johnson administration, the United States began a massive buildup in combat troops in Vietnam. At the same time, Johnson began an aggressive air campaign against North Vietnam. By the end of the war, nearly sixty thousand Americans and approximately two million Vietnamese had died. Over two million Americans had served in the war. The Vietnam War ended the Great Society programs at home, as by 1968, the war was costing U.S. taxpayers some $33 billion a year (not counting veterans' benefits and related expenses).

The Vietnam War, more than other American wars of the twentieth century, was fought by the poor and working class (about 80 percent of the enlisted men) because many middle and upper-class young men received deferments. The U.S. military was more fully integrated in combat than in any previous war, with blacks comprising more of the draftees than whites—30 percent of blacks to 18 percent of whites. Because blacks and Latinos were also more likely to serve in combat positions, they were more vulnerable to casualty. In the early years, blacks made up 23 percent of the fatalities; by 1969, that had fallen to 14 percent. Although only 10 to 12 percent of the population in the southwest, Latinos made up nearly 20 percent of the fatalities from that region. Blacks also made up a disproportionately low share of the officers; while blacks made up 13.5 percent of army enlisted personnel, only 3.4 percent of the army's officers were black.

Facilitated by constant air attacks that did not distinguish between soldier and civilian, the war itself was fueled by a racial ideology that dehumanized the Vietnamese. American GIs regularly referred to Vietnamese as "gooks." When asked about the danger of killing innocent civilians, one GI explained, "What does it matter. They are all Vietnamese." Opposition towards the war grew gradually as notions of racial justice and anti-imperialsim took root. People with less education—black and white—opposed the war more strongly than middle-class people with higher levels of education. For example, between 1966 and 1970, while opposition to the war among college-educated Americans grew from 27 percent to 47 percent, antiwar sentiment among people with a grade school education increased from 41 percent to 61 percent.

By the late 1960s, blacks overwhelmingly opposed the war, an opposition long in developing. One of the first groups to come out against the war, SNCC initially hesitated, worried about breaking so decisively from the Johnson administration and fearing being labeled pro-Communist. Bob Moses linked his opposition to the war to what was happening in the South and joined the first mass mobilization against the war in Washington in 1965. "The South has got to be a looking glass, not a lightening rod" to understanding broader social justice. His action was opposed by other SNCC activists, like Dona Richards, who explained, "While we care a great deal about both Vietnam and civil rights we can't do anything to help the Vietnam situation and we can hurt ourselves by trying."

On January 3, 1966, Sammy Younge, a young SNCC worker, was shot to death while trying to use the "white" restroom at a gas station in Tuskegee. SNCC issued a statement that expressed its opposition to the "aggressive policy in violation of international law" that the administration was pursuing in Vietnam and urged draft resistance. SNCC framed its opposition in terms of its growing sense of Third World solidarity and revolutionary nationalism. "[T]he United States government [is] deceptive in its claims of concern for the freedom of the Vietnamese people, just as the government has been deceptive in claiming concern for the freedom of colored people in such countries as the Dominican Republic, the Congo, South Africa, Rhodesia, and the United States itself." In the next two years, Julian Bond, Martin Luther King, and

Muhammad Ali followed SNCC's lead, taking unpopular public stands against the war.

Julian Bond had been elected to the Georgia legislature in November 1965. On leave from SNCC, he had not helped draft SNCC's statement but supported it publicly once issued. When Bond appeared on January 10, 1966, to take his oath of office, the Georgia House voted not to seat him on the grounds that his support of draft resistance violated the Selective Service Act and brought "discredit to the House." Many members of the House were not keen on having an outspoken black man like Bond as part of "their Legislature" and sought to paint him as a subversive. When Bond appealed this action in court, many civil rights leaders refused to support his struggle. The U.S. Supreme Court ultimately overturned the legislature's action, ruling that Bond could not be denied his seat based on his political beliefs.

King denounced the legislature's refusal to seat Bond and was publicly vilified for his stand and then for his own increasing criticisms of the war. As early as 1965, King had criticized "the madness of militarism" in Vietnam and the expenditure of millions on a war in Vietnam at a time when the government was unwilling to "protect its own citizens seeking the right to vote" in Selma. He even offered to help mediate an international settlement between the United States, Vietnam, Russia, and France. Infuriated at King's criticisms of his foreign policy, President Johnson scoffed at this offer and attempted to ostracize the civil rights leader. For a time, King muted his objections but soon concluded that he must speak out. On April 4, 1967, at Riverside Church in New York, King brought together his criticisms of the racism and imperialism inherent in the United States' position on the war and the ways it diverted money and public attention from the problems at home. King framed his opposition to the war as an extension of his commitment to nonviolence. "I have called for radical departures from the destruction of Vietnam, many persons have questioned me about the wisdom of my path. . . . [S]uch questions mean that the inquirers have not really known me, my commitment or my calling." King's opposition cost him financial support for the SCLC as well as the connections he had to the federal government and other civil rights leaders. Newspapers like the *New York Times* and *Washington Post* castigated him on their editorial pages for speaking out against the war.

Heavyweight boxing champion Muhammad Ali also emerged as a critic of the war. In 1960, then-named Cassius Clay had won an Olympic gold medal. Returning home to Louisville, he was refused service in a restaurant because of the color of his skin. After this incident, Clay threw his medal into the Ohio River. Entering the professional boxing ranks, Clay won a surprising upset over the reigning world heavyweight champion, Sonny Liston, in 1964. After the victory, he publicly announced that he had joined the Nation of Islam (which he had done years earlier) and changed his name to Muhammad Ali, the name given to him by Elijah Muhammad.

The young fighter had been influenced by Malcolm X's example. "My first impression of Malcolm X," Ali remembered, "was how could a black man talk about the government and white people and act so bold, and not be shot at? How could he say these things? Only God must be protecting him. He was so radical at that time, and yet he walked with no bodyguard, fearless. That really attracted me." Many in the sports world resented that Ali had joined the Nation and refused to call him by his new name. Sports commentator Howard Cosell remarked on the hypocrisy behind this opposition, "How selectively we apply our righteous indignation. Nobody calls Betty Perske by that name. She's Lauren Bacall. . . . As part of the sickness of the decade, and as part of the dugout mentality of a certain portion of the press, they would ceaselessly refer to Ali as Cassius Clay."

Verbally quick, Ali praised his own talents. Calling himself "The Greatest" and "The Prettiest," he talked of how he was going to "float like a butterfly and sting like a bee" to demolish his opponents. This bragging—refusing to be deferential or meek—was part of Ali's allure for many young blacks. There on national television and radio was a black man, proud and unafraid, talking about how wonderful and good-looking he was. As Ali himself explained, "We weren't taught like that. We were taught the black man had the bad luck. Black was bad and white was good. So me, being black—'I am the greatest. I'm pretty'—it gave more people confidence." Ali often made up poems about himself and society. Perhaps his most famous rhyme was an off-the-cuff response to reporters on the subject of Vietnam and his own draft status. "Keep asking me, no matter how long. On the war in Viet Nam, I sing this song. I ain't got no quarrel with the Viet Cong . . . ."

His words were quickly and furiously condemned—from the Kentucky legislature to the boxing establishment to national newspapers. The *Los Angeles Times* castigated Ali as the "white man's burden," and the *New York Post* wrote, "Nobody has ever done less with the time and the title, and destroyed his image more." Shortly after making these comments, Ali was reclassified 1-A, fit for combat, and drafted in April 1967. On April 28, 1967, when his name was called, a scared but firm Ali did not step forward, signifying his refusal to be inducted into the U.S. Army. His statement read, "I am proud of the title 'World Heavyweight Champion.' . . . The holder of it should at all times have the courage of his convictions and carry out those convictions, not only in the ring but throughout all phases of his life." Ali's stand made news around the world.

But his claims for conscientious objector status, based on his religious beliefs that the only wars Muslims could fight in were those sanctioned by the religion, were denied. Indicted by a grand jury and sentenced to five years in prison and a $10,000 fine, he was released on $5,000 bail pending his appeal. His boxing title and his passport were taken away. Yet, he told the crowds who gathered to hear him speak, "I have lost nothing. I have gained the respect of thousands worldwide, I have gained peace of mind." Ali was one of 952 men convicted in 1967 for refusing the draft and the first American popular figure to condemn the war in such decisive terms and to accept a heavy loss for his action. In the coming years, the number of conscientious objectors swelled dramatically, reaching more than 100,000 people in 1970—more in one year than in all of World War I and World War II combined.

Three years later, in June of 1970, the Supreme Court upheld Ali's appeal. Although he had lost those years of boxing at the prime of his career, he believed it was the biggest victory of his life. Heroic to some and vilified by many others as unpatriotic, Ali's decision was a momentous one for the antiwar movement. As another sports hero, Kareem Abdul Jabar, explained, "He gave so many people courage to test the system."

Ali's militant stand was not shared by more moderate leaders in the NAACP and Urban League or by prominent blacks such as Jackie Robinson who stood behind the president. They did not want to risk their civil rights work and reputation by speaking out and criticized their counterparts for involving themselves in the war. By the late 1960s, however, more and more blacks denounced the racial imperialism of the war. As James Baldwin explained in 1968, "America is fighting a racist war . . . to protect the material interests of the Western world." Fearful of the growing antiwar sentiment within the black community, General William Westmoreland tried to appeal directly to blacks, telling reporters, "I have an intuitive feeling that the Negro servicemen have a better understanding than whites of what the war is about."

Opposition to the war also grew in the Chicano community. On December 19, 1969, the first Chicano rally against the war was held in Obregon Park, organized by the Brown Berets (a militant Chicano organization) and attended by two thousand people. In February, six thousand people braved the rain to march. This was so successful that organizers decided to call for a national Third Moratorium. On August 29, 1970, in East Los Angeles, between twenty thousand and thirty thousand Chicanos marched to Laguna Park to protest the war in Vietnam. Most Chicanos had initially supported the war but as the draft and the body count disproportionately affected the Chicano community, many began to oppose it. The Brown Berets were instrumental in this shift, as was Rosalío Muñoz, a former UCLA student body president who decided to resist the draft. Although not the first Chicano to do so, he had planned to make his refusal as public as possible and crisscrossed California to turn out support for his decision and to articulate the reasons that Chicanos needed to oppose the war.

Police attacked nonviolent demonstrators at the Chicano Moratorium Against the War.

Thousands came from all over the United States to join the Chicano Moratorium Against the War. Although the protest was peaceful, the police attacked the crowd—firing tear gas, trampling, beating, and arresting people. Some fought back, throwing rocks and tear gas canisters back at the police. Sixty-two demonstrators were injured, and three people died, including journalist Rubén Salazar, who was killed when police threw tear gas into a cafe and one of the canisters hit his head. The first Mexican American to work for the *Los Angeles Times*, to be a foreign correspondent, and to be columnist for a major newspaper where he exposed issues such as educational inequities and police brutality, Salazar was well-respected in the community. His death enraged many Chicanos, particularly when the district attorney decided not to prosecute any of the officers in the case.

The war in Vietnam internationalized the movement for civil rights, broadening the understanding of civil rights as a struggle for human rights. The disjuncture between what government officials publicly proclaimed about American democracy and what the nation practiced was at the heart of the civil rights movement at home—and was clearly revealed in the war in Vietnam abroad. As King lamented, "None of these things that we claim to be fighting for are really involved." He underscored the "cruel irony of watching Negro and white boys on TV screens as they kill and die together for a nation that has been unable to seat them together in the same schools."

THE WAR AT HOME: A FARMWORKER STRIKE

The fight for democracy abroad, moreover, stymied the quest for democracy at home. While the sons of farmworkers were drafted to fight in Vietnam, their families still could not form their own union or be protected on the job. The budding farmworker movement, the NFWA, that Chávez and Huerta had formed in 1964 faced its first real test in September 1965. When the Filipino workers of the Agricultural Workers Organizing Committee (AWOC) in Delano decided to strike, the rank and file of the NFWA voted overwhelmingly to support them. With only $87 in their strike fund, the NFWA was in a tight spot. As Chávez explained, "I had no money. I had no idea [where money for the strike would come]. All I knew was . . . they wanted to strike. . . . [W]e couldn't work while others were striking." This act of solidarity began to build bridges between Filipino and Mexican farmworkers who were often kept segregated in the fields. The coalition that emerged during this strike challenged the ways growers had successfully prevented organizing by pitting different ethnic groups against each other, white against black against Mexican against Filipino.

Many striking families sent the men out of Delano to work while the women kept up the picket lines. Women's roles in organizing and sustaining the strike were questioned as inappropriate. Jessie De La Cruz remembered, "At first it was hard to organize those that believed that women should stay home and do the washing and the cooking. But they never stopped to think about them working out in the fields. So why shouldn't they attend meetings and be involved with the union? It got to the point where most of us out on the picket lines were women." Women's vigilance on the picket lines kept the strike going. Even within the Chávez family, while César organized throughout the state, Helen maintained the union at home in Delano.

The police and sheriff's departments began a concerted campaign to disable the strike. They took photos, recorded license plate numbers, and made picketers fill out identification cards to ensure that they had records of those who were participating. They outlawed shouting, rallying, and any use of the word *huelga,* ("strike" in Spanish). Refusing to be intimidated, on October 13, in front of reporters, Helen Chávez and 12 other women farmworkers yelled, "Huelga, Huelga," while picketing at W.B. Camp Ranch outside Delano. For their act of defiance, they were arrested and spent three days in jail.

Expanding upon the tactics of the black freedom struggle, the farmworkers' movement pursued a strategy to win public support, cognizant of the lack of federal labor protections for farmworkers and the vulnerability of strikes in the past. To increase pressure on the growers and gain national attention, the NFWA organized a march to Sacramento, California's capital, in April of 1966. The march took 21 days, covered nearly 300 miles, and swelled to 10,000 people by the time it reached Sacramento. Some people marched the whole way; according to Angie Hernandez Herrera, one of the marchers who walked the entire time, "Some would keep on walking and you'd see blood coming out of their shoes." Each night they were hosted by local farmworker families and were entertained by Luis Valdez and El Teatro Campesino, a guerilla theater group Valdez started in 1965 to help sustain the movement. Producing one-act plays and traditional songs called *corridos,* El Teatro publicized the struggle, made fun of the growers, built the morale of the movement, and used theater to bring more workers into the cause. Often performing on the back of trucks using car headlights for spotlights, Valdez had written a manifesto especially for the farmworkers' march that he read every night: "Our sweat and our blood have fallen on this land to make other men rich. . . . We do not want charity at the price of our dignity. We want to be equal with all the workingmen in the nation."

The march was coupled with another organizing strategy—a call for a nationwide boycott of Schenley liquors, one of the leading wine grape corporations. A rumor that bartenders were going to honor the boycott gave the farmworkers a surprisingly quick victory when Schenley executives agreed to work out a settlement in the middle of the march. Other wine grape makers, including Gallo, Christian Brothers, Paul Masson, and Almaden, quickly followed. On Easter Sunday, on the heels of its victory with Schenley, the march reached Sacramento. From the capitol steps, Chávez demanded that Governor Edmund Brown "call a special session of the legislature to enact a collective bargaining law for the state of California. We will be satisfied with nothing less." Brown had gone out of town to avoid the march.

The NFWA faced tremendous financial shortages and a challenge from the powerful Teamsters union that also sought to organize their members. In August 1966, the NFWA merged with the Filipino AWOC to become the United Farm Workers Organizing Committee (UFWOC), under the auspices of the American Federation of Labor and Congress of Industrial Organizations (AFL-CIO) and the leadership of César Chávez. This affiliation gave them new resources (an organizing budget of $10,000) and greater power to fight off the Teamsters.

The union's most effective organizing tactic was the national boycott. Bolstered by the Schenley victory, the farmworkers decided to target the biggest table grape producer in the country, the Guimarra Vineyards Corporation, and called for a boycott of Guimarra grapes. Vowing never to negotiate with the farmworkers, Guimarra executives worked hard to break the boycott. When Guimarra began to use the labels of other growers to circumvent the boycott, the UFWOC called for a boycott of all California table grapes. To bring national pressure on the growers and sustain the force of the strike, the UFWOC sent organizers out to form support groups across the country. These national efforts ultimately convinced many Americans to refuse to buy grapes.

Despite growing public support for the grape boycott, strike organizers confronted major problems in sustaining the strike. Most strikers had to work to eke out a subsistence while the growers brought in a constant supply of strikebreakers to harvest the grapes. Farmworkers began to react violently to the continuing willingness of "scabs" to cross their picket lines. Chávez's commitment to nonviolence and the strains on the UFWOC as the strike dragged on led him to make a personal sacrifice in hopes of keeping the movement together. On February 15, 1968, César Chávez began a fast at Forty Acres, near Delano. Inspired by Gandhi, Chávez saw fasting as a way to refocus the movement. With the growers intransigent and vengeful and striking workers growing poorer and angrier, Chávez believed that this individual action could shift the balance. He wanted everyone in the organization to recommit themselves to nonviolence, explaining: "No union movement is worth the death of one farmworker or his child or one grower and his child." Some organizers condemned Chávez's act as naive and ineffective and left the union as a result. Nonetheless, thousands of farmworkers came to Forty Acres to pay their respects to Chávez, to discuss organizing with him, and some to fast themselves. The media came too—and with it the American public. Twenty-five days later, believing that his message of nonviolence had been heard by the union's rank and file, a weakened Chávez, more than 30 pounds thinner, broke his fast with New York Senator Robert Kennedy at his side. His fast had convinced many American consumers throughout the country to honor the grape boycott.

As Chávez's persona grew, so did the surveillance of the movement. Starting in 1965, FBI agents began to monitor Chávez, Huerta, other farmworker activists, and their newspaper *El Macriado*. Growers and some political and police officials labeled the farmworkers Communists.

Chávez deflected these criticisms by drawing on the social justice teachings of the Catholic Church, employing religious holidays and symbols in the daily life of the movement, using a religious song, "De Colores," as their anthem, and calling on clergy as key supporters. Union leaders fully understood the importance of the church to many Chicanos and the ways that church identification helped to shield the strikers from red-baiting charges. The movement also stressed the American-ness of its members. This strategy—by focusing on organizing American citizens as apart from bracero workers—proved to be one of the union's long-term limits because it weakened its base. The union too often framed bracero labor as part of their problem, rather than actively working to bring bracero workers into the organization.

The farmworker movement also faced formidable political foes. President Nixon publicly opposed the boycott. Governor Ronald Reagan, who had been elected governor of California in 1966 on a law-and-order platform opposing many of the gains of the civil rights movement, made a point of eating grapes in public. The U.S. Department of Defense also acted to undermine the strike, sending 468,000 pounds of grapes to the troops in Vietnam in 1966, 555,000 pounds in 1967, 2 million pounds in 1968, and 4 million pounds in 1969.

Still, on July 25, 1970, nearly five years after the strike had begun, Johnny Guimarra, the owner of Guimarra Vineyards, met with the UFWOC. The UFWOC insisted that Guimarra set up a meeting with the 28 other growers in the area. One of the growers, Lionel Steinberg, explained why he succumbed to the economic pressure of the boycott: "They had hundreds and hundreds of people scattered in at least fifty cities . . . so they gradually closed down our outlet for fruit. . . . [I]t was the most successful boycott in American history."

Dolores Huerta was in charge of negotiating the settlement. She described her negotiating style, "I guess the growers complained, they weren't used to dealing with women. . . . People like Jerry Cohen [one of the movement's lawyers] would say, 'You have to be polite.' And my thinking is, Why do we need to be polite to people who are making racist . . . [and] sexist comments? You have to call them at it." By late the next night, farmworkers and growers reached an agreement. Grape pickers would have a hiring hall and a base pay increase from $1.65 to $1.80 an hour. Piece rate bonuses were increased, the employers would contribute a dime per hour into the Robert F. Kennedy Health and Welfare Plan, and a joint grower-worker committee was set up to regulate pesticide use.

Five years later, in 1975, the UFW succeeded in getting the new governor of California, Jerry Brown, to introduce a bill giving farmworkers the right to form their own unions, a protection they had been denied in the 1935 Labor Relations Act. Now farmworkers were legally protected to choose their own union. The law, however, also prohibited secondary boycotts, which had proven key to the union's organizing activities.

"I AM A MAN": THE MEMPHIS SANITATION STRIKE AND THE ASSASSINATION OF MARTIN LUTHER KING, JR.

The UFWOC had shown that labor struggles were often also civil rights battles. This message was brought home in Memphis, Tennessee. In February 1968, when two sanitation workers died on the job, the lack of safety, pension, and benefits prompted workers to act. Thirteen hundred sanitation workers went on strike to gain recognition for their union, to protest differential treatment between white and black city workers, and to demand living wages, benefits, and respect on the job. Nearly all black, the striking sanitation workers risked their livelihoods, because city workers were forbidden under law to strike. And they continued the strike even when the city threatened to begin hiring replacement workers. Underscoring the ways this was a campaign for dignity and respect and not just wages, their signs read, "I am a man." Mayor Henry Loeb refused to talk with the workers, a popular stance in the white community.

As the city's intransigence continued, James Lawson, now a pastor in Memphis, invited Martin Luther King, Jr. to speak to bring national pressure on the city to negotiate. King was moved by the workers' campaign to return to Memphis for a march on March 28. The march turned violent, and King left before it was over. King was tremendously depressed by the violence and worried that this would compromise his efforts to build a national Poor People's Campaign. He vowed to come back and lead a peaceful march.

Since the Montgomery bus boycott in 1955, King's life had been repeatedly threatened; by 1968, King was routinely receiving death threats. Yet he refused to hire bodyguards: "There's no way in the world you can keep somebody from killing you if they really want to kill you." This period was also one of soul-searching for King. Criticized for his stand against the war and his attempts to build a movement for economic justice at home, he remained committed. "If there is no response from the federal government, from the Congress, that's their failure, not those who are struggling for justice." Returning to Memphis on April 3, he met with local leaders to prepare for a march on April 8, despite a court injunction to prevent it. Angered, King told the crowd gathered that night, "All we say to America is: Be true to what you said on paper. If I lived in China or even Russia, or any totalitarian country, maybe I could understand the denial of certain basic First Amendment privileges. . . . But somewhere I read of the freedom of assembly. Somewhere I read of the freedom of

Striking sanitation workers picketing in Memphis.

speech. . . . Somewhere I read that the greatness of America is the right to protest for right." That evening, King called home to arrange his upcoming Sunday sermon, which he entitled "Why America Is Going to Hell."

On the evening of April 4, after a day of meetings, King walked out of his room at the Lorraine Motel in Memphis and was shot and killed. The sniper was James Earl Ray, who, according to the legal case against him, acted alone. When Ray died in 1998, questions remained whether he had acted on his own and about the fairness of his trial. (King's son met with Ray in jail, and the King family publicly pushed for a new trial for Ray.)

King's assassination had a profound effect on the nation, even on activists who had moved away from him politically. King had not been a perfect man. Tormented by fame, he found his growing influence a hard responsibility to bear. He smoked, drank, and womanized. But his influence was immeasurable. A "reluctant leader," as his SCLC associate Andrew Young described him, King led by example. He did not ask others to do what he could not do. The day after he died, Stokely Carmichael declared, "As for Dr. King's murder, I think white America made its biggest mistake because she killed the one man of our race that this country's older generations, the militants and the revolutionaries and the masses of black people would still listen to." Angry and disillusioned, people took to the streets, with riots breaking out in 110 cities.

Two months earlier, King had spoken to his congregation at Ebenezer Baptist Church about his possible death. "If any of you are around when I have to meet my day, I don't want a long funeral. . . . I'd like somebody to mention that day, that Martin Luther King, Jr. tried to give his life serving others. . . . I want you to say that day, that I tried to be right on the war question. . . . I won't have any money to leave behind. . . . But I just want to leave a committed life behind." The process of manipulating his memory and distorting his legacy, however, began even at King's funeral. As SNCC's Cleveland Sellers explained, "We sat a couple rows behind the family, surrounded by dignitaries, most of them rich and white. Hubert Humphrey, our old nemesis from Atlantic City, had a prominent seat. Jackie Kennedy, who had never shown any particular interest in Dr. King or black oppression, was also conspicuously present. Unfortunately, there was no place in the church for the hundreds of thousands of poor blacks who loved Dr. King and believed in his beautiful 'Dream.'" Harry Belafonte recalled a similar feeling, getting particularly angry at a prominent *New York Times* reporter standing next to him at the funeral. "I could not help but tell him that this grievous moment was in part the result of a climate of hate and distortion that the *New York Times* and other papers had helped create. . . . Just coming to grieve the loss was no cleansing of guilt."

A number of parallels can be drawn between King's and Malcolm X's deaths. At the ends of their lives, King and Malcolm were moving closer to each other politically. Broadly criticized for their political stands, both saw the American civil rights struggle in a global context and endorsed the need for profound economic changes within the nation and for local black political empowerment. Neither man nourished the full role that women had and could play in the struggle. Both men, assassinated at the young age of 39, had grown and changed tremendously over the course of their shortened public lives. And both would become more beloved in death than they were at the end of their lives.

Coretta Scott King and many of King's associates were determined to carry on King's work and returned to Memphis for a solemn march. This effort was funded and arranged by Harry Belafonte, who explained, "[I]n the midst of our grief we were still committed to the objectives of the movement . . . the fallen Dr. King did not leave behind a movement that, in the midst of this great tragedy, would lose its courage or its vision." On April 16, with pressure mounting from all sides, the city council agreed to recognize the sanitation workers' union and to grant them higher wages, benefits, and safety standards. Having stood up and won, 63 days after they had walked off the job, Memphis sanitation workers returned to their jobs.

Ralph Abernathy and Jesse Jackson of the SCLC took up the work of the Poor People's Campaign. Four weeks after King's assassination, Rev.

Abernathy set out from Memphis to Washington, D.C., explaining, "For any of you who would linger in the cemetery and tarry around the grave, I have news for you. We have business on the road to freedom. . . . We must prove to white America that you can kill the leader but you cannot kill the dream." On June 19, 50,000 people joined the Solidarity Day March of the Poor People's Campaign. Poor people from across the country set up a tent city named Resurrection City on the Mall in Washington. About 2,500 people stayed at Resurrection City until it was torn down by police on June 24. Although largely a black mobilization, the Poor People's campaign also drew Native Americans, Chicanos, and Puerto Ricans, thus contributing to a growing politicization in these communities.

The riots that swept the nation after King's assassination provided the final impetus for Congress and the president to sign into law an Open Housing Act. The act, first introduced in 1966 but opposed by most whites across the country, prohibited discrimination in buying or renting in much of the nation's housing stock but kept the burden on black litigants to prove discrimination. The uprisings after King's assassination seemed foreboding of an even hotter summer to come and convinced lawmakers to act. President Johnson also linked his support of open housing to the substantial role black soldiers were playing in Vietnam. "Unless there is fair housing . . . I do not know what the measure of their unappreciation would be for the ingratitude of their fellow citizens, after they were willing lay their lives on the altar."

THE FIGHT FOR WELFARE RIGHTS

Most civil rights activists had come to see a link between racial and economic justice but nonetheless avoided the issue of welfare. The stigma associated with welfare and the fact that it primarily affected women led many groups to ignore the issue. Yet welfare was a discriminatory and demeaning institution in need of drastic change. Benefits were low and difficult for black women to claim, particularly in the South. To ensure a ready supply of women for domestic work, black women had long been denied access to the federally-funded AFDC and other social benefits. In 1960, as a result, only 33 percent of the eligible poor received AFDC.

In 1967, the National Welfare Rights Organization (NWRO) was founded to address the unequal and dehumanizing treatment of poor people under AFDC. In a statement outlining their goals, this new organization affirmed, "We are not willing to exchange our rights as American citizens—our rights to dignity—our rights to justice—our rights to democratic participation in order to obtain the physical necessities for our families." Although not constituted as a black group, the NWRO's membership was comprised predominantly of black women but initially led by CORE organizer George Wiley. Johnnie Tillmon, the second chairperson of the NWRO and an African-American woman who had gone on welfare when diabetes and arthritis caused her to lose her laundry job, explained, "In this country, if you are any one of those things—poor, black, fat, female, middle-aged, on welfare—you count less as a human being. If you're all those things, you don't count at all."

In 1969, the NWRO's membership had reached twenty-five thousand, with thousands more participating in NWRO-sponsored local actions. NWRO activists saw benefits as a part of their rights as American citizens and mothers and strove to change public beliefs around welfare. As Tillmon explained, "We understood that what people thought about welfare recipients and women on welfare was that they had no rights, they didn't exist, they was a statistic and not a human being." Welfare regulations outlining minimum standards for people on welfare and providing for special needs were rarely enforced. The NWRO saw this discrimination as the place to start organizing: first by informing welfare recipients of their rights, then by organizing recipients into a group, then to demanding action and, if necessary, demonstrating to uphold the law. To expand these rights, NWRO activists protested in welfare offices, lobbied in Washington, filed suits in courts, and launched campaigns against private businesses such as Sears to press for just treatment of welfare recipients. In Detroit, welfare mothers caused such a disturbance that welfare offices were closed for four days. By 1971, their organizing efforts and political pressure ensured that 90 percent of those eligible received welfare.

The NWRO, in addition, challenged public perceptions of welfare recipients. In 1968, when Senator Russell Long refused to let female welfare rights leaders testify to Congress and called them "brood mares," Johnnie Tillmon and the organization responded with what she termed a "brood mare stampede." They lobbied black church groups to oppose new welfare restrictions and picketed in front of welfare centers, government offices, and the homes of legislators, refusing to be silenced.

The NWRO had organized 540 separate chapters by 1971, increasing to 800 affiliates in 50 states by 1974. Led largely by poor black women, this coalition brought together the poor with middle-class organizers, social scientists, and black and white activists from organizations like CORE. At times, class tensions rippled through the organization, particularly over the question of whether poor women could lead themselves. This came to a head in Tillmon's candidacy for chair; following her election, the organization lost some of its middle-class and foundation support. Still, the NWRO had succeeded in framing the civil rights issues underlying welfare policy and forced local and federal agencies to deal with poor people more justly and equitably.

Chapter 5

RADICAL MOVEMENTS AND THE BACKLASH AGAINST CIVIL RIGHTS

THE BACKLASH TAKES OFFICE: THE ELECTION OF RICHARD NIXON

The backlash against welfare activism and other civil rights gains played a large role in Richard Nixon's election to the presidency and in the third-party candidacy of Alabama Governor George Wallace. Candidates Nixon and Wallace played on the racial fears of white voters by appeals to the "silent majority" who, they argued, worked hard for what they had, obeyed the law, and had been forgotten in the social upheaval of the 1960s. Although Wallace's racial appeals were more overt, Nixon put forth a political discourse and set of policy initiatives that laid the groundwork for New Right racial politics in the coming decades. Nixon extolled the need for "law and order," attacked social activists for weakening America's political and economic order, and blamed the liberal policies of the 1960s for deindustrialization, crime, and the emerging economic downturn. Realizing that many northern and southern whites believed desegregation was moving too quickly, Nixon denounced court-ordered desegregation plans and recommended reductions of $4 million in fair housing enforcement. He preferred the "freedom of choice" plans so popular in the South that had been repudiated by the Supreme Court in May of 1968. The Court overturned "freedom of choice" plans as evasive of the law and ordered schools to dismantle "root and branch" segregation in facilities, staff, faculty, extracurricular activities, and transportation.

Nixon's embrace of racial conservatism appealed to northern as well as southern whites and helped ensure his election. Even though Nixon won the popular vote by a slim margin (43.4 percent to Democratic nominee Hubert Humphrey's 42.7 percent), combined with Wallace's 13.5 percent, the electorate had delivered a resounding 58 percent repudiation of the politics of racial reform. Although Nixon's inaugural speech stressed bringing the country together, the new president cynically played on division. He attempted to stall the Court's desegregation decision by urging officials in the Justice Department, "Do only what the law requires. Not one thing more." His tactics eventually led attorneys in the Justice Department and the chair of the Equal Employment Opportunity Commission to resign in protest. Nixon also promised Senator Strom Thurmond of South Carolina that he would intervene against rules instituted by the Department of Health, Education and Welfare that suspended federal monies to those school districts refusing to desegregate. In effect, Nixon used his power as president to block desegregation. Like former president Eisenhower, Nixon regarded "those who want instant integration" as extremists.

FROM ETHNIC STUDIES TO DESEGREGATION: THE MOVEMENT FOR EDUCATIONAL EQUITY CONTINUES

By the end of 1972, southern schools were less racially segregated than northern ones. These changes in the South were the culmination of efforts led by local blacks. In 1964, only 2 percent of black children attended integrated schools. That year, Congress enacted the Civil Rights Act, barring discrimination in all schools and other institutions receiving federal aid. To maintain the letter (but not the spirit) of the law, most southern districts implemented "freedom of choice" plans, where black families could supposedly choose to send their children to white or black schools. Economic and physical violence—and the threat of such violence—deterred many black parents from exercising the choice to send their children to a white school despite the educational advantages of doing so. Students attending white schools had classes from September to May. Black schools operated on a split session constructed around cotton farming, with school starting in December or January, stopping in early spring for chopping season, and resuming for a couple of months in the summer, ending in September for picking season. The books provided were torn and old, and lunch was provided only once or twice a week.

Little stood to protect those black families who dared to choose a white school. Still, some black families faced these economic and physical dangers and the rejection by many blacks who feared troublemakers in their midst and enrolled their children in white schools. Matthew and Mae Bertha Carter were the first and, for two years, the only black family in Drew, Mississippi, to enroll their children in the white school. As Mae Bertha Carter explained, "Now the black people know what the white man likes before he tells them and some things he don't even have to be told. White man didn't even have to go to the black's house and say, 'Don't send your child to the school,' cause we know what the white man likes."

The seven Carter children braved shouting, angry crowds and hostile teachers and classmates to begin school in September of 1965; that harassment continued unceasingly in the years to come. Lunchtime was especially perilous; for a long time, a number of the Carter children refused to eat lunch because they had to go to the lunchroom. For exercising their choice to send their children to the white school, the family lost their sharecrop. Whites shot into their house and tore down their animal pen. The Carters could not find other work. SNCC, the American Friends Service Committee (AFSC), and the Delta Ministry of the National Council of Churches, however, stepped in and sent food and money to the Carters. In letters to the AFSC, Mae Bertha Carter described the situation. "[D]own here in the lion's den . . . It hard for the poor to stand up for what is right here." Mae Bertha Carter's conviction that her children deserved the best education available sustained her. "[M]y first grader know so much more than my other first graders before, until I don't want them to ever go to another segregated school." The Supreme Court's ruling against "freedom of choice" plans brought some respite for the Carters as more black children began to desegregate Drew's schools.

For even longer than their southern counterparts, many northern whites resisted desegregation, and northern school boards devised numerous ways to evade the law. Even though their children were already being bused to school, many northern whites framed their opposition as antibusing, even though they intended to prevent any sort of desegregation. President Nixon joined forces with this movement, lambasting "forced busing" as antidemocratic.

Faced with such intransigence, civil rights activists explored other approaches to transform their children's educations, ranging from independent black schools, to community control of schools, to curriculum change. Committed to an education that respected their children's background and their intellect, parents and community activists formed the Black Panther school in Oakland and other independent schools in Boston, New York, and Detroit. In the Ocean Hill–Brownsville area of Brooklyn, parents and community members shifted their demands from desegregation of New York's schools, as the city refused year after year to create any plan for desegregation, to local control of schools. Malcolm X had aptly defined a school as segregated when it was "controlled by people who have no interest in it whatsoever"—and thus, parents saw community control as another avenue to attack the effects of segregation. As parent Dolores Torres explained, "We just kept saying, 'Well, they're not representing us. Maybe we should represent ourselves.'"

In 1967, with funding from the Ford Foundation and the support of the liberal Mayor John Lindsay, the United Federation of Teachers (UFT), and many political leaders throughout the city, the board of education established three small experimental school districts—one in Harlem, one on the Lower East Side, and one in the Ocean Hill-Brownsville section of Brooklyn—each to be run by a community-elected board. In August of 1967, the community in Ocean Hill-Brownsville chose an interracial board to oversee the new district; they selected Rhody McCoy, a black administrator with 18 years of experience in New York's schools, as superintendent. At the time, there were no other black superintendents in New York City's school system.

In May 1968, the Ocean Hill-Brownsville governing board decided to transfer 19 teachers and administrators that they thought were not committed to the reform. Dolores Torres, who had been elected to the new board, explained, "[W]hat they were doing was babysitting. We didn't feel that they really had our children's best interest in mind." This decision was denounced by the UFT, whose leadership claimed that the teachers had been unfairly dismissed without a hearing and demanded their reinstatement. When the board refused, 350 teachers in the district went on strike in solidarity with the transferred teachers. Parents and community activists responded by filling in for the striking teachers to keep Ocean Hill-Brownsville schools open and demonstrated outside the schools to prevent the dismissed teachers from returning. McCoy explained, "Now these youngsters, who had previously seen ninety percent of their teachers white, are now looking at their parents or the parents of their friends who are teaching. . . . And this new role model was just fantastic. No more hooky, no more truant playing. Everybody was coming to school." Over the summer, the board of education granted Ocean Hill-Brownsville permission to recruit new teachers to replace the striking unionized ones. Of the 350 new teachers hired, 100 were black and the remaining were white, with half of those Jewish.

Racial tensions heightened. Some teachers believed that the transfer of the 19 teachers was an attempt to expel white teachers from the system. A black judge called in to mediate ruled at the end of the summer that the teachers had been dismissed illegally and ordered their reinstatement. Again, the community board refused. As a result, the UFT called a citywide teachers' strike. UFT President Al Shanker explained,

"To me the civil rights movement was a movement for integration and a movement to eliminate segregation. In a sense, this represented a kind of backward step." The UFT leadership further polarized the situation by accusing the board of Ocean Hill–Brownsville of anti-Semitism. Anonymous anti-Semitic leaflets had been circulated in teachers' mailboxes. Wrongly attributing these sentiments to the Ocean Hill–Brownsville leadership, the UFT accused the district of propagating these sentiments. Even when Jewish and non-Jewish teachers working within the Ocean Hill–Brownsville district took out an ad in the *New York Times* to refute these charges of anti-Semitism, the belief remained. By then, growing numbers of the black community including such diverse groups as CORE and the Black Panthers backed community control, convinced of the impact community-run schools were having on black children. In addition, many blacks across the city who had initially supported the dismissed teachers grew disenchanted with the UFT's tactics.

In contrast, community control lost the backing of some of its white allies. Some white teachers remained committed to the Ocean Hill–Brownsville experiment, splitting with the union to do so. Public sentiment, however, had shifted against the experimental district. Rhody McCoy starkly described the dilemma, "I'm sure that there were several possibilities for a truce with the UFT. One would be to get rid of me. . . . If we would take the teachers back and let them have their regular assignments. . . . But then, what would you have? You wouldn't have had a project. You'd have a shell." At the end of the 1968–69 school year, the New York legislature enacted a new school decentralization bill, abolishing the three demonstration districts, including Ocean Hill–Brownsville. While giving more control to parents and community members across the city and state, the bill was a far cry from the community control briefly allowed in the three experimental districts.

For parents pushing for community control curriculum change was a critical issue. As the black newspaper the *Pittsburgh Courier* pointed out, "How great can the American Negro become in self-esteem and personal dignity if his history and culture are lost, both to him and to his white colleagues?" Racism in textbooks had long troubled the black community, but by the late 1960s, many students of color began to challenge the erasure of the histories and cultures of African Americans, Chicanos, and Native Americans within college curriculum. The exclusion of these histories, they argued, educated people to conform to the racial and economic landscape of the United States.

Student protest won the institutionalization of ethnic studies in universities across the country in the late 1960s and 1970s. Even at a premier, historically black college like Howard University, for example, student Adrienne Manns explained, "there was only one course and that was

'Negro History' and you had to be a history major or an upperclassman to take that." Despite Howard University's role in educating many leaders and professionals in the black community, students were taught that American history and literature were the history and literature of white Americans and were given seminars on manners, etiquette, and attire.

Students began to question this education. In 1966, Robin Gregory's campaign for homecoming queen at Howard galvanized a student movement. As student Paula Giddings explained, "[Robin Gregory] had an Afro, which of course was the statement that she made physically. . . . And Robin talked about the movement." Gregory's victory as homecoming queen spurred a burgeoning movement. As Gregory herself explained, "The coronation . . . energized a lot of people, causing them to begin to question a lot of the issues that we were bringing forward." Students demonstrated when the head of the draft board, General Hershey, came to speak and they succeeded in downgrading the status of ROTC (Reserve Officers' Training Corps) on campus. They demanded that the administration institute curriculum change, establish nonprerequisite courses in black history, abolish Freshman Assembly, establish a black awareness research institute, and recognize Howard as a black university accountable to the black community. They further insisted on greater student governance, the resignation of certain administrators, and the reinstatement of instructors dismissed for political activism. When their demands went unanswered, twelve hundred students occupied the administration building on March 19, 1968. Community groups and local restaurants brought them food, performed plays for them, and lent the students their support. Not all students or faculty favored these actions, however; professor Charles Epps explained his position, "Howard provided a mainstream education which prepared people to be competitive in every field. I don't recognize and I don't think the world recognizes that there is any black physics. . . . [T]here was no such thing as Howard becoming more black than it was." The takeover ended peacefully five days later when the administration agreed to reinstate faculty who had been fired for supporting the students and implementing curriculum change, a black research institute, and increased student governance.

Organized, determined, and challenging an older orthodoxy, the Howard activists transformed the university much like the students who had sat-in at lunch counters in 1960. Their actions inspired many student groups across the country to agitate for ethnic studies in the next few years. Building occupations and demonstrations on many campuses brought together antiwar activism with demands for black student unions, black residential houses, multicultural curriculum, and changes in university recruitment and admissions.

This movement for ethnic studies prompted actions at Columbia University, Harvard University, and San Francisco State University, as students demanded new, diversified curriculum, new faculty of color, and new racial sensitivity. Strikes at Columbia and Harvard also attacked university complicity (and profit) from the war in Vietnam and the exploitative relationship the university had with the community. On April 23, 1968, an interracial group of nearly 1,000 Columbia students seized university buildings to protest the university's ties to the Pentagon and its ongoing encroachment into the working-class and poor neighborhoods that surrounded the university in upper-west Manhattan. The university struck back a week later. One thousand police arrested more than 700 students, injuring 150 in the process. The university's decision to arrest the students galvanized a student strike. When most students struck, the university was forced to shut down for the remaining weeks of the semester.

In 1969, students of the Third World Liberation Front at San Francisco State shut down the campus, demanding the creation of a school for ethnic studies, stronger offerings in black studies, and the institution of an open admissions policy for nonwhite students. The Third World Liberation Front brought together a militant rainbow coalition of white, black, Chicano, Asian-American and Native-American students. Their efforts succeeded in prompting significant curriculum change at the university in the long term. But in the short term, San Francisco State's President S. I. Hayakawa responded by calling out the police and the National Guard to remove students. This drew wide support from conservatives and was a key factor in his subsequent election to the U.S. Senate.

Led by black and Puerto Rican student groups and joined by white students, protests also erupted in 1969 at the various campuses of the City University of New York (CUNY) around the issue of admissions. Not counting the SEEK (Search for Education, Elevation, and Knowledge) program (established in 1964 to provide higher education opportunities to disadvantaged students), blacks and Puerto Ricans comprised about 2 percent of CUNY students under regular admissions even though approximately half of the city's high school students were students of color. Students launched a strike that shut down City College, held a sit-in at the president's office at Brooklyn College, and engaged in similar rowdy mobilizations at Lehman College, Queens College, and Bronx Community College. These protests led to the institution of an open admissions policy within the City University of New York in August 1970. Designed to make the City University system open to all New Yorkers and protect both the white working-class and people of color, the open admissions policy began to make college a reality for many students of color and immigrant and white working-class students. The number of students of color in the freshman class tripled between 1969 and 1972; in absolute numbers the number of whites grew even faster.

Student protest also resulted in the institutionalization of Chicano and Puerto Rican studies. Protests by United Mexican American Students led California State University, Los Angeles, to institute the first Chicano studies program. Subsequent student demands prompted university officials to establish Chicano studies programs at many other California colleges and some Texas schools. Concerns over curriculum extended to secondary education. More than 50 percent of Chicano students in East Los Angeles, for example, never graduated because of expulsion, transfers, or failures because they had never learned to read. The schools Chicanos attended were overcrowded, had few Chicano teachers, and employed many teachers who discriminated against Chicano students. The curriculum contained almost nothing by way of Chicano culture or history.

On March 3, 1968, more than 1,000 students peacefully walked out of Abraham Lincoln High School in East L.A. chanting "Blow Out" and carrying signs that read "Chicano Power" and "Viva La Raza." Students demanded an end to racist school policies and ethnocentric teachers and called for hiring more Mexican-American teachers and administrators and for classes on Chicano history and culture. Sal Castro, a charismatic and politically active teacher who had helped them formulate their plan, joined their demonstration. By afternoon, an additional one hundred students walked out of four other schools—Garfield, Wilson, Belmont, and Roosevelt—and by the end of March, over 10,000 Chicano students had walked out of East L.A. high schools. Partly organized by college students at California State Los Angeles and UCLA and the Brown Berets, these "blowouts" brought the Los Angeles school system to a standstill. Because the walkouts violated public education laws, a grand jury indicted 13 people for conspiracy (including Castro, 7 Brown Berets, and 2 editors of *La Raza* newspaper). At first, the school board suspended Castro, but community protests led the board in October to reinstate Castro.

The walkouts divided many families and the Los Angeles Chicano community. Many opposed the students' militant tactics as confrontational and unproductive. For many older generation Mexican Americans, even the term *Chicano* was distasteful. It had been used pejoratively to describe lower-class Mexicans (and more playfully by working-class people to describe themselves). *Chicano* nonetheless appealed to many young people as a positive, powerful, and unifying name. Ultimately, though, the walkouts garnered support from the Mexican-American adult community. And they led Mexican-American communities across the country to organize to demand similar changes in their schools. In San Antonio, for instance, more than 130 students walked out of two high schools on April 9, 1968.

Rodolofo "Corky" Gonzales was one of those arrested in the East L.A. student walkouts. The son of migrant workers, Gonzales had been a Golden Gloves champion, a Democratic party worker, and then a grassroots community organizer and writer. Appointed director of Denver's War on Poverty in 1965, he was fired the next year for being too radical. Gonzales then worked to promote community control of the schools, published his own newspaper, asserted the importance of Spanish for Chicanos, organized a march on police headquarters to protest police brutality, and pushed for Chicano electoral power. His epic poem *I Am Joaquín* linked the history of Mexican Americans to the history of Mexican peoples and criticized the ways this history had been excluded from the history of the United States. By grappling with the process of identity for Mexican Americans in U.S. society, it became one of the most influential pieces of movement literature. In his introduction, Gonzales explained, "Writing *I Am Joaquín* was a journey back through history, a painful self-evaluation, a wandering search for my peoples and, most of all, for my own identity."

THE MANY FACES OF BLACK NATIONALISM

By the end of the 1960s, rising disillusionment and rising expectations went hand in hand. As more people became active, they grew angrier about the lack of change, the systemic retaliation visited on those who did speak out, and the indifference of the federal government and disagreed over how best to achieve real justice. In the aftermath of the Watts Rebellion, black activists in California gravitated in two directions: towards cultural nationalism (taken up by organizations like US) and revolutionary nationalism (brought forth in groups like the Black Panthers). Harold Cruse elaborated the foundations of cultural nationalism in his 600-page book *The Crisis of the Negro Intellectual* (1967). "There can be no real black revolution in the United States without cultural revolution," Cruse asserted, because "now would be the time for Negro intellectuals to start thinking for themselves as truly independent and original radicals." Sharing this perspective, in September of 1965, Maulana Ron Karenga, born Ronald Everett, founded the US organization. A well-armed nationalist group, and later a rival of the Panthers, US had a unit of strongly disciplined, highly committed young men named the Simba Wachuka ("young lions" in Swahili).

In 1966, Karenga introduced the holiday Kwanzaa to commemorate the African roots of African Americans. Drawing largely on East African traditions even though most African Americans were West African in origin, Kwanzaa (meaning "the first fruits" in Swahili) lasted from the day after Christmas, December 26, to New Year's Day, January 1. Intended to give African Americans a holiday of their own, Kwanzaa affirmed black history to celebrate the seven principles of the African heritage of African Americans: Umoja (unity), Kugichagulia (self-determination), Ujima (collective work and responsibility), Ujamaa (cooperative economics), Nia (purpose), Kuumba (creativity), and Imani (faith). At first, Karenga did not admit that Kwanzaa was created in America because he worried that few blacks would celebrate it. The holiday caught on as a way to mark African-American cultural roots.

To the founders of the Black Panther Party—Huey Newton and Bobby Seale—Karenga's cultural nationalism seemed "a reaction instead of responding to political oppression. The cultural nationalists are concerned with returning to the old African culture and thereby regaining their identity and freedom. In other words, they feel that the African culture will automatically bring political freedom." Taking the Lowndes County Freedom Organization panther as their symbol and a diverse group of revolutionaries from Malcolm X to Chairman Mao to Franz Fanon as their inspiration, Newton and Seale started the Black Panthers in Oakland in October 1966 as a vehicle to transform American society. Looking at class and race in tandem, their 10-point plan ranged from the idealistic to the pragmatic to the revolutionary, calling for full employment, an end to police brutality, an exemption from military service for all black men, and "land, bread, housing, education, clothing, justice and peace." Socialist in philosophy, the Panthers directly attacked capitalism as the economic basis of black oppression.

Yet it was not the Panther's radical program but their uniform and their willingness to carry guns in public that initially caught the attention of the media and the public and helped form the image of them as violent revolutionaries. The Panthers wore black leather jackets, black pants, and black berets because, according to Newton, berets "were used by just about every struggler in the Third World." The Panthers began a campaign to police the police as the first step toward community autonomy, according to Newton, because "we needed to get their attention and give them something to identify with." They asserted a right to armed self-defense and referred to the police as pigs. According to Newton, "We felt that the police needed a label, a label other than that fear image that they carried in the community. So we used the pig as the rather low-lifed animal in order to identify the police." The Panthers trained themselves in the use of guns and began community patrols. Carrying guns, tape recorders, and law books, they took pictures when the police stopped people or made an arrest and recorded evidence of abuse. These acts inflamed the police. Some Panthers also engaged in gun battles with the police.

In May of 1967, a group of fully armed Panthers visited the state legislature—conceived, according to Bobby Seale, as "a media event" to make a public visual statement. They had traveled to Sacramento to protest the police killing of 22-year-old Denzil Dowell and a bill recently introduced in the wake of the Panthers' police patrols that would make carrying a loaded gun in public illegal. The Panthers ended up, mistakenly, on the floor of the legislature and quickly left. Nonetheless, as poet Sonia Sanchez explained, "The whole image that went around the world of Panthers going into the assembly with guns as something that said, simply, 'Don't mess with me.'" Even though no Panthers had used or threatened to use their guns, Seale was arrested and spent the next six months in jail for his role in the protest.

Seale was not the only Panther arrested to try to curb the influence of the organization. In 1967, Huey Newton was convicted of voluntary manslaughter in the death of one police officer, John Frey, and the wounding of another. Claiming self-defense for his role in the confrontation with police that night, Newton was seriously injured with four bullets to the stomach and contended that he had passed out before Officer Frey was shot. After spending three years in prison, his conviction was overturned in 1970 following a national campaign of agitation. The Panthers had realized that to free their leaders they would have to build a mass movement of support for political prisoners, and not rely solely on legal defense. The call to Free Huey became a cornerstone in the Panther's organizing efforts for three years.

During those three years, the Black Panther Party grew tremendously, expanding to include chapters in Chicago and New York. Panthers like Eldridge Cleaver found black nationalism while a prisoner. After being released from prison, he joined the party and published *Soul on Ice,* which became popular among many young black and white radicals and helped augment the party's coffers. Elaine Brown, who joined the Panthers in 1967 and served as their deputy minister of information and later chairperson, explained her decision to join, as "surrendering our lives to something greater, which was the notion of getting rid of oppression, and all the things that oppression meant and means in this country for black people and other people in the country. . . . It means really seeing yourself as part of a whole . . . that you were a soldier in the army. . . . to introduce a socialist revolution into the United States of America."

Panther recruits initially were men, but women soon joined. By 1968, women comprised around 60 percent of the Panthers. Yet, particularly in the early years, sexist comments and harassment, fixed ideas about gender roles (men lead, women step back), demands for sexual favors, and the downplaying of women's intellectual contributions in favor of their domestic ones were common within the party. Eldridge

Cleaver expressed this gendered thinking, when he told women, "you have the power to bring a squeaking halt to a lot of things that are going on, and we call that pussy power. We say that political power, revolutionary power grows out of the lips of a pussy." Cleaver urged women to withhold sex if men were not proper revolutionaries. Initially, men and women served in sex-separated roles (Panthers and Pantherettes) and reported to captains of the same sex. Many women leaders like Elaine Brown, Kathleen Cleaver, Ericka Huggins, Afeni Shakur, Yvonne King, Barbara Sankey, and Audrea Jones became important leaders, but their roles were often limited.

Gender relations in the Panthers in time changed to become more equitable—as many struggled to make it a gender-inclusive organization. Many Panthers began to see that real freedom meant emancipating women and sought to transform the organization's structures. As women began to speak more forcefully about the issues of gender equity within the party, the *Black Panther* published June Culberson's powerful essay on black women's right to self-determination in May 1969. Culberson demanded that men live up to the party's ideals. "You tell us that we are the backbone of the Party and yet you won't allow us to put this into practice for fear that if you really help us get politically educated, we might learn a little more than you do, or may shoot a little straighter." As time went on, the party became more committed to rooting out sexism. When Newton was released from jail in 1970, he stressed that the Panthers "recognize the women's right to be free" and urged Panthers to move away from gendered ideas and see each other as "comrades." Echoing these sentiments, Seale and Cleaver both spoke about the importance of the liberation of women to the revolutionary struggle.

The Panthers' survival programs proved key to their growing community support. "We call the program a 'survival' program," Chairman David Hilliard explained, "survival pending revolution—not something to preface revolution or challenge the power relations demanding radical action, but an activity that strengthens us for the coming fight." These grassroots initiatives included a free breakfast program, free health clinics, sickle cell testing and a free ambulance service, an Intercommunal Youth Institute (or the Oakland Community School as it was better known), free legal aid, and free busing for families to visit their loved ones in prison. These programs broadened public support as the Panthers showed their willingness to address the immediate needs facing the black community. In addition, the Black Panther newspaper, the *Black Panther Intercommunal News Service,* gave much more comprehensive international and local coverage than most other papers and became an invaluable organizing tool as Panther members solicited others to buy the paper.

The Panthers also forged alliances with white groups such as the Peace and Freedom party and Students for a Democratic Society (SDS); white leftists often attended their meetings and rallies. Newton explained the importance of this collaboration. "We were not into a racist bag. . . . We could have solidarity and friendship in a common struggle against a common oppressor without the whites taking over." Focusing on the economic roots of black oppression, the Panthers sought to build cross-racial solidarity, distinguishing between "the Man" and their white allies. The Panthers also sought to turn the alienation and aggression of young criminals and gang members towards political action.

The Young Chicanos for Community Action—later known as the Brown Berets—also recruited gang members and organized community patrols. Started in 1967 through a grant from the Southern California Council of Churches, the group was founded by a group of young people including David Sanchez, Vickie Castro, and Ralph Ramirez. Their emphasis on community defense and police patrols differed from established Mexican-American groups that shied away from issues of police violence. The Brown Berets called for bilingual education, the teaching of Mexican-American history, an end to urban renewal programs that displaced Mexican Americans in favor of high rent homes, and the right to vote regardless of the ability to speak English. Student activist Luis Rodriguez highlighted the ways the Brown Berets and the Panthers channeled the energies of young people into political action: "[F]or a most productive and wonderful time, gang violence stood at a standstill. For a time it appeared the internal warfare had given way to the struggle for land, language and liberty."

A Chicago Puerto Rican group, the Young Lords, further showed how gangs were becoming politicized. Begun in the 1950s as a street gang, the Lords changed in the late 1960s under the leadership of Jose "Cha-Cha" Jiménez. Joining the gang in 1959 and in and out of prison over the next decade, Jiménez had met Fred Hampton while in prison. An extremely charismatic 21-year-old, Hampton was the leader of Chicago's Panthers. The Chicago Panthers had started a free breakfast program for children and a free health clinic and helped establish a truce between many of Chicago's most notorious street gangs. With encouragement from Hampton, Jiménez helped organize the Young Lords to protest the city's urban renewal plans that threatened to displace many blacks and Puerto Ricans. Continuing the connections forged with Hampton and the Black Panther Party, these actions politicized the Young Lords.

A number of New York Puerto Ricans, mostly university students, met Jiménez at political events in Denver and Chicago and were inspired by what he was doing in Chicago. These young people began to organize in New York City, forming the New York chapter of the Young Lords on July 26, 1969. Told by community residents that their first need was garbage pick-up, the Lords began to clean the streets, starting with 110th Street in East Harlem (the heart of New York's Puerto Rican community). The city stood by, refusing to give them brooms and bags to facilitate their work or to pick up the collected trash. On the third weekend, the Lords lugged the bagged garbage into the streets to block traffic, to force the city to remove the garbage. Some set the garbage on fire. The Garbage Offensive, as it became known, gave the Lords a community foothold, as they showed themselves willing to confront authorities on issues important to the community.

Taking very seriously their mandate "to serve the people," the Lords began looking for a place to run a free breakfast program. The First Spanish Methodist Church, located in the heart of East Harlem and unused during the week, seemed perfect. But the pastor refused to let them work out of the church. The next Sunday was a testimonial Sunday, which meant any member of the congregation could speak out. When a number of Lords came to testify, they were arrested by police in the middle of the service. Three weeks later, on December 28, the Lords took over the church, renaming it the People's Church. For 11 days, they ran community programs including free breakfast and clothing programs, health services, and a liberation school. More than 3,000 people occupied the church, ending when the police arrested 106 Young Lords. The People's Church had broadened the Young Lord's base, established it as a community presence, and gained national media attention for the organization. By the end of 1970, the chapter had about 1,000 members.

The Young Lords next moved to address health issues. Every Saturday, members of the Young Lords, accompanied by medical students, went door to door to talk with families about lead paint and to take urine samples from the children. These samples showed the high incidence of lead poisoning in the Puerto Rican community and helped bring public attention to the issue, ultimately resulting in the passage of laws requiring the removal of the paint. Door-to-door testing also revealed that tuberculosis disproportionately affected New York's Puerto Rican community. When the city refused to bring a tuberculosis detection x-ray truck to these neighborhoods, the Young Lords liberated the truck and, with the help of the truck's driver and technician, tested hundreds of people. The Lords twice briefly took over Lincoln Hospital in the South Bronx, which served many working-class Puerto Ricans and blacks: the first time to protest the substandard conditions in the hospital—rats in the emergency room, inadequate supplies, and chronic personnel shortages—and to call for the construction of a new one; the second time to pressure the hospital to create a detoxification program for heroin users.

Although most of the Young Lords were Puerto Ricans, a quarter of the membership was African-American with a smaller number of other Latinos. Women members soon began to challenge the organization's sexism. The original Central Committee was led by five men—Felipe Luciano, David Pérez, Juan González, Pablo Guzmán, and Juan Ortiz—and the original platform called for "revolutionary machismo." But, as Young Lord Iris Morales explained, "[M]achismo could never be revolutionary. That is like saying, 'Let's have revolutionary racism.' It is a contradiction in terms." Demanding that Point Ten of the platform be changed and a woman be part of the Central Committee, women organized a Women's Caucus to push for accountability within the organization around gender issues. The platform was changed to read, "We want equality for women. Down with machismo and male chauvinism." A disciplinary procedure was set up, and many men were disciplined for sexism infractions. Realizing that the problem of sexism was one that men needed to confront on their own, the Lords also started a men's caucus.

A Campaign to Disrupt and Discredit: The FBI's COINTELPRO

Because of their alliances with gangs and other community organizations, their growing base within the community, and their commitment to socialism and self-defense, the Panthers, the Young Lords, and the Brown Berets were subjected to a vigorous campaign of state surveillance and harassment. On August 25, 1967, FBI Director Hoover reconstituted COINTELPRO (begun in 1956 as a domestic surveillance program against Communists) "to expose, disrupt, misdirect, discredit, or otherwise neutralize the activities of black nationalist, hate-type organization and groupings, their leadership, spokesmen, membership, and supporters." Within the next year, FBI agents recruited more than three thousand Ghetto Informants to promote this objective. On March 4, 1968, Hoover followed up with a set of more specific goals for this program, the second of which was to "prevent the rise of a messiah to unite the black community." Hoover feared that Martin Luther King, Stokely Carmichael, and Elijah Muhammad "aspire[d] to this position."

The FBI director soon concluded that the Black Panthers were the "greatest threat to internal security." In response, 233 of the 295 COINTELPRO actions against black groups were directed at the Panthers, and FBI agents intensified their surveillance of US, SCLC, SNCC, SDS, Nation of Islam, the NFWA, the Brown Berets, the Young Lords Party, and other emerging radical organizations like the American Indian Movement. A core tactic was to play on weaknesses and rivalries within and between groups; for example by cultivating distrust of Communists within SCLC and sharpening tensions between Malcolm X and the Nation of Islam and between rival radical groups like US, the Black Panthers, the Young Lords Party, and SNCC. The strategy worked. Violence erupted between US and the Panthers in 1969 over the elections for the Black Student Union at UCLA; three US members shot and killed two Panthers, John Huggins and Alprentice (Bunchy) Carter. FBI agents wrote anonymous letters to help sabotage an emerging political alliance between the Panthers and the Blackstone Rangers of Chicago's Southside.

This harassment and accompanying police raids took a profound toll. In 1969 alone, 28 Panthers were killed by police with hundreds more imprisoned. Between December 1967 and December 1969, the Panther party paid more than $200,000 in bail-bond premiums, money they would never recover. Raids on Panther offices and attacks on their leaders also proved effective in demobilizing the organization. A dramatic example involved Chicago Black Panther leader Fred Hampton. Through the work of paid FBI informant William O'Neal, who became the chief of security for the Chicago Panthers, the bureau amassed a 12-volume, 4,000-page file on Hampton. FBI agents surreptitiously shared this information with the Chicago police, with deadly consequences. In a raid on the Chicago Panther office, the police ripped apart the office, taking a sledgehammer to their typewriters, mimeography machines, and newspapers. As Bobby Seale explained, "The idea on the part of the police was to psych the community up. To terrorize us out of existence." The police also destroyed all the cereal kept on the second floor of the office for the breakfast program. The FBI considered the Panther breakfast program particularly subversive because it built support for the party within the black community and increased the possibility for the "indoctrination" of children. Determined not to let the police shut them down, the Panthers, with the help from the community, rebuilt and reopened the office.

FBI agents and the Chicago police helped convict Hampton of stealing $70 worth of ice cream bars. After serving four months in prison, Hampton returned to his role in the party. Then, on December 4, 1969, with maps supplied by informant O'Neal, Chicago police raided Hampton's apartment at 4:00 in the morning, killing Hampton and another Panther, Mark Clark. Eight months pregnant, Deborah Johnson was asleep next to Hampton when the raid started. "As I walked through these two lines of policemen, one of them grabbed my robe and opened it and said, 'Well, what do you know, we have a broad here.' Another policeman grabbed me by the hair and pretty much just shoved me." Police claimed they were ambushed by Panthers while conducting a search for illegal weapons. However, further investigation contradicted this. Of the more than 80 shots fired during the raid, only one had come from a Panther weapon. Even SCLC head Ralph Abernathy, who had kept a sharp distance from the Panther party, condemned this action: "If the United States is successful in crushing the Black Panther Party it won't be too long before they will crush the Southern Christian Leadership Conference, the Urban League and any other organization trying to make things better."

The FBI's COINTELPRO tactics helped cripple the Panthers organization. Informants gathered information, sowed division within the group and between other radical groups, and acted as agent provocateurs. Their own internal divisions further weakened the Panthers. These included political in-fighting between the Oakland and New York chapters and between Newton and Cleaver, physical disciplining of some members, aggressive and intimidating treatment of other radical groups, violent clashes with rival nationalist groups, and sexual harassment. By playing on these ideological divisions and personal clashes, FBI officials succeeded in driving an irreparable wedge into the organization. The party declined in the mid-1970s, formally ending with the closure of the Oakland Community School in 1982.

PRISON ORGANIZING

Another prominent black radical, Soledad prison inmate George Jackson, was also targeted by law enforcement officials. While serving an indeterminate sentence for a $70 robbery, Jackson began speaking out against biases imbedded in the criminal justice system and started organizing other prisoners. Publication of Jackson's book of letters *Soledad Brother* became one of the most widely read books among militant blacks. In it, Jackson attacked the racial and economic bases of the prison system and described how prisoners were radicalizing in response to their oppression. "[W]ith the time and incentive that these brothers have to read, study, and think, you will find no class or category more aware, more embittered, desperate or dedicated to the ultimate remedy—revolution." His actions caught the attention of prison officials who charged Jackson and two other prisoners, John Clutchette and Fleeta Drumgo, with murdering a prison guard—a charge they denied, claiming to have been framed because of their political activism. A movement grew to demand the freedom of Soledad Brothers (as the three prisoners were called).

Then, on August 7, 1970, Jonathan Jackson, the younger brother of George Jackson, attempted to rescue three other San Quentin prisoners at Marin County Courthouse, taking the judge and jury hostage. While trying to leave the court parking lot, Jonathan Jackson, the judge, and two of the prisoners were killed by guards. Prison policy dictated that guards should shoot to kill when a prisoner is escaping (even if there are hostages involved), and the guards followed those rules.

Since Jackson had died in the shoot-out, the state indicted Angela Davis, a Communist political activist and friend of the Jackson family, for murder, kidnapping, and conspiracy. Davis had not been near the scene of the crime, but the gun Jackson used was registered in her name. A professor of philosophy at UCLA, Davis was well-known because she had been fired by Governor Ronald Reagan in 1969 for her membership in the Communist party and had challenged her dismissal and won. Davis had worked with SNCC and the Black Panthers and was leading the campaign to free George Jackson and other political prisoners. Davis explained what drew her to prison organizing. "[T]here is the tendency also to look at the prisoners as having deserved what they met with . . . And what George Jackson demonstrated with his letters was that prisoners are human beings . . . And at the same time he laid the basis for an important political analysis which was lacking."

Fearful she would not receive fair treatment by the police and the courts, Angela Davis avoided arrest by going underground, eluding the police for two months. Placed on the FBI's Ten-Most-Wanted list, she was picked up by police in New York City and spent a year and a half in jail. The Communist Party, black organizations across the country, her family, the Congressional Black Caucus, and many local citizens built an international movement to win her release on $102,000 bail. Finally the judge, conceding to public pressure, agreed. Aretha Franklin had offered to put up the bail money but at the last moment could not be reached. A white farmer in Fresno—Roger MacAffee—put his land as a property bond for her bail.

At her trial, Davis affirmed her innocence. "The prosecutor has said that this trial has nothing to do with a political frame-up, but, members of the jury, during the entire time I was involved in the movement to free the Soledad Brothers, I was the object of an extensive spy campaign. . . . [The prosecutor] will present no such evidence because, if he did, it would show you the process whereby an innocent person can be set up and accused of outrageous crimes." She was acquitted of all charges.

In August 1971, ten months before Davis's acquittal, George Jackson was shot in the back and killed by prison guards for allegedly trying to escape. Since many prisoners throughout the country had read *Soledad Brother,* his death reverberated across the country—particularly at Attica State Correctional Facility in New York. Inmates there were allowed one shower a week and one roll of toilet paper a month; mail and visits were often censored; and medical care was almost nonexistent. Fifty-four percent of the prison population was black, 37 percent white, and 9 percent Puerto Rican. On September 9, 1971, approximately twelve hundred prisoners seized control of Attica, demanding state minimum wages for prison labor, more educational opportunities, religious freedom, more medical treatment, more showers, better library books, and amnesty for their actions. The inmates took hostages and set themselves up in one of the prison yards. Prison guard Michael Smith, who was taken hostage, explained the inmates' demands. "They were just asking to be treated as human beings." The men developed an organized system to delegate responsibilities for running the prison yard. Assemblyman Arthur Eve, one of the outsider mediators let in to the facility during the uprising, described the order the inmates achieved, "It was almost a community within a community. . . . There was a tremendous amount of discipline there within the yard." *New York Times* reporter Tom Wicker concurred, "The racial harmony that prevailed among the prisoners—it was absolutely astonishing."

Ignoring the advice of the outside observers to continue negotiation or employ limited force, Governor Nelson Rockefeller chose a military end to the prison takeover. On September 13, state troopers stormed the prison, killing 31 prisoners and 10 hostages. None of the inmates or hostages killed that day died at the hands of the inmates; in fact, many inmates tried to protect the hostages once the assault began. Yet, in the aftermath, seeking to justify the raid, state authorities blamed the inmates for cruelties against the hostages and troopers, and Attica guards brutally retaliated against the prisoners. According to Frank Smith, "It was very, very barbaric. They ripped our clothes off. They made us crawl on the ground like we were animals . . . they beat me in my testicles. And they burned me with cigarettes and dropped hot shells on me and then put a football up under my throat, and they kept telling me that if it dropped, they was going to kill me. . . . [T]hey broke glass up in the middle of the hallway and they made people run through the gauntlet. They had police on each side with the clubs they call nigger sticks and they was beating people." The medical examiner's report, however, revealed that the state had lied about the events and that all of the deaths were due to the aggressive actions of the state troopers. Nearly thirty years later, in 1999, a federal judge ordered the state to pay inmates who were beaten and tortured after the Attica takeover $8 million, plus $4 million in lawyers' fees.

THE POLITICS OF LAND:
FROM NEW MEXICO TO WOUNDED KNEE

The inmates at Attica and the Panthers had focused on the economic basis of racial oppression of African Americans; other community activists focused on the denial of economic power and control for Latinos and

Native Americans. In New Mexico, the main issue was land. Many Hispano farmers had grown poorer and poorer as the result of overgrazing, government policy, and the loss of communal lands in the twentieth century, as the U.S. Forest Service came to control access to these lands. For instance, at Kit Carson National Forest, local Hispanos were not allowed to graze their milk cows and draught horses, but the national forest allowed non-Hispano owners of riding horses and beef cattle to graze on park lands. Improved hiking trails and campsites had been added to the forest to encourage its use by outsiders. At the same time the Mexican-American community in New Mexico was deeply fissured. Many of the poorer Mexicans retained their Native American roots and community attachment to the land. Meanwhile, wealthy white and Mexican Americans had long collaborated to protect their class interests often at the expense of poorer farmers.

In the 1960s, a minister born in Texas, Reies López Tijerina, demanded that ancestral land be restored to the New Mexicans. As he later explained, "Our land was stolen, we wanted it back. Our towns were alive and now they're dead, they're frozen, and the commonlands that belonged to the towns were taken away." Tijerina tapped into a growing collective frustration within the community and a long tradition of resistance and sabotage Hispano farmers had engaged against the encroachment of white farmers. In the 1950s, local Hispano farmers had founded the Corporation of Abiquiu to protect their land from further encroachment. Under Tijerina's leadership, in 1963, the group changed into the nonprofit La Alianza Federal de las Mercedes and grew to 20,000 members. Having done research in Mexico into land grants and the Treaty of Guadalupe, Tijerina argued that the United States had violated the terms of the treaty. Thus, parts of the Kit Carson National Forest rightfully belonged collectively to the Hispano people. Tijerina hosted conferences and bought time on the radio for a daily show to build support. He brought suit over these land rights but the courts refused to hear his case.

Then, on October 15, 1966, 350 members of Alianza, including Tijerina, occupied the national forest campgrounds known as Echo Amphitheater to assert their communal rights to the land. They established the Republic of San Joaquin del Rio Chama and arrested forest rangers for trespassing. The demonstrators left peacefully a week later, vowing to come back. The following spring, they announced plans to return. But county attorney Alfonso Sanchez was determined to prevent the group from even meeting to talk about a possible occupation. With Governor David Cargo, who was more sympathetic to Alianza, out of town, Sanchez arrested eight aliancistas on the grounds of unlawful assembly, defined as "three or more persons assembling with intent to take over lands of the U.S Government by force and violence." On June 5, members of Alianza led by Tijerina went to the courthouse at Tierra Amarilla to try to free the jailed protesters and to make a citizen's arrest of Sanchez for violating their civil rights. A shoot-out ensued. Tijerina escaped but was arrested for assault to commit murder, kidnapping, and unlawful assault on a jail. He conducted his own defense and was acquitted of the charges.

Native Americans also demanded land rights and economic autonomy, issues having roots in the displacement of many Indians from native lands and the unwillingness of U.S. officials to uphold its treaties. In 1970, the unemployment rate for Native Americans was nearly 40 percent, almost ten times the national average. Their infant mortality rate was three times the national average; life expectancy was six years shorter for Indians than other Americans; and the suicide rate for Native Americans 100 times that of white Americans. Young people joined forces with the elders in their communities in the struggle for Indian rights, at times taking a more militant stand than many of their parents' generation. As Mary Crow Dog, who was a teenager when she got involved, explained, "The traditional old, full-blood medicine men joined in with us kids. Not the middle-aged adults. They were of a lost generation which had given up all hope. . . . It was the real old folks who had spirit and wisdom to give us."

Many Native Americans had served in Vietnam and utilized their GI benefits to enroll in colleges in the San Francisco Bay and Los Angeles areas. These young people refashioned the contemporary language and methods of the civil rights movement for their own purposes—calling for Red Power, for Indians of different tribes to come together. At a meeting at the San Francisco Indian Center, Richard McKenzie, a Sioux Indian activist, declared, "Kneel-Ins, Sit-Ins, Sleep-Ins, Eat-Ins, Pray-Ins like the Negroes do, wouldn't help us. We would have to occupy buildings before things would change."

And occupy buildings is exactly what they did. In the early morning of November 20, 1969, 89 Native Americans, 70 of whom were UCLA students, landed on Alcatraz Island in San Francisco Bay, the site of a federal penitentiary that had been closed since 1963. The previous month, a fire had claimed the San Francisco Indian Center and American Indian student groups and community activists saw the abandoned Alcatraz as a perfect place for a new center. Calling themselves Indians of All Tribes because they drew from a range of tribal backgrounds and experiences, the group claimed the island by "right of discovery" and by the terms of the 1868 Treaty of Fort Laramie, under which Indians were granted the right to unused federal property that had previously been Indian land. Their press statement read, "We, the native Americans, re-claim the land known as Alcatraz Island in the name of all American Indians . . . [W]e plan to develop on this island several Indian institutions:

1. A Center for Native American Studies . . . 2. An American Indian Spiritual Center . . . 3. An Indian Center of Ecology . . . 4. A Great Indian Training School [and] . . . an American Indian Museum." One of the group's de facto leaders, Richard Oakes, currently was enrolled in the country's first Native American studies programs at San Francisco State College. Indian businessman Adam Fortunate Eagle also played a pivotal role in the early occupation. In the ensuing months, many Indians from across the country joined the occupiers, creating a sense of community and Indian solidarity. Nineteen months later, with its forces dwindling, the occupation ended.

The takeover of Alcatraz and the extensive media coverage it received brought resisting Native Americans into public view. As writer Vine Deloria explained, "The Alcatraz news stories are somewhat shocking to non-Indians. It is difficult for most Americans to comprehend that there still exists a living community of nearly one million Indians in this country. For many people, Indians have become a species of movie action periodically dispatched to the Happy Hunting Grounds by John Wayne on the 'Late, Late Show.'" The consciousness-raising and radicalizing process of coming to Alcatraz prompted many Indian people to engage in a series of militant actions across the country. Short takeovers and militant disturbances took place at Fort Lawton in Washington, at Ellis Island, at an old army communications center in Davis, California, and at Plymouth Rock. On Thanksgiving Day, 1970, activists painted the rock red and proceeded to take over the replica of the Mayflower.

The most militant group to emerge in this period was the American Indian Movement (AIM). Founded in 1968 in Minneapolis by a group of urban Anishinabe (Chippewa), AIM initially organized around urban civil rights issues like police brutality and jobs because by 1960, about half of the eight hundred thousand Indians in the United States lived outside the reservations. In 1953, the Bureau of Indian Affairs had "terminated" thirteen Indian "groupings" under the Termination Act. Having lost title to formerly tribal lands, thousands of Native Americans were forced to relocate to urban centers. AIM was formed to address the dire economic and social situation of these Indians.

Two hundred Native activists convened a meeting during the summer of 1968 to plan a course of action. Founding member Dennis Banks explained, "[Native Americans] were tired of begging for welfare, tired of being scapegoats in America and decided to start building on the strengths of our own people; decided to build our own schools; our own job training programs and our own destiny." Within three years, AIM spread to several other cities beyond Minneapolis, and began to shift its focus to the reservations. One of the organization's early recruits was Russell Means, an Oglala born on the Pine Ridge Reservation. He described his reasons for joining AIM. "Never again would I seek personal approval from white society . . . I would get in the white man's face until he gave me and my people our just due." Means favored militant action to ensure equal rights to Indians. His tactics for shaming the federal government often captured media attention.

Although some activists at the time preferred the name Native Americans, Native Peoples, or First Peoples to the term Indian, others, like Means, preferred the political term Indian. These activists denied that the term Indian derived from Columbus's mistaken belief that he had reached the country of India and foregrounded the Spanish roots of Indian, *in dios*, which meant "of God." For them, calling oneself Indian as a unifying political identity did not negate an individual's tribal identity.

Indian activists focused on treaty violations. As Vine Deloria wrote in his widely read book *Custer Died for Your Sins* (1969), "America has yet to keep one Indian treaty or agreement despite the fact that the United States government signed over four hundred such treaties and agreements with Indian tribes." For example, under nineteenth-century treaties, tribes in the Pacific Northwest could fish in the "usual and accustomed" places, yet when Indians fished in the "accustomed" rivers, they were harassed, beaten, or jailed. And in 1964, the Washington state court closed the rivers to Indian fishing (despite the Supreme Court's legal affirmation of these treaties). To dramatize these treaty violations, in 1965, Native Americans held fish-ins on the Niswually River in Washington. In response, local and state police violently broke up the fish-ins, destroying boats, slashing nets, and beating up and arresting Indians, including women and children. Ramona Bennett, chair of the Puyallup nation, led many of these demonstrations and was teargassed and shot in the stomach while seven months pregnant. Finally, in 1974, the court ruled in favor of her people's right to half of the annual $200 million salmon catch.

At first these actions protesting treaty violations were conducted locally. In the fall of 1972, two thousand Indians from across the country decided to take a collective stand by organizing the Trail of Broken Treaties caravan to Washington, D.C. As Eddie Benton, an Ojibwa medicine man, explained, "There is a prophecy in our tribe's religion that one day we would all stand together. All tribes would hook arms in brotherhood and unite. I am elated because I lived to see this happen." They demanded that President Nixon endorse a 20-point program to change Indian-U.S. relations and reestablish a treaty-making relationship between the United States and Indian nations.

Angry at the government for reneging on its promise to help with logistics of the march (federal officials had also discouraged some local church groups from helping out) and frustrated with the inadequacy of their temporary housing in Washington, the group took over the Bureau of Indian Affairs (BIA) on November 2. This dramatic action was captured on the evening news when Russell Means held a press conference outside the BIA, carrying a makeshift war club and shield made from a portrait of Nixon. Mary Crow Dog explained, "It was on this occasion that I learned that as long as we 'behaved nicely' nobody gave a damn about us, but as soon as we became rowdy we got all the support and media coverage we could wish for." The takeover lasted a week, with protesters installing themselves in the building, caucusing amongst the various groups gathered, and meeting with outsiders. Ready to defend the building by force, they pushed furniture and poured gasoline on the doors, damaging fixtures and graffitiing walls. Damage was estimated at $2.2 million. The occupation ended when federal officials agreed to provide $66,000 in transportation money to help participants return home and to review and reply to the demands. The protesters left peacefully. Explaining that "Indians have every right to know the details of what's being done to us and to our property," they took with them thousands of BIA files and Indian artifacts. A number of Trail activists disagreed with this action, fearing the loss of these records and the damage it would do to the Indian cause. After the files were copied, many were returned to the BIA. On January 9, 1973, the Nixon administration announced its formal response to the Twenty Points, criticizing the November takeover and refusing to address any of the issues presented.

The most dramatic protest occurred on February 27, 1973. On the site of the 1890 massacre at Wounded Knee, South Dakota, about 300 Oglala Sioux, many of them AIM members, claimed the site for themselves to protest conditions on the Pine Ridge Reservation. Fifty-four percent of the adult males on the reservation were unemployed. The life expectancy of an Oglala Sioux was only 46 years. Many on the reservation thought that the leadership did not represent their interests but instead maintained its power with ample support from the BIA. The chairman of the Pine Ridge Reservation, Dick Wilson, was corrupt, and his brutal tactics had destroyed his support on the reservation and led people to demand his impeachment. Wilson blocked these efforts by making himself the head of the review council. The BIA continued to pour money into his administration, including financing the paramilitary Tribal Ranger group, Guardians of the Oglala Nation (GOONs).

A spate of violence against Pine Ridge residents and the lack of judicial redress catalyzed the February 27 takeover. Fearful of Wilson, members of the Pine Ridge Reservation, called on AIM for help. As Mary Crow Dog, who gave birth to her son during the siege, explained, "Wounded Knee was not the brainchild of wild, foaming-at-the-mouth militants, but of patient . . . traditional Sioux, mostly old Sioux ladies." Ellen Moves

AIM activists held Wounded Knee for 71 days.

Camp was one of the elders who invited AIM. "Most of the reservation believes in AIM and we're proud to have them with us. . . . It was mostly the women that went forward and spoke out."

Responding to the siege, more than 200 FBI, BIA, and federal marshals blockaded the town, allegedly on the grounds that Indian activists had taken hostages. Marshals burned all the ground cover around Wounded Knee to prevent supplies from being smuggled in, set up roadblocks, and fired at anyone trying to enter the encampment. But supporters continued to take risks. AIM activists walked miles at night to bring in supplies and arranged two airlifts into Wounded Knee to deliver necessities; the first dropped four hundred pounds of food and the second one ton of supplies. FBI agents arrested the pilot and copilot of the first mission; during the second airlift, a government helicopter shot and killed one man and wounded others gathering the food. On March 11, the occupiers proclaimed the new Independent Oglala Nation, announcing that they intended to send a delegation to the United Nations, and swore in 349 people as citizens. Spiritual leader Leonard Crow Dog affirmed the Independent Oglala Nation's inclusiveness, "We don't want to fight the white man, but only the white man's system."

The siege lasted 71 days, ending on May 7 with the arrests of 120 activists. While the government promised to hold hearings over the occupiers' demands, they reneged, claiming the right of "eminent domain" to negate Oglala claims at Wounded Knee. In the aftermath of Wounded Knee, Wilson's paramilitaries with the sanction of the FBI launched a campaign of repression and violence against Indian activists. The U.S. Commission on Civil Rights subsequently described this period as a "reign of terror" on Pine Ridge. More than 65 AIM members or supporters were killed on the reservation and 350 more assaulted. No one was convicted for any of these murders; the FBI used its resources to surveil activists rather than investigate the murders.

Federal prosecutors brought 185 indictments against Wounded Knee activists, tying up many AIM leaders in litigation for years. While the vast majority of the charges were dismissed or the people acquitted, these trials diverted AIM's organizing and financial resources to fighting these drawn-out legal battles.

"IT'S NATION TIME": INDEPENDENT ELECTORAL POLITICS

By the late 1960s, local political control had become a central goal of militant civil rights activists. Many blacks stepped up voter registration efforts in the North to begin to change the composition of city councils, state legislatures, and the mayors' offices. Recalling black antislavery conventions of the previous century, a black convention movement emerged to demand an independent political voice and real political autonomy for African Americans. Hundreds of meetings were held in the late 1960s, asserting that "It's Nation Time." In March 1972, nearly three thousand delegates and five thousand observers came to Gary, Indiana, for a national black political convention. By equating self-government with control of urban politics, they worked to elect black candidates into previously all-white city governments.

Prior to the late 1960s, no black had ever been elected mayor of a large city. The elections of Carl Stokes in Cleveland, Ohio, in 1967; Richard Hatcher in Gary, Indiana, in 1967; Tom Bradley in Los Angeles in 1973; and Coleman Young in Detroit, Michigan, in 1973 changed that. Many blacks believed that electing black leaders, particularly black mayors, would address discriminatory city financing, health and welfare, housing, and education, while promoting voter registration and political organization. This political movement intertwined local political control with larger political demands, in particular the payment of reparations to African Americans for slavery. In 1969, former executive director of SNCC James Forman took the pulpit at New York's Riverside Church to announce the Black Manifesto, which called on churches and synagogues to pay $500 million in reparations to blacks. "The Black Manifesto is the product of centuries of struggle by black people in an alien land. We will not relinquish our stake, the stake of our labor. With the Black Manifesto, we serve notice on white America and its 'Christian' churches."

The call for black political power, however, was too often a call for black male political power. Some African-American women would find little support for their attempts to open up the political arena. Shirley Chisholm was one of them. A Brooklyn schoolteacher, she became active in the Seventeenth Assembly District Democratic Club and soon realized that although women were the main fund-raisers for Democratic candidates, they were rarely the candidates. She was elected to the state assembly from Bedford Stuyvesant in 1964. With the slogan "Unbought and Unbossed" and a broad coalition of supporters, she defeated CORE's James Farmer to win election in 1968 to the newly formed Twelfth Congressional District seat in Brooklyn. She became the first black woman ever to be elected to the House of Representatives. "We will build a democratic America in spite of undemocratic Americans," she proclaimed. She held this seat for 14 years. In 1972, she became the first black to seek the presidential nomination of the Democratic party, receiving 150 delegate votes. An early member of NOW (National Organization for Women) and a founder of the National Women's Political Caucus and the Congressional Black Caucus, Chisholm received only lukewarm support from black male nationalists and white feminists.

The desire for independent political action surfaced in the Chicano community with the formation of La Raza Unida Party (LRUP) in 1970. LRUP's founding statement rejected "the existing political parties of our oppressors. [We] take it upon ourselves to form LA RAZA UNIDA PARTY which will serve as a unifying force in our struggle for self-determination. . . . [R]eal liberation and freedom will only come about through independent political action on our part." LRUP won a series of elections in Texas towns such as Crystal City and Kingsville but had less electoral success in California and Colorado.

RECLAIMING CULTURE

Black, Latino, and Native American nationalist movements of the late 1960s and early 1970s also reflected broader cultural goals, believing that people of color needed to change the ways they viewed themselves and the ways society portrayed them to gain true liberation. The mass media, schools, books, and popular film and television regularly conveyed demeaning images of people of color—when not totally ignoring the histories and cultures of nonwhite Americans. These representations influenced not only the way whites saw people of color but the ways people of color saw themselves. As Muhammad Ali observed, "They showed us a white Jesus. All the Last Supper is white. All the angels are white. Same with Miracle White. Tarzan, king of Africa, he's white. Angel food cake's white. Devil's food cake chocolate." This cultural emphasis was not uniformly supported within the black, Latino, and Native American communities, but nonetheless influenced how people of color began to view themselves and their histories.

For African Americans, one strand of this cultural movement was an explicit connection to Africa. From wearing dashikis to taking a new African name, many black people sought to reclaim their African ancestry. In January 1977, Alex Haley's miniseries *Roots* premiered on ABC television. Viewed by 130 million viewers over eight evenings, the miniseries attracted the largest television audience in history. Capturing nine Emmy Awards and a special Pulitzer Prize, *Roots* dramatized the story of Haley's ancestors taken from a village in the Gambia and enslaved over generations in the United States. The miniseries revived genealogical interest among whites as well as blacks, many of whom worked to trace their families' African ancestry.

For many Chicanos, reclaiming their cultural heritage meant speaking and learning in Spanish. Most schools discouraged speaking Spanish, and many Chicanos grew up having to disregard their cultural and linguistic roots. Demanding that education be inclusive of all Americans, Chicano activists advocated bilingual education. They produced art and literature in both English and Spanish, publicly celebrated Mexican holidays like Day of the Dead and saints like the Virgin of Guadalupe as well as American-born traditions like jazz and zoot suits.

One by-product of this cultural renaissance was the emergence of a Black Arts movement that strove to change public thought and culture. The Black Arts movement explicitly linked itself to working-class black people and to the radical political struggles of the time, in particular the Black Convention movement. In claiming that culture needed to be changed in order for society to be changed, black artists declared that art would aid in nation building. Born in 1934 in Newark, LeRoi Jones (who changed his name to Amiri Baraka) emerged as a beat poet in Greenwich Village. By the 1960s Baraka had become more African-centered in his art and his political organizing. For Baraka and many other artists at the time, art and culture were crucial sites of political struggle. The new ideas brought forth through revolutionary art would help build independent black power in many cities. The test for art was its political nature—whether art brought the community closer to revolution. This raised the question of what was real Black Art and what was not. These standards of blackness too often cast leadership and struggle in masculine terms.

Many black women challenged this gendered conception and the assumption that black women put aside their concerns for the benefit of the race. Already unhappy with the ways many feminist groups centered on white women's experiences, they objected as well to the ways many black groups focused on black men's needs. Angered by the ways women's issues were overshadowed, many women responded through writing. The early 1970s brought a wealth of black women's writings into the public domain. Maya Angelou published *I Know Why the Caged Bird Sings* (1970); Mari Evans, *I Am a Black Woman* (1970); Toni Morrison, *The Bluest Eye* (1971); and Toni Cade Bambara, *Gorilla, My Love* (1971). These works looked at issues of domestic violence, self-worth, beauty, and identity within the black community.

One of the most controversial and popular works was Ntozake Shange's play *For Colored Girls Who Have Considered Suicide/When the Rainbow Is Enuf.* First performed in 1974, it came to Broadway in 1976. Not since Lorraine Hansberry's play *A Raisin in the Sun,* had a play written by a black woman come to Broadway. Born in 1948 in New Jersey as Paulette Williams, Shange went to Barnard College for her undergraduate education and University of Southern California for her master's degree. She changed her name in 1971 to Ntozake Shange to reclaim an African identity. Influenced by black authors Ralph Ellison, Amiri Baraka, and Claude McKay, Shange criticized the silences in the African-American community around gender issues. Her discussion of rape and sexual harassment in *For Colored Girls* was attacked as hurtful to black men and the community at large. It also earned a 1977 Obie award and opened a space for other black women to speak, write, and perform about these issues.

Artist Faith Ringgold encountered similar pressures. She had attended City College in New York, where she trained in Western high art. Told when she tried to exhibit her own impressionistic work that, as a black woman, she could not possibly create good Western art, she retrained herself, reading extensively from black authors like James Baldwin and Amiri Baraka and studying various African art techniques. Her works *The Flag Is Bleeding, U.S. Postage Stamp Commemorating Black Power,* and *Flag for the Moon: Die Nigger,* along with murals and portrait masks of women from Harlem interwove criticisms of the U.S. treatment of blacks with a vision of women speaking out. Criticized by many whites as being political and by black male artists of being too soft and African-inspired, Ringgold challenged the racism and sexism imbedded in the art world and in the black community. As she explained, "In the 1970s, being black and a feminist was equivalent to being a traitor to the cause of black people." She helped organize a demonstration against the Whitney Museum of American Art for its failure to include black artists in an exhibit of art from the 1930s. On November 17, 1968, approximately thirty artists picketed the Whitney, calling for a show of African-American artists and an exhibit featuring Romare Bearden. Realizing that many of her male colleagues had gained professionally from these protests, Ringgold, Kay Brown, and Dinga McGannon helped organize a show of black women artists called "Where We At."

Cumulatively, these movements changed the contours of American politics and culture, cultivating pride, self-determination, and new meanings of democracy. The refusal to be silent—to hide cultural specificity and ethnic identification for fear of being castigated in a white-dominated world—was one of these movements' most powerful legacies. As AIM supporter Karen Baird-Olsen wrote, "AIM destroyed and/or seriously undermined dangerous prejudices about the First Peoples and provided new choices and alternate paths for Indians all across the country. American Indians were given an alternative to the pervasive image of the silent, apathetic, helpless, dumb, pagan Indian to emulate." Pablo Guzmán of the Young Lords continued, "Certainly the organization stamped everyone involved. In almost everything I do today . . . I am incorporating what I learned as a Young Lord." Bernice Johnson Reagon described how she had been empowered by the movement. "There was a sense of power, in a place where you didn't feel you had any power. . . . So you were saying in some basic way 'I will never again stay inside these boundaries.'"

Chapter 6

THE RISE OF DISSENT

The civil rights movement of the 1960s was a catalyst to the women's movement. Women's inequality, and the discriminatory effect of administrative and cultural biases, had not been major national priorities prior to the 1960s. Between 1940 and 1960, economic opportunities for women and the increase in the number of working women had improved, and barriers to women's admission to law, medical, and professional schools and into the business world had been breached. Women's organizations formed during the 1920s, the National Woman's Party and the Women's International League for Peace and Freedom, had also failed to attract young members. Their issues—enactment of a federal Equal Rights Amendment (ERA), ratification of the United Nations Covenant on Human Rights, curbs on the militarization of U.S. foreign policy, and denigration of the United Nations as an instrument for averting world conflict—commanded limited support. The formation in November 1961 of the Women's Strike for Peace to lobby for a treaty banning atmospheric testing of nuclear weapons highlighted women's roles as mothers. Questioned about their loyalty during hearings of the House Committee on Un-American Activities in 1962, women activists decried the adverse effect of nuclear testing on children.

By the end of the decade, however, women's rights had become a major national issue, and age-old discriminatory practices were curbed. Women activists effected these changes, symbolized by the formation first in 1966 of a nationwide organization that focused on women's issues, the National Organization for Women (NOW), and then the appearance of a less centralized, radicalized women's movement that demanded women's liberation. For militant feminists, gender equality would not be achieved solely by the end to discriminatory legal and administrative barriers; traditional conceptions of women's role and sexuality would have to be repudiated.

THE QUEST FOR EQUALITY

The political initiatives of the newly elected Kennedy administration brought some tentative advances in women's rights. On assuming office, President John F. Kennedy did not intend to end systemic practices limiting women's opportunities but to prohibit glaringly discriminatory practices. At the suggestion of Esther Peterson (his highest woman political appointee, who headed the Women's Bureau in the Department of Labor), Kennedy on December 14, 1961, created the President's Commission on the Status of Women. The commission was to investigate and offer recommendations to combat the "prejudices and outmoded customs [that] act as barriers to the full realization of women's basic rights." This limited mandate, and the individuals whom the president appointed, ensured that the commission would focus on promoting gender equality. The commission's report of October 1962, *American Women,* documented the glaring disparity in women's education and wages (most notably, that employed women earned 40 percent less than men) and identified the various laws that discriminate against women.

The report focused national attention on the status of women and on the reality of sexual discrimination. Creation of this presidential commission led to the appointment of state commissions on women that evolved into an informal network of women experts nationwide. Then, on November 1, 1963, President Kennedy established an Interdepartmental Committee on the Status of Women (a federal interagency task force to coordinate action on federal employment issues) and a Citizens' Advisory Council on the Status of Women to which he appointed 20 prominent private citizens. By 1971, these two presidentially appointed groups sponsored four national conferences attended by representatives from state commissions that in turn published a series of reports identifying practices that adversely affected women's rights.

In 1962, moreover, Kennedy reversed civil service policies dating from the 1880s where separate lists for male and female federal employees were compiled, a practice that served to bar women from high-level federal employment. In 1963, Kennedy successfully lobbied for passage of the Equal Pay Act, which became effective in June 1964 to prohibit paying women lower wages than men for the same job. Because federal wage laws did not cover executive, administrative, and professional appointments, the Equal Pay Act's impact was limited to the 61 percent of women employees holding low-level service, factory, and clerical jobs.

Kennedy's most important legislative initiative affecting women's rights was the by-product of congressional politicking around legislation prohibiting racial discrimination. When the legislation that became the Civil Rights Act of 1964 was undergoing committee review, conservative southern Democrat Howard Smith introduced an amendment to the proposed ban in Title 7 against discrimination based on "race, color, religion and national origin" to include the category of "sex." Smith hoped to sabotage the Civil Rights Bill, believing the addition of "sex" was so far-fetched that it would weaken support among the bill's liberal advocates. Congresswoman Martha Griffin enthusiastically endorsed the principle of the proposal on its merit, and succeeded in mobilizing sufficient support from liberals (the majority of whom had initially feared that the amendment would undermine the goal of banning racial discrimination) to ensure House approval of Smith's amendment by a vote of 168–133. Unwilling to complicate passage of a civil rights bill (already made difficult by the need to override a southern-led filibuster in the Senate), Senate proponents endorsed the amended House bill.

To monitor compliance with the act's guarantee of equal employment opportunities for all employees and job applicants, the act created an Equal Employment Opportunity Commission (EEOC). The newly appointed head of EEOC, Henry Edelsberg, publicly announced his intent not to enforce the sex discrimination clause, deeming its passage a "fluke" and declaring that he would not deny "female secretaries" to men. Edelsberg's position was not shared by other members of the commission. Indeed, during the EEOC's first year of operation, 25 percent of all complaints of employment discrimination came from women.

Concurrently, on September 24, 1965, President Lyndon Johnson, by Executive Order 11246, established an Office of Federal Contract Compliance to supervise and coordinate compliance of federal contracting agencies with the act's nondiscriminatory requirements. Under the president's order, all recipients of federal contracts (comprising one-half of the nation's workforce) must not discriminate in their employment practices and, further, must undertake affirmative action programs to rectify the effects of past discrimination. Johnson's order explicitly covered discrimination based on race, religion, and ethnicity. Responding to pressure from an emerging women's movement, on October 13, 1967, President Johnson issued Executive Order 11375 to bar explicit discrimination based on sex and to preclude sex discrimination in federal appointments.

President Richard Nixon extended this legislative ban on sexual discrimination. On January 14, 1969, the outgoing Johnson administration's Office on Federal Contract Compliance published proposed guidelines to combat discrimination. Fleshing out these requirements in February 1970, the Department of Labor required that all federal contracts include specific goals and timetables and called for an analysis of the racial composition of the workforce and applicants. Because the new guidelines did not specifically refer to sexual discrimination, women's rights activists immediately protested this omission. In response, Secretary of Labor James Hodgson announced that federal contracts would contain a clause mandating the employment of a specified quota of women. Then, in 1972, Congress enacted the Educational Act, Title IX of which prohibited sex discrimination in all federally funded educational programs. In addition, Congress expanded the jurisdiction of the U.S. Commission on Civil Rights (created under the 1957 Civil Rights Act) to include sex discrimination.

The various legislative and administrative changes combined to break down long-held barriers limiting women's social and economic opportunities. Title IX, for example, forced universities to initiate athletic programs for and provide athletic scholarships to women. These initiatives had a trickle-down effect, opening athletic opportunities for women at the high school and grade school levels. The quality of women's team sports improved dramatically (women had previously excelled in individual sports such as tennis, figure skating, swimming, golf, and track and field), leading to women's teams winning gold medals in soccer, softball, and basketball at the 1996 Olympics. More substantively, the number of college-educated women earning bachelor's degrees in business and management between 1971 and 1981 increased from less than 3 percent to 16 percent. In contrast, the number of women who majored in education (previously believed to be women's traditional role) during that decade declined from 36 percent to 17.5 percent. The opening up of the professions occurred across the board. The number of women earning professional degrees increased from 3 percent in 1960 to 24 percent in 1979. The number of women applying for admission to law school increased by 500 percent during the 1970s, while between 1970 and 1981 the number of women employed as lawyers and judges increased from 4.7 percent to 14 percent and as physicians from 8.9 percent to 13.8 percent.

THE RISE OF A FEMINIST MOVEMENT

Women had become more assertive of their rights, creating formal and informal networks to publicize their demands for gender equality. Women did not need commission studies or administrative rulings to learn of their second-class status, highlighted by their response to Betty Friedan's 1963 book, *The Feminine Mystique.*

In her seminal book, which sold more than one million copies, Friedan challenged the conception of women, promoted in the popular culture of the 1950s, as contented housewives and mothers. Early marriages and increased birthrates of the postwar years, the rise of suburbia and the resultant isolation of married women, and the invention of labor-saving appliances that ostensibly increased leisure time had not brought satisfaction to many middle-class women. Friedan's disparagement of the "feminine mystique" struck a responsive chord for them—showing that their frustration was a collective problem not a personal shortcoming—and underlay their overwhelming response to the announced decision in 1966 of the formation of NOW.

The early women's movement had also incubated in the civil rights movement. Like their male counterparts in the civil rights (SNCC) and radical student (SDS) movements, college-age women were attracted to organizations that promoted freedom and equality—to challenge racial discrimination and antidemocratic policies. Many women, black and white, had become skilled as organizers and, in the process, gained a new self-awareness. In time, with the radicalization of the civil rights and student movements, their adherents located the obstacle to freedom and democracy (whether racial discrimination in the South and urban North or U.S. involvement in the Vietnam War) as systemic, requiring the overthrow of a corporate-dominated capitalist society.

Women had taken leadership roles in civil rights and antiwar organizing. On November 1, 1961, fifty thousand women in over sixty cities walked out of their homes in a housewives' strike against nuclear testing. The five women behind the organization of the November strike called themselves Women Strike for Peace. They would grow into one of the strongest early voices against the war. In January 15, 1968, Women Strike for Peace helped organize an all-women demonstration against the war called the Jeanette Rankin Brigade. Named after Congresswoman Jeanette Rankin, who had voted against America's entry into both world wars, their goal was to bring thousands of women to Washington to petition Congress calling for an immediate withdrawal of American troops from Vietnam. New York Radical Women joined the protest, adding their own militant twist on the proceedings. Holding a Burial of Traditional Womanhood in Arlington Cemetery, they protested the war not as peaceful mothers but as militant feminists. Even though none of the speeches at the Jeannette Rankin Brigade spoke to women as mothers, the split between older and younger feminists was pronounced.

As part of their own reassessment of the systemic source of inequality and injustice, women activists in the civil rights, antiwar, and radical student movements became sensitive to issues of gender oppression and demanded that these organizations address women's issues. At a

November 1964 SNCC meeting, two white women, Mary King and Casey Hayden, presented an anonymous position paper on the treatment of women in SNCC. Mary King explained, "We who had come to grips with death, we were afraid of what our fellow SNCC staff members were going to say when they read this paper about women." The paper and the issue of gender inequalities within the organization, at the time, commanded little consideration. A year later, seeking "to define our own freedom" and using the ideas of democratic organizing they had learned from Ella Baker and SNCC, King and Hayden revised this paper, signed it, and sent it to forty activist women around the country. Many responded enthusiastically, and their memorandum was published the next year in the magazine *Liberation.*

Responding to King's and Hayden's anonymous paper, SNCC leader Stokely Carmichael poked fun at his own and other SNCC males' misogynist attitudes, joking that "the only position for women in SNCC is prone." As the joke was repeated, Carmichael's remark took on a more dismissive nature. It reflected a conviction of many civil rights activists that the movement should confine its focus to issues of race and captured a sentiment held by many male leaders that men should be assigned leadership roles and women traditional housekeeping, secretarial, and sexual functions within SNCC.

This experience recurred within the radical student movement. In time, radical female students demanded that organizations like SDS move beyond working to end corporate dominance and address the oppression of women. They encountered indifference, at times hostility from their male counterparts. These differences came to the fore at the National Conference on New Politics, convened in Chicago in August 1967 to consider the launching of a national radical party. After women activists had reached an agreement with the conference's organizers to set aside time for a floor debate on their resolution on women's issues, the presiding officer refused to recognize the women standing at microphones prepared to initiate the discussion. In a particularly galling action, he patted one of the women on the head and told her, "Cool down little girl, we have more important things to talk about than woman's problems."

Questions about the Johnson administration's commitment to enforce the 1964 Civil Rights Act's ban against sex discrimination provided the catalyst to forming a national, action-oriented women's civil rights organization. At a 1965 national conference of state commissions on the status of women, the attendees were told that the presidentially established council could not ensure the enforcement of the sex discrimination ban. By then, an informal national network of women activists had evolved, committed to evaluate and recommend changes to challenge sex discrimination. It was a natural step for this informal network to create a formal organization. Adopting the direct action model of the racial justice community, many women concluded that only through a national lobbying organization could women achieve the political voice to secure equal rights for women. NOW's formation triggered an overwhelming response. Between 1967 and 1974, NOW grew from a national organization with 14 chapters and a membership of 1,000 to 700 chapters and 40,000 members.

This grassroots response confirmed a heightened interest in and commitment to women's issues. Between 1965 and 1975, for example, the number of women's studies courses offered by the nation's colleges increased from 100 to over 15,000, and the number of women's studies programs from 270 to 1,500. This interest also shaped the meteoric success of the national women's magazine *Ms.*

Ms. began in December 1971 as a special section of *New York* magazine devoted to women's issues. The positive response led to the one-time publication in January 1972 of an independent issue. With articles ranging from "The Housewife's Moment of Truth" to "Women Tell the Truth about Their Abortions" to "Welfare Is a Woman's Issue," this issue sold over 250,000 copies within eight days at newsstands nationwide. This response led to the formal launching in April 1972 of *Ms.*, a magazine for, by, and about women. The newsletter of the Women Action Center, *Ms.* was edited by Gloria Steinem, an activist journalist who had opposed the Vietnam War and supported the United Farm Workers. By 1973, *Ms.* was self-supporting, commanding a subscription base of 200,000 and having a long list of advertisers.

Although the readership of *Ms.* and the membership of NOW were predominantly white, middle-class housewives and professional women, women's rights commanded broader support. Women across racial lines differed in their views of the goals and issues of women's liberation. For instance, Friedan's description of "the problem with no name" (the stultifying isolation of staying home and caring for their own children) was not a pressing issue for many women of color and working-class white women who had never had the option to stay home and care for their children. Pay equity, child care, and welfare rights were more pressing issues for them. Many women of color also resented the ways white women appealed to a common sisterhood without acknowledging how race and racial privilege fractured such bonds. Black women sometimes chose to raise gender issues in black organizations and at other times joined organizations with white women. Nonetheless, black women consistently supported the goals of the women's movement more heartily than did white women—by a factor of two to one. Raising gender issues within the Black Panthers, the Young Lords, and the Chicano movement, women of color sought to address the double jeopardy of being nonwhite and female. In

1973, black women founded the National Black Feminist Organization, and in 1974, a group of black lesbians broke away from the National Black Feminist Organization to form the Combahee River Collective.

Women's experiences in the civil rights movement, radical student movements, and even the early women's movement led many activists to challenge the premise that attacking discrimination only required the passage and enforcement of new laws. To many women activists, male chauvinism and a patriarchal family system that treated women as inferior and as sex objects were another source of women's inequality and required changes in popular attitudes about women. Kate Millett's 1970 book *Sexual Politics* promoted this awareness by challenging cultural myths about female sexuality, identifying sexism as the source of women's inequality, and urging women to recognize their unique identities.

This demand for women's liberation did not lead to a cohesive nationwide feminist organization but to a series of ad hoc, locally based groups—Redstockings, WITCH (Women's International Terrorist Conspiracy from Hell), Radical Women, the Jeannette Rankin Brigade. Many younger activists, who criticized NOW's focus on legislative solutions (particularly when there seemed to be little public will to enforce the new laws), believed that women could only come into their own politically apart from men. They held consciousness-raising meetings and conferences, attempting to break the silence around issues facing women—such as domestic violence, rape, and abortion. Such consciousness-raising had a profound effect. Between 1968 and 1972, public support for abortion increased from 15 percent to 64 percent, and services for battered women and rape victims were established.

Despite their limited numbers and lack of a national organization, radical feminists' direct action tactics commanded media attention. Invariably negative, this coverage portrayed militant feminists as sex-obsessed and irrational. One such example, which led to the popular stereotype of feminists as bra burners, involved the widespread publicity given to a demonstration organized by young feminists at the 1968 Miss America pageant in Atlantic City. In a strategy to command attention, the women activists had set up a Freedom Trash Can (inviting women to discard items of women's oppression: bras, girdles, high-heeled shoes, false eyelashes) and crowned a sheep Miss America. In accordance with the request of the Atlantic City police, the trash can was never set on fire, but feminists from then on were dismissively labeled bra burners—trivializing the movement. The protest was intended to highlight how certain standards of beauty became the measure by which a woman's worth was defined over intelligence, creativity, and commitment; the racism of the contest; and how the position of Miss America was used to support the Vietnam War and consumerism at home.

Women protested the Miss America Pageant.

Radical women used guerrilla theater and direct action to dramatize other issues as well. WITCH protested a bridal fair at Madison Square Garden by carrying signs reading "Always a Bride, Never a Person" and "Here Comes the Bribe." Dressed as witches, they showed up at the New York Stock Exchange to put a hex on the proceedings. They protested the firing of a feminist professor, Marlene Dixon, by the University of Chicago and attacked the United Fruit Company for its policies in Central America and its treatment of women clerical workers. In New York, a group of women held an Ogle-In, heckling, whistling, and loudly describing the physiques of the passing men to dramatize how women were regularly harassed when walking on the street. At the University of California, women invaded the men's locker room chanting and banging pots and pans, demanding weight-training and self-defense classes. Feminists protested at magazines from *Newsweek* to *Ladies Home Journal* and took over radio station KPFA to demand the hiring of more female journalists and more programming about women. By the early 1970s, women's groups had formed in countless towns and cities across the country to deal with issues ranging from sex discrimination on the job to gender-neutral curriculum in public schools to day care and other support services for women.

A Conservative Backlash

As civil rights activists shifted from nonviolence to black power, as anti-war activists adopted confrontational tactics to shut down the Pentagon and stop troop movements, as students challenged conventional morality about extramarital sex, use of drugs, and dress style, radical feminists challenged traditional conceptions of women's identity and sexuality. The militancy of these equal rights groups provoked a powerful backlash. As in the case of the civil rights movement, in the early and mid 1960s women activists at first commanded support for proposals to ensure elemental rights and to remove discriminatory barriers to equal rights. This rights consensus did not mean that a majority of Americans endorsed the principle of gender (or racial) equality. Nor had a national consensus emerged to support any proposed ameliorative change. The limits of this consensus soon became clear when many Americans questioned whether the changes in women's status had gone too far and whether tactics of mass demonstrations had created an atmosphere of permissiveness that ensured disorder and anarchy. The decade of the 1960s ended with a debate over the need to preserve traditional values and civic morality. Still, despite this resistance to the militancy of women activists, public ideas about gender roles and women's rights had been reshaped.

The history of the Equal Rights Amendment highlights this reversal. First introduced in 1923 by the National Woman's Party, this proposed amendment to the U.S. Constitution—"Equality of rights under law shall not be denied or abridged by the United States or by any State on account of sex"—had languished until the 1970s. An amendment to bar any form of federal or state discrimination was no longer controversial in the rights-oriented atmosphere of the 1960s and received well more than the required two-thirds support: 354–23 in the House in October 1971 and 84–8 in the Senate in March 1972. Within ten days of Senate passage, 6 states ratified the amendment, another 22 states did so before the end of the year, and another 8 followed in 1973. By the 1978 deadline for ratification, however, only 35 of the needed 38 states had ratified the amendment. Congress subsequently extended the deadline to June 30, 1982, but no additional state voted in favor of ratification.

The Equal Rights Amendment fell victim to a new cultural conservatism invigorated by the abortion issue. Abortion rights emerged as a major concern for activist women during the 1960s. Reflecting the new sensitivity to women's rights, between 1967 and 1971 17 states revised their laws governing abortions. Between 1968 and 1972, moreover, public support for liberalizing abortion laws increased from 15 percent to 64 percent.

Then in January 1973, the Supreme Court, in *Roe v. Wade,* struck down a Texas law prohibiting abortion as an unconstitutional violation of a woman's privacy rights. In his majority opinion, Justice Harry Blackmun ruled that the right to privacy included a woman's right to an abortion in consultation with her physician. Blackmun did not find the right to an abortion to be absolute, dividing the term of a pregnancy into three trimesters, with the state's right to protect the fetus increasing as the pregnancy advanced.

Denouncing the Court's ruling in *Roe v. Wade,* a militant antiabortion movement grew to include many who had heretofore not actively opposed the changes in women's status instituted during the 1960s. Opposition to abortion became part of a broader New Right religious movement, one that reshaped the politics of the 1970s, 1980s, and 1990s. This New Right movement condemned the Court's decision as state-sanctioned murder and increasingly questioned the consequences of the changes in women's status. Endorsing traditional conceptions of women as mother and housewife, New Right activists decried the radical individualism of the women's rights movement as subverting social responsibility and the legitimate communitarian interests of the broader society.

Phyllis Schlafly championed this position when founding a new national organization in October 1973, Stop ERA, to rally opposition to ratification of the Equal Rights Amendment. Two years later, in 1975, Schlafly formed the Eagle Forum (adopting the national symbol of the eagle to convey the defense of traditional values) to challenge the broader influence of the women's rights movement. Her core message was that the quest for equality threatened to undermine traditional American values. The growth and militancy of antifeminist movements, however, were not alone responsible for the defeat of the Equal Rights Amendment or the broader national reassessment that evolved. At best, the early 1960s had only led to a new consensus supportive of the principle of antidiscrimination but not gender equality. The nation remained divided over the role the federal government should play in promoting gender equity.

GAY RIGHTS: A NEW CONSENSUS

A politics of civil rights provided an important impetus to the women's rights movement; in contrast, a politics of civil liberties proved to be more important to changing the status of gays and lesbians. Homosexual activists encountered seemingly insurmountable barriers in their quest to end discrimination. Homosexuality was uncritically perceived to be sinful; homosexuals were seen as abnormal and mentally diseased; and, consistent with these widely held beliefs, homosexual activities were criminalized. Literature about homosexuality could be seized under federal and state antiobscenity laws, and antisodomy laws were enacted by all 50 states and the District of Columbia. Finally, given prevailing moral and security concerns, coming out as gay or lesbian invited ostracism and the loss of employment. Creation of a national organization to lobby for an end to discrimination against gays and lesbians would at minimum require so-called closeted homosexuals to reveal their sexual orientation and join organizations promoting homosexual rights. These barriers explain the small membership, in 1960, of the Mattachine Society and the Daughters of Bilitis—230 and 100 respectively.

Attitudes toward homosexual activism became less hostile during the 1960s and 1970s. In 1961, the American Law Institute published its model penal code which included eliminating antisodomy statutes. Decriminalizing homosexual activities remained controversial—indeed, only two states (Illinois in 1961 and Connecticut in 1969) adopted the model code in its entirety, while opposition of the Catholic Church hierarchy in New York led to the overwhelming defeat of a proposal to repeal that state's antisodomy statute. The institute's recommendation, however, changed the debate over laws governing private consensual sexual activities. Between 1962 and 1986 (the date of the Supreme Court's ruling in *Bowers v. Hardwick*), nearly half the states repealed their antisodomy statutes by legislation or executive order. Antisodomy laws, moreover, were rarely enforced and were primarily of symbolic value (for religious conservatives in upholding the immorality of homosexuality; for homosexual activists in symbolizing their second-class status).

Simultaneously, the American Civil Liberties Union (ACLU), the nation's premier civil liberties organization, reversed its earlier position that homosexuality could be criminalized. The ACLU affirmed instead, in 1967, that the constitutional right to privacy protected sexual activities between consenting adults. Abandoning another earlier position, the ACLU opposed as a violation of due process the federal employment policy of automatically barring homosexuals. Then, in 1973, the ACLU created the Sexual Privacy Project to fight discrimination against gays and lesbians.

Tolerance for homosexuality extended beyond the civil liberties community. In 1969, the American Sociological Association adopted a resolution opposing all forms of discrimination, including discrimination against homosexuals. In 1970, the National Association for Mental Health endorsed the decriminalization of homosexual activities. Most importantly, the American Psychiatric Association Council voted in 1973 to remove homosexuality from its *Diagnostic and Statistical Manual*, its official listing of mental disorders, in effect challenging the science that homosexuality was a mental disease. Indeed, the Department of Defense had cited the *Manual*'s listing when denying security clearances to homosexuals. Conservative members of the association immediately demanded a referendum, conducted in 1974, of the members. The council's decision won overwhelming support, with 58 percent favoring deletion and 37 percent retention.

A series of Supreme Court obscenity case rulings also paved the way for a public debate over gay rights by restricting the censorship of sexually offensive speech. In *Roth v. U.S.* (1957), the Court upheld the conviction of publisher Stanley Roth on obscenity charges, but required that convictions establish the fact that the offensive material "taken as a whole appeals to prurient interest." The Court extended this limitation on the enforcement of obscenity statutes in *Memoirs v. Massachusetts* (1967), when overturning the suppression of the classic *Fanny Hill*. Writing for the majority, Justice William Brennan held that a book "cannot be proscribed unless it is found to be *utterly* without redeeming social value." The Court's civil libertarian rulings extended to homosexual publications. In January 1953, the Mattachine Society began publication of a journal, *One,* intended to promote awareness and support for gay rights. The post office immediately barred this journal's distribution as violating federal obscenity laws. The Court in 1958 ruled that this ban violated First Amendment rights.

These changes emboldened people like Frank Kameny, a former federal employee fired because of his sexual orientation, to oppose publicly the dismissal of homosexual federal employees and demand respect for the rights of gay people. This assertiveness revived interest in the Mattachine Society and the Daughters of Bilitis, leading to an increase in the number of members and chapters by the late 1960s. Capitalizing on the rights atmosphere of the 1960s, gay activists demanded that they be treated no differently than other individuals. In 1968, a new journal, the *Advocate,* promoted this growing militancy, while the Mattachine Society and the Daughters of Bilitis abandoned their earlier more cautious stance to challenge homophobic attitudes and demand greater tolerance for homosexuality.

The new boldness culminated at the Stonewall Inn in Greenwich Village on June 27, 1969. That night, New York police raided a well-known gay bar to arrest its patrons for violating local antihomosexual ordinances. This raid was not atypical; New York police routinely shut down, temporarily, gay and lesbian bars, having raided five gay bars in the three weeks prior to Stonewall. On this night, however, the patrons of the Stonewall Inn—most of whom were working-class gay men, including many people of color and a number of drag queens—did not surrender quietly to avoid public exposure. Instead they fought back, and the bar was burned down.

More than four hundred police officers were eventually called in to contain a riot that extended beyond the bar's patrons to involve two thousand individuals. Although police raided gay bars in the immediate aftermath of Stonewall, the Stonewall riot brought to an end open police harassment of gay and lesbian establishments in New York City.

GAY LIBERATION

The gay community's response to the Stonewall raid marked a shift in the attitudes of gays and lesbians, reflected in the formation of a militant gay organization appropriately named the Gay Liberation Front (GLF), and within a year, a second was formed, the Gay Activist Alliance. Abandoning the caution of the leaders of the Mattachine Society, the GLF's organizers sought to motivate gay people to disclose their sexual orientation publicly and to insist on respect for their right to equal treatment. Part of this process was reclaiming the word *gay* itself. Just as activists had reclaimed the terms *Chicano* and *black* to denote a sense of militancy and pride, so gay and lesbian activists reclaimed the words *gay* and *queer* to signify their openness and pride in their identity. In 1971, the first Gay Liberation National Conference was held in Austin, Texas, attended by more than three hundred activists from 20 cities, to discuss the oppression of homosexuals. Soon after the formation of the Gay Liberation Front, lesbians, who had grown angry at the homophobia of many feminist groups and the sexism of many gay groups, formed a women's caucus that soon became the Radicalesbians. Stonewall, moreover, became a revered anniversary and was the occasion for annual parades at which participants willingly revealed their sexual orientation. In the first such anniversary parade, one thousand to three thousand persons marched through New York City's Central Park, with similar parades (commanding hundreds) in Chicago and Los Angeles. The anniversary, unofficially known as Gay Pride Day, was thereafter commemorated on the last Saturday in June, with marches and rallies held across the nation.

By 1973, many gays and lesbians had asserted a new public voice. That year also marked the formation of Dignity, a national organization established to give comfort and voice to gay Catholics. Nonetheless, the premise that public policy should be changed to foreclose discrimination based on sexual orientation commanded limited public support. The principal changes of the 1960s, then, were greater public acceptance of the right to privacy, a new visibility of gay and lesbian people, and the lifting of bans on the dissemination of literature about homosexuality.

A New Politics of Civil Liberties

The changed status of homosexuals highlights the symbiotic relationship of civil liberties and civil rights. The Supreme Court's rulings in the *Brown* case (striking down racial segregation) and in the *Yates* case (curbing federal prosecution of radicals) shared in common the principle that unpopular minorities should be free of majoritarian restraint.

Roe v. Wade affirmed this limitation on state police powers and endorsement of privacy rights. The Court removed the state's ability to control women's bodies, allowing women to decide to end an unwanted pregnancy in consultation with a doctor. Earlier Supreme Court rulings, notably in *Poe v. Ullman* (1961) and *Griswold v. Connecticut* (1964), affirmed this limitation on state control. In *Poe,* Justice John Harlan argued that legislation against contraception was "an intolerable and unjustifiable invasion of privacy in the conduct of the most intimate concerns of an individual's personal life." Then, in *Mapp v. Ohio* (1961) and *Miranda v. Arizona* (1966), the Court prohibited the use of evidence obtained through a warrantless search and required state police to advise suspects of their right to counsel and to remain silent during police interrogations. At the same time, the Court also affirmed certain positive rights. In *Gideon v. Wainwright,* the Court guaranteed the poor a public defense and in *Escobar v. Illinois* granted defendants the right to a lawyer during questioning. Last, in *Berger v. New York* (1966) and *Katz v. U.S.* (1967) the Court required warrants as a condition for state and federal wiretapping.

Wiretapping and Bugging Policy: Privacy Rights

The Court's balancing of individual liberties and security considerations reflected a new public commitment to civil liberties. During the early 1960s, these new priorities prompted changes in Justice Department electronic surveillance policy instituted under Attorneys General Nicholas Katzenbach and Ramsey Clark.

In contrast to their predecessors, Katzenbach and Clark limited FBI wiretapping and bugging practices. On March 30, 1965, Attorney General Katzenbach required the attorney general's prior approval for each FBI tap and bug and limited such authorization to a six-month period (after which reauthorization must be sought). Katzenbach further required the listing of all individuals whose conversations had been intercepted by FBI taps or bugs in a special index. Attorney General Ramsey Clark extended these administrative restrictions on June 16, 1967, to ensure that all authorized taps and bugs not be used in an illegal manner and "that even legal use . . . be strictly controlled." Under Clark's guide-lines, all FBI requests (initial and then reauthorization) had to be sub-mitted in writing, specify why less intrusive techniques could not be used, and the value of the expected information.

Katzenbach's and Clark's administrative rules had direct and indirect civil liberties consequences. Tighter oversight and record keeping requirements significantly reduced the number of such installations: FBI national security wiretaps declined from highs of 519 in 1945, 322 in 1954, and 244 in 1963 to 82 in 1968, whereas FBI bugs declined from a high of 102 in 1955 to 0 in 1967 and 9 in 1968. The attorneys general's stricter rules and decisions to advise the courts of such installations also precipitated a bitter internal conflict between FBI and Justice Depart-ment officials.

Frustrated by the attorneys general's civil liberties priorities, FBI offi-cials in 1966 privately complained that Justice Department officials were willing to disclose to the press and the courts "the existence of micro-phones [bugs] regardless of whether or not this coverage had any bear-ing on the case under consideration." Because of this "propensity," FBI officials decided not to advise Justice Department officials of the extent of their bugging practices, concluding that this would "result only in the Department running to the courts with resultant adverse publicity to the Bureau which could give rise in the present climate to a demand for a Congressional inquiry of the Bureau." FBI officials decided to advise Jus-tice Department officials of bugging practices only "where prosecution is imminent." During the period 1960 through 1966, department officials were advised of only 158 of the FBI's 738 bugging installations.

FBI officials' concern about adverse publicity dovetailed with a change in both press and congressional interest in governmental wire-tapping practices. More sensitive to privacy rights, reporters closely mon-itored court cases and congressional hearings in which FBI wiretapping and bugging practices were revealed. FBI officials became particularly alarmed by a 1965 decision to initiate hearings into federal surveillance tactics. In preparing for public hearings, the Long Subcommittee demanded that all federal intelligence agencies specify the extent of their use of wiretaps, bugs, mail opening, and the records practices they adopted governing use of and access to this intercepted information.

Had FBI officials truthfully answered the subcommittee's questions, they would have exposed the extent of such FBI uses and the special records procedures (Do Not File, June Mail) that had been devised to avert discovery of recognizably "clearly illegal" practices. When instituting these separate records procedures in the early 1940s, FBI officials sought to ensure that records documenting their approval of illegal investigative techniques could be safely destroyed and thus would not be vulnerable to court-ordered discovery motions or congressional subpoenas (because technically not maintained in the FBI's central records system).

Then, in 1971, another subcommittee of the Senate Judiciary Committee, chaired by North Carolina Senator Sam Ervin, initiated a broader inquiry into the impact of data banks and computers on the Bill of Rights. In the course of this investigation, the Ervin Subcommittee publicized the illegal surveillance practices employed by military intelligence agents during the 1960s to monitor civil rights and anti–Vietnam War activists. (Military surveillance of domestic groups had been banned by the Posse Comitatus Act of 1878.) Although the Ervin Subcommittee did not examine FBI surveillance activities, FBI officials became concerned that the subcommittee might do so in the future. Indeed, these hearings into how technology and national security claims affected First Amendment rights previewed a later investigation, also headed by Senator Ervin, into the so-called Watergate Affair. Combined these hearings were a catalyst to the enactment of two legislative initiatives in 1974: the Privacy Act and key amendments to the 1966 Freedom of Information Act.

FBI Director Hoover responded to the attorneys general's administrative rules and Congress's belated willingness to examine surveillance practices by reassessing FBI procedures. Hoover feared both that adverse publicity might lead to an intensive congressional inquiry into FBI practices and that the FBI could no longer rely on the unquestioned support of the attorney general. Accordingly, in a series of secret orders of 1965 and 1966, the FBI director imposed numerical ceilings on FBI wiretaps and bugs; prohibited the continued resort to break-ins, mail opening, and trash covers (rummaging through the garbage of a targeted individual or organization); and raised the minimum age of recruited FBI informers from 18 to 21 (to decrease the possibility that an immature college recruit might expose the FBI's monitoring of student activists).

THE CRISIS OF "LAW AND ORDER"

This politics of civil liberties, however, soon gave rise to a politics of "law and order." The outbreak of urban race riots, the emergence of militant black leaders advocating black power and revolutionary change, the onset of violent anti–Vietnam War demonstrations combined with radical student activists' condemnation of conventional morality and advocacy of revolutionary change precipitated a counterreaction. The Supreme Court's rulings limiting police powers further heightened public fears about crime. The nation seemed on the verge of disintegration as radical students pledged to disrupt the Democratic National Convention in Chicago, and in the aftermath of Martin Luther King's assassination in

April, race riots broke out in more than a hundred cities. Attorney General Clark intensified these anxieties when he rebuked Chicago Mayor Richard Daley for his remark (that future riots could be averted if police were allowed to shoot looters), counseling against "loose talk of shooting looters."

In the crisis atmosphere of the time, Clark's reasoned comment proved to be impolitic. His antipathy toward the use of excessive force seemed to confirm an unwillingness to reestablish order. Capitalizing on public fear over the breakdown of law and order, Republican presidential candidate Richard Nixon won election in 1968 in part by charging that oversensitivity toward the rights of lawbreakers undermined the rights of law-abiding citizens. In his acceptance speech at the Republican National Convention, Nixon personalized the issue: "If we are to restore order and respect for law in this country, there's one place we're going to begin: we're going to have a new Attorney General of the United States of America." Further claiming that the Supreme Court's civil liberties rulings advanced the rights of criminals at the expense of hardworking, loyal Americans, Nixon promised to appoint strict constructionist justices to the Supreme Court.

Law and order fears provoked a major change in public policy. Consistently throughout the twentieth century, conservative southern Democrats and Republicans had opposed the expansion of federal regulatory powers as intruding on states rights. These concerns also fueled a belief that local and state police should be responsible for law enforcement. By the late 1960s, conservatives abandoned states rights principles to support an increased federal role in law enforcement.

One immediate result was passage in 1968 of the Omnibus Crime Control and Safe Streets Act. That act provided federal financial and training assistance to local and state police, made it a federal crime to cross state lines to engage in or promote a riot, and legalized the use of wiretaps and bugs during criminal investigations. Congress, however, sought to limit the potential for abuse when rescinding the ban of the 1934 Communications Act against wiretapping by requiring federal agents to obtain a prior court warrant for each wiretap and bug. Proponents of this legislation, reflecting still-prevalent national security concerns (that subversive influences shaped radical activities), affirmed that the warrant requirement not impair president's "inherent" powers to safeguard the nation's security. The statutory language, however, did not define whether such "national security" powers extended to domestic critics of internal security measures or of the president's foreign policy.

Richard Nixon's election to the presidency on a "law and order" platform ensured an extensive and unilateral use of this undefined authority. The Nixon administration moved quickly to prosecute radical anti–Vietnam War activists under a provision of the 1968 act that made it a federal crime for individuals to cross state lines to promote unrest or riot. Justice Department officials unilaterally authorized FBI wiretapping of these activists. Use of wiretap evidence during the ensuing trial precipitated an appeal that challenged whether the president had inherent power to authorize warrantless wiretaps. In June 1972, in *U.S. v. U.S. District Court*, the Supreme Court denied that the president could order warrantless wiretaps during "domestic security" investigations.

FEDERAL SURVEILLANCE: A NEW SKEPTICISM

The Supreme Court's 1972 ruling did not directly challenge Cold War federal surveillance practices. This rebuff to executive wiretapping practices was exceptional, the consequence of a decision to employ wiretaps during an investigation that resulted in prosecution (a situation purposefully avoided by previous presidents and their attorneys general). The court's ruling, moreover, did not address a far more serious civil liberties problem: namely, that the FBI monitored individuals (using taps and bugs) not to prosecute them but to contain their influence.

By the 1960s, FBI investigations were not confined to law enforcement but also collected what was euphemistically termed *intelligence*—that is, information about the noncriminal personal and political activities of a broad range of individuals and organizations. Such investigations, at first, were intended to inform executive officials about the plans of targeted individuals and organizations (ranging from the conservative America First party to the radical German American Bund and U.S. Communist Party). FBI agents also monitored the radical press, critics of the bureau, and private citizens (including prominent personalities like First Lady Eleanor Roosevelt and popular singer Frank Sinatra). FBI intelligence investigations exploded during the early Cold War era and much of the acquired information was covertly disseminated to conservative reporters and members of Congress in order to contain the influence of individuals and organizations deemed subversive. During the 1960s these containment efforts were intensified in response to the upsurge of the civil rights, student, and anti–Vietnam War movements.

For one, FBI officials expanded COINTELPRO, formerly directed only at the Communist party, to civil rights, student, and antiwar activists. Specific programs were instituted against the Trotskyite Socialist Workers party (in 1961), white supremacist organizations like the Ku Klux Klan (in 1964), militant black power organizations like the Black Panther party (in 1965), and New Left student organizations like the Students for a Democratic Society and the Weathermen (in 1968). These containment objectives were predicated not on these groups' actual influence but future potential. Indeed, FBI Director Hoover rationalized the need to institute the COINTELPRO–Socialist Workers Party in 1961 to discredit this revolutionary group for promoting "its line on a local and national basis through running candidates for public office and strongly directing and/or supporting such causes as Castro's Cuba and integration problems arising in the South."

The major tactics employed under these so-called COINTELPROs included mailing anonymous letters to provoke factionalism within the targeted organization or to divert the attention of key leaders (such as writing to wives that their husbands were having an affair or to the parents of student activists that their son/daughter was experimenting with drugs or engaging in illicit sex). FBI agents also leaked derogatory information to reporters and columnists to ensure the publication of unfavorable news stories about the personal morality or political objectives of these activists.

This disruptive purpose underlay the response of FBI officials to the 1964 congressional debate over the Johnson administration's proposed Civil Rights Bill. FBI Director Hoover ordered FBI officials to summarize all the information that agents had collected about subversive influence on the civil rights movement. His stated premise for preparing these summaries was that because civil rights had become "the primary domestic issue on the political front today," the FBI should be in a position to provide "both sides" of the debate with "proper presentation of the facts" about "communist penetration."

This covert political containment effort failed to avert congressional passage of the Civil Rights Act of 1964. FBI officials next sought to contain the growing national prominence of Martin Luther King Jr. by launching a multifaceted campaign to discredit a man whom they considered "the most dangerous and effective Negro leader in this country." FBI agents were pressured to develop evidence to expose King "for the clerical fraud and Marxist he is." (The FBI was never able to document that King was a Communist Party member or had acted under the influence of Communists.) FBI officials concurrently sought to identify "a more manageable black leader" to replace King.

FBI interest in King dated from the Montgomery bus boycott. As King's national and international influence increased, so too did the intensity of FBI surveillance and containment efforts. FBI officials deemed suspicious King's close association with radical activists, his strategy of civil disobedience when challenging racial segregation, and his questioning of the FBI's professionalism and commitment to enforce the nation's civil rights laws. In October 1963, FBI Director Hoover successfully pressured Attorney General Robert Kennedy to authorize a wiretap of King and then, on his own, directed agents to bug King's motel rooms and meeting places as the civil rights leader traversed the country to rally support for ending racial segregation.

Already troubled by King's civil rights activities and associations with radical activists, the moralistic FBI director was appalled by the information developed by these bugs—both King's political strategy and plans and his "immoral conduct." The FBI director sought to exploit this illegally obtained information, in December 1964 ordering the preparation of transcripts of the "highlights" from the intercepted conversations obtained through FBI bugging of King's hotel rooms. (The highlights included an "incident" at the Willard Hotel in Washington, D.C., recording "dirty jokes and bawdy remarks . . . plus the sounds of people engaged in sex.") The resultant transcript, numbering 321 pages, was first incorporated in a composite tape and then mailed, with an anonymous cover letter, to King's wife, Coretta. (An agent mailed the letter and tape from Florida to avert any suspicion that the FBI was the source.) FBI officials offered to *Newsweek* reporter Ben Bradlee transcripts of King's sexual activities; to *Los Angeles Tribune* reporter David Kraslow a similar transcript placing King in the midst of a sex orgy; to *Chicago Daily News* reporter James McCartney photographs allegedly showing King leaving a motel in the company of a white woman with the implication that they had had sexual relations. These efforts—and others involving *New York Times* reporter John Herbers, *Chicago Daily News* columnist Mike Royko, *Atlanta Constitution* editors Ralph McGill and Eugene Patterson, and *Augusta* (Georgia) *Chronicle* reporter Lou Harris—did not elicit the desired press coverage. Still, while these reporters rebuffed this sleazy attempt to impugn King's character, none filed alternative stories disclosing that the FBI had collected such personal information and had sought to promote its dissemination.

This effort to discredit King was unique only in intensity. FBI officials also sought to contain the influence of other civil rights leaders, but again only if assured that their collection and dissemination of derogatory information could be kept secret. Thus, the FBI investigated the "moral character" of Andrew Young and Jesse Jackson and, in the weeks following King's assassination in Memphis, of King's principal aide and SCLC successor, Ralph Abernathy. Responding to senior FBI officials' "recent request for information dealing with immoral activities on [Abernathy's] part," the FBI's Atlanta office reported on April 29, 1968, that "little information has been developed regarding promiscuous activity on the part of Abernathy." Hoover thereupon asked the FBI's Washington office to check into allegations that Abernathy was "involved in illicit relations with white women" and had been "beaten by five Negroes who surprised him in bed with a white woman." The FBI's Washington field office reported back that none of these allegations could be confirmed through the Bureau's confidential sources or contacts with the Washington, D.C., police department and the U.S. Park Police. In 1970, moreover, (this time responding to a 1970 request of Vice President Spiro Agnew for assistance in "destroying Abernathy's credibility" in view of his "inflammatory pronouncements"), FBI officials sent Agnew a report "about sexual immorality, Abernathy's luxurious accommodations during the Poor People's Campaign and his support of the Black Panther party."

THE NIXON ADMINISTRATION: THE BREAKDOWN OF THE COLD WAR CONSENSUS

The FBI's assistance to the Nixon administration was not atypical. Throughout the 1960s and early 1970s, FBI Director Hoover regularly volunteered such information in addition to servicing other White House requests for information about liberal and radical activists, journalists, and members of Congress. Hoover's reports both detailed the critics' political strategies and plans and their personal character and conduct.

President Kennedy requested FBI investigations in 1961 and 1962 to identify the sources of stories written by *New York Times* reporter Hanson Baldwin and *Newsweek* reporter Lloyd Norman. The FBI wiretapped both reporters but was unable to identify the source of the suspected leaks. FBI officials responded to an even more sensitive Kennedy administration request, wiretapping the offices of a law firm (hired as lobbyists by the Dominican Republic government) and bugging a meeting in a Washington, D.C., hotel attended by the chairman of the House Agriculture Committee, Harold Cooley. At the time, the administration was lobbying Congress not to grant a sugar quota to the Dominican Republic under proposed legislation regulating the importation of sugar. (Administration officials hoped that this denial would force that government to institute democratic reforms.)

The FBI's intelligence role exploded during the Johnson administration. Disturbed by critical press reporting about the increasingly controversial Vietnam War, President Johnson requested FBI background checks of NBC correspondent David Brinkley, AP (Associated Press) reporter Peter Arnett, *New York Times* reporter Harrison Salisbury, syndicated columnist Joseph Kraft, *Life* magazine Washington bureau chief Richard Stolley, *Chicago Daily News* Washington bureau chief Peter Lisagor, and *Washington Post* executive Ben Gilbert.

President Nixon shared Johnson's obsession over critical media coverage. Richard Nixon had won the presidency in 1968 by capitalizing on widespread public antipathy toward the Johnson administration's duplicity and arrogance (captured in presidential statements of the success of military operations in Vietnam followed by increases in troops and promises that the costs of the war would not produce inflation followed by increasing inflation). This distrust did not dissipate with Johnson's departure from office. Nixon himself confronted the further problem of Democratic congressional opposition to his various foreign and domestic policy initiatives. Concerned over the fragility of his public support, and the possible effect of public cynicism on his reelection prospects in 1972, Nixon viewed the Washington press corps as a potential political liability.

Nixon pursued a strategy intended to minimize public dissent over an unpopular war and pressure the North Vietnamese to accept a negotiated settlement that would ensure an independent, non-Communist South Vietnam. Under this strategy, American troops would be gradually withdrawn from South Vietnam while American air bombing increased—secretly bombing North Vietnamese supply lines in Cambodia.

Incensed over a May 8, 1969, *New York Times* story filed by William Beecher recounting U.S. bombing attacks on Cambodia, the Nixon White House demanded an FBI investigation to ascertain the reporter's source. The FBI wiretapped four Washington-based reporters (Beecher and his colleague at the *New York Times* Hedrick Smith, *London Times* reporter Henry Brandon, and CBS correspondent Marvin Kalb) and 13 government officials, including members of Nixon's White House and National Security Council staffs. Owing to the sensitivity of wiretapping prominent individuals (reporters and Nixon's own appointees), great care was taken to prevent discovery. The transcripts of the intercepted conversations were hand-delivered to the White House, the wiretap logs themselves were maintained separate from other FBI national security wiretaps in the office of FBI Assistant Director William Sullivan, and, finally (in contravention of departmental policy), the names of the individuals whose conversations had been intercepted were not included in the FBI's Elsur Index.

Nixon's antipathy toward the Washington press corps intensified following the 1970 congressional elections. The president had hoped that Republicans would win control of the Senate in the 1970 elections by employing a "law and order" strategy against vulnerable incumbent Democratic Senators who had been elected in traditionally conservative states during the atypical 1958 and 1964 elections. These Democrats, however, won reelection. Convinced that biased press coverage was the cause of this failed strategy, the Nixon White House shifted tactics to focus on discrediting reporters. Vice President Spiro Agnew became the point man for an assault on the "nattering nabobs of negativity."

As part of this antimedia strategy, senior White House aide H. R. Haldeman on November 25, 1970, relayed a particularly sensitive request to FBI Director Hoover. The president wanted the FBI to prepare a report listing "the homosexuals known and suspected in the Washington press corps" as well as "any other stuff" the president would be interested in. Nixon believed, Haldeman added, that a "specific" FBI investigation would not have to be conducted, as the FBI director would already have such information "pretty much at hand." The president assumed correctly; within two days the requested report was hand-delivered to Haldeman.

These efforts failed to stymie a public debate over the relationship between national security claims and First Amendment rights. Instead, in 1971, Daniel Ellsberg leaked a copy of a classified history of U.S. involvement in Vietnam to the *New York Times* and to other national newspapers and members of Congress. As a Defense Department aide during the Johnson administration, Ellsberg had in 1968 participated in the drafting of a 47-volume Defense Department history of U.S. policy in Vietnam dating from the 1940s (the so-called Pentagon Papers). Retaining his security clearance, Ellsberg had access to one of the 15 copies of this still-classified history and intended in 1971 to precipitate a public debate by releasing this internal history documenting the duplicity of administration pronouncements and the erroneous assumptions behind U.S. involvement. Ellsberg failed to convince influential congressional critics (notably, Senator J. William Fulbright) to publicize the Pentagon Papers but found a willing recipient in *New York Times* reporter Neil Sheehan and his editors at the *Times*. Taking care to avoid compromising legitimate secrets, Sheehan and his editors worked secretly to prepare a multipart history that included reprinting actual documents. The first installment was published in the *Times*' Sunday edition on June 13, 1971.

The published story did not directly affect the political interests of the Nixon administration (because the history stopped at 1968). Ellsberg's leaking of the Pentagon Papers, however, threatened presidential control over classified information, and the administration struck back in two ways. On June 14, Attorney General John Mitchell demanded that the *Times* suspend publication and return the "top secret" classified documents to the Department of Defense. The *Times* refused to honor this request (on the grounds of "the interest of the people of this country to be informed of the material contained in this series of articles"). The administration then filed suit to stop the *Times* from publishing the Pentagon Papers—thereby raising the question of the intersection of national security and First Amendment rights.

Federal Judge Murray Gurfein at first enjoined further publication (the first case of prior restraint). Gurfein ultimately concluded that the government had failed to prove that by publishing the Pentagon Papers, the *Times* "would seriously breach the national security." The *Times* had done nothing more than "vindicate the right of the public to know." The Nixon administration appealed Gurfein's decision to the Supreme Court.

On June 30, the Court endorsed the *Times'* First Amendment right to publish the Pentagon Papers. "The dominant purpose of the First Amendment," Justice William Douglas argued, "was to prohibit the widespread practice of governmental suppression of embarrassing information." Justice Potter Stewart concurred. The government did have a legitimate security interest in keeping national defense information secret, Stewart conceded, but should enforce that secrecy rather than resorting to prior restraint against publication. In a glancing criticism of excessive secrecy and overclassification, Stewart added: "For when everything is classified, then nothing is classified, and the system becomes one to be disregarded by the cynical or the careless, and to be manipulated by those intent on self-protection or self-promotion."

The Nixon administration was not content to rely on the courts. The White House concurrently sought to discredit Ellsberg, casting his actions not as those of a principled individual motivated by a desire to promote a public debate but as unbalanced and unpatriotic. This necessitated acquiring damaging personal information about Ellsberg. Nixon's broader purpose was to deter other government officials having access to secret information from undermining his policies.

In this case, the Nixon White House did not turn to the FBI for assistance. The president, instead, relied on a special group of White House aides and private citizens financed through leftover 1968 presidential campaign funds. Nicknamed the White House Plumbers, its mandate was to plug leaks. White House aide Egil Krogh headed this group to find out "all it could about Mr. Ellsberg's associates and motives." Krogh turned to two current White House aides, G. Gordon Liddy (a former FBI agent) and E. Howard Hunt (a former CIA officer). Through their contacts within the Cuban exile community in Florida, Hunt and Liddy recruited four Cuban Americans to break into the office of Ellsberg's psychiatrist to photocopy records that could raise questions about Ellsberg's personality and character.

This operation was unprecedented, the president having avoided seeking FBI assistance. Had such a request been made, FBI officials would have honored the request but in the process created records of both the request and their response. FBI Director Hoover had regularly conducted sensitive investigations targeting presidential critics since Franklin Roosevelt's presidency. Nixon's desire for complete control by making this a strictly White House operation arose from his desire to ensure that these actions never become known.

Since 1969, President Nixon had regularly solicited FBI assistance to monitor a variety of political activists and prominent personalities (ranging from the liberal Americans for Democratic Action chairman Joseph Duffy to anti-Nixon film producer Emil D'Antonio). Indeed, the FBI's earlier informal liaison relationship whereby "presidents and attorneys general were furnished important intelligence information on an individual basis" was expanded under Nixon in a formal program, code-named INLET. Dating from November 1969, FBI field offices were ordered to "flag" for automatic forwarding to the White House any information that would be of "interest" to the president. Relevant collected information was sent to ensure that the president and the attorney general received "high level intelligence data in the internal security field on a continuing basis" and "items with an unusual twist or concerning prominent personalities which may be of special interest to the President or the Attorney General."

In June 1969 the Nixon administration instituted another special program to ensure that Internal Revenue Service (IRS) tax audit investigations targeted "dissidents" and "extremists." A special staff was established within the IRS and eventually more than eight thousand individuals and three thousand organizations were targeted, including the Ford Foundation, the National Urban League, Common Cause, and the John Birch Society; Senators Charles Goodell and Ernest Gruening; and syndicated columnists Joseph Alsop and Jimmy Breslin. An internal IRS memorandum emphasized the need to prevent discovery of the political use of the IRS: "We certainly must not open the door to widespread notoriety that would embarrass the Administration."

FBI officials, on their own, had intensively monitored the civil rights, radical student, antiwar, and radical feminist movements throughout the 1960s. FBI officials then briefed Presidents Johnson and Nixon about the plans, and suspect associations of their radical critics. In turn, the appreciative presidents exploited the FBI's vast resources to promote their own political objectives.

FBI Director Hoover willingly honored President Johnson's request for advance intelligence about planned demonstrations at the 1964 Democratic National Convention in Atlantic City. A special FBI squad, masquerading as reporters and wiretapping key civil rights leaders, was dispatched to monitor civil rights activists and their supporters among convention delegates. This squad's findings were immediately relayed to the Johnson White House through a direct communication line. The resultant advance intelligence about the strategy of supporters of the seating of the Mississippi Freedom Democratic Party delegation and of liberals seeking to draft Robert Kennedy as vice president enabled the president to determine convention policy.

Such FBI surveillance and dissemination activities raise serious civil liberties issues. By the late 1960s, opposition to the Vietnam War was no longer confined to radical activists but included the liberal religious, academic, and business communities. Fearful that these activists might influence public opinion and the Congress, Johnson administration officials sought to tar these critics as disloyal.

As part of this political operation, President Johnson asked FBI Director Hoover to "brief at least two Senators and two Congressmen, preferably one of each Party," about the subversive character of the anti-Vietnam demonstrators "so that they might in turn not only make speeches upon the floor of Congress but also publicly." FBI officials complied, actually drafting a speech that Congressman Howard Smith delivered about the subversive nature of the antiwar movement and then disseminating copies of the speech to university and corporate executives. FBI officials also prepared a "good strong memorandum" for prominent administration officials assigned to speak in various parts of the country. Beginning in 1968, FBI field offices prepared "on a continuing basis" a series of reports for "prompt . . . dissemination to the news media . . . to discredit the New Left movement." "Every avenue of possible embarrassment," about New Left activists, FBI Director Hoover emphasized, "must be vigorously and enthusiastically explored."

The FBI was unable to uncover convincing evidence that the civil rights and antiwar movements were directed and controlled by the Soviet Union. Accordingly, in 1967, President Johnson directed the CIA to establish this Communist connection. CIA officials in response initiated a code-named Operation CHAOS program, in the process knowingly violating the 1947 National Security Act's ban against CIA internal security investigations. Under this program, CIA personnel infiltrated domestic civil rights and antiwar organizations. Following Richard Nixon's election, and under increased pressure to confirm Communist influence, CIA officials refined and expanded this program in 1969. CIA officials were also unable to confirm Soviet (or Communist) direction and control, concluding instead that these protest activities were indigenous in origin.

The inability of CIA and FBI officials to document Communist direction led them to solicit the National Security Agency's (NSA) assistance in 1967. As the Defense Department's intelligence agency, the NSA could intercept international messages transmitted electronically. Beginning in 1967, the NSA intercepted the messages of organizations and individuals (such as SDS and SNCC leaders but also actress Jane Fonda) who were named by FBI and CIA officials because they "may foment civil disturbances or otherwise undermine the national security" or "are employed in activities which may result in civil disturbances or otherwise subvert the national security." NSA officials nonetheless worried that their involvement could prove to be politically harmful since by so doing they violated the agency's charter (confining their mission to foreign intelligence and counterintelligence) and the ban against intercepting electronic communications of American citizens. Accordingly, CIA and FBI officials were asked to destroy or return to the NSA these reports within two weeks of receipt.

By the late 1960s, dissent over the Vietnam War extended to prominent members of Congress and the mainstream media. In the mid-1960s, Senator J. William Fulbright had preferred to express his serious reservations about the president's Vietnam policy in private. By February 1966, Fulbright decided to employ his powers as chair of the Senate Foreign Relations Committee to convene public hearings to challenge the wisdom and costs of U.S. policy in Vietnam. Concerned over the public impact of these nationally televised hearings, President Johnson asked the FBI to monitor them and prepare a report about whether Senator Fulbright and other congressional critics were "receiving information from Communists." The FBI director was unable to uncover any evidence that the Communist party "or any other subversive group" had furnished materials to the senators or prompted their criticisms.

Frustrated by the FBI's inability to produce the desired evidence, President Johnson demanded that the FBI "constantly keep abreast of the actions of representatives of Soviet and Soviet bloc embassy officials in making contact with senators and congressmen and any citizens of a prominent nature." "Much of this protest concerning his foreign policy," the president explained, "particularly the hearings in the Senate, had been generated" by Communist officials.

Having wiretapped the Soviet embassy and the embassies of Soviet bloc countries, FBI officials prepared a detailed 67-page report of the telephone contacts of senators and representatives and congressional staff with these embassies during the period between July 1965 through March 1966. (Such telephone contacts were quite innocent, relating to attendance at embassy social functions or background meetings over legislative issues of interest to diplomatic personnel.) Thereafter, all subsequent congressional and congressional staff contacts with these embassies were reported on a biweekly basis until this practice was temporarily terminated with Richard Nixon's inauguration. The practice was resumed in July 1970 when White House aide Larry Higby requested information on any "contacts" of members of Congress and congressional staff with Soviet and Soviet bloc embassy officials.

Despite the intensity of the FBI's investigative efforts (and the unprecedented solicitation of CIA and NSA assistance), no evidence was developed to confirm that Soviet or Chinese officials either ordered or controlled the antiwar activities of radicals, liberals, members of Congress, or congressional staff. CIA and NSA reports did cite the contacts of American radicals with Communist officials but, then, these contacts were not secret because activists publicly traveled overseas to meet with Cuban and North Vietnamese officials.

President Nixon grew increasingly concerned over continued public criticism of his Vietnam policy, criticism that intensified following his April 1970 decision to send U.S. troops into Cambodia. The Cambodian invasion precipitated nationwide protests on college campuses, which turned violent when the Ohio governor sent in the National Guard to quell an uprising at Kent State, resulting in the deaths of four students. Student opposition became so bitter that college administrators suspended classes for the academic year.

As White House liaison to the intelligence community, Tom Huston met regularly with the FBI's liaison to the White House, FBI Assistant Director William Sullivan. Dissatisfied by the FBI's inability to link dissent with Communists, Huston at first redefined the criteria confirming Communist influence to include "all information possibly relating to foreign influences and financing of the New Left." Any contacts, ideological sympathy, or shared objectives would constitute evidence of Communist influence. The resultant FBI (and CIA) reports failed to satisfy Huston, who complained to Sullivan about the quality of FBI reports. Sullivan had by then developed a close working relationship with Huston and confidentially advised the White House aide that the source of the problem was restrictions that FBI Director Hoover had imposed in 1965–66 on the FBI's use of illegal investigative techniques.

Huston and Sullivan devised a crafty strategy to resolve the Hoover problem. According to Sullivan, the FBI director had become exceedingly cautious, having reached the mandatory retirement age of 70 in 1964. Fearing that discovery of the FBI's continued use of illegal tactics could in the climate of the time lead to his forced retirement, Hoover had limited FBI wiretapping and bugging installations and had prohibited break-ins and mail opening in 1965–66. To reverse these Hoover-imposed restrictions, Huston and Sullivan urged the president to appoint a special interagency committee (on which they would play key roles) to study and recommend changes in current intelligence agency collection procedures.

Working under tight secrecy, the interagency task force identified a series of "clearly illegal" activities that the president could approve to improve the quality of intelligence reporting: authorization to intercept international communications, increased use of wiretaps and bugs, lifting restrictions on mail opening and break-ins, lowering the age of recruited informers to 18, and creating a permanent interagency committee operating under the authority of a White House representative to "coordinate intelligence gathering within this committee."

As a member of the parent committee (to which the task force was to report), FBI Director Hoover first learned of the task force's specific list of options immediately prior to the proposed meeting at which its report was to be submitted to the president. Lacking veto authority, Hoover wrote a series of footnoted objections to this report. The FBI director's footnotes first defended the adequacy of the FBI's coverage of dissident activities and then added that he "would not oppose other agencies" (namely the CIA and NSA) "instituting such coverage themselves" after seeking the attorney general's approval. Hoover was no longer willing to have the FBI perform such "clearly illegal" services for other intelligence agencies and stressed the political risks of "leaks to the press," with the possible loss of public support for the intelligence agencies.

Hoover's objections were not based on legal or civil liberties considerations. Should the FBI perform such "clearly illegal" activities, its reputation could suffer, precipitating further scrutiny of FBI operations and authority. The astute FBI director was keenly sensitive to the changed political climate of the 1960s, with the emergence of a more independent and critical media and Congress.

Huston was not dissuaded by Hoover's footnoted objections. Instead, the White House aide urged the president to invite the FBI director to the White House for a "stroking" session to explain his reasons for endorsing the changes, announce his approval of the recommended changes at another meeting of the heads of all the intelligence agencies, and then issue an "official memorandum setting forth the precise" changes. Nixon rejected this course of action (preferring to ensure presidential deniability) and instead ordered Huston to send the authorization memorandum under his (Huston's) signature (thus the characterization of this as the Huston Plan). Should any of the recommended "clearly illegal" activities be publicly compromised, there would be no record of explicit presidential authorization.

Huston complied with the president's course of implementation. On July 23, 1970, he sent a memorandum to the heads of all the intelligence agencies authorizing the proposed changes. This action did not settle the matter, since no presidential directive (even highly classified) had been issued. Concluding that the absence of explicit presidential authorization put the FBI at risk, Hoover acted to safeguard his own and the bureau's interests. On July 27, he outlined to Attorney General John Mitchell how he intended to act in the future. He opposed the proposed "lifting of the various investigative restraints" and "creation of a permanent interagency committee" but nonetheless was willing to "implement the instructions of the White House at your [the attorney general's] direction." Prior to conducting any proposed operations (mail opening, wiretap, bug, break-in), he would seek Mitchell's "specific authorization." Hoover's intent to create a written record that each action was conducted pursuant to the president's program with the attorney general's prior approval would have effectively subverted President Nixon's strategy of deniability.

Mitchell became immediately alarmed and met that day with the president. The attorney general emphasized the "sensitivity" of the various techniques (wiretaps, bugs, mail opening, break-ins) and the likelihood that their use would "generate media criticism if they were employed." On balance, Mitchell counseled, "the risk of disclosure of the possible illegal actions . . . was greater than the benefit to be achieved." Convinced by this reasoning, President Nixon recalled Huston's memorandum.

The Huston Plan's proposed authorization of "clearly illegal" investigations did not become known at the time. The president's decision to rescind Huston's authorization memorandum within two weeks after it had been sent to the heads of all the intelligence agencies, however, was no victory for civil liberties, for FBI Director Hoover's reservations and Attorney General Mitchell's counsel were not based on due process concerns or on the need to respect privacy rights and constitutional limits. The ultimate irony of the Huston Plan was that an FBI director who had secretly acted since the early 1940s to expand FBI surveillance of political activities (to include the use of illegal investigative techniques) had served as a brake against future abuses in the changed political climate of the 1970s. Another by-product of Hoover's independence was that it became the catalyst for the creation of the White House Plumbers.

By 1971, President Nixon faced a delicate problem stemming from his earlier efforts to exploit the FBI to advance his administration's political objectives. The president could not be sure that the wily FBI director might leak information of the FBI's earlier servicing of the Nixon administration's politically questionable requests. Hoover's independence also underlay FBI Assistant Director William Sullivan's covert collaboration in formulating the Huston Plan. Indeed, Sullivan privately advised the White House that Hoover's caution and continued obsession with the Communist Party had effectively hamstrung the FBI's ability to monitor New Left activists and organizations. Sullivan's continued frustration over Hoover's actions soon led him to break publicly with the FBI director in September 1971.

Prior to this formal break, Sullivan had forged an alliance with officials in the Nixon administration. In July 1971, he briefed Assistant Attorney General Robert Mardian about the blackmail potential of the FBI wiretap records he had maintained in his office since 1969 involving reporters and NSC, White House, and State Department and Defense Department officials suspected of leaking information to *New York Times* reporter William Beecher. Sullivan warned that Hoover had "used wiretap information to blackmail other presidents." This wiretapping operation had become even more sensitive after its inception. The FBI had continued to wiretap NSC aides Morton Halperin and Anthony Lake after they had left the NSC staff (when they no longer would have access to classified information) and became foreign policy advisers to Democratic Senator Edmund Muskie (at the time perceived to be the front-runner for the 1972 Democratic presidential nomination). These wiretaps continued even after the FBI had reported, "Nothing has come to light that is of significance from the standpoint of the leak in question." By then, however, these wiretaps provided invaluable intelligence about the president's political adversaries in the Democratic Party. White House aide John Ehrlichman enthusiastically counseled senior aide Haldeman about one such report: "This is the kind of early warning we need more of—your game planners are now in an excellent position to map anticipatory action."

The duration (from 1969 until 1971) and targets (Nixon's own appointees to the NSC and White House staffs) of the NSC operation posed potentially serious political problems. The targets were not suspected Soviet agents or politically suspect radical activists but prominent Americans who were either members of the Washington press corps or former staff who had received a security clearance. The disclosure of the existence and operation of these taps would raise privacy concerns and questions about presidential abuses of the FBI, call into question national security concerns, and highlight President Nixon's antipathy toward an independent and critical press. For these reasons, when briefed in July 1971 of Sullivan's possession in his office of the wiretap logs, Mardian ordered the FBI assistant director to turn them over to be secreted in White House aide John Ehrlichman's office safe.

Already concerned about Hoover's independence, in September 1971, the Nixon White House convened a special meeting to discuss Hoover's continuance as FBI director. There, the participants concluded that Hoover should be pressured to resign. Believing that only the president could make such a request, a personal meeting between Hoover and Nixon was arranged for September 20, 1971. At the last minute, the president hesitated to ask Hoover to retire.

Hoover's death of a heart attack in May 1972 resolved this problem and at the same time provided an opportunity and an unanticipated dilemma for the White House. To fill this vacancy Nixon appointed L. Patrick Gray III (at the time an assistant attorney general heading the criminal division) as Acting FBI Director. Nixon advanced two interests by appointing Gray. First, because he was only acting director, Gray would serve at the pleasure of the president and thus would have an interest in demonstrating his loyalty to Nixon (and, as an outsider, would have no institutional loyalty to the FBI). Second, legislation enacted in 1968 required Senate confirmation of the FBI director. By not making a permanent appointment, Nixon ensured that the policies of the new FBI director (and questions about Hoover's directorship) would not become an issue in the 1972 political campaign.

THE WATERGATE AFFAIR:
ITS LEGACY FOR CIVIL LIBERTIES

In June 1972, Washington, D.C., police arrested four individuals associated with the Nixon reelection campaign whom they discovered in the headquarters of the Democratic National Committee. Further investigation established that the break-in had been financed through 1972 Nixon campaign funds and had been coordinated by former Nixon White House aides E. Howard Hunt and G. Gordon Liddy. By 1973, questions were being raised whether high-level Nixon campaign and White House officials (including President Nixon) had coordinated an elaborate cover-up to contain the FBI's investigation into the break-in and ensure that the six arrestees remain silent about the involvement of higher-ups.

These questions were first raised during hearings conducted by the Senate Judiciary Committee into Gray's confirmation as FBI director, Nixon having formally appointed him in January 1973. Responding to pointed questions about the FBI's investigation into the Watergate break-in, Gray admitted to having allowed White House counsel John Dean III to sit in during FBI interviews of White House aides and to having met with Dean 33 times to brief him on the progress of the FBI investigation. Then, in a more electrifying statement, Gray admitted having personally destroyed sensitive records turned over to him by White House aide John Ehrlichman the preceding summer. Gray claimed that these records had no relationship with the Watergate break-in. (Among these records were the NSC wiretap logs formerly maintained in FBI Assistant Director Sullivan's office.) Gray's admission to destroying records led him to withdraw his name from consideration for FBI director. More importantly, his admission (and description of the relationship with Dean) raised questions about the FBI's political independence.

The Gray hearings were a preview to a series of even more dramatic revelations that spring and summer. Responding to questions about the role of high-level officials in the Nixon White House and 1972 reelection committee in the Watergate break-in, the Senate in 1973 established a special investigative committee. Chaired by North Carolina Senator Sam Ervin, the special Senate committee focused on whether the president had known, authorized, or participated in the break-in and resultant cover-up. Commencing televised hearings on May 17, the committee inquiry soon publicized troubling evidence about the White House–FBI relationship. The catalyst for this shift came when former White House Counsel John Dean sought a plea bargain with the committee and prosecutors in the spring of 1973. In return for immunity, Dean disclosed to the prosecutors and the Senate committee the actions that he and senior White House officials (including the president) had taken to contain the Watergate inquiry. Dean, in addition, turned over classified White House documents relating to the Huston Plan, the creation and activities of the White House Plumbers, and the NSC wiretaps. These documents broadened the issue from the Watergate break-in and cover-up to whether the president had used the intelligence agencies for political purposes and had willingly undermined the law.

President Nixon and senior White House aides Haldeman and Ehrlichman immediately denied Dean's allegations of a White House-orchestrated cover-up. At the same time, President Nixon claimed that "national security" interests were the reasons for instituting the Huston Plan, White House Plumbers, and NSC wiretaps.

White House aide Alexander Butterfield's subsequent disclosure that since 1971, all Oval Office conversations had been taped dramatically changed the dynamics of the hearings. The tapes could help resolve whether Nixon or Dean was telling the truth. Almost immediately President Nixon claimed the right of "executive privilege" to withhold from the Senate committee specified tapes of Oval Office conversations (identified from White House logs or from Dean's testimony). Nixon's claim was immediately challenged in court. In a unanimous ruling of July 1974 in *Nixon v. U.S.*, the Court denied that the president had an absolute right to secrecy, ruling that "an absolute unqualified [executive] privilege" would "plainly conflict with the functions of the courts" in criminal proceedings. Oval Office tapes released following this ruling documented that since June 1972, Nixon had sought to contain the FBI's investigation into the Watergate break-in.

The crescendo of revelations during the summer months of 1973 led to Nixon's resignation as president and heightened public skepticism about the scope of presidential powers, federal secrecy, and the prioritization of national security over civil liberties. By shattering the wall of secrecy that had shrouded federal surveillance activities and laying bare the questionable basis for national security secrecy claims, these revelations ushered in a politics more sensitive to privacy rights and more skeptical of secret, centralized government.

Part Three

1973–2000

The militant tactics of antiwar and civil rights activists and the urban race riots of the late 1960s precipitated a conservative backlash against reform politics. In their campaigns for the presidency in 1968, Republican nominee Richard Nixon and American Independence party nominee George Wallace tapped into this antiliberal mood. Nixon's electoral victory confirmed that a new consensus had emerged, one that questioned whether the federal government should actively promote equality (through increased federal spending and regulation) and whether dissent undermined public order.

This new consensus shaped the politics of the 1970s through the 1990s. During the 1980s and 1990s, affirmative action programs to offset discrimination in hiring and in higher education were sharply challenged through court cases and popular initiatives. Judicial mandates to remedy desegregation through court-ordered busing came under attack. The Supreme Court pulled away from vigorous desegregation, at a time when many of the nation's urban school systems experienced white flight, leaving the public schools in many cities effectively segregated. In addition, programs originally enacted under the New Deal and expanded under the Great Society to provide a safety net against extreme poverty were curtailed in the 1980s, and AFDC was rescinded in 1996, on the premise that public welfare programs sustained dependency and contributed to the decline in social and economic conditions in the nation's inner cities.

Religious conservatives forged a broad movement that blamed the women's rights and other liberal social movements for the nation's social and economic problems. To them, the Supreme Court's historic ruling in

Roe v. Wade, striking down state restrictions on abortions, marked the nation's moral decline. They demanded the restoration of traditional values and the reversal of those policies that had curbed discrimination against women, gays and lesbians, and racial minorities. Articulating this moral protest, Rev. Jerry Falwell (the founder of the Moral Majority, renamed the Christian Coalition in the 1990s) argued, "God Almighty created men and women biologically different and with differing needs and roles." Falwell maintained that "[g]ood men who are godly men are good leaders. Their wives and children want to follow them." The neoconservative intellectual Allen Bloom extended this attack in his bestselling critique of American higher education, *The Closing of the American Mind* (1986), decrying the growth of multiculturalism and women's and ethnic studies.

The religious conservative movement reached its zenith in the 1980 presidential campaign. Republican presidential nominee Ronald Reagan publicly championed the Moral Majority's moralistic objectives. And, delegates to the 1980 Republican National Convention adopted platform planks opposing abortion and ratification of the Equal Rights Amendment and endorsing legislation on voluntary prayer in schools to preserve the "sanctity of the family."

The calls of religious conservatives for individual responsibility and respect for established authority initially commanded support. Their coercive tactics to ensure a society based on traditional values, in time, alienated many Americans who favored privacy rights and less government. Having come to reassess Great Society/New Deal liberalism, in reaction to the successes and excesses of the movements of the 1960s, many Americans found equally anathema the demands of religious conservatives to legislate morality—whether through amending the Constitution to ban abortion and to ensure prayer in public schools, posting the Ten Commandments in public offices, or regulating pornography and the contents of television shows and movies.

Many other Americans who had themselves been energized by the civil rights, student rights, gay and lesbian rights, and women's rights movements of the 1960s also came to reassess Great Society programs. These people criticized the tokenism of these efforts. Militant activists questioned whether liberal politicians were committed to needed systemic changes (both legislative and appropriations) essential to achieving equality. They remained committed to the goals of racial justice and human rights. Multiracial coalitions came together to demand that the nation live up to its creed of justice and equality. Receiving far less media attention than their 1960s counterparts, and responding to the new language and tactics of post–civil rights politics, these coalitions continued the work of earlier civil rights activists with a broadened vision of economic and political equality.

Proponents of civil rights and civil liberties discovered that a new public consensus celebrated the goals of the civil rights movement while rejecting the steps to achieve those goals. By the 1990s, this consensus stressed personal privacy—both an aversion to state-imposed social engineering (whether to promote equality through Great Society programs or to legislate morality by banning abortion or requiring school prayer) and an increased respect for orderly dissent. This new politics was also influenced by the end of the Cold War and the collapse of Communist governments in Eastern Europe and the Soviet Union. The Watergate Affair proved to be a defining event, heightening concerns about how secrecy had permitted abuses of power and how presidents and intelligence agency officials had purposefully exploited national security concerns to repress movements challenging the status quo. As the public came to demand both less secrecy and more accountability, privacy rights and skepticism about government-imposed reform framed national politics.

Chapter 7

NEW SOCIAL MOVEMENTS AND POST–CIVIL RIGHTS POLITICS

The mid-1970s were a paradoxical time: the movements of the 1950s and 1960s had provoked significant change and yet encountered palpable intransigence. The United States had gone to war in Vietnam to protect democracy while civil rights and civil liberties movements challenged the reality of democracy within the United States. Revelations about Watergate and COINTELPRO underscored the extent to which federal officials had attempted to squash public dissent. As Americans faced difficult economic times in the 1970s and 1980s, many whites found the civil rights movement a convenient scapegoat for their own economic vulnerability. The politics that emerged under the Reagan, Bush, and Clinton presidencies began to roll back the gains of the civil rights movement.

Framing civil rights gains as *reverse discrimination* and racism as largely a problem of the past, post–civil rights politics hinged on a new language of race that emphasized culture and strong values as the marker of successful groups in America. These discourses celebrated individual people of color and blamed the economic and social problems of people of color on family dysfunction, poor values, and a "culture of poverty" rather than economic dislocation, public disinvestment in cities, and the continuing structures of racism. This political shift did not go unchallenged. Civil rights activists continued to press for changes in education, public services, and economic opportunity and reformed their strategies and coalitions to pressure the country to live up to its democratic ideals.

The Fight for Educational Equity Encounters Further Resistance

The issue of school desegregation remained contentious, in the South and in the North. Many northern whites supported the goals of the civil rights movement—until it moved into their own backyards. Then, their commitment to integration faltered. In the North, white and nonwhite children largely attended separate schools in districts that were predominantly controlled by a white leadership who evinced little interest in ensuring educational excellence for students of color. For instance, despite the campaign that the black community had waged since 1960, Boston's schools remained segregated and were still controlled by the School Committee, who refused to admit any responsibility for the second-class education black students received. Community activists organized meetings, sit-ins, and school boycotts and started their own small busing programs, but these efforts made little headway with the Boston School Committee. Community members succeeded in getting the state legislature to pass a law prohibiting racially imbalanced schools, but the School Committee sued to avoid following the law. As a last resort, the NAACP filed suit in federal court on behalf of black parents. In June 1974, U.S. District Court Judge W. Arthur Garrity ordered Boston Public Schools to begin desegregation. Majority black schools were paired with nearby white schools to minimize busing.

Enraged by what they saw as an infringement of their civil rights, a group of whites led by city council member Louise Day Hicks formed ROAR (Restore Our Alienated Rights). They vowed to fight desegregation of "their schools" and to keep their children at home. These white parents believed that desegregation would ruin their children's educations and that Boston's black neighborhoods threatened their children's safety. Fears of interracial mixing also ran high. According to one white father, "The question is: Am I going to send my young daughter, who is budding into the flower of womanhood, into Roxbury [a black neighborhood] on a bus?" Drawing many of its members from home and school associations, ROAR urged white parents to keep their children home and held numerous rallies from July to September to demonstrate their resistance to integration.

This was a movement against desegregation, not busing. Thirty thousand Boston students were already bused to school, including 50 percent of Boston's middle schoolers and 85 percent of its high schoolers. Rejecting the School Committee's claim of preserving neighborhood schools, Judge Arthur Garrity cited extensive busing, open enrollment, magnet schools, citywide schools, and widespread high school feeder programs (all of which were already going on in Boston Public Schools) as "antithetical" to a neighborhood school system. His decision cited overcrowding and underutilization in Boston's schools, the use of districting to preserve segregation, the creation of a dual system of secondary education, the use of less qualified and lower-paid teachers in predominantly black schools, and the restricting of black teachers largely to black schools as intentional segregation and cause for legal action. District lines had been drawn to ensure all-white schools, requiring thousands of white children to travel farther to school. The label "anti-busing" conveniently but deceptively distinguished northern resistance to desegregation from southern.

Determined not to shoulder the blame for desegregation, Mayor Kevin White adopted this language of neighborhood schools. White had received 90 percent of the black vote in the 1968 election and was confident of his reputation in the black community. Accordingly, he concentrated his attention on whites, particularly white mothers, and over the summer scheduled a hundred meetings to calm their fears and convince them he was behind them. He had previously committed $200,000 of city finances towards a futile appeal of the Racial Imbalance Act. White's approach left the black community on its own. In late 1973, black community activists formed the Freedom House Institute on Schools and Education to work with parents and students on the desegregation process. They set up a hotline for parents to call for information about desegregation and received hundreds of calls before school began.

Much of the city's leadership worked against the court's desegregation order. The School Committee did little to plan for desegregation. On September 1, hundreds of teachers were still not assigned to a school. Adamantly opposed to desegregation, the Boston Teacher's Union and the Boston Police Patrolmen's Association also publicly opposed desegregation and committed funds to appeal the decision. Many city council members also openly condemned desegregation. Council members Hicks, Dapper O'Neill, Christopher Ianella, and Patrick McDonough each displayed the letters R-O-A-R in their office windows to spell the acronym of the antidesegregation organization and let ROAR use their chambers to meet. Furthermore, the police department assigned a low priority to enforcement for desegregation and did not commit enough officers to the job.

Given this lack of leadership, some of the ugliest antidesegregation demonstrations in the nation's history erupted with the start of school on September 12, 1974, even though most Boston schools desegregated without incident. Crowds of whites harassed black students trying to desegregate white schools, and their harassment often turned violent. Buses carrying elementary school students were stoned. Nine children were injured and 18 buses damaged. A mob of whites confronted the

Thousands of people joined the NAACP to protest the continued resistance to desegregation in Boston.

black students desegregating South Boston High School, throwing rocks, bottles, eggs, and rotten tomatoes and yelling "Niggers Go Home." One student, Phyllis Ellison, who attended school that day, explained, "And there were people on the corners holding bananas like we were apes, monkeys. 'Monkeys get out, get them out of our neighborhood.'" Many white parents kept their children home. The attendance plan for South Boston High School included 941 African-American students and 1,604 white students. Yet, on the first day, only 40 black students and 25 white students attended. The plan for Roxbury High School included 523 whites and 453 blacks. Forty white students and 400 black students attended the first day.

More than 1,100 people called the black community center Freedom House that first day. The NAACP counseled black parents not to send their children to school until assured of city protection. Many black students were determined to go back, believing their actions would ultimately benefit the black community and the city as a whole. Ellison continued, "[A]t that time it did frighten me somewhat, but I was more determined then to get inside South Boston High School. . . . I felt that the black students were making history." With many black parents fearful of letting their children continue with desegregation, parents and other community organizers decided to monitor the buses themselves—not trusting the police to protect their children—and held meetings, marches, and rallies throughout the year in support of desegregation.

Although the bulk of media attention focused on the white working-class neighborhood of South Boston, racial violence also erupted in the white middle-class neighborhoods known as the High Wards—Hyde Park, Roslindale, and West Roxbury. The first race riot at school happened at Hyde Park High School on September 19, 1974. In October, a crowd of whites chased a group of black students out of a Roslindale restaurant, and two men were arrested for carrying Molotov cocktails outside Hyde Park High School.

Not all schools, however, were plagued with violence. The boycott failed in most schools, with 66 percent of students attending school. The Jeremiah Burke High School, a formerly black high school, was desegregated peacefully. A teacher observed, "There was a lot of education, a lot of learning, a lot of teaching going on in the building, and the kids realized it." Nor did all South Boston whites resist busing. South Boston mother Tracy Amalfitano sent her two boys to school, despite the anger it caused within the community and the violence directed against her family. "The community basically was talking about kids not being safe going into the minority communities, but because I went in and out every day myself, I knew that they were safe there. And my concern was that they were safe when they got off, when my older son got off the bus in his own community." Amalfitano's efforts were "lonely," unsupported by local politicians, while "political leaders [met] quite routinely with those that boycotted." Many white mothers who went along with desegregation met in secret, afraid of the reactions of their families and friends should they find out. One mother explained, "ROAR doesn't represent all white people." She did not tell her husband about the meetings but was committed to continuing them. "The Black students face quite a bit of abuse but they have as much right to go to school here as my kids do . . . I can feel what the Black parents are going through now, and I know we have the same concern for our children."

White leaders such as Louise Day Hicks cited the violence to justify their opposition, urging the city to stop desegregation because it was too dangerous. As many whites continued to keep their children at home,

ROAR set up alternate schools and tutoring sessions for these students. The turning point in the struggle came more than a year later. Ruth Batson and other black leaders concluded that real change within Boston's school system could be ensured only by removing Boston Public Schools from the control of the School Committee and putting the schools under the jurisdiction of the court and an outside administration. As NAACP chair Thomas Atkins testified to the U.S. Commission on Civil Rights of the vacuum of leadership from officials and the white community. "The black community, throughout the period from last summer through now, has had to bear the burden of leading the whole city." On December 9, 1975, Judge Garrity took the school system out of the control of the School Committee, ousted the principal at South Boston High School and seven other administrators, and put the system into receivership. On that day, the NAACP office was firebombed. Many black leaders felt receivership marked a real turning point as busing opponents realized that the judge meant business. Louise Day Hicks lost her seat on the city council in 1977, and a black man, John O'Bryant, was elected to the School Committee, the first in 76 years.

The resistance to Boston's desegregation highlighted the limits of northern support for desegregation. Mirroring public recalcitrance around civil rights nationwide, the Supreme Court's support of desegregation and educational equity also waned. In 1974, in *Milliken vs. Bradley,* the Court overturned federal district judge Stephen Roth's desegregation decision, the first time the Court reversed such a decision since *Brown.* Judge Roth had joined the city of Detroit and its 53 predominantly white suburbs, creating superdistricts between city and suburb to enable effective desegregation. The suburbs appealed to prevent the implementation of this decision. In a 5-4 ruling, the Supreme Court reversed Roth's decision. Despite pervasive housing discrimination in the suburbs, the economic interdependence between Detroit and its suburbs, and the fact that the Fourteenth Amendment applied to the state and said nothing about cities, the Court ruled that suburbs were not responsible for segregation and should not be tied to the city through these superdistricts. The city would have to desegregate within its own borders. Justice William Douglas's dissent pointed out that had this been a sewage problem or a water problem rather than a problem of segregation, the necessity of a metropolitan solution would not be debated. Thurgood Marshall also dissented, characterizing the majority decision as "more a reflection of a perceived public mood . . . than it is the product of neutral principles of law." In effect, *Milliken* legalized white flight to the suburbs as a means to avoid desegregation.

The Court's ruling previewed a growing public backlash against civil rights that profoundly affected affirmative action and the movement for educational and job equity. First mentioned by President Kennedy in a 1961 order requiring firms with federal contracts to recruit blacks, President Johnson outlined the rationale for affirmative action in June 1965: "You do not wipe away the scars of centuries by saying: Now you are free to go where you want, do as you desire, and choose the leaders you please. We seek . . . not just equality as a right and a theory but equality as a fact and equality as a result." Only 4.8 percent of all U.S. college students were black in 1956; barely 1 percent of law students were black, and 2 percent of medical students were black (three-quarters of these attended two historically black schools, Howard University and Meharry Medical School). This new policy of affirmative action moved from dismantling discriminatory laws to encouraging full access to jobs and education. The Equal Employment Opportunity Commission began to look at discrimination not only in terms of intentional bias against a certain individual but statistical analyses of proportional representation. "Equality as a result" was accomplished when women and people of color were admitted to universities, elected to office, and hired for jobs in proportion to their rate in the population.

Martin Luther King, Jr. defended the necessity of affirmative action, arguing: "It is impossible to create a formula for the future which does not take into account that our society has been doing something special against the Negro for hundreds of years." For King, removing the legal barriers of discrimination did not constitute real equality. "It is obvious that if a man is entered at the starting line in a race three hundred years after another man, the first would have to perform some impossible feat in order to catch up with his fellow runner." President Johnson agreed: "You do not take a person who, for years, has been hobbled by chains and liberate him, bring him up to the starting line in a race and then say, 'you are free to compete with all the others,' and still justly believe that you have been completely fair."

Faced with continuing intransigence in the all-white skilled trades in Philadelphia, the U.S. Department of Labor, in its Philadelphia Plan in 1967, mandated that the area's government construction contractors adopt affirmative action. In 1968, the Department of Labor instructed major contractors to set timetables to achieve "full and equal employment opportunity" for people of color and women. As a result of these requirements, by 1973, blacks held 21 percent of skilled trades positions on federal construction sites in the Philadelphia area.

Affirmative action plans blossomed under the more conservative Republican President Richard Nixon. Nixon's cabinet helped put in place a national policy based on "visible measurable goals to correct obvious imbalances" in the labor force. Contractors had to show "a good faith effort" to meet these standards or risk having their contracts revoked.

The Nixon administration also established the Office of Minority Business Enterprise to enable people of color to obtain government grants and contracts. These policies increased the numbers of people of color and white women in colleges, graduate and professional schools, business, and the professions. In the first decade of affirmative action policies, 850,000 blacks found jobs in city, state, and federal government social services. Whereas only 227,000 blacks were enrolled in college in 1960, by 1970 that number had increased 100 percent. By 1977, 1.1 million African Americans attended the nation's universities. Indeed, after 10 years of affirmative action policies, blacks and whites were attending college in the same proportion.

Nixon supported these initiatives partly to promote division between civil rights groups (pushing for black access to jobs in the skilled trades) and labor unions (seeking to protect the preferences of white workers). Affirmative action offered the Nixon administration a way to mitigate further social unrest in the nation's cities more cheaply than job training and education. At the same time, Nixon cynically attacked the programs he had helped create, mischaracterizing them for his own political gain: "When young people apply for jobs and find the door closed because they don't fit into some numerical quota, despite their ability, and they object, I do not object. I do not think it is right to condemn those young people as insensitive or even racist."

This antipathy towards affirmative action led to a legal challenge to the biracial admissions policy of the University of California–Davis medical school filed by Allan Bakke. A 33-year-old white medical school applicant, Bakke sued UC–Davis for "reverse discrimination." Sixteen of the 100 spaces in UC–Davis's medical class were reserved for blacks although these were not always filled. Bakke did not object to the five spaces in the medical class that were set aside for relatives of faculty, state politicians, and important business people and contributors. Indeed, Bakke's age likely affected his admissions chances, as medical schools shied away from accepting older students. (Bakke was turned down by a dozen medical schools.)

In their 1978 ruling on the case, the Supreme Court justices set out a complicated decision, neither fully repudiating nor endorsing affirmative action. Mandating that UC–Davis admit Bakke, the Court struck down separate admissions processes as a violation of the Equal Protection Clause of the Fourteenth Amendment. But the Court majority also held that race could be a factor in admissions decisions for the purpose of encouraging diversity within an entering class. Justice Thurgood Marshall dissented from the majority's reasoning, saying that the Fourteenth Amendment allowed for special remedies for groups as evidenced by the Freedman's Bureau. Justice Blackmun agreed, arguing "to get beyond racism, we must first take account of race." The ways that the case was covered and litigated (through words like *racial preferences* and *reverse discrimination*) defined the terms of the debate around affirmative action in the years to come and opened the door to white legal challenges to affirmative action.

In response to the Supreme Court's *Bakke* decision and the accompanying public anxiety, universities scaled back their newly implemented efforts to recruit African Americans and Latinos. At the same time, the cost of attending college shot up more than 75 percent, as President Reagan and Congress slashed funding for Pell grants and other forms of financial assistance. The progress made in the 1960s and early 1970s in black college education rates reversed in the years after *Bakke.* By 1991, 41.7 percent of white high school graduates enrolled in college, compared with 31.5 percent of blacks. In 1992, 12 percent of blacks, compared with 22 percent of whites, had completed a bachelor's degree. The number of black Ph.D.s also declined from 4.5 percent in 1977 to 3.7 percent in 1992. Real educational equity that had seemed attainable in the mid-1970s had become an increasingly distant possibility.

Opponents of affirmative action funded by conservative think tanks such as the Center for Individual Rights and the Bradley Institute stepped up their assault against affirmative action during the 1990s—and increasingly, the courts took their side. Twelve years of Reagan's and Bush's appointments had transformed the federal judiciary; together, they had filled over half of the federal judgeships and appointed five Supreme Court justices. In *Hopwood v. Texas* in 1996, the Fifth Circuit Court of Appeals overturned the University of Texas Law School's affirmative action program, holding that ensuring a diverse student body was not enough to justify the program. The court discounted that factors other than race had played a role in denying the plaintiff Hopwood's admission to the law school class (one hundred whites with scores lower than hers had been admitted).

In California and Washington, voters approved state referendums to prohibit any use of race or gender with regard to employment, contracts, or admission. Supported by African-American conservatives, such as Ward Connerly, these initiatives reappropriated the discourse of civil rights into a campaign against "reverse discrimination." The California Civil Rights Initiative (CCRI), as it was disingenuously named, passed despite the organizing efforts of groups like Californians for Justice and opposition from blacks, Latinos, and Asians. President Clinton's and the Democratic Party's silence about the CCRI aided its passage. These initiatives and court decisions had a significant effect on admissions, with the number of blacks and Latinos admitted to the University of Texas and to the University of California at Berkeley and at Los Angeles dropping dramatically after *Hopwood* and the approval of the CCRI. For example, the numbers of African Americans admitted at the University of California–Berkeley in the year after the CCRI declined 64.3 percent, Chicanos 56.3 percent, and Native Americans 58.9 percent.

A New Day in Politics?:
The Emergence of Post–Civil Rights Politics

In 1976, with strong support from blacks, Georgia Governor Jimmy Carter became the Democratic nominee for president. Many saw Carter's candidacy, as a "new southerner" not wedded to segregation, to be a sign of a new day in American politics. Blacks played a historic role that year at the Democratic National Convention, with Congresswoman Barbara Jordan giving the keynote address and Rev. Martin Luther King Sr. closing the convention. A diverse array of blacks campaigned for Carter, from poet Nikki Giovanni to Detroit Mayor Coleman Young to SCLC's Andrew Young. The NAACP launched Operation Big Vote to register new voters in 36 states. In the November election, Carter carried Mississippi with 11,500 votes more than Gerald Ford. While Ford won 59 percent of white voters, Carter won more than 90 percent of black Mississippi voters. SCLC leader Andrew Young noted the historic importance of this victory, "[T]he hands that picked cotton finally picked the president." Black support, 94 percent for Carter, also proved decisive in northern states such as Ohio, Pennsylvania, and New York; meanwhile, Chicano support at 81 percent gave Carter the edge in Texas.

Yet, although he did appoint people of color to a record number of federal positions, including Andrew Young as ambassador to the United Nations, Patricia Harris as the Secretary of Housing and Urban Development, and Leonel Castillo to head Immigration and Naturalization Services, Carter failed to advance a civil rights agenda. Many of Carter's policies aimed at helping working blacks and Latinos stalled in Congress, while his tax reforms primarily benefited the wealthy and large corporations.

By the late 1970s, racial violence and KKK membership were again on the rise. In 1978 and 1979, Klansmen bombed black churches, homes, and schools in over a hundred cities and attempted to assassinate a number of southern NAACP officials. The most violent eruption of Klan violence occurred on November 3, 1979, in Greensboro, North Carolina. Seventy-five Klan and Nazi members attacked an anti-Klan demonstration, killing 5 people and wounding 11 others. The police had known of the planned attack on the civil rights activists (many of whom were members of the Communist party), and yet the on-duty officers were on lunch break during the time of the attack. Although the event was captured on videotape, an all-white jury concluded that there was insufficient evidence to convict the Klan members.

In this volatile political climate, California Governor Ronald Reagan secured the Republican presidential nomination in 1980. Reagan polished the racially motivated conservatism of Barry Goldwater, Richard Nixon, and George Wallace into a palatable but still divisive form of racial politics. What distinguished Reagan's triumph was not the political power of white backlash—this had much longer roots throughout the nation's history—but the repackaging of white resistance into new language and new targets. Reagan ran on a campaign that celebrated America, disparaging those who talked of the country's flaws or problems. Claiming to be the real egalitarian, Reagan called on America to "stand tall" against enemies domestic and foreign. He kicked off his campaign in Philadelphia, Mississippi, in August of 1980, the town where Goodman, Schwerner, and Chaney had been killed in 1964, pledging to defend "states rights." The subtext of his cheery, flag-waving campaign was clear: to return America to white Americans. Even his campaign slogan—"It's morning again in America"—underscored the darkness of the previous decades. In the 1980 election, 22 percent of Democrats, many who opposed the special programs that they believed people of color were receiving, switched party allegiance to vote for Reagan. Pollsters found in 1980 and then again in 1984 that many Reagan supporters attributed their economic vulnerability and the nation's domestic problems to blacks.

Reagan's message resonated well with many white middle and working-class voters faced with changes shaking the foundations of the U.S. economy. Beginning in the 1970s, the abandonment of manufacturing centers in the East and Midwest and the expansion of a low-wage service sector and subcontracting economy in the Sunbelt profoundly transformed the U.S. labor market. Private divestment and capital flight cost over 38 million American jobs. Unemployment soared from 2.8 million in 1968 to 7.6 million in 1980, while the number of people living in poverty grew by 8 million between 1979 and 1984. The shift from manufacturing to service and high-tech information industries, and the deployment of just-in-time production techniques, made it easier for employers to replace full-time employment with part-time and temporary jobs. In addition, immigrants from Latin America, the Caribbean, and Southeast Asia increasingly came to occupy the bottom end of the service and assemblage industries. The 1965 Immigration Act had changed the demographics of the U.S. immigrant population. In three decades, the percentage of Europeans among legal immigrants dropped from 80 percent to less than 20 percent. The steady growth of Third World migration to coastal cities like New York and Los Angeles fueled the booming high-tech, financial, and tourism industries eager for a steady stream of vulnerable immigrant labor who worked for minimal wages and few labor protections.

Corporate restructuring devastated African and Latino communities. "Last hired, first fired" rules disproportionately affected workers of color who had only recently gained entry into the skilled trades through the federal antidiscrimination policies of the 1960s, and who lived either in Rustbelt cities abandoned by manufacturing or Sunbelt cities that welcomed low-wage industries and open shop policies. The reorganization of cities like New York and Los Angeles into centralized command centers for global economic activity produced a highly bifurcated labor market divided between high-income and low-income workers, particularly evident in black and immigrant communities. In 1990, nearly 20 percent of blacks were employed as managers or in the professions, compared with 5 percent in 1950, yet black poverty had increased. By Reagan's second term, one-third of black families earned incomes below the poverty line; for black teenagers, unemployment increased from 38.9 percent to 43.6 percent. Black unemployment overall had risen by 1985 to a crisis level of 15.1 percent, followed by Latino unemployment at 10.5 percent. The effects of deindustrialization and economic globalization were clearly evident in the altered class structure of U.S. urban centers and in rising poverty among low-income women and communities of color. As the bottom half of the U.S. economy became increasingly feminized, poverty grew rapidly among female-headed households as women accounted for two-thirds of the nation's poor adults by the early 1980s.

President Reagan blamed this economic crisis on New Deal and Great Society programs. Reagan claimed that the black and Latino beneficiaries of the liberal programs of the 1960s were undermining the American tradition of individualism and self-reliance and were the cause of capital shortage and declining investment. As one commentator observed, the president treated "people in trouble as people who make trouble." Reagan's administration instead initiated a series of tax cuts for wealthy Americans and U.S. corporations, claiming that these subsidies would grow the economy and trickle down to the less fortunate. The effect of his tax policies was to transfer $25 billion from the least well-off to the richest fifth.

Calling for a return to an American tradition of self-help and voluntary associations, Reagan rolled back the welfare state. He abolished the public service jobs program, cut almost half a million people from the food stamp program, and reduced or eliminated funds for public housing and Medicaid for the working poor. Unemployment insurance was cut 6.9 percent, AFDC 12.7 percent, food stamps 12.6 percent, child nutrition 27.7 percent, and low-income energy assistance 8.3 percent.

In two years, Congress cut $18 billion from AFDC, Medicaid, supplemental security income (SSI) for elderly and disabled poor, free lunch programs, legal services, and food supplements for pregnant mothers, infants, and children under five. Thus, Reagan made the behavior of poor people the cause of the nation's problems, while celebrating the market as the solution for all economic troubles. Claiming that racism was a problem of the past, the president appointed people to the Civil Rights Commission and the EEOC who reversed the racial policies of the past administrations, withdrew federal support to promote desegregation, affirmative action, and open housing, and tried to roll back enforcement on voting rights and antidiscrimination laws.

President Reagan also initially opposed a popular movement demanding a federal holiday to commemorate the legacy of Martin Luther King, Jr. "We could have an awful lot of holidays if we start down the road . . . there's no way we could afford all those holidays." Congress, however, repudiated the president, approving in 1983 a bill designating the third Monday of every January as a federal holiday in honor of Martin Luther King. When the state of Arizona refused to honor the day, civil rights groups launched a boycott of the state. Conventions and groups totaling more than 134,000 visitors canceled their meetings in Arizona, leading the state to lose an estimated $77 million in tourist dollars. Succumbing to this political and economic pressure, the state eventually reversed its position.

NEW BLACK POLITICS

Black political mobilization continued throughout the 1970s, 1980s, and 1990s. In 1976, Unita Blackwell, one of the former leaders of the Mississippi Freedom Democratic Party, was elected mayor of Mayersville, Mississippi, the town where she had once been denied the right to vote. Local activists like Blackwell formed the backbone of Jesse Jackson's bid for the Democratic presidential nomination in 1984. Former SCLC organizer and founder of Operation PUSH (an organization dedicated to economic justice for African Americans), Jackson tapped into and inspired grassroots organizing throughout the country. Although other Democratic candidates focused on swing voters, Jackson sought to bring new voters into the party: "Reagan won Alabama by 17,500 votes but there were 272,000 unregistered blacks. He won Arkansas by 5,000 votes with 85,000 unregistered blacks. . . . [T]he numbers show that Reagan won through a perverse coalition of the rich and the unregistered. But this is a new day." Jackson hoped to build a Rainbow Coalition, allying whites, blacks, and Latinos. He was not supported by mainstream civil rights organizations such as the NAACP and the Urban League, who feared that his candidacy would undermine increasing black influence within the Democratic party, while his decision to meet with the Palestinian Liberation Organization and his friendship with Nation of Islam minister Louis Farrakhan fractured his support among liberal Jewish voters.

Although Walter Mondale captured the Democratic nomination, Jackson's speech electrified the 1984 Democratic Convention, exhorting that "our time has come." He called for a new social movement emerging from the campaign that repaired divisions among whites, Jews, blacks, and Latinos. "We must turn from finger-pointing to clasped hands. . . . Twenty years later, we cannot be satisfied by just restoring the old coalition. Old wine skins must make room for new wine." That same night, Unita Blackwell—who 20 years earlier with the MFDP had been refused a seat—also spoke to the convention. "I felt tears because Fannie Lou Hamer should have been standing there, she was standing there in us, in me, in Jesse, in all of us, because in 1964 she testified . . . for the right for me to stand there at the podium." Jackson sought the Democratic presidential nomination again in 1988. With widening support from Latino and black politicians, Jackson received seven million votes—nearly 24 percent of the primary vote. Massachusetts Governor Michael Dukakis instead won the nomination, receiving 43 percent of Democratic primary voters. Jackson's focus on voter registration brought millions of new voters to the polls in 1984 and 1988 but did not lead to a more progressive politics or the defeat of Republican nominees Ronald Reagan (1984) and George Bush (1988).

Other civil rights leaders had greater success building new coalitions. On April 12, 1983, black Congressman Harold Washington was elected mayor of Chicago. A voter-registration campaign in Chicago brought in a hundred thousand new black voters in 1982 and convinced Washington to enter the mayor's race. Long considered one of the most segregated cities in the nation, Chicago had been tightly controlled by white machine politics. By building a coalition between liberal whites and people of color in the city, Washington won a surprising upset in the Democratic primary against the incumbent Mayor Jane Byrne and Richard Daley, son of the late mayor, and defeated Republican Bernard Epton in the general election. At his inauguration, Washington celebrated the election and what lay ahead for the city, "My election was the result of the greatest grassroots effort in the history of the city of Chicago. . . . [T]here is a fine new spirit that seems to be taking root. I call it the spirit of renewal." Washington, however, faced a tough first term—trying to clean up bias, corruption, and mismanagement within Chicago's municipal government with little support from the city council or the police. Reelected for a second term, Washington died unexpectedly of a massive heart attack on November 25, 1987.

In another important victory for the Rainbow movement, David Dinkins was elected mayor of New York City in 1989. His long history of Democratic party activism and commitment to bringing the city together enabled Dinkins to defeat three-term mayor Ed Koch in the primary and Republican nominee Rudolph Giuliani in the general election. Celebrating the "gorgeous mosaic" of New York City, Dinkins polled 88 percent of the black vote, 64 percent of the Latino vote, and less than 30 percent of the white vote. Latino voting power proved central to Dinkins's victory and in other political races throughout the country. Between 1976 and 1996, Latino voter registration increased 164 percent compared with 31 percent for non-Latinos; voter turnout grew 135 percent among Latinos in contrast to 21 percent among non-Latinos. The number of Latino voters more than doubled from 2.1 million in 1980 to 5 million by the late 1990s. Strong Latino support helped bring Dinkins into office; a lower Latino turnout and only 55 percent support helped propel Rudolph Giuliani to a slim victory four years later.

Multiracial coalitions also came together to promote the candidacies of women of color. Carol Moseley-Braun became the first black woman ever elected to the U.S. Senate in 1992. Running in the Illinois primary against incumbent Senator Alan Dixon and Albert Hofeld, Moseley-Braun was mostly ignored. Her hearty support from white women and more than 99 percent of the black vote ensured her victory in the primary. She then defeated Republican Richard Williamson in the general election. In 1992, Nydia Velazquez of Brooklyn, New York, also drawing on a rainbow coalition of voters, became the first Puerto Rican woman elected to Congress.

RADICAL ACTIVISM, PROFOUND REPRESSION

FBI agents continued to harass militant racial organizations. By the mid 1970s, the American Indian Movement had replaced the Black Panther Party as the FBI's "number one terrorist organization in America." While only a few FBI agents were stationed in South Dakota before the siege at the Pine Ridge Reservation at Wounded Knee in 1973, the number grew to 60 by 1975. After Wounded Knee, tribal leadership, with help from the Bureau of Indian Affairs and the FBI, violently repressed Pine Ridge activism, leading to 60 deaths on the reservation. In response to this violence, the activists armed themselves and called on AIM for protection. A number of AIM activists came to Pine Ridge and set up a spiritual camp on the land of Harry and Cecilia Jumping Bull.

At the time tribal leader Dick Wilson was preparing to sign over one-eighth of the reservation (a portion rich in uranium) to the federal government, a deal that AIM strongly opposed. On the evening of June 25, 1975, two FBI agents came to the Jumping Bulls' house on the pretense of arresting 17-year-old AIM supporter Jimmy Eagle on a theft charge. (All charges against Eagle were subsequently dropped.) Fearing bigger trouble, AIM supporters solicited assistance from activists across the reservation. The next morning, when 150 BIA police and FBI men raided the Jumping Bull house, they were met by 30 AIM activists. In the ensuing firefight, 2 FBI agents and 1 AIM member were killed.

Out of the 30 AIM activists present at the Jumping Bull residence, U.S. attorneys decided to prosecute 3 for the murder of the 2 FBI agents: Leonard Peltier, Bob Robideau, and Darrelle Butler. Robideau and Butler were tried first. During their trial, both testified that they did shoot during the June 26 raid as a matter of self-defense, and their attorneys revealed that FBI agents had coerced and manipulated witnesses prior to the trial to try to ensure their conviction. Butler and Robideau were acquitted, as the jury concluded that "it was the government, not the defendants or their movement, which was dangerous." The jury foreman explained, "We felt that any responsible person would have reacted the same way when the agents came in there shooting."

Leonard Peltier was tried separately in 1977. Doubting that he would get a fair trial after the shoot-out, Peltier sought refuge in Alberta, Canada. Extradited to the United States on a falsified affidavit, he returned too late to stand trial with the other two defendants. Having lost with Robideau and Butler, U.S. prosecutors changed their strategy. The case was removed from Cedar Rapids to a more conservative judge in North Dakota, who ruled inadmissible much of the defense used in the earlier trial, including the acquittal itself and the evidence of FBI misconduct. Claiming that "the FBI is not on trial," the judge allowed no mention of the "reign of terror" on Pine Ridge, the falsified affidavit, or the FBI's treatment of witnesses leading up to the trial. Nor did he allow Peltier to plead self-defense as had Robideau and Butler. Peltier was convicted of the murder of the two agents and was sentenced to two consecutive life terms. Peltier protested to the judge in his presentencing statement, "you were unwilling to allow even the slightest possibility that a law officer would lie on the stand. Then how could you possibly be impartial enough to let my lawyers prove how important it is to the FBI to convict a Native American activist in this case?"

Peltier's lawyers immediately appealed the decision and, through the Freedom of Information Act, requested the FBI files on the case. The 12,000-page files revealed that the ballistics of the gun introduced as

Peltier's (which the FBI knew was not his) did not match the bullets that killed the two FBI agents. U.S. prosecutors admitted they "do not know who shot the agents" and to having falsified documents submitted to Canadian authorities to secure Peltier's extradition. Peltier's first appeal was denied by the Eighth Circuit Court. Subsequent courts have conceded that "there is evidence in this record of improper conduct on the part of some FBI agents, but we are reluctant to impute even further improprieties to them" by ordering a new trial. The position of the prosecutors, moreover, has changed over the years. Accusing Peltier of "aiding and abetting" (when he was originally convicted for murder, not aiding and abetting), they denied that the discrepancies in the evidence exonerated him or necessitated a new trial. Amnesty International classified Peltier a political prisoner, attributing his imprisonment and the denial of his appeals to his role in AIM (a group the U.S. government opposes).

Amnesty International has also questioned the trial and imprisonment of another American prisoner—Mumia Abu-Jamal. In 1981, journalist and political activist Mumia Abu-Jamal was arrested and charged with the killing of Philadelphia police officer Daniel Faulkner. A former Black Panther and award-winning radio commentator who had been critical of police harassment, Abu-Jamal became involved in a late-night confrontation with police officers during their attempt to arrest his brother. In the confrontation, Abu-Jamal was shot by police and then subsequently beaten while Officer Faulkner was also shot and killed. Ballistics experts could not match any of the bullets at the scene or in the officer's body to Abu-Jamal's legally registered gun. Four eyewitnesses had described a person fleeing the murder scene, but Abu-Jamal was injured too severely to have fled. Charged with the murder of Faulkner, Abu-Jamal was found guilty and sentenced to death. His case triggered an international grassroots movement to demand a retrial for him and to call attention to the unfairness of the death penalty. As Abu-Jamal wrote, "Why is it that Pennsylvania's African-Americans who make up only 9 percent of its population, comprise close to two-thirds of its death row population? . . . They are not administering justice. . . . They are simply revealing the partiality of justice." In 2001, Judge William H. Yohn Jr. of federal district court threw out the death sentence, finding the presiding judge's instructions to the jury to be unconstitutional. Yohn, however, upheld Abu-Jamal's murder conviction.

Local activists and lawyers with the National Task Force for COINTELPRO Litigation and Research did succeed in overturning the conviction of another political prisoner, Geronimo ji Jaga (Pratt). A decorated Vietnam veteran and former head of the Los Angeles Black Panthers, ji Jaga spent 27 years in jail for the murder of white school teacher Karen Olson. Viewing ji Jaga's Black Panther leadership as a threat, FBI

officials and government prosecutors had adopted a two-pronged strategy, manipulating evidence and testimony during the trial while at the
same time promoting internal division within the Panther party itself.
During his trial, ji Jaga and his lawyers asserted that he had been in Oakland during the murder, 350 miles north of Santa Monica where Olson
was killed, and that he had been under FBI surveillance at the time. FBI
agents knew this to be true, their own wiretaps placed him in Oakland
at the time. This evidence was withheld during the trial and subsequent
appeals. Panther activist Julius Butler, one of the key witnesses for the
prosecution, testified that ji Jaga had admitted to the crime. Although ji
Jaga's legal team suspected Butler was an FBI informant, Butler denied
under oath that he was working for the FBI. Ji Jaga's defense was further
compromised by fissures within the Black Panther Party. Panther leader
Huey Newton excommunicated ji Jaga and his wife, Sharon Pratt, and
ordered that "any Party member or community worker who attempts to
aid them or communicate with them in any form or manner shall be considered part of their conspiracy to undermine and destroy the Black Panther Party." As a result, nearly a dozen Panthers, who could have cor-
roborated ji Jaga's story that he was in Oakland, remained silent during
ji Jaga's first trial. On May 29, 1997, after 27 years of imprisonment, ji
Jaga was released. A California judge overturned his conviction based on
the new evidence that Julius Butler had indeed worked for the Bureau
and that FBI records put ji Jaga in Oakland at the time of the murder.

The most decisive case of state repression of black radicals occurred
in Philadelphia. For nearly a year in 1977-78, police had blockaded the
headquarters of black nationalist organization MOVE in Powelton Village.
A radical, naturalist, utopian community, MOVE members lived together
in communal fashion and were dedicated to revolutionary change "to
show people how corrupt, rotten, criminally enslaving this system is."
MOVE members did not encourage violence but asserted their right to
self-defense if attacked. This stand-off ended with the death of one officer and injuries to both the police and MOVE members.

Following the siege and increased surveillance, MOVE members for-
tified their house at 6221 Osage Avenue. Then, in May 1985, Mayor Wilson Goode, himself black, authorized an attack and bombing of the
Osage house. Neighborhood complaints about the bullhorn and loud-
speaker system MOVE members had set up, the stray dogs and cats the
organization took in, their sanitary practices and dreadlocks hairstyles,
the way they raised their children, and overall danger to society were
cited as justification for the ensuing police attack.

Early in the morning on May 13, 1985, Police Commissioner Sambor
announced the police raid, shouting through his bullhorn, "Attention
MOVE! This is America!" Aware of the daily routine of the children living

The bombing of a MOVE house in Philadelphia killed 11 MOVE members and destroyed 61 houses.

at the MOVE house, authorities could have intercepted the MOVE leaders or their children outside of the house prior to the siege but chose not to do so. Following 12 hours of continuous assault where police fired ten thousand rounds of ammunition, a Pennsylvania state police helicopter dropped a bomb containing highly classified explosives onto the roof of the MOVE house, igniting a fire measuring 7,200 degrees Fahrenheit. The tar roof turned to liquid, parts of the house flew off like kindling, and the fire raced down the avenue, devouring houses on both sides of the street. In the first hours, firefighters held off—or were told to hold off—putting out the fire. While everyone else but MOVE had been evacuated from the block before the attack began, the attack killed 11 MOVE members, including 5 children, and destroyed 61 houses. Two people in the MOVE house lived—Ramona Africa and 13-year-old Birdie Africa.

Mayor Goode justified the attack the next day. "I would make the same decision because I think we cannot permit any terrorist group, and revolutionary group in this city, to hold a whole neighborhood or a whole city hostage." City authorities discovered only four guns and no explosives, despite having labeled MOVE as armed and dangerous. The only living adult from the Osage house, Ramona Africa, was tried on 12 counts of conspiracy, rioting, and aggravated assault. She was convicted and sentenced on 2 counts of riot and conspiracy but was acquitted of the other charges.

CHALLENGING BLACK ELECTED OFFICIALS

While some black Philadelphians gave the Goode administration the benefit of the doubt, many civil rights supporters throughout the city and the nation condemned the bombing. Black activists, artists, and intellectuals launched a "Draw the Line" campaign and attempted to place an ad in various newspapers to demonstrate their opposition to Mayor Goode's actions. The *Philadelphia Inquirer* refused to run the ad, as did the black-owned *Philadelphia Tribune*. Months later, with pressure building and as more facts leaked out about Goode's role in the bombing, the *Tribune* ran the paid ad, which read, "When Black elected officials use their positions of power to attack Black people, or to cover up for or excuse such attacks, they are no friends of ours and don't speak for or represent the interests of Black people. In the past, lines were clearly drawn on this question. Those who attack Black people were counted among our enemies. This line must be firmly drawn again. Murder is murder, no matter whether those responsible are Black or white."

The disillusionment many in the black community felt toward Mayor Goode mirrored the feelings of blacks in other cities. The election of black mayors in many cities kindled high hopes that city hall would be responsive to the needs of the black community. Change proved more difficult and slower in coming. As Maynard Jackson, Atlanta's first black mayor, explained, "[W]e had to deal with that tremendous expectation in the black community. Now, equally important and equally difficult was what we found in the white community: exaggerated anxiety. . . . I've seen bad press. But for the first two years that I was mayor, the press was almost hysterical."

Although black mayors brought with them fresh ideas and a committed staff, municipal governance from city bureaucracy to the police had not changed. Many city workers were not committed to the reforms that had brought these mayors into office. Mayor Jackson, for example, campaigned on making city hiring fair and open to all Atlantans. He immediately faced stiff opposition when he sought to open up the awarding of construction contracts in the planned $750 million airport expansion to African Americans. As black mayors sought to hold onto the coalitions that had brought them into office, they often felt that they had to take a tough stance on crime and unions to retain the support of white voters. Los Angeles's Mayor Tom Bradley, for example, remained silent when civil rights activists protested the harassing tactics of the Los Angeles Police Department (LAPD), allowing Police Chief Daryl Gates and the police to run roughshod over the civil rights of the city's black and Latino community.

In part because of the opposition he faced over affirmative action in the airport construction, Maynard Jackson took a very hard line when

1,300 sanitation workers, 98 percent of them black, struck for wage increases. Willie Bolden, an organizer for the municipal employees union AFSCME (American Federation of State, County, and Municipal Employees) who had worked hard to elect Jackson, explained the strike, "We made up in our minds, even though we had a lot of respect for Maynard, that we were not going to exchange a white slave master for a black master. . . . And whatever it took to get for our people what they rightfully deserved, we were going to do that—including a strike . . . our folks were picking up garbage working among maggots, and we felt that they needed to get paid for doing that." Jackson responded by firing the striking workers, although most were rehired when the union accepted the city's offer three months later. Detroit's Mayor Coleman Young, despite his labor background, cultivated strong ties with Detroit's business community even before he was elected. He pursued those ties once in office, often ignoring the needs of his black constituents.

"STRUGGLE DOES NOT END AT THE BORDERS OF THE UNITED STATES"

In the 1980s civil rights activism also took on international dimensions, as activists contrasted the nation's democratic rhetoric with its antidemocratic foreign policy. Many people saw that protecting civil rights at home meant protecting them abroad and broke the law to demonstrate their opposition to U.S. policy in South Africa and Central America. On Thanksgiving Eve in 1984, Randall Robinson of Trans-Africa, Mary Frances Berry of the U.S. Commission on Civil Rights, Eleanor Homes Norton of the Georgetown Law Center, and District of Columbia delegate to the Congress Walter Fauntroy launched daily sit-ins at the South African embassy in Washington, D.C., to protest South Africa's apartheid policy. As political activism within South Africa heated up and the National Party government grew more repressive, many Americans sought to intensify the international pressure on the South African government, drawing connections between U.S. and South African racial policies. Hundreds of Americans, including scores of celebrities and politicians, were arrested over the following year in front of the embassy.

A parallel movement grew on college campuses. Students built shantytowns, led sit-ins, held rallies and demonstrations, and disrupted corporate meetings to pressure their universities to divest holdings in companies doing business in South Africa until apartheid was ended. Students charged that many U.S. corporations benefited economically from apartheid and that the system of racial separation could not sustain itself without international investment. Eleanor Holmes Norton linked the civil rights movement to this burgeoning antiapartheid movement. "Struggle does not begin or end at the borders of the United States. . . . Blacks get their moral authority not only because they were pressing for their own rights, but because they did so in a way that wrote equality lessons large. And they wrote those lessons large enough for people throughout this country and throughout the world to understand the meaning of equality." Congress bowed to pressure (from students and hundreds of thousands of Americans) to pass limited economic sanctions against South Africa in 1986, overriding President Reagan's veto.

The Reagan administration's policy in Central America and the Caribbean also provoked widespread opposition from human rights activists. From 1981 to 1989, the U.S. poured $3.7 billion into El Salvador to prop up a military dictatorship that murdered thousands of its own citizens each year. Yet in 1982, only a minority of Americans—one poll saying 16 percent—supported this policy in El Salvador. When nearly a half million Salvadorans fled this repression and torture to come to the United States and when the Reagan administration sought to deport them (even though many faced severe punishment and possible death if they returned), church groups along with a network of Salvadorans began a Sanctuary movement, promising food, shelter, and safety to Salvadoran refugees.

Many Americans protested the inconsistencies of the government's refugee policy, deporting Salvadorans and Haitians but welcoming refugees from Communist Cuba. Human rights activists questioned why Cuban boat people were granted asylum while darker-skinned Haitians, fleeing the dictatorship of Jean-Claude Duvalier, were sent back. For them, refugees should be admitted whether or not their government was a friend of the United States or their skin color not white.

A WAR ON DRUGS OR A WAR ON COMMUNITIES OF COLOR?

The Reagan administration's War on Drugs also undermined the democratic vision of equal justice that had given rise to the civil rights movement. Through it, the country found a new language to stigmatize communities of color. Whites and blacks had equal rates of drug abuse and whites used alcohol and drugs at higher rates than blacks, nonetheless black and Latino users and dealers—and by extension black and Latino communities—were targeted during the 1980s. While white users were steered towards rehabilitation centers, blacks and Latinos were pushed into jail as racial fears and moral panic justified increased policing, longer sentences, and more jails. The War on Drugs also provided a distraction from the economic problems facing many Americans as deindustrialization, suburban flight, and public disinvestment led to rising unemployment and poverty rates and to declining housing stock in many cities.

The portrayal of cities as sites of moral breakdown and young people as delinquent provided cause to suspend civil liberties to get "these hoodlums" off the streets. An individual's color often led to a search and arrest. Once in the criminal justice system, people of color were more likely to receive longer sentences and to serve prison time rather than parole. By the end of the 1990s, half of all inmates were black and 17 percent were Latino. Racial biases within the legal system posed a more chilling problem following the Supreme Court's 1977 ruling legalizing the death penalty. Disproportionate numbers of people executed or on death row were people of color. And because most states blocked prisoners from voting while in prison and 14 states barred persons convicted of a felony from voting, felony convictions had critical political impact in reducing the voter rolls.

The explosion of crack cocaine onto the American drug scene in the mid-1980s and the violence that accompanied this lucrative market led to the enactment of "three strikes" laws, mandatory higher sentences, and a dramatic increase in aggressive policing tactics and high-tech surveillance. Ironically, the Reagan administration indirectly enabled this drug-related violence by weakening laws regulating the sale and distribution of guns. By the mid-1980s, a $30 fee, plus a loose background check, was sufficient to buy a gun.

Drug-war policies also spurred tremendous growth in the prison industry and in state and federal spending. Since the beginning of the War on Drugs in the 1970s, the United States spent $300 billion on prisons, with little reduction in drug sales or drug abuse. By the end of the century, corrections cost the nation $40 billion per year. The construction of new prisons cost states approximately $54,209 per bed, while federal construction costs ran as high as $78,000 per inmate. Excluding new construction, prisoners cost the state almost $25,000 per person per year. And, whereas the prison population in the United States numbered 200,000 in 1972, it had increased six-fold by 1997 to nearly 1.2 million, with another half a million awaiting trial or serving short sentences in local jails.

Towns and cities hit hard by deindustrialization clamored to be the sites of these new prisons. More than 600,000 guards, administrators, and other personnel worked for the prison system, providing a powerful economic and political incentive to continue high rates of incarceration. When President Reagan changed a 60-year-old policy of prohibiting for-profit prisons because they often led to abuses of prisoners, private companies entered the business of building and running prisons and of using prison labor. In 1996, paid 80 percent less than minimum wage since their wages were garnished to pay for "room and board," prisoners produced $9 billion worth of products for companies such as TWA, IBM, Microsoft, AT&T, Eddie Bauer, Spalding, and Starbucks. While unemployment rates for young people of color remained high, incarcerated young people of color labored for companies in prison. Prison education programs, libraries, and newspapers were also defunded.

The War on Drugs also heightened tensions between the police and communities of color. These tensions reached a breaking point for Miami's black community in 1980. On December 17, 1979, while riding his motorcycle, Arthur McDuffie slowed instead of stopping for a red light. Thirty-three-years old, unarmed, and father of two, McDuffie was a black ex-Marine and insurance agent. McDuffie's refusal to stop for police led to a high-speed chase. He was heavily beaten after being pulled over and died four days later as a result of these injuries. On May 17, 1980, an all-white jury acquitted the four police officers of all charges in McDuffie's death, despite extensive, graphic testimony of the beatings that McDuffie sustained. The black communities of Miami—Liberty City, Overtown, and Coconut Grove—erupted in violence over this verdict and their frustration with their own economic and social marginalization in the city. Many black neighborhoods had been cut through by highway construction, and black unemployment reached as high as 50 percent, while greater economic opportunities were opened up to light-skinned, middle-class Cubans. As Miami's Puerto Rican–born Mayor Maurice Ferre explained, "all of the many problems that Miami had in the black community—poverty, the underclass, racism—all of these things were coming together. . . . [T]his is the tinderbox that somebody strikes a light and all of a sudden there's an explosion." In the next several days, 18 people were killed, 400 wounded, and 1,250 people arrested, with property damage estimated at $50–100 million.

The demographics and heavy-handed tactics of the New York Police Department (NYPD) precipitated similar protest. In the early 1960s, at a time when larger numbers of blacks and Puerto Ricans were moving to the city and looking for sustainable employment, the city repealed its law requiring city residence for municipal employees. This perpetuated an overwhelmingly white police force (many members of which did not live in the city) in an increasingly nonwhite city. In 1980, black and Puerto Rican city residents sued the 90 percent white NYPD. Ruling for the plaintiffs, the court of appeals required that a third of all newly hired officers be black or Latino to correct this discriminatory hiring pattern.

A series of killings by police aggravated the already tense police-community relations. In September of 1983, Michael Stewart died in police custody following his arrest for painting graffiti on a subway wall.

Stewart's family contended that he was choked and beaten by the police. But the medical examiner ruled the death had been caused by unrelated heart failure despite conceding that Stewart had sustained bodily injuries. Then, on October 29, 1984, police officer Stephen Sullivan shot Eleanor Bumpers twice at close range. The first shot badly injured the hand in which Bumpers allegedly held a knife, threatening Sullivan. Nonetheless, Sullivan was also found not guilty.

The Stewart and Bumpers cases highlighted the difficulty of successfully prosecuting police and magnified community concern over police brutality. Two New York mothers—Iris Baez and Margarita Rosario—in response formed Parents against Police Brutality in 1995 to draw attention to their sons' cases and the lack of police accountability. Baez's son Anthony had been killed by an illegal police chokehold, while Anthony Rosario and Hilton Vega (Margarita Rosario's son and nephew) were killed execution style, laying face down on the floor. As Rosario explained, "We gave ourselves a name just to have a name. Then calls started. Press, families: It turned out to be something the community needed." Visiting other families who had lost loved ones through police violence, Baez and Rosario offered consolation, community, and political action. Family by family, they built a political network. Baez regularly showed up at public events that Mayor Giuliani attended, demanding justice be brought against Officer Francis Livotti in the death of her son. At the time of her son's death, Livotti was the subject of several civilian complaints. Her efforts finally secured an investigation that led to Livotti's conviction on federal civil rights charges. The Baez family also won a civil suit against the city for $3 million. No criminal charges were brought against the two officers involved in Anthony Rosario's death.

Parents against Police Brutality emerged as a leader in the movement that blossomed in the wake of the police shooting of an unarmed African immigrant, Amadou Diallo. On February 4, 1999, Diallo was shot 41 times outside his apartment in the Bronx by the NYPD's Street Crime Unit (established as an elite unit to fight the War on Drugs). In response, a multiracial group of New Yorkers, led by the Reverend Al Sharpton and a coalition of civil rights and civil liberties groups across the city, began daily rallies and civil disobedience outside police headquarters in downtown Manhattan. The four officers were indicted for murder. Their attorneys convinced the state to move the trial to Albany; on February 25, 2000, the four officers were acquitted of all charges.

Charges of police brutality also arose in Los Angeles. Under the leadership of Police Chief Daryl Gates, the Los Angeles Police Department stop-and-frisk, zero-tolerance procedures targeted urban communities, and young black and Latino men in particular. In one incident in 1979, police officers killed Eula Mae Love. A 5'4", 39-year-old African-American woman, Love grabbed a kitchen knife to prevent a gas maintenance man from turning off her gas. Although she had not actually stabbed anyone, the police arriving on the scene shot her 12 times. This incident inflamed the black community, with Congresswoman Maxine Waters demanding Gates's resignation. A group of several hundred clergy demanded that the Justice Department review this killing and the killings by the police of three hundred other people of color in Los Angeles over the past decade. A community group, the Coalition against Police Abuse, collected tens of thousands of signatures to demand a civilian review board and independent oversight of the police. Chief Gates dismissed charges that the Los Angeles police had used excessive force, specifically concerning the deaths of 15 blacks during police chokeholds. "We may be finding," Gates explained, "that in some blacks when the carotid choke hold is applied the veins or arteries do not open up as fast as they do on normal people."

Gates's initial success in precluding any meaningful investigation of police tactics was undermined by an unprecedented confirmation of police brutality. In March 1991, black motorist Rodney King was pulled over following a police chase, severely beaten, and then released without being charged. What distinguished this incident was that the 56 blows police officers rained on King in 81 seconds were captured on videotape by George Holiday, a local man experimenting with his new videocamera. The videotape was broadcast and rebroadcast throughout the city and the nation. The guilt of the officers seemed photographically clear, and many Angelenos demanded that the LAPD be held accountable for the kind of justice it had long practiced. Defense attorneys, however, convinced the judge that, given the publicity, the officers could not receive a fair trial in Los Angeles. The trial was moved to Simi Valley, a largely white suburban community friendly to law enforcement. It ended on April 29, 1992, when the jury acquitted the officers of all charges. Enraged, a multiracial group of Angelenos took to the streets in a rebellion that lasted four days. Fifty-eight people were killed (26 African Americans, 18 Latinos, 10 whites, 2 Asians, and 2 unknown), 2,300 were injured, 5,000 were arrested (52 percent of whom were Latino and 39 percent black), and damage was estimated at more than $500 million. Although police brutality was the catalyst, the widening gap between rich and working-class Angelenos was at the heart of the riot. Rodney King himself held a press conference to try to stop the violence. "People, I just want to say, can we all get along. . . . We'll get our justice. They've won the battle, but they haven't won the war." Public outrage over the Simi Valley verdict led officials in the Civil Rights Division of the Department of Justice to indict and try the four officers on civil rights charges. Two of the officers were convicted, and two others were acquitted.

From "Willie" Horton to Colin Powell: George Bush's Post–Civil Rights Policies

The stereotype of black criminality proved politically useful for Republican nominee George Bush in the 1988 presidential campaign. In an influential ad about "Willie" Horton, he attacked the Democratic presidential nominee, Massachusetts Governor Michael Dukakis. Governor Dukakis had let Horton (a black man) out of prison on a Massachusetts furlough program, and Horton then raped a white woman. Horton's actual name was William, but Bush's advisors opted for "Willie" because it better conveyed Horton's race in the ad. Using a demeaning mug shot resembling the caricatured images of blacks in the Jim Crow South, the Horton ad effectively portrayed Dukakis as dangerously soft on crime. By playing on long-held white fears of black crime (and black rapists in particular), Bush's campaign transformed one crime into a parable of marauding blacks that would be unleashed by a Dukakis presidency. The Horton ad proved to be emblematic of the new politics of race (where race is invoked in malignant ways but not spoken of directly), and was pivotal in Bush's victory.

In 1992, President Bush responded to the Los Angeles riots by blaming liberal social programs of the 1960s and proposing Operation Weed and Seed—a federally funded initiative to weed out urban crime while seeding cities with increased socioeconomic opportunities. Promises were made to help rebuild Los Angeles and alter the social conditions that had produced the rebellion. What resulted, however, was more funding for weeding—80 percent of the $500 million allocated was for the police—than for seeding cities with the kinds of jobs, educational opportunities, after-school programs, and health care denied to many residents.

The calculations underpinning President Bush's racial politics emerged most clearly in his appointment of Clarence Thomas to the Supreme Court. To replace the distinguished Thurgood Marshall, who retired from the court in 1991, Bush nominated Thomas, an extremely conservative black jurist. Despite personally benefiting from affirmative action policies that opened up racially exclusive institutions like Yale Law School, Thomas opposed this and a number of other civil rights initiatives instituted during the 1960s. As head of the Equal Employment Opportunity Commission during the Reagan administration, Thomas had shown little enthusiasm for enforcing racial and sexual equality. He claimed that he had never discussed the landmark abortion decision of *Roe v. Wade*. Thomas even catered to public scorn around black welfare recipients by slandering his own sister, Emma Mae Martin. "She gets mad when the mailman is late with her welfare check." Thomas had made up this story. Martin was not on welfare at the time and had stayed in

Georgia to care for their mother and an older aunt while Thomas pursued his education.

The Senate Judiciary Committee had almost completed its hearings into Thomas's confirmation when a congressional aide leaked the news that a former employee at the EEOC, a black lawyer named Anita Hill, had previously told Congressional investigators that Thomas had sexually harassed her while she worked for him at the Department of Education and at the EEOC. Pressure from women's groups forced the committee to delay voting on Thomas's confirmation until a hearing into the charges could be completed. This process was flawed from the start: other women who also had accused Thomas of sexual harassment were not allowed to testify nor was any expert testimony on sexual harassment allowed. Senator Joe Biden ran the proceedings like a criminal trial rather than as a hearing to determine the qualifications of a potential life appointment to the bench. The matter was turned into a public spectacle, with the committee juxtaposing the conflicting accounts of Hill and Thomas into a "he said, she said" scenario for national television. Hill, a black conservative herself and a law professor at the University of Oklahoma, testified how Thomas on numerous occasions had propositioned her, boasted about his sexual skills, and made sexually explicit remarks to her while she was working for him, even though she asked him not to do so.

Having long argued that racism was a thing of the past but now faced with Hill's damaging testimony, Thomas claimed racism and called the proceedings a "high-tech lynching." Although black groups had split around Thomas's confirmation, Hill's charges and Thomas's claims of racial victimization brought many to Thomas's side. Ultimately, the Senate voted 52–48 to confirm Thomas. In the aftermath of the hearings, 1,600 African-American women took out a *New York Times* advertisement and organized a conference to document how Anita Hill—and, by extension, African-American women—had been disparaged during the hearings. Criticizing the silences of many traditional black organizations around Hill's charges, the ad stated: "We are outraged by the racist and sexist treatment of Professor Anita Hill, an African American woman who was maligned and castigated for daring to speak publicly of her own experience of sexual abuse."

The Thomas appointment revealed another feature of post–civil rights racial politics. Blacks in leadership positions seemed to confirm that the racial situation was becoming more fair, even while their own success did not necessarily represent larger systemic change (many of these leaders had been chosen for their conservative politics). Such symbolism helped in advancing other controversial policies, for instance masking the role of blacks in the military. In January 1991, President Bush prepared to take the United States to war against Iraq, defending this action as necessary to protect democracy and U.S. oil interests in the Kuwaiti emirate. The U.S. commitment to self-determination and racial advance was embodied in the leadership role of the conservative black Chairman of the Joint Chiefs of Staff Colin Powell. Powell's position at the helm of the operation obscured inequities within the armed forces: blacks, while only 13 percent of the U.S. population, comprised 25 percent of the troops but a small minority of the officer corps. The war also brought forth a wave of ethnic intolerance across the nation, as Arab Americans of various ethnicities found themselves the targets of harassment and even violence. Some Americans put bumper stickers on their cars reading "I Don't Brake for Iraqis," and political cartoons and editorials played on anti-Arab stereotypes.

OLD STRUGGLES, NEW ACTIVISM

Just as post–civil rights politics turned on the idea that racism was largely a remnant of the past, so too was civil rights activism seen as a movement of the past. Although public focus on these movements lessened, the quest for racial justice and equality continued, often in new forms. Many of the activists of the sixties were joined by young new allies to continue the work of local organizing. Key issues of the civil rights movement such as public transportation and education remained crucial battlegrounds for community activists and student leaders in the 1980s and 1990s. These movements succeeded in forging multiracial coalitions to press for social change.

The Bus Rider's Union (BRU) in Los Angeles exemplified this marriage of the goals and tactics of civil rights movements of the 1950s and 1960s to the new issues and strategies of the 1990s. The BRU came out of the Labor/Community Strategy Center, whose founders began their political activism in the 1960s. Using the bus as a space for organizing and as a symbol of the broader problems that confronted working-class whites and people of color, the BRU assembled a multiracial base of fifty thousand supporters to challenge the racial and class inequities in Los Angeles's public transportation system. In a car-dominated city, poor and working-class Angelenos relied on an overcrowded bus system as their means of transportation. The BRU was moved to act when the Metropolitan Transportation Authority (MTA) announced in 1994 that it planned to raise bus fares by $.25 and eliminate the $42 monthly pass while cutting back on bus service. Building a constituency across the city against this plan, the BRU won a class action suit against the MTA, arguing that the city had created a separate and unequal system of public transportation in violation of Title 6 of the Civil Rights Act. Eric Mann, one of the center's founders, compared the suit, which challenged "transportation racism and the creation of racist separate and unequal public transportation systems," with *Brown v. Board of Education* . The city's buses, accounting for 94 percent of the MTA's passengers, received less than a third of the MTA's resources. Eighty-one percent of the bus riders were people of color, 60 percent had incomes under $15,000, and 57 percent were women. The city's commuter rails connecting L.A. to its white, middle-class suburbs (many still in the process of completion) accounted for only 6 percent of the riders but 70.9 percent of the MTA's resources. The Bus Rider's suit was litigated by the NAACP–Legal Defense Fund and the SCLC, joined by the Korean Immigrant Workers Advocates. In a pretrial compromise, the MTA agreed to keep the monthly pass and raise the price to $49 and the individual fare by $.25. The court subsequently ordered the MTA to add more buses to alleviate the pervasive overcrowding. BRU activist Della Bonner saw the organization's purpose to pressure politicians elected because of the struggles of the 1960s to make good on their commitments. "We have to remind them. 'The policies that you helped create and implement are not meeting the needs of the people who did the protesting. We are still around.'"

In the 1980s and 1990s, movements for ethnic studies reemerged to protect the gains won in the late 1960s and to institute real change to diversify the curriculum. Some universities had waned in their commitment to ethnic studies while others had established black and Chicano studies programs with grant money and were willing to let the programs slide as funding and student protest died down. At institutions like Harvard, Columbia, and Berkeley, students held sit-ins and hunger strikes, took over buildings, and met with administrators to pressure the university to substantiate their professed commitment to multicultural education. By the late 1980s, the Afro-American Studies department at Harvard had been decimated; only one professor remained and plans were afoot to downsize the department into a program. Student demonstrations, sit-ins, and negotiations with the administration led to the hiring of Dr. Henry Louis Gates Jr. and the department's rejuvenation. At Columbia University, students demanded a systematic ethnic studies curriculum, particularly regarding Latino and Asian-American studies, and the diversification of the much-celebrated Core curriculum. To draw attention to these educational shortcomings, students briefly occupied the dean's office in February 1996. On April 1, four students began a hunger strike, and, nine days later, 150 students occupied the library. The arrest of 22 students by the police galvanized the student body. Two days later, several hundred students took over Hamilton Hall. Following negotiations over the next four days, university officials agreed to make new commitments to Asian-American and Latino studies but refused to establish an ethnic studies department or make fundamental changes in the Core curriculum.

Movements for curriculum change were not limited to higher education. As the United States prepared to celebrate the 500th anniversary of Columbus's voyage to the Americas, activists and educators mobilized to challenge the celebration and the heroic narrative of Columbus presented in most elementary and secondary school textbooks and classes and public festivities. The magazine *Rethinking Schools,* started in Milwaukee as a journal for progressive teachers and concerned parents across the country, for example, published a 100-page special issue entitled *Rethinking Columbus.* Selling more than two hundred thousand copies in the first few months, *Rethinking Columbus* brought together autobiographical writings by Native Americans, critical historical essays by teachers, bibliographic suggestions, and poetry to counter the quincentenary celebrations and to provide a more substantive exploration of Native-American experiences and perspectives. To link antiquincentenary activities throughout the country, Native-American activists also started a newspaper entitled *Indigenous Thought.*

Open enrollment policies also came under attack. For example, by the mid-1990s, 65 percent of the students at the City University of New York were people of color and over 50 percent were immigrants. The City University had become a university serving all New Yorkers. Mayor Giuliani, however, saw this as a decline in standards. In 1998, he proposed ending open admission at CUNY by cutting all remedial classes. Under open admissions at CUNY, students had been able to take noncredit remedial classes (if they did not pass entering tests on reading, writing, or math) as they began their college coursework in other subjects. Despite the fact that 80 percent of all public colleges (including the State University of New York) and 63 percent of private colleges offered remedial courses, CUNY's admissions policy was attacked as lowering standards. Mayor Giuliani's criticisms resonated with many throughout the city and state who believed the new demographics of CUNY had corrupted this formerly excellent "Harvard of the poor." Faculty members, through the New Caucus (the reform wing of the faculty union), and students, most notably Hunter College's SLAM, pressed to stop a plan that could shrink the student population of CUNY's four-year colleges by 45 percent, including nearly 75 percent of the students of color. Governor George Pataki and the CUNY Board of Trustees, however, endorsed Giuliani's recommendations and ended the 30-year policy of open admissions.

With public and judicial mandates for desegregation on the wane, educational segregation and resource shortages remained the same in some places—and returned with a vengeance in others. In 1991–92, 66 percent of blacks and 73 percent of Latino students attended schools where the majority of students were students of color. This segregation was accompanied by vast differentials in resources between schools that served white students and those that served students of color. Substantial discrepancies in public resources also separated suburban and city schools, while academic magnet programs found within many large school systems often took a greater share of the resources and the white students. For instance, in New York in 1990, per-pupil spending in the city was about half what it was in the wealthy Long Island suburbs of Great Neck, Jericho, and Manhasset. Elite magnet high schools like Stuyvesant High and Bronx Science received far superior materials and state-of-the-art facilities to those of the majority of the city's high schools. In January 2001, State Supreme Court Judge Leland DeGrasse ruled that New York State's system of financing public schools, by disproportionately hurting minority students, deprived New York City students of a "sound, basic education" and violated federal civil rights laws. He ordered an overhaul of the formula for financing. In states such as New Jersey, Alabama, North Carolina, Ohio, Connecticut, and Florida, parents and community activists also fought resource inequities by initiating suits for equalization and improvement in education.

THE LIBERAL FACE OF POST–CIVIL RIGHTS POLITICS

Despite his set of black advisors and New South background, President Bill Clinton's commitment to civil rights proved not to be as deep as his campaign promises. During the 1992 presidential campaign, Clinton returned to Arkansas to preside over the execution of Rickey Ray Rector, a mentally disabled black man who had killed a policeman, to negate any attack that he was soft on crime. In one of his first appointments as president, Clinton nominated University of Pennsylvania law professor Lani Guinier as assistant attorney general for civil rights. Guinier's support of affirmative action and proactive government action to ensure voting rights came under swift condemnation from many Republicans and media personalities who labeled her the "quota queen" (even though she disavowed quotas). Unwilling to meet the controversy head-on, two months later, Clinton withdrew Guinier's nomination. Having known Guinier personally for more than 20 years, he now claimed that her views were racially polarizing and scoffed that she believed "that minority rights cannot always be guaranteed under majority rule." Clinton's unwillingness to stand behind Guinier proved characteristic of his unwillingness to stand behind the civil rights gains of the 1960s in affirmative action, fair immigration policy, or social programs to alleviate the economic and social conditions that relegated many people of color to poverty.

But it was President Clinton's support of welfare reform that put a liberal stamp on the civil rights backlash. Playing on stereotypes of welfare recipients as lazy and dependent, Clinton had pledged during his 1992 campaign to "end welfare as we know it." Upon assuming office, he proposed no program to provide assistance to enable those on welfare to acquire the education and training to compete for skilled jobs in a high-tech economy, nor did he challenge popular perceptions that equated welfare with black and Latino women when most welfare recipients were white, lived in the suburbs or rural areas, and were in their twenties.

Blacks and Latinos disproportionately were the victims of poverty; in 1996, 28.4 percent of blacks and 29.4 percent of Latinos lived in poverty, more than double the rate for whites. These distressing statistics were cited during the ensuing debate over welfare not to spur the nation to action but to blame blacks and immigrants for their values and, by extension, their own condition. Contrary to the popular myth that welfare recipients kept having children to increase their welfare check, families on welfare were slightly smaller than the average U.S. family. Many women on welfare had been battered—and went on welfare to escape an abusive situation. Three-quarters of welfare recipients did not remain long on welfare but moved from welfare to underpaid work. And, although the debate focused on the overwhelming tax burden of welfare, welfare funding comprised less than 1 percent of the national budget; even including food stamps, it only made up 2.5 percent of the budget. The average welfare payment for a family of three was $388 per month, for a year $4,656—or, half of the poverty level. In contrast, corporate welfare in the form of tax breaks and public subsidies of private corporations was five times greater than welfare programs for the poor.

Numerous studies underscored how women on welfare wanted to work, did so when they could find jobs, and turned to welfare when stable work was not available. Still, work was often not a route out of poverty primarily because the minimum wage had not kept up with inflation. In the 1970s, a full-time, minimum-wage worker with two children lived above the poverty line. By the mid 1990s, the same family earned $8,840 a year—far below the 1995 poverty line of $12,188. For many parents in minimum-wage jobs, public assistance had become a necessary means to supplement what they were denied in the private sector: an income and health benefits on which their family could survive.

Despite this contrary reality, the political campaign for welfare reform hinged on popular myths that welfare and the culture it bred—not poverty—was hurting the poor. The lexicon of post–civil rights America—"culture of poverty," "welfare queens and deadbeat dads," "family values"—pathologized nonwhiteness without speaking it. As a Democratic president, Clinton legitimated the post–civil rights backlash by ushering in a postwelfare world that played on racial imagery while disavowing that race had anything to do with it.

In August 1996, President Clinton signed into law the Personal Responsibility and Work Opportunity Reconciliation Act (PRA). Dismantling the 60-year-old federal cash assistance program, Aid to Families with Dependent Children, this legislation replaced AFDC with Temporary Assistance to Needy Families (TANF), block grants to states governed under a new set of time limits and restrictions. Popularly known as "welfare reform," the PRA radically transformed the character of public assistance. No longer a social safety net, welfare became a temporary program designed to encourage marriage and other so-called family values among the nation's poor and to move welfare recipients as quickly as possible into the workforce. The PRA implemented strict restrictions on welfare eligibility, imposed strict work requirements, and banned large sectors of the American public (including teenage mothers, newborn babies, convicted felons, and legal immigrants) from receiving public assistance.

The new federal rules established a five-year lifetime limit on cash benefits and required that at least 80 percent of each state's welfare recipients work a minimum number of hours within two years. Those welfare clients who could not find a job were given a choice: lose their benefits or work in the public sector in exchange for monthly benefits *(workfare)*. Workfare jobs, however, were not necessarily newly created jobs, and no minimum-wage provisions or national fair labor standards applied to them. States were not required to provide basic education or skills development to their welfare clients or to track employment outcomes and wages over time. The program's definition of *work* or *training program* did not include higher education, only vocational programs approved by the state.

President Clinton declared welfare reform a success in the summer of 1999, citing new evidence that 35 percent of all welfare recipients had moved into work or work-related activities. The celebration seemed premature, given that these statistics confirmed that the majority of welfare recipients had not found work. On the same day that the president celebrated the success of the PRA, the Urban Institute released a study that showed that nearly one-third of those who had left public assistance since August of 1996 had returned at least once and that one-fourth of those who initially found jobs were no longer employed and had no working partner. The study also found that health insurance, which had formerly been provided to recipients through the Medicaid program, had been severely impacted by the 1996 reforms. The majority of those who had found work received no health coverage. Reviewing the wages earned by welfare recipients who had moved into work, the Congressional General Accounting Office concluded that these earnings averaged far below the poverty level.

Welfare reform depressed wages and affected jobs in the lower end of the workforce. In New York City, for example, Mayor Giuliani cut 22,000 municipal workers since 1995 and replaced them largely with workfare workers. By 1999, part-time workfare workers made up three-fourths of the labor force in the city's Parks Department, one-third of the Sanitation Department, and helped staff the city's welfare agency, housing authority, and public hospitals. The principal beneficiary of welfare reform was the city: the average New York City clerical worker's hourly wage was $12.32 not including benefits, but a workfare worker cost the city $1.80 an hour for a 20-hour work week and earned no benefits. Thirty thousand New York City workfare workers earned as low as $68.50 in cash and $60 in food stamps every two weeks for their work. Because the PRA's definition of *training* did not include higher education, twenty thousand students had been forced to drop out of the City University of New York.

These changes provoked protest and a new civil rights activism. From workfare organizing in New York City to community protests in Mission Hill, Boston, to the Economic Human Rights campaign of the Kensington Welfare Rights Union (KWRU), welfare recipients and their allies continued the work of the National Welfare Rights Organization to demand that state and federal policy recognize the rights of the poor. Based in Philadelphia, KWRU was founded in 1991 by a group of poor women and led by a former welfare recipient, Cheri Honkala. Through collective action, civil disobedience, and a commitment to addressing the daily survival needs of its members, KWRU built a national political movement around the position that poverty and homelessness were human rights issues. A multiracial movement of poor people led by poor people, this movement challenged the stereotypes of poverty in America, called for a politics of economic human rights, and combined providing services with political action to dramatize the inequities of contemporary society. An affiliate of AFSCME, KWRU cultivated connections to unions and the labor movement. In seeking to make poverty visible and uncomfortable, KWRU activists built tent cities, took over houses, protested at sites ranging from the Liberty Bell to the governor's mansion, and leafleted at welfare offices.

In the summer of 1998, KWRU launched a national tour, the New Freedom Bus, to document the human rights abuses of poverty and welfare across the United States. Honkala explained, "We're trying to polarize things in churches, labor unions, student organizations, campuses, and begin to have people take a position. . . . We're going to have millions of additional [poor] people on the streets of this country and you have a moral responsibility to do something." Crisscrossing the nation, hearing stories of toxic pollution in Mississippi, 80 percent unemployment in Appalachia, the demolition of public housing in Chicago, and the effects of time limits on poor people in Los Angeles, KWRU publicized the drastic effects of poverty and welfare reform. They brought these testimonials to the United Nations to argue that the United States had violated the 1948 Universal Declaration on Human Rights.

POST–CIVIL RIGHTS NATIVISM

The backlash against civil rights that fueled welfare reform also influenced immigration policy. The PRA itself served as a covert attack on the rights of immigrants, drawing sharp distinctions between the rights and entitlements of citizens and noncitizens and instituting unprecedented information sharing between government agencies. Whereas a green card had formerly ensured access to public benefits, legal immigrants arriving in the United States after August of 1996 had to wait five years before applying for cash assistance, food stamps, Medicaid, and public housing. Undocumented immigrants were not eligible for public assistance under AFDC, although their U.S.-born children were. This distinction remained in place, but federal and state agencies in charge of public benefits (including welfare, emergency health services, prenatal care, etc.) were required to report any person known to be illegally residing in the United States to the Immigration and Naturalization Service, making it dangerous for undocumented immigrants to apply for any benefits for their U.S.-born children.

The PRA was part of a broader nativist politics that had grown in the 1980s and 1990s. Responding to a growing clamor against the racial ideas that determined U.S. immigration since 1924, Congress passed the Hart-Cellar Act in 1965, putting an end to a system of ethnic quotas. Family reunification and job skills were now the priorities to govern immigration. By repealing the numerical limits on particular ethnic groups, the 1965 law opened the doors to much larger numbers of Asian, Caribbean, and Latin-American immigration, ended the preferential treatment Western European immigrants had received, and helped make the population of immigrants in the United States more multiracial.

Immigrants comprised a far smaller percentage of the population at the end of the century than at the beginning (14.7 percent of the population in 1910 compared with 7.9 percent in 1990). Yet, by the 1990s, many Americans felt that the country was being overrun by the new immigrants. The race of these new immigrants affected public perception; many Americans felt threatened by the increasing diversity of the United States. Half of the nearly 20 million people who migrated legally to the United States since 1965 came from Latin America and the Caribbean and another quarter from Asia and Africa. Although many businesses and the U.S. economy generally relied on a stream of undocumented labor, increased border patrols with Mexico also found popular support in the United States. In 1997, the United States deported 110,000 people; over 90 percent of whom were Latinos.

This anti-immigrant fervor triggered the passage of the Immigration Reform and Control Act (IRCA) in 1986, which allowed for significant legal Mexican immigration, provided amnesty for some undocumented workers who would have to prove their work history in the United States, and introduced civil and criminal sanctions against employers employing undocumented workers. IRCA made special exceptions for farmworkers by offering legal status to agricultural workers who could prove that they had spent at least 90 "man-days" during a qualifying period doing agricultural work. The law's employer sanctions were rarely enforced. Between 1989 and 1994, the number of INS agents to enforce the employer sanctions was cut in half, with fewer than 350 agents responsible for overseeing 7 million employers. Nonetheless, by legitimizing workplace raids, IRCA stepped-up the campaign against undocumented workers because these workers, rather than their employers, often lost their jobs or were arrested if the company was investigated.

In the early 1990s immigrants were vilified as a threat to American culture and values. In his campaign for the Republican presidential nomination in 1992, Pat Buchanan called the United States a "European country." "Our Judeo-Christian values are going to be preserved and our Western heritage is going to be handed down to future generations and not dumped on some landfill called multiculturalism." Sharing these sentiments, Californians resoundingly approved Proposition 187 in 1994 to deny undocumented immigrants and their families access to health care, welfare, and public education. Sponsored by a group calling itself SOS (Save Our State), Proposition 187 promised to save the state from an "illegal alien invasion." One proponent who drafted the proposition explained: "the people are tired of watching their state run wild and become a third world country." Proposition 187 neither increased employer sanctions nor closed the border to illegal immigration. Rather, it identified immigrants as a burden to the American taxpayer and the system of social privileges to which American citizens were entitled. Two out of three whites, nearly 50 percent of Asian Americans and African Americans, and 23 percent of Latinos supported the measure. After it passed, Proposition 187 was immediately challenged in court as a violation of constitutional guarantees to education and a state infringement on federal jurisdiction. When the California Supreme Court ruled that the proposition was unconstitutional, civil rights groups like Californians for Justice pressured Democratic Governor Gray Davis not to appeal the decision.

Rising nativism also led to passage of the Illegal Immigration Reform and Immigrant Responsibility Act (1996). The act aimed to reduce legal and illegal immigration and to speed up deportation for those immigrants whom the government saw as undesirable. It increased funding for border patrol, heightened civil penalties for illegal entry, and allowed the INS to wiretap and conduct undercover operations to ferret out immigrant smuggling and document-manufacturing rings. It put in place new grounds for deportation (including suspected terrorist activity and false claims of citizenship), restricted class action suits by undocumented immigrants against the INS, imposed new limitations on judicial review of INS decisions, and eased sanctions against employers. All in all, it gave added power to the INS, demonized undocumented immigrants, and turned a blind eye to companies that profited from their work.

This backlash against the immigration reforms of the 1960s also led to a debate about language. Chicano activists had successfully shown how using Spanish was a civil rights issue and a matter of cultural preservation. In 1968, Congress enacted the Bilingual Education Act, Title 7, which provided federal funding for the first time for bilingual education. Six years later, the Supreme Court, in *Lau v. Nichols,* unanimously affirmed that language was a civil rights issue. The Court found that students with limited English were deprived of their civil rights when schools did not address these linguistic issues. Citizens' groups funded by conservative foundations like the Heritage Foundation emerged to reverse these changes. In 1986, Californians approved a proposition declaring English to be the official language, and 17 states were quick to follow. Several "English only" bills were introduced in Congress although none passed.

Labor unions responded to the changing nature of work, at the same time reversing their own long history of nativism, by systematically organizing documented and undocumented immigrant workers in the 1980s and 1990s. Faced with meager wages and treacherous working conditions, many immigrant workers who had long histories of labor militancy in their home countries were nonetheless vulnerable to deportation if they participated in any kind of organizing within the United States. Unionizing these workers required a direct and proactive style of organizing. One of the most successful efforts came about through Justice for Janitors (SEIU Local 399) in Los Angeles in 1987.

Blacks and immigrants primarily from El Salvador and Guatemala, these janitors worked for large building service corporations as subcontractors hired by building managers. Justice for Janitors used direct action, a corporate campaign, and work stoppages rather than petition for a National Labor Board Relations election to pressure companies to recognize the union directly. They began by focusing on the world's largest cleaning contractor, International Service System (ISS), in the Century City section of Los Angeles. The Los Angeles police responded to a peaceful march of striking janitors and their supporters, attacking and injuring 90 demonstrators, 19 seriously. The violence made national news. Nine days later, ISS executives agreed to a contract. Threatened by a sympathy strike of janitors in New York City, ISS further agreed to a wage increase. Over the next several years, Justice for Janitors succeeded in unionizing the janitorial workforce in Los Angeles. When the union began their campaign in 1987, only 10 percent of the janitors in Los Angeles were unionized; by 1995, that figure had risen to 90 percent. Massive civil disobedience and a strike in 1995 with support from community organizations and churches produced a major contractual victory: a uniform minimum wage of $6.80 per hour and a fully paid family health care plan for each member. Unions across the country emulated these tactics as documented and undocumented workers joined forces from Florida to New York to demand standard wages and safer conditions.

Chapter 8

A NEW POLITICS OF DISSENT AND PRIVACY RIGHTS

One legacy of the 1960s civil rights revolution was a changed conception of the role of women in society. By the 1970s, court rulings and legislative and administrative reforms banned discriminatory practices that limited employment and educational opportunities. The Supreme Court expanded these rights in two separate rulings of 1987. *Board of Directors of Rotary International v. Rotary Club of Duarte* required all-male Rotary Clubs to admit women to membership whenever states had enacted laws upholding equal access to public accommodations; *Johnson v. Transportation Agency* upheld a voluntary affirmative action program allowing employers to favor women and minorities over males and whites to correct "a conspicuous imbalance in traditionally segregated job categories."

Women fully exploited these new opportunities. In 1981, women made up 14 percent of judges and lawyers, up from 14 percent in 1971; 22 percent of doctors, up from 9 percent; and 30 percent of Ph.D.s, up from 10 percent. And, whereas in 1960, approximately 30 percent of women worked outside the home, by 1990, 60 percent did. Symbolizing these gains, Jane Pauley was appointed co-anchor of NBC's *Today* show, Lesley Stahl CBS's White House correspondent, and Judy Woodruff one of PBS's national correspondents.

The working wife and mother had become the norm. By the 1990s, approximately 67 percent of married women held jobs as did 68 percent of married women with children. Responding to this new situation, in 1993 President Bill Clinton signed a family leave bill to provide 12 weeks of unpaid leave for pregnancy, temporary disability, or care for family members without loss of job or health benefits. Women's earnings lagged substantially behind those of men, increasing from $.59 to a man's dollar in 1970 to $.74 in 1996. In 1974, clerical workers formed Nine to Five to defend their right to fair treatment, to highlight practices of sexual harassment, and to ensure respect from their predominantly male supervisors.

Women's employment status and opportunities nonetheless improved. Between 1970 and 1996, the proportion of women earning bachelor's degrees increased from 43.1 percent to 53.1 percent, medical degrees from 8.4 percent to 40.9 percent, law degrees from 5.4 percent to 43.5 percent, engineering degrees from .8 percent to 16.1 percent, and M.B.A.s from 3.6 percent to 37.6 percent. Furthermore, the percentage of women employed as managers and executives increased from 16.7 percent to 45.4 percent and as college professors from 28.6 percent to 42.3 percent. The new consensus on women's abilities also recast higher education. Whereas in 1987, men had earned 57 percent of all degrees awarded by four-year colleges, by 1997, women became the new majority, earning 55 percent. Nonetheless, few women headed the nation's largest corporations, law firms, and universities.

Women experienced similar gains in politics. Women were elected mayors (in Chicago, Honolulu, and Houston) and governors (in New Hampshire, New Jersey, Texas, and Arizona); two were appointed to the Supreme Court (Sandra Day O'Connor and Ruth Bader Ginsburg), while Geraldine Ferraro won the 1984 Democratic vice-presidential nomination. Nine women were elected to the U.S. Senate (including Barbara Mikulski of Maryland, Diane Feinstein and Barbara Boxer of California, Susan Collins and Olympia Snowe of Maine), while the number of women appointed to the cabinet or elected to state legislatures and the House of Representatives increased substantially.

A Conservative Backlash, but Privacy Rights

These changes in women's social and economic status, and the increasing number of women who sought full-time careers in business and politics catalyzed religious conservatives. To them, women's new status and the militancy of women's rights activists threatened traditional values and undermined the institution of the family. In his 1980 book *Listen America,* fundamentalist minister Jerry Falwell denounced feminism as the product of "a minority core of women, who were once bored with life, whose real problems are spiritual problems. Many women have never accepted their God-given roles." The conservative activist Phyllis Schlafly similarly contrasted the women's liberationist—whom she characterized as "imprisoned by her own negative view of herself and of her place in the world around her"—with her "Positive Woman," whom she affirmed "understood that men and women are different, and that these very differences provide the key to her success as a person and fulfill-ment as a woman."

Religious conservatives specifically focused on abortion as the defin-ing threat to family values. Their opposition made abortion rights a deeply divisive political issue and motivated women activists, through groups like Planned Parenthood and National Abortion Rights Action League, to work to repulse efforts to reverse the social and political gains they had achieved during the 1960s.

A more conservative Congress and Supreme Court seemed poised to rescind *Roe v. Wade.* During the late 1970s and early 1980s, Congress enacted a series of laws narrowing access to abortions. Attorneys in fed-erally funded agencies were prohibited from representing women seek-ing abortions, foreign aid funds could not be used for abortions, federal funds were prohibited for any domestic program in which abortion was an included service in family planning, and federal funding for abortions at military hospitals was denied to military personnel.

One of these legislative restrictions, the so-called Hyde Amendment of 1977, prohibited Medicaid funding for abortions except in cases where the mother's life was in danger or when a rape or incest had been promptly reported to police or a public health agency. Challenged in court, this restriction was upheld by the Supreme Court in *Harris v. McRae* (1981).

In 1983, however, in *City of Akron v. Akron Center for Reproductive Health,* the Court struck down an Akron, Ohio, ordinance restricting women's access to abortion. This law instituted a 24-hour waiting period, compelled doctors to inform any patient that "the unborn child is a human life from the moment of conception," and required all second-trimester abortions to be performed at hospitals rather than clinics. The Court majority held that the required waiting period was "arbitrary and inflexible," the informed consent requirement not intended to "promote" but "withhold" consent, and the second-trimester hospital requirement imposed a "heavy and unnecessary burden on women's access to a rela-tively inexpensive . . . and safe abortion."

President Ronald Reagan, elected on a platform that denounced abortion, seemed to have furthered the goals of the antiabortion move-ment when appointing three conservative jurists (Antonin Scalia, Sandra Day O'Connor, Anthony Kennedy). Nonetheless, his more conservative appointees never commanded a majority to reverse *Roe v. Wade.* In *Web-ster v. Reproductive Health Services* (1989), the Court upheld a Missouri statute forbidding any institution receiving state funds from performing abortions. The Court's divided majority nonetheless reaffirmed a woman's right to an abortion.

This ruling inflamed an already contentious debate over abortion—over the rights of women to privacy and of the states to regulate the conditions governing abortions. A more militant antiabortion movement emerged with the formation of Operation Rescue in 1986. Antiabortion activists sought to stop abortions by conducting sit-ins and picketing and blocking abortion clinics and the homes of abortion providers. They lobbied state legislators to enact legislation restricting access to abortions and Congress to adopt a constitutional amendment banning abortions. Their efforts led a number of state legislatures to enact laws imposing various restrictions on abortions.

One such Pennsylvania law provided a clear test whether the Court would rescind *Roe*'s privacy rights guarantee. This law required doctors to counsel any woman seeking an abortion about the specifics and risks of the procedure (including describing the state of fetal development and alternatives to abortion) and to obtain the woman's written consent before performing an abortion. The law instituted a 24-hour waiting period before an abortion could be performed and required minors younger than 18 to obtain the written consent of a parent or a judge and to be accompanied by a parent during abortion counseling. In its 5–4 ruling in 1992 in *Planned Parenthood of Southeastern Pennsylvania v. Casey,* the Court reaffirmed that "the essential holding of *Roe v. Wade* should be retained and again affirmed." Women had a right to an abortion, the Court held, "before viability . . . without undue interference from the State." The divided majority also affirmed the State's "power to restrict abortions after viability" unless the mother's life or health was endangered based on the "principle that the State has legitimate interests from the outset of the pregnancy in protecting the health of the women and the life of the fetus that may become a child." To reconcile these competing rights of the individual and the state, the Court proposed a balancing test whereby state restrictions could not impose an "undue burden" on a woman's right to an abortion.

The *Casey* ruling did not resolve this issue. Abortion opponents continued to lobby state legislatures to institute other restrictions that could pass the "undue burden" standard, such as a ban on so-called partial-birth abortions. The Court's ambivalence mirrored a new consensus about women's rights shaping national policy, a consensus that acknowledged the importance of moral concerns but also the priority of nondiscrimination and privacy rights.

GAY AND LESBIAN RIGHTS

The politics of women's rights in the post-1973 era was shaped by a reassessment of whether the federal government should remedy past discriminatory practices against racial minorities and women. This reassessment did not directly affect the status of gays and lesbians. Gays and lesbians had not benefited directly from the recently enacted civil rights laws barring racial and sexual discrimination or mandatory affirmative action programs. Gays and lesbians, moreover, encountered organized opposition to the proposed laws prohibiting discrimination based on sexual orientation. This opposition centered around whether antidiscrimination laws sanctioned inherently immoral conduct.

The nation's religious communities in particular divided over whether gays and lesbians should be granted equal rights. The more tolerant attitudes of the 1950s and 1960s challenged the belief that homosexuality was inherently immoral. Nonetheless, organized religious communities remained deeply divided over whether government (local, state, federal) should explicitly ban such discrimination. Within the mainline Protestant churches, the divisive issue became whether gays and lesbians should be allowed to marry (thereby entitled to the same pension and death benefit rights as heterosexual couples) and to be ordained as ministers. Historic teachings of the church, notably sections of the Old Testament, provided a biblical rationale for rejecting the full acceptance of gays and lesbians as tantamount to legitimating an immoral life style. American Catholics were similarly conflicted. In 1973, a group of Catholics, with tacit approval of the church, formed Dignity, a national organization that welcomed gays and lesbians to full church membership. Catholic leaders, however, distinguished between the sinner and the sin, and the church's formal position, as articulated in an October 1986 Vatican letter to American Catholic bishops, maintained that homosexuality was "intrinsically evil from the moral point of view and should therefore be considered objectively disordered."

The strongest opposition to antidiscriminatory proposals, moreover, came from fundamentalist Christians. Dating from its formal organization in 1980 to promote a "spiritual rebirth" in the nation, the Moral Majority specifically attacked President Carter's "lack of moral leadership" for allegedly supporting gay and lesbian rights. Endorsing a moral antipathy toward homosexuality, the 1980 Republican presidential nominee Ronald Reagan criticized the gay and lesbian movements for seeking "a recognition and acceptance of an alternative life style which I do not believe society can condone, nor can I."

This debate over the morality of homosexuality underlay a broader debate about whether to ban discrimination against homosexuals. This debate shifted after the 1970s, partly in response to the militant tactics of conservative Christians.

The rights revolution of the 1960s had given rise to a militant, organized gay and lesbian movement. Far better organized and willing to go public to demand equal rights and respect for their basic humanity, gay and lesbian activists lobbied local, state, and federal officials to ban

discrimination based on sexual orientation. Their efforts at first won a
series of limited victories at the local and state level because their
demands for antidiscriminatory ordinances seemed elementarily fair and
would entail no increase in public spending. By 1976, one-third of the
states repealed antisodomy laws, while common councils in numerous
towns and cities (Eugene, Oregon; Wichita, Kansas; Champaign-Urbana,
Illinois; Iowa City, Iowa; and Aspen, Colorado) enacted ordinances banning discrimination based on sexual orientation. In 1979, moreover, California Governor Jerry Brown issued an executive order barring discrimination against homosexuals in state government hiring practices.

PRIVACY RIGHTS
AMID A CONSERVATIVE BACKLASH

Achieved without direct public support, these local ordinances were vulnerable to an organized counterreaction. The specific catalyst was the
decision of the Dade County (Florida) Commission to bar discrimination
based on "affectional or sexual preference" in housing, public accommodations, and employment. The popular singer Anita Bryant protested
the commission's action as sanctioning immorality and threatening family values. Under the banner Save Our Children, she launched a petition
drive to repeal this ordinance by a public referendum. Her referendum
won overwhelming public approval by a vote of 202,319 to 89,562. This
electoral success kindled similar repeal efforts in St. Paul, Eugene, and
Wichita.

California State Senator John Briggs, hoping to capitalize on this
issue to advance his candidacy for governor, introduced a statewide initiative to ban homosexuals from teaching in the public schools. Briggs's
vaguely worded initiative (the ban would apply to those who sanctioned
homosexuality) provoked bitter opposition. Opponents framed the issue
as one of personal privacy and liberty. The initiative was overwhelmingly
rejected—58 percent to 42 percent. That same day Seattle voters rejected
a local initiative to repeal that city's gay rights ordinance by a vote of 63
percent to 37 percent.

The Bryant-Briggs initiatives provoked a counterreaction from citizens who resented the efforts of moralistic Christians to impose their particular religious beliefs on the community. Gay and lesbian activists were
also moved in 1982 to organize the Human Rights Campaign Fund, a political action committee dedicated to advancing gay rights through funding
candidates sympathetic to their community's concerns. Gays and lesbians
were elected as delegates to the Democratic National Conventions of
1980, 1984, 1988, and 1992. Whereas delegates to the Republican

National Convention of 1984 responded to demands by the Moral Majority by adopting a plank endorsing "family values," the Democratic National Convention approved a strong gay rights plank.

The new tolerance of homosexual rights soon acquired another dimension, triggered by the medical crisis with the announced discovery in July 1981 by the Center of Disease Control of the AIDS (Acquired Immunodeficiency Syndrome) virus. As AIDS afflicted many gay men, it first intensified public fears about the promiscuity of homosexuals. Political and religious conservatives tapped into these fears. Some, such as the political commentator (and perennial Republican presidential aspirant) Patrick Buchanan, claimed that "the sexual revolution has begun to devour its children." Homosexuals, Buchanan continued, "have declared war on nature, and now nature is exacting an awful retribution." Fundamentalist ministers in Houston urged city officials to close gay bars while Rev. Falwell, addressing a Moral Majority rally in Cincinnati in July 1983, demanded that the Reagan administration shut down gay bathhouses and prohibit gays from donating blood. AIDS was the "judgment of God," Falwell warned. "You can't fly into the laws of God and God's nature without paying the price."

Forming ACT-UP (Aids Coalition to Unleash Power), gay and lesbian activists mobilized to demand increased federal funding for research to find a cure or alleviate the AIDS crisis. Federal funding for medical research increased. Popular health fears quickly dissipated as the medical crisis proved to be containable through "safe sex," monitoring the supply and distribution of donated blood, and drugs that delayed the onset of full-blown AIDS. Rejecting the intolerance of religious conservatism, Wisconsin became the first state to enact legislation banning discrimination based on sexual orientation in 1987 (followed by Massachusetts in 1989, Hawaii and Connecticut in 1991, and Vermont, New Jersey, and Minnesota in 1993); governors of Ohio and New York also issued executive orders banning discrimination in state agency hiring practices.

National attitudes toward homosexuals had changed radically, highlighted by the public's reaction to the Supreme Court's 1986 ruling in *Bowers v. Hardwick.* Michael Hardwick had been arrested for violating the state of Georgia's antisodomy law when police barged into his home. With the help of the ACLU, Hardwick challenged Georgia's law. Writing for the majority Justice Byron White questioned "whether the Federal Constitution confers a fundamental right upon homosexuals to engage in sodomy and hence invalidates the laws of the many States that still make such conduct illegal and have done so for a very long time." Justice Harry Blackmun's minority opinion, in contrast, defined the issue as whether individuals had "the most comprehensive of rights and the right most valued by civilized man, namely 'the right to be let alone.'" In a Gallup poll, respondents opposed the Court's ruling by 47 percent to 41 percent, and by 57 percent to 34 percent opposed the premise that "states shall have the right to prohibit sexual practices conducted in private between consenting adults." In a 1994 poll, 83 percent of the respondents held that homosexual relations between consenting adults was a private matter, with only 30 percent agreeing that "homosexuality is wrong and there should be laws against it."

By the 1990s, gays and lesbians were no longer cloistered and their sexual practices automatically condemned. Indeed, the first department of gay and lesbian studies was established at San Francisco State College in 1989, with that same college creating the first full-time tenure-track position in the field in 1991. By the end of the decade, such programs were no longer unique.

Colorado voters, however, in 1992 approved by referendum an amendment to the state constitution prohibiting state and local governments from enacting laws protecting homosexuals from discrimination. But the Supreme Court in *Romer v. Evans* (1996) ruled that this amendment unconstitutionally imposed a "special," "broad and undifferentiated disability" on homosexuals, denying them "the safeguards that others enjoy and may seek without constraint."

Gays and lesbians, moreover, had become a politically powerful interest group. Democratic presidential nominee Bill Clinton publicly sought their support, championing the right of gays and lesbians to be treated fairly and nondiscriminatorily. Clinton's defeat of the incumbent Republican President George Bush in 1992, however, was no mandate for gay and lesbian rights. Public attitudes towards gay and lesbians remained conflicted—although the majority rejected the antigay sentiments of Patrick Buchanan and televangelist Pat Robertson, who called on the Republican party to lead a "cultural war for the soul of America."

This ambivalence was reflected in the public reaction to two executive orders issued by President Clinton in 1995 and 1993. In 1995, Clinton reversed a long-standing employment policy instituted by President Eisenhower barring homosexuals from federal employment as "security risks." Clinton rescinded this rule that had denied security "solely on the basis of the sexual orientation of the federal employee." While this order was noncontroversial, Clinton's decision in 1993 to ban discrimination against gays in the military was immediately challenged. The Joint Chiefs of Staff decried this policy change as undermining military morale and discipline, and Congress responded by rescinding the president's order.

A chastened president proposed a compromise where gays and lesbians could serve in the military so long as they did not disclose their sexual orientation ("don't ask, don't tell"). Despite this new policy, the number of gays and lesbians dismissed from military service increased in the ensuing years. A survey of military personnel conducted by the Pentagon's Inspector General in 2000 questioned the military service's commitment to precluding harassment of suspected homosexual personnel. The survey was triggered by the bludgeoning death of a gay soldier, Pfc. Barry Winchell, by members of his military unit, and uncovered that 80 percent of respondents had heard antigay remarks and 37 percent had witnessed or experienced sexual harassment based on sexual orientation in the past year, whereas 85 percent believed that "offensive" antigay comments were to some extent tolerated within the military. In addition, 50 percent of respondents claimed not to have received any training in the Defense Department's antiharassment policy. Secretary of Defense William Cohen, in response, reaffirmed his intention to enforce the antiharassment policy.

A NEW POLITICS OF CIVIL LIBERTIES: ANTISECRECY AND PRIVACY RIGHTS

The underlying antipathy toward government regulation and the new priority of privacy rights provided the lodestar for a new politics of civil liberties. The Watergate Affair and opposition to the Johnson and Nixon administrations' Vietnam War policies undermined public confidence in the presidency and the intelligence agencies. Watergate and Vietnam sharpened public anxieties about government secrecy and the accountability of presidents and intelligence agency officials. These concerns shattered a Cold War consensus that valued secrecy and national security over the right to advocate and organize to advance unconventional political and social ideas.

Recent technological developments intensified these libertarian concerns—particularly, the invention and expanded use of data banks and computers (and by the late 1980s, personal computers). This new technology ensured more efficient communication across vast distances but at the same time increased the risk that personal communications or previously discrete or inaccessible information could be intercepted, correlated and disseminated. Such privacy concerns sharpened public uneasiness about how government surveillance and secrecy could threaten individual liberties.

The militancy of religious conservatives—symbolized by the formation of the Moral Majority in 1980 and the Christian Coalition in the 1990s—enhanced support for civil liberties as many Americans came to value tolerance over moral control. These concerns coincided with a changed international context with the collapse of the Soviet Union and the end of the Cold War in the period 1989-91 and followed disclosures of presidential and intelligence agency abuses during the 1973 Senate Watergate and 1974 House impeachment hearings.

Long convinced that opposition to the Vietnam War and support for civil rights and economic justice was monitored by the FBI, radical and liberal activists had their worse fears confirmed in the early 1970s. In 1970 it became known that FBI agents had monitored Earth Day rallies (organized by Senators Edmund Muskie and Gaylord Nelson) and these liberal Senators' leadership role in seeking to develop a national ecology movement. Senator Nelson responded to this disclosure by introducing a resolution to create a joint congressional committee to investigate the federal intelligence agencies. Nelson's resolution commanded little support and died in committee.

That same year, however, a Senate Judiciary subcommittee conducted public hearings to examine the impact of data banks and computers on civil liberties. The hearings soon uncovered that military intelligence officials had responded to the upsurge in anti-Vietnam war demonstrations and urban race riots by launching in 1965 an expansive Continental United States Intelligence program, headquartered in Fort Holabird, Maryland. By the late 1960s, this massive surveillance program was staffed by a network of 1,500 military agents in over three hundred bases around the country, supported by a sophisticated and comprehensive communication system. Military agents accumulated information about approximately eight hundred organizations and 5,500 individuals, which they computerized for easy retrieval and dissemination.

Concurrently, in March 1971, an activist antiwar group, the Citizens' Commission to Investigate the FBI, broke into an FBI regional office in Media, Pennsylvania, and photocopied thousands of pages of FBI documents. Copies of these documents were then mailed to members of the Congress and the media. The pilfered documents confirmed that the FBI had intensively monitored dissident political activities, resorted to unethical and illegal investigative techniques, and purposefully sought to discredit dissident political activists and organizations. One of the photocopied documents contained the caption COINTELPRO-New Left. Unaware of this secret FBI program, NBC correspondent Carl Stern filed a Freedom of Information Act request for the FBI's COINTELPRO files. When his request was rebuffed by the Justice Department, Stern filed suit in court. In September 1973, Federal Judge Barrington Parker ordered the release of the COINTELPRO files.

Stern had inadvertently stumbled upon one of the FBI's more questionable programs. The released documents, for one thing, discredited the national security rationale originally advanced by Nixon administration officials to allay questions raised with the publication of the Media

FBI documents. The released COINTELPRO files instead documented the containment and harassment purposes behind this program. These revelations were followed by a series of other critical news stories, detailing FBI monitoring of members of Congress and extensive use of informers and wiretaps—the latter of which were publicized in court cases that raised further questions about the Nixon Justice Department's abuse of grand juries.

On assuming office in 1969, the Nixon administration launched a full-scale campaign to prosecute radical activists. To do so, personnel in the Justice Department's Internal Security Division were increased tenfold. Between 1970 and 1973, Internal Security Division attorneys exploited the latitude allowed to government prosecutors in the conduct of grand jury proceedings to indict radical anti-Vietnam War activists. Their practices included laundering illegal wiretap information, holding simultaneous grand juries in different cities to force witnesses to answer potentially incriminating questions, and pressuring witnesses to inform against their associates. Through discovery motions and interrogating government informers (in trials held in Camden, New Jersey; Gainsville, Florida; Detroit, Michigan; Fort Worth, Texas; and Harrisburg, Pennsylvania), defense attorneys publicized the abusive tactics of government prosecutors. In the process, they convinced jurors not to convict their clients.

These revelations influenced how the public responded to the Senate Watergate Committee and the House Judiciary Committee hearings of 1973-74. The Watergate hearings documented that key White House and Nixon campaign officials had first authorized the break-in to the Democratic National Committee's headquarters in 1972, then orchestrated a campaign to contain the investigation into the break-in, and finally pressured others to commit perjury. The hearings confirmed that these abuses were part of a pattern of official misconduct that included wiretapping prominent members of the Washington press corps (and even members of the president's White House and National Security Council staffs), authorizing the Huston Plan's proposed use of "clearly illegal" investigative techniques, and creating a special White House group (the Plumbers) funded from leftover 1968 campaign funds to monitor those suspected of leaking classified documents to the media. The revelations in time precipitated impeachment proceedings by the House Judiciary Committee, culminating in President Nixon's forced resignation in August 1974. Nixon's resignation, however, did not staunch public and congressional concerns about the adverse consequences of unchecked presidential power and secrecy for civil liberties and constitutional government, concerns intensified by additional disclosures of December 1974 and February 1975.

In a December 1974 *New York Times* article, Seymour Hersh reported that the Central Intelligence Agency (in violation of its legislative charter banning any "internal security" role) had, during the 1960s and early 1970s, monitored civil rights and antiwar activists. CIA officials and the Ford administration at first refused to confirm or deny Hersh's story. Faced with the prospect of a sweeping congressional inquiry, CIA Director William Colby in January 1975 publicly confirmed the accuracy of Hersh's story. Hoping to co-opt any congressional inquiry into the scope of the CIA's intelligence activities, President Ford appointed a special presidential commission with authority limited to investigating CIA domestic surveillance activities.

Ford's preemptive strategy failed, in part because of another revelation the next month. During February 1975 testimony before a House subcommittee, Attorney General Edward Levi announced that former FBI Director J. Edgar Hoover had maintained a secret office file containing dossiers on the personal and political activities of prominent Americans, including presidents and members of Congress. Levi's disclosure confirmed what many members of Congress and reporters already suspected—that the former FBI director had monitored the activities of prominent Americans and had particularly sought information about their personal lives.

LIBERTY AND SECURITY: THE PROPER BALANCE

Until the mid-1970s, demands for a searching independent inquiry into the practices of the intelligence agencies had been successfully rebuffed. The series of disclosures between 1970 and 1975 led the Senate on January 21, 1975, to create a special Senate committee to investigate the "intelligence activities carried out by or on behalf of the Federal Government." This committee, chaired by Senator Frank Church, was authorized to obtain all agency records needed to address a series of pointed questions. Had the CIA conducted "illegal domestic intelligence" operations within the United States? Had the FBI "or any other Federal agency" (the CIA and the National Security Agency) conducted "domestic intelligence or counterintelligence operations against United States citizens?" What had been the "nature and extent of executive branch oversight" of all federal intelligence activities? What had been the specific legislative or executive authority for federal intelligence activities? Had any intelligence agency violated "any State or Federal statute . . . including but not limited to surreptitious entries [break-ins], surveillance, wiretaps, or eavesdropping, illegal opening of the United States mail, or the monitoring of United States mail?"

Because of the more skeptical political climate of the mid-1970s, the Ford administration could not resist the Church Committee's demands for access to relevant presidential, CIA, NSA, and FBI records. The resultant unprecedented access to records of secret activities led to the committee's discovery of the scope and political purposes of FBI, CIA, NSA, and White House practices dating from Franklin Roosevelt's presidency. The committee's public hearings of 1975 and massive reports of 1976 offered a numbing account of the FBI's now infamous COINTELPROs, of the FBI's extensive wiretapping, bugging, and break-in practices, and of FBI officials' campaign to discredit civil rights leader Martin Luther King Jr. The congressional inquiry uncovered how presidents and intelligence agency officials had ensured "deniability" and subverted congressional oversight through sophisticated separate records and record destruction procedures. The committee further uncovered how responsible executive officials purposefully avoided their responsibility to ensure that the programs and practices of federal intelligence agencies conformed with the law or ethical principles.

To preclude the recurrence of these abusive practices, the committee recommended that Congress enact legislative charters defining the parameters of the federal intelligence agencies' authority. More rigorous congressional oversight could ensure that future surveillance would not intrude on First Amendment rights.

Coming at a time of increased public cynicism about presidential power and claimed national security authority, the Church Committee highlighted three crucial issues. First, presidents and intelligence agency officials had successfully shielded questionable decisions from public and congressional scrutiny. Second, many of the discovered abusive practices were not grounded in law (some explicitly illegal) and were based on secret, vaguely worded executive directives. Third, executive guidelines did not explicitly prohibit abusive practices, and presidents (and the attorneys general) preferred deniability and willingly avoided their responsibility to ensure that intelligence agency practices were legal and ethical.

The Church Committee's recommendations, released in the midst of the 1976 presidential campaign, were not immediately acted upon. Members of Congress nonetheless at the time differed over whether the proposed charter legislation should specify permissible activities or simply outline permissible parameters. They agreed that at minimum the intelligence agencies' authority should be defined by statute and that closer congressional oversight should replace the current system of presidential discretion. Indeed, in 1976 both the House and the Senate in 1976 established permanent Intelligence Committees to monitor the intelligence agencies.

President Ford, however, was unwilling to defer to Congress. To restore public confidence in the intelligence agencies and at the same time institute what he believed to be responsible administrative reforms, Ford by Executive Order 11905 in February 1976 spelled out new rules to limit FBI (and CIA and NSA) foreign intelligence and counterintelligence operations to obtaining information about the plans and purposes of the nation's foreign adversaries. His proposed reforms were to ensure tighter administrative control and efficiency.

The next month, Attorney General Edward Levi issued guidelines that would govern FBI "domestic security" investigations. Levi allowed the FBI greater latitude for FBI internal security than criminal investigations. Internal security investigations would not have to meet a "probable cause" standard that the suspect violated a federal statute. Balancing competing interests of liberty and security, Levi sought to ensure that such investigations would neither be interminable nor monitor First Amendment activities.

Under the Levi guidelines, FBI agents could initiate "domestic security" investigations based upon "allegations or other information that an individual or group may be engaged in activities which involve or will involve the violation of federal law." Such "preliminary" investigations were to be limited to a 90-day period and confined to confirming or refuting the allegation. "Full" domestic security investigations, in contrast, had to be based on "specific and articulable facts giving reason to believe that an individual or group is or may be engaged in activities which involve or will involve the use of force or violence and which involve or will involve the violation of federal law." These investigations were to be subject to departmental oversight. Senior Justice Department officials would have to authorize all full investigations at least annually, and "determine in writing whether continued investigation is warranted." This requirement of a written record of review and approval negated the practice of deniability that had defined the FBI–Justice Department relationship since the 1940s.

While never enacting an FBI charter law, Congress did enact laws to limit specific governmental surveillance and dissemination practices. In 1974, Congress amended the 1966 Freedom of Information Act (FOIA) making it easier for citizens (and journalists) to obtain FBI records. Exploiting the act's mandatory disclosure requirements, journalists and academic researchers could obtain FBI files and in the process publicize the scope and political purpose of past FBI surveillance of prominent Americans and radical activists.

That same year, Congress enacted the Privacy Act to empower individuals to obtain any record of their activities maintained by federal agencies. Federal agencies were required to describe how they collected and maintained information on individuals and to describe their purpose in collecting and in the "routine use" of such information. Information could be collected only to accomplish a lawful purpose. The act addressed a problem of increasing public concern in the computer age— the ease by which personal information could be accessed and collated, and then widely disseminated, without the knowledge of the individual. Enactment of the Privacy Act reflected a new priority of the post-1973 period: individuals had a fundamental right to privacy and such privacy rights were "directly affected by the collection and maintenance, use and dissemination of personal information by federal agencies."

Then, in 1978, Congress enacted the Foreign Intelligence Surveillance Act. This legislation corrected a deficiency, exposed during Congressional hearings and court cases of the early 1970s, of the 1968 Omnibus Crime Control and Safe Streets Act legalizing wiretapping. Dating from 1968 the Nixon administration had claimed an "inherent" presidential power to wiretap domestic groups and activists without a court-approved warrant. Seeking a warrant would disclose such wiretapping, Nixon had then argued, and thereby alert foreign spies and their agents to the government's surveillance activities. By 1978, Congress was no longer willing to defer to such expansive claims of presidential powers or acquiesce that any external review inevitably compromised legitimate security interests. All foreign intelligence and counterintelligence interceptions required the prior approval of a specially established court, and these proceedings would be conducted in secret. The national security exemptions of this act, as in the case of the 1974 amendments to the Freedom of Information Act, were nonetheless intended to subject executive decisions to external, independent scrutiny. Such scrutiny would theoretically increase the likelihood of discovering, and thereby deterring, abuses of First Amendment rights (previously conducted secretly in the name of national security).

Two developments of 1979–80—the Iranian hostage situation and the Soviet invasion of Afghanistan—soon led many in the public and Congress to question whether the post-Watergate reforms had gone too far and undermined national security interests. These international crises seemingly confirmed that an undue concern over the rights of dissenters and an insistence on publicity had compromised the nation's intelligence activities. Republican presidential nominee Ronald Reagan capitalized on these concerns during the 1980 presidential campaign, calling for a more militant foreign policy and the "unleashing" of the intelligence agencies. His election to the presidency and Republican congressional gains (winning control of the Senate) accordingly killed congressional action on proposed legislation to charter the intelligence agencies.

The newly elected president moved quickly to rescind the restrictions that Presidents Ford and Carter had imposed on the FBI's and CIA's foreign intelligence and domestic surveillance activities. President

Reagan issued Executive Order 12333 in 1981 to expand the FBI's and the CIA's intelligence activities. Whereas President Carter's guidelines had prohibited intelligence operations that could contravene federal laws or First Amendment rights, Reagan's order relaxed these restrictions to promote more effective "foreign intelligence" and "foreign counterintelligence" operations. Any proposed foreign intelligence or counterintelligence activity would no longer require the attorney general's review to confirm that it did not violate the nation's criminal laws or First Amendment rights.

Then, in March 1983, Attorney General William French Smith rescinded the strict oversight and authorization requirements of the Levi guidelines. Smith's guidelines abandoned the distinction between preliminary and full investigations and the requirement predicating FBI internal security investigations on a "probable cause" standard. Investigations could henceforth be initiated whenever "facts or circumstances reasonably indicate that two or more persons are engaged in an enterprise [to further] political or social goals wholly or in part through activities that involve force or violence and a violation of the criminal law of the United States." The FBI could launch investigations to "anticipate or prevent crime" and whenever uncovering information that individuals or organizations "advocate criminal activity or indicate an apparent intent to engage in crime, particularly crimes of violence." Smith's guidelines in addition limited Justice Department's oversight responsibilities. FBI officials need only "notify" the Justice Department's Office of Intelligence Policy whenever instituting "domestic security/terrorism" investigations, while the attorney general's oversight role was now "may, as he deems necessary request the FBI to prepare a report on the investigation."

CIVIL LIBERTIES AND THE END OF THE COLD WAR

By the 1980s, the Reagan administration offered a different rationale for government surveillance activities than the need to investigate and contain Communist subversion. The new rationale emphasized instead the need to address the problem of international and domestic "terrorism." This new terminology encompassed both an internal threat posed by nativist groups (survivalists, white supremacists), members of militia groups, and militant opponents of gun control and abortion and an external threat posed by American citizens and alien residents who were either influenced by Islamic fundamentalism, identified with the objectives of militant Middle Eastern nationalists (Iranians, Egyptians, Palestinians, or supporters of Osama bin Laden), or were ideologically sympathetic toward Marxist revolutionary movements. The FBI, moreover, continued to monitor liberal and radical activists who challenged the nation's domestic priorities and foreign policy decisions. This latter practice was revealed through a series of law suits filed in New York, Seattle, Detroit, and Chicago during the late 1970s and 1980s to challenge the surveillance practices of so-called Red Squads, special local and state police units that had since the 1930s monitored radical political and labor union activists and had worked closely with FBI and military intelligence agents. One such case, brought against the Chicago police, the FBI, and military intelligence, *Alliance to End Repression v. City of Chicago,* exposed how the Chicago police and their FBI counterparts intensively monitored political activities, shared the acquired information with the media and each other, and disseminated this information in ways that adversely affected First Amendment rights.

In her 1985 ruling in the *Alliance* suit, Federal Judge Susan Getzendanner explicitly banned future police and FBI surveillance unless based on the standard of "a reasonable suspicion of criminal conduct" and unless senior police officials in writing stipulated that such surveillance had a lawful policing and intelligence purpose. In addition, the court awarded the plaintiffs (which included the ACLU and the American Friends Services Committee) a monetary settlement of $641,250 as compensation for the Chicago police's violation of their First Amendment rights. These Red Squad cases, in addition, had raised questions whether in fact FBI investigations of radical activities had been scaled back. FBI officials admitted during the Chicago trial that their investigations formerly classified as "domestic security" had been reclassified "foreign counterintelligence" following the issuance of the Levi guidelines.

FBI investigations of dissident activities, however, did not stop. When issuing the Smith guidelines, Reagan administration officials announced that FBI investigations would target individuals or organizations that "may be or will involve violence" or had the "potential" to overthrow the government. Those subject to such monitoring included individuals active in the nuclear freeze movement, primarily middle-class, religiously-motivated peace activists who sought to rally opposition to the Reagan administration's increase in spending on nuclear weapons. No evidence of subversive influence was uncovered. By spring 1983, the nuclear freeze had garnered support from numerous referendums, 368 city and county councils, 444 town meetings, and (according to Harris and Gallup polls) the vast majority of Americans.

Individuals (mostly students) active in Amnesty International were also investigated, FBI agents having learned of their activities through letters they had written to officials in the Soviet Union and Eastern Europe protesting those governments' treatment of political prisoners. FBI agents even monitored Lance Lindblom, the president of a major philanthropic foundation who met regularly with foreign leaders and political dissidents. FBI investigations soon expanded to organizations formed in the 1980s in response to a new set of issues and concerns. These included the radical environmentalist group Earth First! and the militant gay rights organization ACT-UP. In 1988, FBI officials launched a formal Library Awareness program under which librarians were contacted for information about readers of unclassified technical and scientific journals. Librarians were specifically encouraged to be wary of the "suspicious activity of library patrons, particularly foreigners" or persons with "East European or Russian-sounding names" and those seeking books or periodicals on "underground tunneling, military installations, or technological breakthroughs." This program proved risky, both because the holdings of public and college research libraries were unclassified and because librarians, given their traditional interest in First Amendment rights and in protecting the privacy rights of library users, were likely to compromise this initiative. The resultant critical publicity led to the program's formal termination.

The most intensive FBI investigation initiated during the 1980s centered on critics of the Reagan administration's Central America policies. In 1981, Justice Department officials ordered an FBI investigation into whether the Committee in Solidarity with the People of El Salvador (CISPES) should register as an agent of a foreign power under the 1940 Foreign Agent Registration Act. Composed of American citizens, predominantly college students and religious activists, CISPES activists openly criticized the Reagan administration's support of the military government of El Salvador. Their criticisms mounted following the assassination of three American Catholic nuns and a lay person working with the impoverished peasantry of El Salvador. These liberal and socially conscious religious activists suspected that the Salvadoran military (and by extension the U.S. military) was responsible for these deaths and thousands of others. The FBI's resultant investigation failed to substantiate that CISPES was a foreign agent.

Since the Foreign Agent Registration Act investigation had failed to uncover evidence of foreign direction, FBI officials launched another, intensive investigation in March 1983, ostensibly to ascertain whether CISPES was involved in international and domestic terrorism. This FBI investigation failed to uncover any evidence of terrorist plans or activities but quickly strayed beyond the stated purpose of ascertaining "the extent of CISPES support of terrorism in El Salvador, and the potential of committing terrorist operations in the United States." When publicly released in 1988, FBI reports pertaining to this investigation documented that FBI agents closely monitored individuals "actively involved in demonstrations," and recorded their positions articulated in radio programs and other interview formats, support of local ballot initiatives, and distribution of literature to the public "urging U.S. citizens to write their representatives [in Congress] to express their concern over increasing U.S. involvement in El Salvador." This investigation had expanded to other religious, trade union, and political groups mobilizing public opposition to the administration's Central America policies. These included Oxfam America, the Southern Christian Leadership Conference, two Catholic religious orders (the Sisters of Mercy and the Maryknoll Sisters), the National Council of Churches, the American Civil Liberties Union, the U.S. Catholic Conference, the United Automobile Workers, the National Education Association, and Amnesty International. The reports confirmed an FBI interest in these activists' political beliefs; one FBI agent characterized the writings of a church leader as those of a "mind totally sold on the Marxist Leninist philosophy," whereas another agent deemed it "imperative at this time to formulate some plan of attack upon CISPES and specifically upon individuals . . . who defiantly display their contempt for the U.S. government by making speeches and propagandizing their cause." FBI officials, moreover, responded to an agent's recommendation that an investigation of a targeted organization be discontinued because no evidence of violent conduct had been uncovered but only nonviolent political education, by ordering him to "consider the possibility" that the group "may be a front organization for CISPES."

The CISPES investigation underscored how security considerations continued to shape FBI practices—and how secrecy could immunize such investigations from public scrutiny. Only because the FBI investigation of CISPES was closed in 1985 were FBI files on CISPES vulnerable to release under the Freedom of Information Act. Their release in 1988 precipitated a flurry of critical news stories that, in turn, became the catalyst to a congressional review that year of the FBI's CISPES investigation.

Then, when the Bush administration initiated a massive air and land campaign against Iraq in January 1991, its military strategy precipitated limited public criticism. Some of these critics became the subject of FBI interest. In this instance, FBI officials adopted a different surveillance strategy of interviewing prominent Arab-American citizens and Arab alien residents about their knowledge of terrorist activities. The extensive interviewing was intimidating for many within the Arab-American community who muted their dissent. The interviews, moreover, were not predicated on any evidence that the subjects either knew about any terrorist activities or might themselves have been willing to engage in terrorism.

The so-called Gulf War interviews comported with a new focus on supporters of Palestinian causes and militant Islamic fundamentalists. Beginning in 1979 and continuing through the 1980s, the FBI launched an investigation of the General Union of Palestinian Students, a student organization committed to Palestinian independence. This investigation continued despite FBI officials' awareness that the organization's purpose was to assist "Palestinian students in their education and settlement in the United States and to report, explain, correct and spread the Palestinian cause to all people." In their quest to identify all chapters and leaders of this student organization, FBI agents inevitably monitored First Amendment activities. One FBI report, for example, described other groups with "any interest in PLO [Palestinian Liberation Organization] issues," meetings and conferences sponsored by the organization, and the fliers, literature, and articles in college newspapers describing the organization's events and plans. FBI agents purposefully ensured that adherents of the organization were aware of the FBI's "interest," and attempted to recruit some adherents to serve as informers.

FBI monitoring of Arab Americans and alien residents of Middle Eastern descent intensified during the 1990s in response to a series of terrorist incidents within the United States and abroad. These included the 1993 truck bombing of the World Trade Center in New York City; an aborted conspiracy to bomb a federal building, the United Nations, and the Lincoln and Holland tunnels in New York City in 1994; and terrorist bombing attacks on the Khobar Towers in Saudi Arabia (housing U.S. airmen stationed at the base there) in 1996; on two U.S. embassies in Africa in 1998; and on the destroyer USS *Cole* in a Yemen harbor in 2000. In the case of the international incidents, U.S. officials suspected that Saudi exile Osama bin Laden (then living in Afghanistan) had funded and planned these attacks.

THE 1990S: PRIVACY RIGHTS AND LIMITED GOVERNMENT

The formal end of the Cold War in 1989–91 (with the collapse of Communist governments in Eastern Europe and the dissolution of the Soviet Union) did not end FBI surveillance of radical activists. Instead, the focus of FBI intelligence investigations shifted from suspected Communists and Communist sympathizers to domestic or international terrorists. Those targeted also included right-wing activists.

By the 1990s, anti-FBI and antigovernmental criticisms were no longer confined to the radical left. Many conservatives—militia groups, white supremacists, and antiabortion activists—viewed federal policies in general, and the FBI in particular, with deep skepticism and suspicion. The popularity of Oliver Stone's film *J.F.K.* and the television series *X-Files* confirmed how many Americans suspected that U.S. intelligence agencies might have been involved in conspiracies to assassinate President

Kennedy and civil rights leader Martin Luther King. Many conservatives now held more cynical views about FBI activities, an outlook that contrasted strikingly with their counterparts of the 1950s who eulogized the FBI as a protector of the nation's security from spies. Legislation enacted during the 1990s led to FBI investigations of militant conservative activists involved in bombing abortion clinics or violating the nation's antigun laws.

The Freedom of Access to Clinic Enterprises Act, enacted in May 1994, criminalized acts of violence against physicians who perform abortions or abortion clinics. In 1993, Congress enacted the Brady Law, imposing restrictions on the sale of handguns and outlawing specified types of semiautomatic weapons. Responsibility for enforcing antigun laws lay with the Bureau of Alcohol, Tobacco and Firearms (ATF), nonetheless many opponents of gun control laws and adherents of various white supremacist, antitax, antiabortion, and militia movements suspected that FBI agents were monitoring their activities. In reality, FBI investigations were confined to those individuals who, if they were in fact members of militant militia, white supremacist, or antitax groups (the Order, the Freemen, Posse Comitatus), had either bombed abortion clinics, robbed banks to finance their activities, publicly announced their intention not to pay federal taxes, or counseled others how to avoid tax payments.

The suspicions of conservative activists about FBI surveillance heightened in response to two highly publicized actions of the FBI's Hostage Rescue Team in 1992-93. In 1989, ATF agents entrapped Randall Weaver (who had become a target of their investigative interest owing to his association with the white supremacist Aryan Nations) into selling them an assault weapon, thereby violating federal gun laws. Indicted in December 1990, Weaver was arrested about two months later but was released on his own recognizance. When Weaver failed to appear for his trial, ATF officials solicited the assistance of U.S. marshals in arresting him. At the time, Weaver was holed up in an isolated mountain cabin near Ruby Ridge, Idaho. The marshals surrounded the cabin and soon engaged in a gun battle, which ended with the deaths of one of the marshals and Weaver's son. Deeming Weaver dangerous, and cognizant of the difficulty of effecting his surrender, in August 1992 ATF officials sought the assistance of the FBI's well-trained Hostage Rescue Team. During the resultant siege, FBI sharpshooters accidentally killed Weaver's wife before effecting his surrender.

The Ruby Ridge shoot-out was soon followed in February 1993 by an even more dramatic siege. ATF actions were again the catalyst. In an attempt to arrest David Koresh, the leader of a religious cult called the Branch Davidians, on gun charges, ATF agents devised a secret plan to storm the compound of the group near Waco, Texas. Koresh and leaders of the heavily armed Davidians, however, almost immediately learned of the ATF's planned raid. Four ATF agents and six Davidians were killed in the ensuing shoot-out. ATF officials thereupon again sought the assistance of the FBI's Hostage Rescue Team. Following a 51-day standoff, FBI officials eventually lost patience in negotiating Koresh's surrender and opted to raid the compound, using heavily armored combat engineering vehicles to teargas the occupants. Rather than surrender, Koresh and Davidian leaders set fire to the compound. The fire spread quickly, resulting in the deaths of 80 Davidians, including 25 children under the age of 15.

The Ruby Ridge and Branch Davidian raids provoked sharp media and congressional criticism of the FBI. These criticisms differed from those of the mid-1970s, which had centered on the FBI's tactics to discredit radical activists. Critics now condemned the FBI's Hostage Rescue Team's seemingly excessive use of force and the militarization of federal law enforcement. Furthermore, when responding to media and congressional inquiries about the FBI's "rules of engagement" and their own supervisory role, senior FBI officials either withheld or destroyed relevant FBI documents, rekindling suspicions of a cover-up and about their accountability.

This skepticism did not mean that security concerns ceased to define public policy during the 1990s. The terrorist bombing of the World Trade Center in New York City in February 1993; the discovery in 1994 of an aborted conspiracy to bomb the United Nations building, a federal building in New York City, the Lincoln and Holland Tunnels, and the George Washington bridge; and the 1995 bombing of the Albert Murrah Federal Building in Oklahoma City renewed concerns about a terrorist threat (whether foreign-directed or domestic).

The bombing attack of 1993 of the World Trade Center devastated the building, causing a crater five stories deep. Miraculously, only six individuals died although more than a thousand were injured. The resultant investigation led to the conviction of four militant Islamic fundamentalists. Following upon this investigation into the World Trade Center bombing, FBI agents uncovered another conspiracy; militant Islamic fundamentalists planned to bomb the United Nations and other federal and state facilities in New York City. This terrorist plot was aborted; FBI agents arrested (and later obtained the conviction of) 11 militant Islamic fundamentalists and the charismatic cleric Sheik Omar Abdel Rahman. In the highly publicized trial, which began in January 1995, government prosecutors portrayed the defendants as part of a wider, religiously motivated movement, under the spiritual leadership of Sheik Rahman, which planned to resort to terrorist bombings to pressure the government to change U.S. policy in the Middle East.

Another quite different in purpose terrorist bombing attack occurred later that year in April, resulting in the total destruction of the Murrah Building, the death of 168 people, and the wounding of another 850. Immediately many suspected that Islamic fundamentalists were responsible for this attack. FBI agents, however, soon apprehended and subsequently secured the conviction of Timothy McVeigh and Terry Nichols, two right-wing former soldiers who held strong antigovernment views. McVeigh, in particular, bitterly resented the FBI's (and the ATF's) roles in the Branch Davidian raid. He was greatly influenced by a 1978 novel, *The Turner Diaries,* that had become a virtual bible for right-wing antigovernmental activists. In this fictional account of an armed citizenry at war with a Washington-based Zionist conspiracy, the bombing of FBI headquarters set off a white Aryan revolution.

McVeigh purposefully chose the anniversary of the fiery FBI raid on the Branch Davidian compound to bomb a symbol of governmental power, the federal building in Oklahoma City. No evidence was uncovered that McVeigh had acted in concert with other right-wing militia or white supremacist activists. Because of McVeigh's and Nichols's native birth, avowed patriotism, and conservative beliefs, the Oklahoma City bombing raised a different question than that posed following the 1993 and 1994 New York cases—was terrorism an exclusively foreign-directed phenomenon, or did it have domestic roots as well?

Prior to the Oklahoma City bombing attack, the Clinton administration had drafted legislation to expand federal authority to deport militant Arab activists, ostensibly to preclude future terrorist activities. Criticisms of the proposed bill delayed congressional approval. The devastating bombing of the Murrah Building kindled interest in the proposed restrictions, the more so because this attack followed the recent convictions of Islamic fundamentalists for their role either in bombing the World Trade Center or plotting to bomb other structures in New York City. New provisions were added to this bill to enhance federal law enforcement powers. The more controversial provisions would have made it easier for federal agents to monitor suspected terrorists through roving wiretaps, to identify the source of bomb components, and to identify the funding sources and contacts of individuals suspected of international or domestic terrorism.

The law enforcement provisions provoked opposition from an unusual coalition of traditional civil liberties activists (such as the American Civil Liberties Union) and conservatives who identified with the anti–gun control movement (such as Republican Congressmen Tom DeLay and Bob Barr). Their criticisms led Congress to strip the bill of those provisions that directly threatened the rights of American citizens: authorizing roving wiretaps, increasing access to credit card records, and tagging components that could be used in making bombs (components that had other commercial and agricultural uses). The major changes of the stripped-down Anti-Terrorism and Effective Death Penalty Act of 1996 were limited to alien residents and visitors who might have links with foreign radical government and movements. Any alien who sympathized with or had been a member of a foreign terrorist organization could be denied a visa or deported. Evidence for such sympathies could include financial contributions to any foreign group designated by the secretary of state as "terrorist," even if that support was for lawful and humanitarian purposes. Immigration officials could introduce secret evidence during deportation hearings to document the individual's terrorist proclivities without that individual's counsel having the right to challenge the reliability of this source. The debate over the proposed antiterrorist bill, however, did have further civil liberties consequences. Conservative senators introduced an amendment to this bill to curb the use of writs of habeus corpus during death penalty appeals. This provision made it more difficult for prisoners to seek redress in federal courts in those cases where state court proceedings violated constitutional standards.

The World Trade Center and Murrah Building bombings also triggered an expanded FBI foreign intelligence role. Between 1992 and 1999, the number of FBI agents assigned to analyze and collect national security information increased from 224 to 1,025, and the number of court-approved wiretaps and break-ins authorized under the Foreign Intelligence Surveillance Act increased from 484 to 886.

Despite the expanded use of foreign intelligence wiretaps and the more permissive standards of the Smith Guidelines, on September 11, 2001, 19 alien residents (13 of whom had entered the country on student or business visas) hijacked four commercial jets. Two of the commandeered jets were crashed into the twin towers of the New York City World Trade Center, with the resulting fires imploding the building. The third jet crashed into a wing of the Pentagon in Washington, D.C. The fourth jet crashed in western Pennsylvania, passengers having overpowered the four hijackers.

The surprise attack and its devastating consequences, including the deaths of 3,062 individuals and billions of dollars in property losses, shocked and infuriated the American public. In response, the Bush administration introduced a far-reaching antiterrorist bill, and Attorney General John Ashcroft pressured Congress to approve it within the same week.

Congress approved a slightly modified version of the administration's bill, which President George W. Bush signed into law on October 26, 2001. The antiterrorist act, formally titled the USA Patriot Act, broadly expanded federal surveillance powers. The authorization of wiretaps under the Foreign Intelligence Surveillance Act of 1978 was revised from cases in which "the purpose" is foreign intelligence gathering to "significant purpose" and to permit roving wiretaps as well. In addition, federal agents were empowered to monitor computer and e-mail communications, to search the premises of suspected terrorists without their presence, to investigate individuals suspected of "harboring" or "supporting" terrorism, to share information (including grand jury testimony) with other intelligence agencies, and to obtain access to bank accounts used to launder funds for terrorist operations. The act also empowered the attorney general to detain for seven days immigrants suspected of terrorism (after which, criminal charges or deportation proceedings would have to be initiated). To allay fears that these expanded powers would threaten civil liberties and privacy rights, Congress authorized suits against government officials who leaked information obtained through the expanded wiretapping and surveillance powers and adopted a sunset provision. The wiretapping and computer monitoring provisions would expire in four years unless Congress later specifically extended this authorization.

CONCLUSION

On November 7, 2000, Americans went to the polls to elect the 43rd president of the United States. For six weeks the nation watched while the results in Florida were contested and recontested. Charges of voter intimidation by police, closed voting booths, blacks and Latinos being turned away at the polls, disproportionate numbers of ballots cast by blacks and Latinos being disqualified, and black voters being purged from the voting lists led the Commission on Civil Rights to hold hearings on voting discrimination and the NAACP and other civil rights leaders to file suit under the Fourteenth Amendment and the 1965 Voting Rights Act against the state of Florida.

At the end of the twentieth century, the United States celebrated itself as the greatest democracy in the world. Yet the close of "the American century" bequeathed an ambivalent legacy of civil rights and civil liberties. From World War II through the Cold War to the dissolution of the Soviet Union, the United States portrayed itself internationally as the beacon of democracy. Yet within its borders, movements for civil rights and civil liberties exposed the sharp limits of democracy at home, and federal and state officials too often compromised these rights in the name of tradition, political expediency, economic gain, or national security. As Martin Luther King Jr. again demanded of the United States the night before his assassination, "Be true to what you said on paper."

The movements for civil rights and civil liberties outlined in this book never commanded majority support while they were happening. Most Americans, regardless of their background or political beliefs, avoided disruptive challenge to the status quo. But over time, these movements reshaped the meanings of American democracy—and pushed the country's leaders to begin to make real the nation's commitment to "liberty and justice for all." The very definitions of civil rights—the very American-ness of civil rights—shifted over the course of these fifty years. It is perhaps the ultimate success of these movements that popular memory has largely erased the unpopularity of many of these struggles. Martin

Luther King, Jr. and Malcolm X—two men feared or despised by most Americans at the time of their deaths—were celebrated at the close of the century.

Looking back on these struggles, it is easy to assume we would have been the ones to sit-in, not the ones to tell Rosa Parks to get up; we imagine that we would not have informed on colleagues for their political views or fired someone for getting pregnant. But the ability to think and act outside of societal norms required courage and a willingness to face social ostracism, the daily tedium of organizing year after year, economic repression, and physical violence—courage that many Americans, at the time, did not have. This history also reminds us that the struggle to make American democracy real for *all* Americans was led and peopled by men and women who have not often made it to the history books and who were considered crazy by many of their peers. Countless Americans in towns and cities who refused to be silent, and not charismatic leaders like Martin Luther King or Malcolm X, were the key to moving the nation to endorse civil rights.

At the same time, the forces of resistance and backlash that continue to undermine these gains (whether school desegregation, abortion, privacy rights, the right to dissent, or equal protection) have recast the language and practice of political, racial, and gender repression into new and dangerous forms. The need to compromise civil liberties in the fight against communist subversion changed to the need to do so in the fight against terrorism; popular resistance to school integration became institutionalized as a call to resist busing and the court's protection of suburban schools from desegregation and resource sharing. In post–civil rights America, the belief that racism is largely over has been used to countenance social policies that have racially inequitable results. The belief that feminism is irrelevant to this generation of women masks pervasive and continuing social and economic disparities between men and women.

This history reveals the impact of small groups of individuals—whether they worked for the FBI or sat-in at Woolworth's. The study of grassroots political struggles and federal agencies over the past fifty years—a history from the bottom up and the top down—is a study of the nature of power and the diverse forms it takes. The immense power of the federal government, particularly through agencies like the FBI, to monitor and contain dissent was matched only by the willingness of many individuals to dissent, whatever the cost. And the costs were unimaginably high.

This history also unveils the political position fear occupied over the past fifty years. From the grassroots to the highest seats of power, fears over miscegenation, racial mixing and the dangers of black neighborhoods, the decline of the family and American values, the immorality of

Communism, the irrational moralism of Islamic terrorists, and the contagion of homosexuality undergirded political action and public policy. Legitimized as common sense and written into law from *Korematsu v. U.S.* to *Bowers v. Hardwick,* fear often masked political and economic interests committed to maintaining the status quo.

Examining the denials of civil rights over the past fifty years, moreover, reveals the tenuousness of civil liberties in a country that has long celebrated its commitment to these ideals. The very concept of civil rights has been used to highlight the ways that certain peoples have been denied civil liberties—in other words denied the protections and privileges of the state. The red-baiting of Paul Robeson, the NAACP, and gay federal employees in the 1950s was about punishing people not just for what they stood for but for who they were; it was also about protecting political, racial, and gender power. Thus, just as the silencing of unpopular views is rooted in maintaining the status quo, the protection of unpopular views is also the protection of marginalized people. The introduction of unpopular views recasts the meaning of democracy, not simply protecting dissenting views for the sake of pluralism. As can be seen from the continuing struggles around voting rights, real democracy means more than saying that every American can vote.

This history of civil rights and civil liberties blurs the lines between these two concepts even as it shows how the struggles for civil rights and civil liberties diverged. Civil liberties has long been framed as constraining governmental action to protect the individual citizen, but it is more complex than just limiting governmental power. Enabling the freedom of the individual has *sometimes* meant restricting government power (such as in *Roe v. Wade*) while other times it has meant enacting new government provisions to ensure equity in access to justice (such as in *Gideon v. Wainwright*). While protecting civil liberties means ensuring freedoms of speech, press, and association, it also requires examining the economic and political structures that distribute these freedoms, as the passage of the 1964 Civil Rights Act showed. Claiming one's civil liberties, for instance the right to privacy in one's bedroom, is, at its root, about claiming a public identity entitled to rights under the law. Protecting one's civil rights and liberties thus rests on an affirmation of that public identity. The history of racial discrimination has rested on defining the public interest as white; the struggle for civil rights was therefore a struggle to redefine the public.

Redefining the American public meant challenging the ways that diversity and tolerance were celebrated as American ideals but not practiced. As many of these struggles revealed, individual rights were inextricably tied to group rights. In a country that defined *American* as the individual and denied rights based on membership in a group (whether being nonwhite, gay, or female), challenging a legal and social system that demonized group identity meant challenging the idea of the individual as white, male, and straight. From the Young Lords to the Gay Liberation Front, activists marked and celebrated group identity, convinced that protecting the individual meant changing the status of the group. As Justice Harry Blackmun wrote in his dissent in the *Bakke* case, "In order to get beyond racism, we must first take account of race. . . . And in order to treat some persons equally, we must treat them differently."

In some ways, the struggles for civil rights and civil liberties sustained and encouraged each other in the late 1950s and 1960s. But particularly in post-1973 America, a limited but powerful notion of civil liberties—favoring privacy, limits on government, and the belief that individual rights are undermined by group protection—has been used to undermine civil rights. Civil liberties have been divorced from the people who must be protected by them.

These fifty years contradict two dominant narratives in American history: first, that the history of the United States is one of progress and continual improvement; second, that all things remain the same. Rather, the history of civil rights and civil liberties over the past fifty years is a history of contestation: of the very definitions of civil rights and liberties and how they should be distributed, of who should be entitled to them, and of when they would be enforced. The flowering of activism from the Anita Hill controversy to Justice for Janitors to the campaign to free Mumia Abu-Jamal reveals that movements for civil rights and liberties did not end in the 1970s. The belief that problems of racial and gender discrimination are now largely in the past is sharply contradicted by the discrepancies in school funding, prison sentences, poverty rates, and access to jobs and housing between whites and nonwhites, men and women. To see the limits of change, however, does not obscure the significance of the change that has occurred.

RECOMMENDED READING

There is no study that comprehensively surveys the history of civil rights and civil liberties since 1945. Peter Irons, *A People's History of the Supreme Court* (New York, 1999) is a critical analysis of important legal decisions, Arthur Schlesinger Jr., *The Imperial Presidency* (Boston, 1973), surveys how foreign policy concerns led to the growth of presidential power and secrecy and Howard Zinn, *A People's History of the United States* (New York, 1995), surveys the politics of civil rights and civil liberties in this period.

The impact of the New Deal and World War II on civil rights and civil liberties is outlined in David Kennedy, *Freedom from Fear* (New York, 1999); Mary Dudziak, *Cold War Civil Rights* (Princeton, 2000); Ron Takaki, *Double Victory:A Multicultural History of America in World War II* (New York, 2000); and Roger Daniels, *Concentration Camps, U.S.A.* (New York, 1972).

The impact of Cold War national security concerns and secrecy on civil rights and civil liberties is also indirectly surveyed in Melvyn Leffler, *A Preponderance of Power* (Stanford, CA, 1992); Michael Hogan, *A Cross of Iron* (New York, 1998); Daniel Moynihan, *Secrecy* (New Haven, CT, 1998); and Athan Theoharis, ed., *A Culture of Secrecy* (Lawrence, KS, 1998).

While no book surveys civil rights activism over the fifty-year postwar period, there are a number of useful surveys of the 1950s through 1970s. The most detailed are the Eyes on the Prize series: *Eyes on the Prize Civil Rights Reader* (New York, 1991); Henry Hampton, *Voices of Freedom* (New York, 1990); and Juan Williams, ed., *Eyes on the Prize* (New York, 1987). Manning Marable, *Race, Reform, and Rebellion* (Jackson, 1991); Philip Klinker with Rogers Smith, *The Unsteady March:The Rise and Decline of Racial Equality in America* (Chicago, 1999); and Robert Weisbrot, *Freedom Bound* (New York, 1990) provide a useful foundation for this period as well. Alexander Bloom and Wini Breines, eds., *"Takin' it to the streets":A Sixties Reader* (New York, 1995) and

Howell Raines, *My Soul is Rested* (New York, 1977) complement these historical surveys with primary sources and oral histories from the period.

Juan González, *Harvest of Empire* (New York, 2000); Kenneth Jackson, *Crabgrass Frontier: The Suburbanization of the United States* (New York, 1985); Robin Kelley, *Race Rebels* (New York, 1994); and Tom Sugrue, *The Origins of the Urban Crisis: Race and Inequality in Postwar Detroit* (Princeton, 1996) lay out important views of the racial landscape and the politics of place and race in postwar America.

Useful autobiographies of civil rights movement participants include Rosa Parks, *Rosa Parks: My Story* (New York, 1992); John Lewis, *Walking with the Wind* (New York, 1998); Endesha Ida Mae Holland, *From the Mississippi Delta* (New York, 1997); Assata Shakur, *Assata: An Autobiography* (Chicago, 1987); Melba Patillo Beals, *Warriors Don't Cry* (New York, 1995); Angela Davis, *Angela Davis: An Autobiography* (New York, 1974); Elaine Brown, *A Taste of Power* (New York, 1994); David Hilliard, *This Side of Glory* (Chicago, 2001); Amiri Baraka, *The Autobiography of LeRoi Jones/Amiri Baraka* (New York, 1984); Septima Clark, *Ready from Within* (Navarro, CA, 1986); Jo Ann Robinson, *The Montgomery Bus Boycott and the Women Who Started It* (Knoxville, 1987); Eldridge Cleaver, *Soul on Ice* (New York, 1968); and Cleveland Sellers, *The River of No Return: The Autobiography of a Black Militant and the Life and Death of SNCC* (New York, 1973).

There has been a flowering in recent years of work on movements in the South. Some of the best are Clayborne Carson, *In Struggle: SNCC and the Black Awakening of the 1960s* (Cambridge, 1996); Timothy Tyson, *Radio Free Dixie: Robert F. Williams & the Roots of Black Power* (Chapel Hill, 1999); John Dittmer, *Local People* (Urbana, 1995); Charles Payne, *I've Got the Light of Freedom* (Berkeley, 1995); Cynthia Griggs Fleming, *Soon We Will Not Cry: The Liberation of Ruby Doris Smith Robinson* (New York, 1998); and Chana Kai Lee, *For Freedom's Sake: The Life of Fannie Lou Hamer* (Urbana, 1999).

We are just beginning to see an outgrowth of scholarship on black struggles outside of the South. Mike Marquese, *Redemption Song: Muhammad Ali and the Spirit of the 1960s* (New York, 1999); Dan Georgakas, *Detroit, I Do Mind Dying: A Study in Urban Revolution* (Boston, 1998); Komozi Woodward, *A Nation within a Nation: Amiri Baraka (LeRoi Jones) & Black Power Politics* (Chapel Hill, 1999); Charles Jones, ed., *The Black Panther Party Reconsidered* (Baltimore, 1998); Matthew Countryman, Jeanne Theoharis, and Komozi Woodard, eds., *Freedom North* (New York, 2002); and Joshua Freeman, *Working Class New York* (New York, 2000) each contribute to a fuller understanding of the variety of struggles, tactics, and ideologies of black liberation outside the South.

The best comparative analysis of Martin Luther King Jr. and Malcolm X is James Cone, *Martin & Malcolm & America: A Dream or a Nightmare* (Maryknoll, NY, 1991). Michael Dyson, *I May Not Get There with You: The True Martin Luther King Jr.* (New York, 2001); James Washington, ed., *A Testament of Hope* (New York, 1986); Malcolm X with Alex Haley, *The Autobiography of Malcolm X* (New York, 1965); and George Breitman, ed., *Malcom X Speaks* (New York, 1965) provide an important foundation into the lives, work, and philosophies of Martin Luther King Jr. and Malcolm X. Vicki Crawford, ed., *Women in the Civil Rights Movement: Trailblazers and Torchbearers, 1941–1965* (New York, 1990) corrects much of the early work on the civil rights movement that ignored women's pivotal leadership and organizing roles.

Useful work on the Chicano movement includes F. Arturo Rosales, *Chicano: The History of the Mexican American Civil Rights Movement* (Houston, 1997); Susan Ferriss, *The Fight in the Fields: César Chávez and the Farmworkers Movement* (New York, 1997); and Rudolfo Acuña, *Occupied America: A History of Chicanos* (New York, 1988). Young Lord's Party, *Palante: Young Lord's Party* (New York, 1971) and Andrés Torres and José Velázquez, eds., *The Puerto Rican Movement* (Philadelphia, 1998) provide an introduction to the work of the Young Lords and other Puerto Rican activist groups. Vine Deloria, *Custer Died for Your Sins* (New York, 1969); Troy Johnson et al., eds., *American Indian Activism* (Urbana, 1997); Paul Chat Smith and Robert Alan Warrior, *Like a Hurricane: The Indian Movement from Alcatraz to Wounded Knee* (New York, 1996); Mary Crow Dog, *Lakota Woman* (New York, 1994); Leonard Peltier, *Prison Writings: My Life is My Sun Dance* (New York, 2000); and Russell Means, *Where the White Man Fears to Tread* (New York, 1997) give a good introduction to American Indian politics during this period.

Dan Carter, *From George Wallace to Newt Gingrich: Race and Conservative Counter-Revolution* (New Orleans, 1999); Maurice Isserman and Michael Kazin, *America Divided: The Civil War of the 1960s* (New York, 2000); and Thomas and Mary Edsall, *Chain Reaction: The Impact of Race, Rights and Taxes on American Politics* (New York, 1991) assess the conservative backlash against civil rights during the 1970s, 1980s, and 1990s. The War on Drugs and the racial politics of security, incarceration, and policing are illuminated in Mike Davis, *City of Quartz* (New York, 1992); Christian Parenti, *Lockdown America* (New York, 1999); Margot Henry, *Attention MOVE! This is America* (New York, 1987); Mumia Abu-Jamal, *Live from Death Row* (New York, 1996); Jimmie Reeves and Dick Campbell, *Cracked Coverage* (Durham, 1994); and David Cole, *No Equal Justice*. For more on post-Fordism and the American economy, see Saskia Sassen, *The Global City* (Princeton, 1991).

Jonathan Kozol, *Savage Inequalities* (New York, 1991) and Gary Orfield, Susan Eaton, and the Harvard Project on School Desegregation, *Dismantling Desegregation: The Quiet Reversal of Brown v. Board of Education* (New York, 1996) look at the racial inequalities in contemporary public education; William Bowen and Derek Bok, *The Shape of the River: Long-Term Consequences of Considering Race in College and University Admissions* (Princeton, 1998) is an important study of affirmative action. Juan Perea, ed., *The New Nativism* (New York, 1996) and Alejandro Portes and Rubén Rumbaut, *Immigrant America* (Berkeley, 1996) illuminate the politics of post-1965 immigration.

Michael Katz, *In the Shadow of the Poorhouse: A Social History of Welfare in America* (New York, 1996); David Zucchino, *The Myth of the Welfare Queen* (New York, 1997); Deborah Gray White, *Too Heavy a Load: Black Women in Defense of Themselves, 1894–1994* (New York, 2000); and Dorothy Roberts, *Killing the Black Body* (New York, 1997) are useful histories and critical analyses of the politics of welfare and welfare rights activism. Robin Kelley, *Yo Mama's Disfunktional* (Boston, 1997) is the best survey of civil rights struggles in the 1990s. Kimberly Springer, ed., *Still Lifting, Sill Climbing: African American Women's Contemporary Activism* (New York, 1999) also looks at black women's contemporary activism.

Until the 1960s, the role of women in American society was downplayed, if not ignored, except in accounts of women's roles in the abolition movement, in the campaign for women's suffrage and Prohibition amendments, and humanitarian causes (mental health, the settlement house movement, nursing). Women's history first commanded serious historical interest and research in the 1970s. Some of the earlier works are William Chafe, *The American Woman* (New York, 1972); Judith Hole and Ellen Levine, *Rebirth of Feminism* (New York, 1971); Jo Freeman, *The Politics of Women's Liberation* (New York, 1975); and Sara Evans, *Personal Politics: The Roots of Women's Liberation in the Civil Rights Movement and the New Left* (New York, 1979). By the 1990s, women's history had become a major area of study. Students might profitably consult Ellen DuBois, ed., *Feminist Scholarship* (Urbana, IL, 1987) and Vicki Ruiz and Ellen DuBois, eds., *Unequal Sisters: A Multicultural Reader in U.S. Women's History* (New York, 2000). Useful surveys include Barbara Ryan, *Feminism and the Women's Movement* (New York, 1992); Rosalind Rosen, *Divided Lives* (New York, 1992); Ruth Rosen, *The World Split Open: How the Modern Women's Movement Changed America* (New York, 2000); Linda Kerber and Jane Sherron DeHart, *Women's America* (New York, 1995); and William Chafe, *The Paradox of Change* (New York, 1991). More specialized works include Susan Faludi, *Backlash* (New York, 1991); Leila Rupp and Verta Taylor, *Survival in the Doldrums: The American*

Women's Rights Movement, 1945 to the 1960s (New York, 1987); Joanne Meyerowitz, ed., *Not June Cleaver:Women and Gender in Postwar America, 1945-1960* (Philadelphia, 1994); Stephanie Coontz, *The Way We Never Were:American Families and the Nostalgia Trap* (New York, 1992); and Rochelle Gatlin, *American Women Since 1945* (Jackson, MS, 1987).

Research into the history of gays and lesbians, and changing societal attitudes first began to command interest during the 1980s. Useful surveys include John D'Emilio, *Sexual Politics, Sexual Communities* (Chicago, 1983); Barry Adam, *The Rise of a Gay and Lesbian Movement* (New York, 1995); Martin Duberman, *Midlife Queer* (New York, 1996); Donn Teal, *The Gay Militants* (New York, 1971); and Dudley Clendinen and Adam Nagourney, *Out for Good* (New York, 1999).

There is no work that comprehensively surveys the history of civil liberties since 1945. Students might profitably consult Samuel Walker's history of the premier civil liberties organization, the American Civil Liberties Union, *In Defense of American Liberties* (New York, 1990) and Philippa Strum, *Privacy: The Debate in the United States since 1945* (Fort Worth, 1998).

Until the late 1970s, most historical research focused on federal and state loyalty programs, the so-called Smith Act cases, the House Committee on Un-American Activities, the blacklisting practices in the entertainment industry, and McCarthyism. State loyalty programs and investigations are surveyed in Harold Hyman, *To Try Men's Souls: Loyalty Tests in American History* (Berkeley, CA, 1959) and Walter Gelhorn, ed., *The States and Subversion* (Ithaca, NY, 1952). Federal loyalty programs are surveyed in Eleanor Bontecou, *The Federal Loyalty-Security Program* (Ithaca, NY, 1953) and Ralph S. Brown Jr., *Loyalty and Security* (New Haven, CT, 1958). The Smith Act cases are surveyed in Michal Belknap, *Cold War Political Justice* (Westport, CT, 1977); Peter Steinberg, *The Great "Red Menace"* (Westport, CT, 1984); and Arthur Sabin, *In Calmer Times* (Philadelphia, 1999). Walter Goodman, *The Committee* (New York, 1968) is a useful, if somewhat dated history of the House Committee on Un-American Activities, while Kenneth O'Reilly, *Hoover and the Un-Americans* (Philadelphia, 1983) extends this history by exploring the covert relationship between the committee and the Federal Bureau of Investigation. The Hollywood blacklist is surveyed in John Cogley, *Report on Blacklisting* (New York, 1956) and Larry Ceplair and Steven Englund, *The Inquisition in Hollywood* (Garden City, NY, 1980). McCarthyism is surveyed in David Oshinsky, *A Conspiracy So Immense* (New York, 1983) and Richard Fried, *Nightmare in Red* (New York, 1990), while Ellen Schrecker, *Many Are the Crimes* (Boston, 1998) and Athan Theoharis, *Chasing Spies* (Chicago, 2002) extend this assessment by exploring as well the role of the Federal Bureau of Investigation.

The O'Reilly, Schrecker, and Theoharis studies highlight a major shift in recent historical scholarship to focus on the FBI. Useful histories include Sanford Ungar, *F.B.I.* (Boston, 1976); Frank Donner, *The Age of Surveillance* (New York, 1980); and Athan Theoharis, *Spying on Americans* (Philadelphia, 1978). Biographies of FBI Director J. Edgar Hoover provide useful insights into the FBI's impact on civil liberties; see, for example, Curt Gentry, *J. Edgar Hoover* (New York, 1991) and Athan Theoharis and John Cox, *The Boss* (Philadelphia, 1988). More specialized studies have focused on academic freedom issues, including Sigmund Diamond, *Compromised Campus* (New York, 1992); Jessica Wang, *American Science in an Age of Anxiety* (Chapel Hill, NC, 1999); and Mike Keen, *Stalking the Sociological Imagination* (Westport, CT, 1999). FBI surveillance of prominent writers is surveyed in Natalie Robins, *Alien Ink* (New York, 1992) and Herbert Mitgang, *Dangerous Dossiers* (New York, 1990). The FBI's controversial COINTELPRO is the subject of a number of studies; see, for example, Brian Glick, *War at Home* (Boston, 1988). The recent history of the FBI, specifically continued controversies or reforms in rules and procedures, is surveyed in John Elliff, *The Reform of FBI Intelligence Operations* (Princeton, NJ, 1979); Tony Poveda, *Lawlessness and Reform* (Pacific Grove, CA, 1990); John Kelly and Phillip Wearne, *Tainted Evidence* (New York, 1998); and James Dempsey and David Cole, *Terrorism & the Constitution* (Los Angeles, 1999).

The FBI's surveillance of prominent civil rights activists and organizations is surveyed in David Garrow, *The FBI and Martin Luther King, Jr.* (New York, 1981); Taylor Branch's two-volume biography of King, *Parting the Waters* (New York, 1988) and *Pillar of Fire* (New York, 1998); Clayborne Carson, ed., *Malcolm X: The FBI File* (New York, 1991) and *In Struggle: SNCC and the Black Aawareness of the 1960s* (Cambridge, MA, 1981); Robert Hill, *The FBI's Racon* (Boston, 1992); Kenneth O'Reilly, *Racial Matters* (New York, 1989); Gerald Horne, *Black and Red: W. E. B. DuBois and the Afro-American Response to the Cold War* (Albany, NY, 1986); and Adam Fairclough, *To Redeem the Soul of America: The Southern Christian Leadership Conference and Martin Luther King, Jr.* (Athens, GA, 1987).

INDEX

PHOTO CREDITS

Page xix   © AP/Wide World Photos

Page 25   © AP/ Wide World Photos

Page 58   © Bettmann/CORBIS

Page 97   © AP/Wide World Photos

Page 114   © Bettmann/CORBIS

Page 120   © Bettmann/CORBIS

Page 148   © Bettmann/CORBIS

Page 162   © AP/Wide World Photos

Page 195   © Bettmann/CORBIS

Page 210   © Bettmann/CORBIS